Opening The Musical Box

A Genesis Chronicle

FIRE FLY
PUBLISHING

Opening The Musical Box

A Genesis Chronicle

Alan Hewitt

First published in 2000 by Firefly Publishing
Firefly is an imprint of SAF Publishing Ltd. in association with
Helter Skelter Publishing Ltd.

SAF Publishing Ltd.
Unit 7, Shaftesbury Centre,
85 Barlby Road,
London.
W10 6BN

ENGLAND

ISBN 0 946719 30 6

A CIP catalogue record for this book is available from the British Library.

Printed in England by Cromwell Press, Trowbridge, Wiltshire.

Contents

Acknowledgements

A project such as this is never the work of one person, and this is no exception to that rule. Many people have helped with the preparation of this book and I would like to take this opportunity to thank a few of them. First of all; my grateful thanks to Peter Morton, Ted Sayers; Jonathan Dann; Matthew Skelland; Jonathan Guntrip; Jeremy Brown and Warren Watts who collectively with myself, have over the last twelve or so years made *The Waiting Room* the success that it is now. They have put up with my tantrums when things didn't go according to the 'plan' and their work on both the magazine and this project has been invaluable and their patience has been truly remarkable! Special thanks also must go to Gerald Dann whose design skills have enabled us to bring you the magazine in a far more legible form than would otherwise have been possible and who has contributed significantly to this project in much the same spirit.

I could not have begun this without the active participation of band members past and present who have contributed material and time in abundance. I am particularly grateful for the input given by Tony Banks; Steve Hackett; Anthony Phillips; Mike Rutherford; Ray Wilson and Nir Tsidyakhu whose contributions over the last few years have formed the backbone of this book. Nothing could have been achieved without the support which has been given by the management of the various artists and the people whom the band have worked with who have also given time and information to me. In particular I would like to thank the following; Carol Willis-Impey; Joanne Greenwood; Annie Callingham; Billy Budis; Tina at "FOPG"; Rob Ayling at "Voiceprint"; Verena Magitteri at Fundamental; Harry Williamson; Peter Cross; Richard MacPhail; Simon Hopkins; Jeremy Silver; Tony Goodwin and Glen Colson at Virgin Records; David Thomas; Rupert Hine; John G Perry; Chris Stewart; John Silver; Armando Gallo and Paul Whitehead all of whom have been unstinting in their generosity and have put up with our constant badgering for information about one thing or another. All of the extracts from interviews quoted within the text of this book are from interviews which have been carried out personally by myself, Peter, Ted or Jonathan for either *The Waiting Room* or *The Pavilion* magazines and websites unless otherwise stated. To those numerous others whose work I have drawn upon I offer my grateful thanks.

The following have also made a considerable contribution to this project, in tangible or less tangible ways; Peter Gozzard (the press cutting king extraordinaire), Richard and Andrew Nagy for all their chauffeuring and photographic work, Mike Jackson; Phil and Richard Morris; Simon Pound; Mel Huang; Jack M Beerman; Serge Morissette (le plus gentile homme dans tout le monde!!) George German III; Tom Oastler; Mansoor Khaleeluddin; Stephanie Stratton; Gary Myer; Amanda Gardner; Kevin Powell; Jon "Armando" Guntrip; Asemund Hanevik; David Birtwell; and others too numerous to mention; you all know who you are! Special thanks also to Thomas Holter; Mario Giammetti; Helmut Janisch; Bernd Zindler and Peter Schutz, who together with myself, Peter; Ted and Jonathan write for the various Genesis fan clubs which collectively form the Worldwide Genesis Fanclub Network, keeping interest about the band going and to Vernon Parker whose "Annotated Genesis Chronology" was a Godsend!

Continuing thanks as well to Bill Brink for being a persistent pain in the neck and for his enthusiasm and work on the Internet. I would also like to express my personal gratitude to Geoff Parkin, who for almost fifteen years ran the Official Genesis fanclub: "Genesis Information" which was the inspiration for us to form "TWR" in the first place and gave impetus to the creation of this book. Sadly, Geoff passed away in November 1994 and will not see the end result of his encouragement. To me and all the fans who knew him Geoff was a true gentleman and a fan amongst fans, who will be greatly missed and this book is dedicated to his memory.

Finally; a big thank you to all the fans everywhere who have over the years been a continuing source of amazement and inspiration and encouragement. This is my attempt at a thank you to all of them and to the band and its members whose various careers we have followed and which bring so much pleasure to us all, as well as providing the soundtrack to all our lives, I hope that this brings you as much pleasure in the reading as it did to me in the writing.

Introduction

Project Genesis

Early August 1987, some three or four weeks after the end of Genesis' most successful tour to date in support of their *Invisible Touch* album, marked the beginning of what was has since become something of an obsession which has increasingly taken over most, if not all, of my spare time. I found myself ensconced in my home with a couple of friends, Ted Sayers and Peter Morton, both of whom had shown an interest in trying their hand at a Genesis 'fanzine'. My natural scepticism got the better of me and I refused to have anything to do with such a hare-brained scheme. After all, there was already a fan club in existence and, frankly, I didn't think that there was anything we could possibly produce that would be better than that. Undaunted, both Peter and Ted continued to insist that we could and should make a go of it. Ted had the benefit of experience in writing a magazine about Peter Gabriel in the early eighties, so I was persuaded, somewhat reluctantly, to throw some ideas together to see what would emerge from our collective brainstorming.

Two weeks later, I was confronted with an amazing pile of articles written by the three of us amounting to what looked suspiciously like the outline of a magazine. Whether it would stand up to the test of fans actually 'buying' it was another matter. However, I was now convinced that something could be made out of our ramblings and, during numerous telephone calls and visits to and from the others' houses, a magazine emerged. The writing had proven surprisingly easy to do, the tricky bit now was to think of a convincing title and sell it to the punters. Numerous suggestions came and went for our little publication, reminiscent in fact of the band's early search for an identity. Eventually, Ted suggested the name which stuck and our magazine was christened *The Waiting Room* much to my chagrin, because two of my suggested titles had been shot down in howls of raucous laughter! So it came to pass that in late August 1987, the first issue of *The Waiting Room* (or *TWR* as it soon became abbreviated to) came into existence.

Looking back on that initial issue now, I cannot help but wonder how we ever got beyond it; it was amateurish in the extreme and sported a garish home-made cover by yours truly that still makes me cringe when I see it. The fans didn't see it that way however, and with one small ad in one of the official fan club's contact sections, we managed to sell out our meagre initial print run of fifty copies which are now collector's items in their own right — or so I am told. The reaction was favourable and people actually started asking when the next issue was due. Our first hurdle had been successfully cleared. We had proven to ourselves that we could write a magazine. That was the easy bit in many ways. Now we had to go and write another one; a daunting prospect with as yet no firm contact with any member of the band or their management(s).

Our first break came in January 1988 when I received a letter from Anthony Phillips whose address I had kindly been given by a fellow fan. I had written to him in the hope that he might be prepared to contribute something to our next issue or perhaps do an interview? Not only was he amenable to this but a firm date was arranged. Before this took place however, another stroke of luck gave us contact with Steve Hackett when Ted and I bumped into him and his manager at one of his shows during his *Momentum* UK tour. Once again an interview was duly arranged and it soon became apparent that the magazine would have several exclusives for its next issue. Over the next couple of years, Anthony and Steve became regular contributors, always approachable and soon they were joined by Tony Banks and Mike Rutherford.

By now we, like the band, had experienced personnel changes. Ted had left due to other commitments and had been replaced by Jonathan Dann and his irrepressible father whose work has been invaluable ever since. The magazine was now selling well in the UK, Europe and further afield too and had a sister in the shape of *The Pavilion* which covered Anthony Phillips and acted as his own official fanclub. To us it seemed as if we had found our own niche in the world of fan magazines. Our fortune had been to secure the help and generous assistance of a wide range of people who, like the three of us, were interested in the music that makes Genesis and its component parts so special. Now that we were successfully writing a magazine, the next step was logical enough – a book. It sounds straightforward enough when mentioned like that. The reality is much different however. For instance; how could we hope to improve upon the books already written about the band? I am thinking particularly of the three volumes by Armando Gallo which, as far as Genesis fans are concerned, are still the yardsticks by which all other such books are measured. Did we simply want to trot out another reiteration of the same facts as previous publications or did we want to try and add another dimension. And if so, what? The answer to this question was given to us by the readers of the magazine. If we were to try and do this properly, a work of biography would not be the answer. While producing the magazine we had drawn upon many other facets of the band's career not normally written about. Hence the rationale behind this project was not solely to create a biographical picture of the band and its individual members, although that is, of course, a necessary component.

My aim within this book is to cast the net a little bit wider and draw into it many more of those strands of the Genesis 'web' to create a bigger picture of the band. I also wanted to include the people who work for them, the fans who follow both the band and their solo projects, and in so doing answer as many of the questions that I have been asked about the band. This is a book written by fans FOR fans. Neither myself, nor any of the people associated with either magazine, are professional journalists, we all have to earn our crust in widely different ways. The one thing that binds us together is our passion for all things Genesis.

Unlike others, we make no claim to be "experts", although, certainly in my own and Ted and Peter's cases, we have followed the band and its members for over twenty one years, and I am sure that counts for something. Anyway, I hope that you like the finished result, it could not have been written without you.

Alan Hewitt
Liverpool
2000

Genesis: A Chronology

The following is a somewhat brief guide to the key events in the history of Genesis and the band's various solo off-shoots over the last thirty or so years.

February 12th 1950:	Stephen Hackett born.
February 13th 1950:	Peter Brian Gabriel born.
March 27th 1950:	Anthony George Banks born.
October 2nd 1950:	Micahel John Cleote Crawford Rutherford born.
December 23rd 1950:	Anthony Edwin Phillips born.
January 30th 1951:	Philip Collins born.
September 1963:	Peter Gabriel and Tony Banks enter Charterhouse Public School.
September 1964:	Mike Rutherford enters Charterhouse Public School.
April 1965:	Anthony Phillips enters Charterhouse Public School.
December 16th 1965:	Anon perform their first gig at Charterhouse.
Summer 1966:	Anon record "Pennsylvania Flickhouse" at Tony Pike Sound.
August 1967:	Genesis (as yet un-named) sign publishing contract with Jonjo Music.
2nd February 1968:	The Silent Sun single released by Decca Records.
15th May 1968:	A Winter's Tale single released by Decca Records.
8th September 1968:	Ray Wilson born.
March 1969:	From Genesis To Revelation album released by Decca records.
27th June 1969:	Where The Sour Turns To Sweet single released.
23rd September 1969:	Genesis' first gig at Mrs Balme's dance Chobham.
October 1969:	Guide Me Orion (Flaming Youth's first single) released on Fontana Records.
November 1969:	Ark Two album released by Flaming Youth (featuring Phil Collins) on Fontana Records
November 1969:	Genesis' first "professional" gig at Brunel University.
22nd February 1970:	BBC "Night Ride" session recorded.
March 1970:	Genesis sign to Charisma Records.
11th March 1970:	Genesis gig at the Roundhouse London filmed.
July 18th 1970:	Anthony Phillips' last gig with Genesis at Haywards Heath.
August 30th 1970:	Phil Collins joins Genesis.
21st October 1970:	Trespass album released on Charisma Records.
January 1971:	Steve Hackett joins Genesis.
February 1971:	First Charisma Package tour of UK.
March 7th 1971:	Genesis' first gig overseas at "La Ferme" Woluwe St Lambert Belgium.
26th June 1971:	Genesis appear at the Reading Festival for the first time.
September 1971:	"The Knife" single released.
November 20th 1971:	Nursery Cryme album released.
April 1972:	Genesis' first overseas tour starts in Italy.
May 26th 1972:	Great Western Festival Lincoln.
October 21st 1972:	Foxtrot album released.
December 16th 1972:	Genesis' first US gig at Brandeis University Boston.
April/May 1973:	Genesis' first headlining tour of Europe.
June 1973:	Genesis Live album released.
17th June 1973:	Zox and the Radar Boys gig Aylesbury (featuring Phil)
October 1973:	Selling England By The Pound album released.
December 1973:	Genesis' first US tour.

February 1974:	"I Know What I Like" released as single charts at no 19 in the UK, the band's first UK hit.
January/May 1974:	Genesis' first headlining tours of the USA and Europe.
November 1974:	The Lamb Lies Down On Broadway album released.
November 20th 1974:	First gig of The Lamb Lies Down On Broadway tour in the USA.
February 19th 1975:	First European gig of The Lamb Lies Down On Broadway tour.
May 23rd 1975:	Last gig of The Lamb Lies Down On Broadway tour.
August 18th 1975:	Peter Gabriel announces his departure from Genesis.
August 1975:	Steve Hackett's first solo album; Voyage of the Acolyte released.
September 1975:	Beyond An Empty Dream album released featuring the hymn "Take This Heart" co-written by Anthony Phillips and Mike Rutherford.
December 1975:	Brand X first gig at London School of Economics
February 1976:	A Trick Of The Tail album released.
March 30th 1976:	First gig of the "A Trick Of The Tail" tour in London Ontario.
10th July 1976:	Last gig of the "A Trick..." tour at Luton Sports Centre England.
July 1976:	Unorthodox Behaviour Brand X's first album released.
January 1st 1977:	Wind & Wuthering album released and band commence world tour by playing a series of sell-out shows at London's Rainbow Theatre.
February 1977:	Peter Gabriel releases self-titled first solo album.
March 1977:	Anthony Phillips's first solo album: "The Geese & The Ghost" released.
March 1977:	"Moribund The Burgermeister" first solo single from Peter Gabriel reaches no13 in the UK charts.
5th March 1977:	Peter Gabriel's first solo gig at Passaic New Jersey USA.
April 1977:	Moroccan Roll album released.
May 1977:	Genesis play their first gigs in South America.
3rd July 1977:	Last gig of Genesis' Wind & Wuthering world tour in Munich.
8th October 1977:	Steve Hackett announces his departure from Genesis.
15th October 1977:	Seconds Out live album released.
November 1977:	Livestock album released.
March 1978:	"Follow You Follow Me" released becoming Genesis' biggest hit to date reaching No 7.
30th March 1978:	Genesis begin their massive And Then There Were Three world tour in the USA.
April 1978:	And Then There Were Three album released.
May 1978:	Steve Hackett's second solo album: Please Don't Touch released.
June 1978:	Peter Gabriel's second solo album released.
June 1978:	Anthony Phillips's second solo album Wise After The Event Released with bonus edition of the first album in the Private Parts & Pieces series.
24th June 1978:	Genesis headline the Knebworth Park Festival.
August 1978:	Pete Gabriel's second solo tour begins in UK.
24th December 1978:	"Rob & Gab" Christmas show featuring Peter Gabriel and Tom Robinson along with Phil Collins at London's Hammersmith Odeon.
August 1979:	Peter Gabriel premieres material from his third solo album at the Reading and Glastonbury Festivals.
September 1979:	Brand X Product album released.
September 1979:	Tony Banks' first solo album: A Curious Feeling released.
September 1979:	Steve Hackett releases Spectral Mornings album.
September 1979:	Anthony Phillips releases Sides album.
February 1980:	Mike Rutherford's first solo album: Smallcreeps Day released.
February 1980:	"Games Without Frontiers" single released (video banned by BBC).
21st February 1980:	Gabriel starts his tour in support of his third solo album in Oxford.
3rd March 1980:	"Turn It On Again" single released.
17th March 1980:	Duke tour begins at the Festival Hall Paignton.
March 1980:	Steve Hackett releases the Defector album.
March 1980:	Defector tour starts in UK.
28th March 1980:	Duke album released.

June 1980:	Private Parts & Pieces II: Back To The Pavilion released.
December 1980:	"In The Air Tonight" single released reaching no 2 in UK chart.
11th February 1981:	Face Value Phil Collins' first solo album released.
March 1981:	Anthony Phillips' 1984 album released.
August 1981:	Abacab single released.
September 1981:	Abacab album released.
25th September 1981:	Genesis commence Abacab tour in Barcelona Spain.
23rd December 1981:	Final show of Abacab tour at the NEC Birmingham.
3rd May 1982:	3 x 3 EP released.
16-18th June 1982:	First WOMAD Festival Shepton Mallet.
July 1982:	Private Parts & Pieces III: Antiques released.
August 1982:	Mike Rutherford's second solo album: Acting Very Strange released.
2nd August 1982:	Genesis commence the Three Sides Live tour in Peoria USA.
August 1982:	Three Sides Live album released.
6th September 1982:	"Shock The Monkey" single released.
September 1982:	Peter Gabriel's fourth solo album released.
September 1982:	Phil Collins' second solo album: Hello, I Must Be Going" released.
2nd October 1982:	"Six Of The Best" reunion concert at Milton Keynes Concert Bowl.
28th October 1982:	Peter Gabriel commences tour in support of his fourth solo album in Boston USA.
21st November 1982:	Phil Collins' first solo gig at Den Haag Holland.
April 1983	Steve Hackett releases Highly Strung album.
15th April 1983:	Tony Banks releases Wicked Lady soundtrack.
19th April 1983:	Highly Strung tour commences in Worthing UK
June 1983:	Peter Gabriel Plays Live album released.
September 1983:	Anthony Phillips's musical Alice opens in Leeds.
September 1983:	Anthony Phillips' Invisible Men album released in USA.
24th September 1983:	Genesis release "Genesis" album.
26th October 1983:	Steve Hackett releases Bay Of Kings album and tour of UK universities begins
7th November 1983:	First gig of the Mama Tour at Normal Illinois USA.
29th February 1984:	Last gig of Mama Tour at the NEC Birmingham UK.
May 1984:	Anthony Phillips' Invisible Men album released in UK.
August 1984:	Anthony Phillips' Private Parts & Pieces IV: A Catch At The Tables" released.
August 1984:	Steve Hackett's Till We Have Faces album released.
October 1984:	Anthony Phillips' Private Parts & Pieces V: Twelve released.
12th February 1985:	Phil Collins' No Jacket Required album released.
14th February 1985:	No Jacket Required tour starts in Nottingham UK.
March 1985:	Mike + The Mechanics debut album released.
May 1985:	Anthony Phillips' Harvest Of The Heart compilation album released.
May 1985:	Peter Gabriel releases the Birdy soundtrack.
13th June 1985:	Live Aid Wembley Stadium and JFK Stadium Philadelphia Phil Collins flies Concord and plays both gigs.
August 1985:	Anthony Phillips' Private Parts & Pieces VI: "Ivory Moon" released.
3rd October 1985:	No Jacket Required tour ends in New York USA.
March 1986:	Gabriel releases So album.
May 1986:	Tony Banks releases Soundtracks album.
June 1986:	"Invisible Touch" single released.
June 1986:	Peter Gabriel takes part in the Conspiracy of Hope tour of USA for Amnesty International.
June 1986;	Mike Rutherford's first solo tour with the Mechanics the "Miracle Tour" takes place in USA.
10th September 1986:	Invisible Touch album released.
17th September 1986:	Invisible Touch World Tour commences in Detroit USA.
17th September 1986:	Peter Gabriel plays concert at the United Nations Building in New York.

7th November 1986: Peter Gabriel commences the "This way up" tour, Rochester NewYork.
November 23rd 1986: Genesis play first ever gigs in Australia and New Zealand completed on December 17th
20th December 1986: Peter Gabriel plays benefit gigs for "University for peace" in Tokyo Japan.
July 4th 1987: Genesis' Invisible Touch world tour ends at Wembley Stadium UK.
August 1987: Anthony Phillips' Private Parts & Pieces VII: Slow Waves Soft Stars released.
October 30th 1987: Peter Gabriel's This way up tour ends in Athens Greece.
25th April 1988: Steve Hackett commences tour in support of new Momentum album.
May 1988: Steve Hackett releases the Momentum album.
August 1988: Phil Collins stars in Buster film with Julie Walters.
2nd September 1988: Peter takes part in the Human Rights Now! Amnesty International tour which begins at Wembley Stadium UK.
15th October 1988: Human Rights Now! tour ends in Buenos Aires Argentina.
November 1988: Mike + The Mechanics' second album "The Living Years" released.
November 18th 1988: Anthony Phillips releases the Tarka album.
22nd February 1989: Mike + The Mechanics' first UK/European tour commences in Zurich Switzerland.
14th August 1989: Tony Banks releases the Bankstatement album
September 1989: Peter Gabriel releases the Passion soundtrack to Martin Scorsese's Last Temptation of Christ film.
21st November 1989: Phil Collins releases the But Seriously album.
December 1989: Anthony Phillips releases the cassette- only Missing Links Volume 1 album.
16th April 1990: Phil Collins commences the But Seriously world tour in Brussels Belgium.
November 1990: Peter Gabriel releases the "Shaking The Tree" compilation album.
25thMarch 1991: Mike + The Mechanics' Word Of Mouth album released.
7th June 1991: Tony Banks releases the Still album.
21st November 1991: Genesis release the We Can't Dance album.
16th May 1992: We Can't Dance tour begins.
2nd August 1992: We Can't Dance tour ends.
10th August 1992; Steve Hackett begins first tour of USA in almost four years.
24th August 1992: Anthony Phillips releases Private Parts & Pieces VIII: New England.
21st September 1992: Peter Gabriel releases Us album.
23rd October 1992: Genesis begin series of provincial UK theatre shows at Southampton Mayflower Theatre.
2nd November 1992: Genesis play six shows at Earls Court Arena London.
16th November 1992: Genesis release The Way We Walk Volume One: The Shorts album.
17th November 1992: Genesis' last theatre show at the Civic Hall Wolverhampton.
11th January 1993: Genesis release The Way We Walk Volume Two: The Longs" album.
13th April 1993; Peter Gabriel commences Secret World tour in Stockholm Sweden.
17th May 1993: Steve Hackett releases Guitar Noir album.
21st May 1993: Steve Hackett commences first UK tour in five years at Liverpool's Neptune Theatre.
18th September 1993: Phil Collins' last gig with Genesis at Cowdrey Ruins.
2nd November 1993: Phil Collins releases Both Sides album.
April 1st 1994: Phil Collins' Both Sides world tour commences in Utrecht Holland.
May 1994: Anthony Phillips releases the Sail The World soundtrack.
June 1994: Anthony Phillips releases Missing Links Volume Two: The Sky Road album.
14th August 1994; Peter Gabriel's Secret World tour ends at the "Woodstock II" concert Saugerties NY
15th August 1994: Genesis re-issue Trespass to The Lamb Lies Down On Broadway re-mastered albums.
19th September 1994: Steve Hackett releases Blues With A Feeling album.

4th October 1994: Genesis re-issue A Trick Of The Tail to Three Sides Live re-mastered albums.
24th November 1994: Steve Hackett commences Italian tour at Congeliano Veneto.
January 1995: Anthony Phillips releases Gypsy Suite album.
February 1995: Mike + The Mechanics release Beggar On A Beach Of Gold album.
17th March 1995: The second leg of Phil Collins' Both Sides world tour titled "The Far Side" commences in Johannesburg South Africa.
May 15th 1995: Phil Collins' "Far Side" tour ends in Manila.
3rd June 1995: Mike + The Mechanics commence their Beggar On A Beach Of Gold tour in Durban South Africa.
August 1995: Anthony Phillips releases Anthology album.
August 1995: Steve Hackett releases There Are Many Sides To The Night album.
11th September 1995: Tony Banks releases -Strictly Inc album.
16th October 1995: Anthony Phillips releases Echoes album.
28thFebruary 1996; Mike + The Mechanics commence their UK "Hits" tour in Belfast.
4th March 1996; Mike + The Mechanics "Hits" album released.
29th March 1996: Press announcement detailing Phil Collins' departure from Genesis.
June 1996 GTR release King Biscuit Flower Hour live album.
11th July 1996: Phil Collins commences first Big Band Jazz tour at the Royal Albert Hall London.
22nd August 1996: Anthony Phillips releases Private Parts & Pieces IX: Dragonfly Dreams album.
September 1996: Anthony Phillips releases The Meadows Of Englewood album.
October 1996: Steve Hackett releases Genesis Revisited album initially in Japan only.
21st November 1996: Phil Collins releases "Dance into the light" album.
December 16th 1996: Steve Hackett performs handful of shows in Japan to promote Genesis revisited album.
28th February 1997: Phil Collins commences the Dance Into The Light tour at Tampa Florida USA.
6th June 1997: Genesis announce Ray Wilson as replacement for Phil Collins, also new album: Calling All Stations and tour plans for 1997/98.
26th July 1997: Anthony Phillips releases Survival The Music Of Nature album.
15th August 1997: Congo single released.
26th August 1997: Genesis play acoustic promotional show at the Telecom Tower in Berlin.
28th August 1997: Genesis play acoustic promotional show at Kennedy Space Centre Florida.
August 1997: Anthony Phillips releases "Live Radio Sessions" album.
2nd September 1997: Genesis release "Calling all stations" album.
September 1997: Steve Hackett releases "A Midsummer night's dream" album.
22nd September 1997: Steve Hackett releases UK version of "Genesis revisited".
22nd October 1997: Anthony Phillips releases "Missing Links Three: Time and Tide" album.
15th November 1997: Genesis radio show Hotel Richmond Copenhagen Denmark.
13th December 1997: Genesis radio show at RTL Studios Paris France.
23rd January 1998: Genesis play first full gig with Ray Wilson as singer to invited audience at Bray Films Studios.
28th January 1998: First gig of "Calling All Stations" tour at the Sportovinhala Prague Czech Republic.
25th February 1998: First UK gig of "Calling all stations" tour at NEC Birmingham.
5th April 1998: Final gig of "Calling all stations" tour at Hartwell Arena Helsinki Finland.
11th May 1998: Genesis "reunion" at Heathrow Airport London for promotion of "Genesis Archive 1967-75" Boxed set.
30th May 1998; Genesis perform at the "Rock in Ring" Festival Germany.
31st May 1998: Genesis perform at the "Rock in Park" Festival Germany.
12th June 1998: Phil Collins commences his second Big Band Jazz tour in Santa Barbara USA.

22nd June 1998:	Genesis "Archive 1967-75" 4CD set released.
24th July 1998:	Phil's last Big Band show at the Symphony Hall Birmingham UK.
5th October 1998:	Phil Collins "Greatest Hits" album released.
November 1998:	Anthony Phillips' "Archive Collection Volume One" album released.
8th February 1999:	"Another Day" first single by Ray Wilson's band 'Cut' released.
8th March 1999:	"Millionairhead" first solo album by Ray Wilson's band 'Cut' released.
5th April 1999:	Virgin Japan re-issue entire Genesis back catalogue as limited edition CDs with restored artwork, gatefold sleeves and other original details.
27th April 1999:	Cut's first gig at Room at the Top night club Bathgate Scotland.
30th April 1999:	Cut's tour as "Special Guests" of The Scorpions begins at Deggendorf Eisstadion Germany.
26th April 1999:	Steve Hackett releases his "Darktown" album.
10th May 1999:	Mike + The Mechanics showcase gig for new album at The Hanover Club London.
13th May 1999:	First date of Mike + The Mechanics' UK tour at The Barbican Centre York.
17th May 1999:	"Now That You've Gone" first single from Mike + The Mechanics' fifth album released.
24th May 1999:	"A Hot Night In Paris" Phil Collins' Big Band Jazz live album released.
24th May 1999:	"A Joyful Noise" Chester Thompson's solo album re-released.
31st May 1999:	"Mike & The Mechanics" 5th studio album by Mike & The Mechanics released.

Genesis

Anon: The Band That Time Forgot

Britain in the 1960's can be likened to the England of the Tudor period, which saw the blossoming of the "English Renaissance" that gave us Shakespeare, Donne, Byrd and so many others. The England of the second Elizabeth was likewise in the throes of a cultural upheaval the like of which had never been seen before as the nation gradually threw off the shackles of austerity, the after-effects of six years of war and began to breathe again. Into this atmosphere of burgeoning creativity a group of public schoolboys began a love affair with music which would span four decades.

History has already related how the formative line-up of Genesis emerged out of the ashes of two school groups at Charterhouse; Anon fronted by Mike Rutherford and Anthony Phillips, and The Garden Wall which included Tony Banks and Peter Gabriel. In the cloistered atmosphere of Charterhouse the individual members of the band were drawn to music as an escape from the repressive regime that permeated school life. Their earliest efforts at musical creativity were divided between the various school bands which sprang up in the wake of the musical revolution going on outside the walls of Charterhouse.

The history of Anon can be traced back to the now legendary group formed by Phillips at St Edmunds Preparatory School in Hindhead; it was in The Spiders that Phillips first teamed up with Rivers Job, an older boy at the school. In fact, his first experience of performing in front of an audience was as lead singer of a group that pre-dated the formation of The Spiders. It was a memorable occasion but for all the wrong reasons as Phillips recalls: "Someone had heard 'My Old Man's a Dustman', so we went and rehearsed it, but I forgot the words and so was sacked as the singer..!"[1] As a result, he became more interested in playing the guitar, and met Rivers whereupon the two of them discovered a common interest in pop music. The formation of The Spiders soon followed as Phillips and Rivers joined forces with Richard Francis who was known as "Sid", and "Bonehead" Goldsmith whom Phillips describes as "the legendary drummer" having been thrown out of school for a variety of nefarious activities. Phillips also remembers that "Bonehead" was "years ahead of his time as he didn't worry about a regular rhythm!"[2] It was obvious that The Spiders were not destined for greatness but a longstanding friendship was forged between Phillips and Rivers which survived his departure to Charterhouse and the disbanding of The Spiders.

Rivers' arrival at Charterhouse was opportune, as he soon teamed up with another pupil, Richard MacPhail, who had similar interests. During the Easter holidays of 1965 Rivers took McPhail to Phillips' house in Putney for a rehearsal where it soon became patently obvious that McPhail was not cut out to be a drummer. However, he did know the words to The Rolling Stones' songs which formed the fledgling band's repertoire: "That's basically how I became the singer in the band",[3] McPhail confirms.

At the same time, another Charterhouse pupil, Rob Tyrrell found himself equally drawn to music and by the time that Phillips, Rivers and McPhail were looking for a drummer, he had become more than competent. Another budding drummer at the school, Chris Stewart could only marvel at Tyrrell's natural ability and remembers, "Rob was absolutely superb! He was a natural. I was terribly jealous of him".[4]

Phillips clearly recalls the first time that he, Rivers and Tyrrell played together in an empty classroom, but at that stage Tyrrell didn't have his drums with him, so Phillips asked an older boy in his House if he would lend Rob his kit. As Phillips recalls, "this chap was quite kind to lend us his drums although he was almost a brooding presence as it were, quite understandably, as he didn't want his drums to be broken up! Of course, it was Peter Gabriel!"[5]

Phillips also remembers the material which comprised the band's set, "The early stuff was just Stones' numbers and it really had that kind of raw quality to it"[6] Another pupil, Mick Colman also has some fond memories of those days, "Ant and I started to collaborate on songs. I wrote one called 'She's Got Those Lopin' Shoulders', the first and by far the worst song I ever wrote. The first memory I have of actually playing with Anon was probably my initial rehearsal with the band, which I think took place in the room under the stage (Green Room) of the main hall one afternoon. I used to get a little bit frustrated by having to play little more than 'ker-chunk, chunk, chunk, chunk, ker-chunk, chunk, chunk' etcetera and even then being allowed the use of only the bottom two strings of the guitar in time-honoured twelve bar fashion. For relief I sometimes got to play 'did-dee, did-dee, did-dee, did-dee,' on the same two strings, typical of the early Stones sound. I found it very difficult not to embellish or overplay here and there, with the result that I would be rounded upon with cries of: "For Christ's sake, Mick, can't you just play 'did-dee, did-dee, did-dee, did-dee?" Ah, those were the days!"[7]

Suitably inspired, the band were now on the lookout for both a name and a rhythm guitarist. The search was short and Phillips remembers being impressed by new guy

Mike Rutherford as he was slightly more sociable than others, "I don't know what happened with Mike. I think he was basically in the pub! He was a bit of a lad in those days. He was unlike the others; he was with the 'in' crowd".[8]

Rutherford's first band had been The Chesters formed while he was at Preparatory School. His first public appearance had been memorable but once again for all the wrong reasons, as Rutherford remembers, "I couldn't really tune my guitar, but there was a master who could. At that show, between his tuning in the early evening and me playing it, it went out of tune, so it sounded pretty horrible. I was singing 'Travelling Light' with an out of tune guitar but I was fairly uninhibited in those days and I wasn't shy about performing."[9]

Soon Anon set about establishing an audience, making their debut performance at a concert held at Charterhouse on 16th December 1965. The show itself comprised a mixture of comedy sketches; music and a film made by the pupils. Anon were due to perform three songs, and even at this debut the spectre of the technical problems which were to later dog Genesis raised its head. Rutherford's guitar lead failed and the replacement was too short for him to play in his proper place. Panic over, Anon started their first number "We've Got A Good Thing Going", and after initial nerves had subsided, it was followed by "Talkin' About You" and "Mercy Mercy". The brief set was well received by the pupils, but not apparently by the school's headmaster Mr Van Oss who spent the entire set with his fingers in his ears.

Other performances followed – usually at friends' parties – including a now legendary gig at a fancy dress party at Rob Tyrrell's parents' house where guests were invited to turn up as pub signs. Mike couldn't resist joining in and he arrived dressed as a highwayman complete with Tricorn hat and mask!

Further gigs ensued (although more difficult to catalogue) the frequency of which soon led to other difficulties within the band. Richard MacPhail's parents were increasingly worried about their son's involvement, to the point where he was forced to leave. This meant that Anon needed a new lead singer and Mike Rutherford suddenly found himself in the spotlight, "It was a nightmare. I couldn't really reach the notes. I remember one particular moment when we were doing a Stones' song like 'Mercy, Mercy' and I sang so high that my Adam's Apple kind of came out of place!"[10]

Rutherford's stint as singer was also short-lived, as his House Master, Mr Chare, banned him from playing the guitar. With Rutherford out of the group, the search was now on for someone who could fill his role as rhythm guitarist. Fortunately Richard MacPhail was able to rejoin and he introduced a music scholar from Rutherford's House called Mick Colman. McPhail remembers: "Mick had his own guitar and amp which was quite something. He played the introduction to 'The House of the Rising Sun' which we all thought was very impressive".[11]

Eventually the group decided to try and record some of these gems with the help of fellow Charterhouse pupil, Brian Roberts who had set up a home recording facility in two rooms over a pair of garages next door to his father's surgery in Wellesley Road, Chiswick. Roberts recalls the set up "If you were sitting in the rooms above the garage you could hear all the traffic from the road as clear as day. Air-tight didn't come into it, it was more a case of wind-open!"[12] Extensive rehearsals had taken place before the group took themselves down to Chiswick where they recorded a set of demos during a couple of days in April 1966. Among the titles they put down were a version of The

Stones' "Lady Jane" and at least three Anon originals. This included the recording of Anthony Phillips' first song of any worth (his words, not mine) "Patricia" which eventually became "In Hiding" on the first Genesis album, along with two other Anon originals; "Pennsylvania Flickhouse" and "Don't Want You Back". Anthony Phillips also remembers some of the antics which went on at this very primitive recording studio. "Brian had this garage. He was the guy with the German mother who used to call them both, the husband and the son, by their surname (laughter). 'Roberts you get ze tea'. She was wild actually. I remember a policeman came in once to see what we were doing because we were sort of sitting on this balcony and I've never seen a guy sent packing so quickly. He was just gone!"[13]

With McPhail's encouragement, the idea of an end-of-term concert featuring the various Charterhouse bands took shape. To gain a wider acceptance amongst the sceptical authorities at the school, it was agreed that all the bands would be playing for charity, and having got this far, Richard now set about finding other bands suitable to share the bill. Two others were found: The Climax (the band that Rutherford had joined during his brief exile from Anon); and another called The Garden Wall including both Peter Gabriel and Tony Banks, joined by Chris Stewart who by this time had had drum lessons from Gabriel. They were lacking a bassist and lead guitarist so Phillips and Rivers agreed to fill in.

The Climax opened the show before The Garden Wall took the stage. The piano in the hall proved too difficult to move so Tony Banks played it from off-stage, with the result that no one knew he was there until he played the intro to the fourth song; "When A Man Loves A Woman" apparently from nowhere.

Anon, having already tasted the excitement of recording their own material, decided to have another go, and by pooling their resources had managed to raise the grand sum of twenty Guineas with which to record two of their songs at a local studio: Tony Pike Sound in Putney. Having resolved problems in the band's line-up by re-enlisting Rutherford to replace Mick Colman who was unable to attend the session, the band recorded "Pennsylvania Flickhouse" and "Don't Want You Back", two of the songs they had previously recorded with Brian Roberts which featured frequently in their set. Upon arriving at the studio in Drybergh Road, the group soon found that their previous methods of obtaining a sound they were happy with were not suitable on this occasion as Phillips recalls, "We were used to playing our amps quite full so we got a lot more power from the overloading."[14] The noise that the band were making was too much for Tony Pike to bear and he issued his now famous injunction: "You mind my compressors!"

Having completed the session, the band took away with them a master tape with their two songs on it, but the question of what to do with it still remained. The suggestion arose that an acetate should be cut from the tape so that the band members would, in effect, have their own record as a souvenir of their first experience in a proper recording studio. No one can recall clearly why the eventual acetate was a one-sided affair with only "Pennsylvania Flickhouse" on it, but six copies were duly cut from the master tape, plus one for Brian Roberts Two of these still survive today in the hands of Mike Rutherford and Richard MacPhail.

By the autumn of 1966, Anon seemed to have run their course, when, whether by accident or design, they managed to get themselves a slot at the Charterhouse end-of-term concert in December. With McPhail, Rivers and Mick Colman out of the picture, Mike Rutherford was free to rejoin after the dissolution of The Climax, taking up bass duties and a fair proportion of the vocals again. And there, effectively the story of Anon ends, as this was to prove to be their final gig.

With the band now defunct, the ex-members were free to take part in various sessions and it was while recording at Brian Roberts' garage studio that fate played its part in bringing the fledgling Genesis together, as Phillips himself remembers. "Mike and I went to record our songs and I got Tony Banks to come and play some keyboards on it and he was going to bring Peter his vocalist, who I hadn't really heard sing, to do one song. He was kind of a wild guy who used to stand on tables and so on. The deal was that Banks would come along and play keyboards if we recorded one song of theirs and, of course, their song was far better than any of our stuff and we eventually got the publishing deal on the basis of their song which was called 'She Is Beautiful' which became 'The Serpent'. Mike and I were writing dreadful songs. I mean, we wrote one called 'Listen On Five' which was ghastly!"[15]

In The Hall Of The Studio King

Ghastly or not, the group had managed, through the auspices of a friend of theirs at Charterhouse, to attract the ear of Jonathan King, a Charterhouse old boy who had already gained a degree of chart success. He had written, produced and sung the mournful classic "Everyone's Gone To The Moon" which went on to be a UK hit in 1966 and subsequently followed it up by writing and producing another hit for Hedgehoppers Anonymous called "It's Good News Week". Hardly the most impressive credentials for a progressive band like Genesis, but King had two significant points in his favour. First of all he was enthusiastic about the music the band were producing (so enthusiastic that he tried to sign the group to a five-year contract in September 1967 before parental objections reduced this to one year), and secondly he was able to give them recording time through his connections with Decca Records.

Anthony Phillips remembers the compromises that the young composers had to make. "We went progressive and I really liked a lot of that and then when the other boys did 'Silent Sun' I thought it was a terrible sell-out and I really hated it to start with. I thought it was a real sort of Jonathan King… he loved the seven chord trick, basically that was all he knew (laughter). I wasn't with that stuff, I thought it was OK but nothing special."[16]

Under King's auspices, the band now comprised Anthony Phillips, Tony Banks, Mike Rutherford, Peter Gabriel and John Silver (Chris Stewart having checked out before the album came to be recorded). They began to write much more intricate and complex music. Phillips recalls, "Peter's lyrics went very cosmic and there were songs like 'Barnaby's Adventure' and 'The Mystery Of The Flannen Isle Lighthouse.'"[17] Even in those early days the band members had very strong ideas of what they wanted their music to sound like and consequently there was some division of opinion when they finally got to record their first album in 1968. Anthony Phillips: "We were dead naïve and some of the playing on that album was pretty rough but it seemed to sound pretty good to most of us. We had this idea that putting strings on meant a lovely sort of string wash… and I thought we were getting it with our twelve string sound and rich chords. But the worst thing about the way it was recorded was that when they stuck all the backing tracks on, it all went left in the stereo and the strings were suddenly on their own with the vocals dominating the whole thing."[18]

Tony Banks also remembers: "We did the album in a day and a half, we worked on it and then came back the following day to finish it. Then later we did a mono mix of it which sounded good, but then these arrangements were added. We were involved in writing some of the parts, the awful thin string lines as opposed to the big banks of strings which we'd hoped for. It all sounded cheesy in the end."[19]

The band's first single coupled "The Silent Sun" with "That's Me" and was released to an indifferent public reaction by Decca on 2nd February 1968. The album itself was recorded in September 1968 at Regent Sound Studios and it was at this time that the unnamed band began looking for gigs to bring their brand of music to an audience. They began with an inauspicious gig at a local Sunday School teacher's home which Phillips still has vivid memories of "Peter singing that song 'Babies' in the corner and we couldn't hear him! He has this style, which has obviously become a very endearing style, but in those days it wasn't very confident. He appeared to pick at the piano and that would have been fine if it was obvious to us what tempo he was in and, of course, that relied on us being able to hear him. But he tended to drift and he was over in the corner where a lot of people were talking, and he just drifted out of the frame really… he was still going but I don't think anybody else was listening to him!"[20]

Life on the road soon beckoned and consequently a realisation of the increased level of commitment this would require. Not surprisingly the decision to go "professional" was one which the band agonised over. Richard MacPhail secured a place for them to rehearse and it was there that the formative Genesis really began to take shape. Tony Banks recalls, "It was a slow process as both Peter and I were a bit unsure about going professional. We borrowed £150 from each of our parents, most of which went into buying a Hammond organ and we continued to rehearse. We had already written some material and we tried to get people to act as our agent or manager. We took some of the songs from the *From Genesis to Revelation* period such as 'Visions of Angels' as well as some of the things we'd written more recently and just slowly embellished them. We had this song which became 'The Knife' which was originally written on the piano, and was then transferred to the organ and through that we found it sounded great."[21]

Ever the perfectionists, the young group honed their craft with scant regard to the effect their single-mindedness was having on the personal relationships within the band. The strain soon began to tell and this was to have grave consequences as Anthony Phillips recalls. "It was definitely a formative period that the group had to go through. I look back on it and think that we made an awful lot of mistakes in terms of how it was handled, which meant that personality difficulties were going to be inevitable, in the sense that we never stopped working. We never left the place. You have to get away from it, and from the people in order to keep the freshness and to stop things going sour. The music got better obviously, but the personalities started to fray and to move apart. It's certainly *not* true to say that when I left I was the dissenting voice and everyone else was hunky dory – very much not so at all. I had grown apart from Mike Rutherford and Tony Banks, who I don't think would mind me saying, had grown even further apart from Peter Gabriel."[22]

John Silver also recalls this period being one of intense work. "We were all taking it quite seriously. The nexus of the band really comprised Mike, Peter and Ant. I had become friendly with Peter in London and I'd said that I had been a drummer in a series of bands so he said, 'Well, come and meet the other guys'. After meeting at various flats and apartments in London, eventually I did some playing with them and we all hit it off. I think we all knew that it was quite possible that we would be successful but although we all wanted the success a great deal, we weren't willing to compromise on the publicity and commercial side for that success."[22a]

During this period, Decca released a second single from the as yet unreleased album and took the unusual step for the time of coupling two non-album tracks. The single "A Winter's Tale"/ "One-Eyed Hound" appeared on 10th May 1968 – once again to public indifference. Decca finally released the album in March 1969 although not without problems. Jonathan King, having given the group the concept of the creation of the world to work around, decided it would be fitting to call the band "Genesis", although several other names were suggested including "Gabriel's Angels" and "The Champagne Meadow". Decca pointed out that there was already a band by the name of Genesis in the USA insisting that King change the name, which he refused to do. Hence upon its release, the album carried the title *From Genesis to Revelation* which condemned it to being relegated to the "Religious" sections of most record stores – consequently it sold a lacklustre 649 copies.

A final single was issued on 27th June 1969 coupling a further two album tracks; "Where The Sour Turns To Sweet" / "In Hiding" but to no avail. The band were not disheartened however, as by this time they had put all their energy into sharpening their craft and further embellished their repertoire of songs in preparation for a "proper" gig to a paying audience starting at London's Brunel University in November 1969. This was soon followed by a series of gigs in a wide variety of different venues, some more savoury than others.

Having no experience of playing to an audience led to several highly amusing incidents as Phillips recalls. "Well I think you remember the terrible ones and the good ones. There was one that summer in the East End where there was only one guy in the audience and Peter said, 'Any requests?' That was a legendary one! I also remember one at this awful night club called Blaises which had a teeny small stage. In those days Mike used to play the cello and he bowed up a woman's skirt! That's obviously one that you couldn't forget! Another terrible gig was when we had a showcase at The Marquee and my amp went wrong. The twelve string used to feedback badly so when we got to the quiet bit in 'Stagnation' it was just a complete funnel of sound! So they whipped the lead out of the amp as I was playing the lead guitar part. I wasn't sure what had happened and so I turned the volume up rather than down, so when they plugged the lead back in there was a terrible roar!"[23]

Even at this early stage of their development the band were creating their own brand of music which was often perplexing to audiences who wanted something they could dance to. It's fair to say that the songs that they were writing weren't always to their putative audience's tastes, but it's also true that the band themselves weren't always sure about some of the tracks. Phillips recalls, "Mike and I came into our own in 1969 when we first went on the road. Tony Banks found the organ a tricky proposition and didn't naturally adapt to it straight away, so Mike and I suddenly found ourselves with the lions share of the songwriting for a while. We were also responsible for some of the more average material because our electric stuff was still forming the basis of some of our louder songs. It wasn't the best stuff and I think 'Going Out To Get You' was probably a hotch potch of Blues riffs and I don't really remember much more about it. We had loads of nice acoustic songs all of which were basically butchered, although not deliberately, by tech louts, the musical equivalent of lager louts.

"We had a good second set at one time. I remember playing at Brunel University with Fairport Convention – effectively blowing them off stage with a second set which consisted of 'Visions of Angels', 'Twilight Alehouse', 'Pacidy', probably 'Stagnation' and finally 'The Knife'. It was a good set. 'Pacidy' was dropped in the end because it was too slow and ponderous. The pressure came to accelerate everything because the people we were playing to weren't proper concert audiences and you had to get a move on."[24]

Tony Banks recalls, "I used to play guitar in the middle of 'Let Us Now Make Love' and I think that song went through its best phase in the early version of it when Ant used to play it on the piano to us and it sounded great. It was a very good song, it sounded great live."[25]

By the beginning of 1970 the band had parted company with Jonathan King and were on the look out for a new record deal and new management. Their enforced exile at the MacPhail cottage led to the creation of a plethora of pieces, many of which are now sadly lost, although a handful have recently been issued as part of the band's retrospective *Genesis Archive 1967-1975* four disc set. Many others have eluded fans and Tony Banks recalls some of them:

"For some reason 'Let Us Now Make Love' wasn't recorded for *Trespass*. It wasn't left off because we didn't think it was good. I think we'd seen it as a possible single, so we left it behind. Everyone seemed to want us to record 'Twilight Alehouse' but we didn't particularly want to as we didn't think it was as good as some of the other ones. 'Pacidy' sounded good live as well, but part of the problem was that we had too much material. Some of those early songs most people would never have heard of; things like 'Jamaica Longboat', 'Digby Of The Rambling Lake'. There was also a song called 'The Light' which later became 'Lilywhite Lilith', and an instrumental piece called 'Moss' which we used to call 'The Epilogue'. 'The Light' was a popular live song as was the long version of 'Going Out To Get You' and 'The Knife' so it was a toss up between those two as to which would make it on to the album. 'Going Out To Get You' started out with a riff of Ant's, but we made it a much bigger thing and it went on for about twenty minutes."[26]

It was the band's extended version of 'The Knife' which convinced record engineer John Anthony to take his boss at the newly formed Charisma Records, Tony Stratton-Smith, to see a gig and the band were signed to his label within a matter of weeks. Another witness to this formative period in the band's story was the artist responsible for the covers to their first three Charisma albums, Paul Whitehead.

"I met them through John Anthony. At the time I was Art Director for a magazine called *Time Out* and John said, 'I'm producing this band and you're a natural: a perfect fit'. The first time I met them I went to the Charisma office and they were very naïve, and basically I had an interview with them and I had no idea what they did. You've got to understand the English class structure; English Public School boys are twits (laughter). The only guy that was real was Mike. It was kind of weird. I remember them going on the road with a picnic hamper as they didn't trust the food in the transport cafes! They were definitely *not* rock 'n' roll, you know! However, after I spent time with them and listened while they wrote songs, I gave them my feedback and I brought books for them to look at. To me it was like they had the musical language and I had the visual language."[27]

The band's performances at this time are hard to document, although apparently their show at London's Roundhouse on 11th March 1970 was filmed and still exists somewhere. The band also managed to secure a spot on the BBC's prestigious *Night Ride* programme in February 1970, which turned out to be the first of a series of sessions for the BBC that lasted until 1972 and captured the band at several important points on their rise to fame. This is a session which Mike Rutherford remembers particularly well. "The first one with Alec Reid sticks in my mind the most. We were just writing and writing then, with very little to work towards, and suddenly that first session appeared and we had a goal. I remember being very impressed with the way everyone was worried about the levels not peaking, whereas normally you don't worry as long as it sounded good".[28]

With so much material to choose from, the band's problems were exacerbated by their continuing attention to detail and there were several disagreements during the recording of the new album as Phillips recalls. "I remember having an argument with the engineer about the twelve string sound. I remember him telling me, 'That doesn't sound like a twelve string'. I'd been playing this thing on the road for nine months and I had developed my own sound which wasn't everybody's idea of a twelve string sound. I didn't go for the percussive, all-plectrum kind of stuff, I was trying to aim toward the more orchestral thing."[29]

Gradually, the band began to gain an audience with their non-stop round of playing any and every university and college hall they could, and the band's musicianship improved enormously. However, a serious problem loomed on the horizon. Anthony Phillips was beginning to have doubts about the direction in which the band was going and about his own position within the group. Also, playing live was proving difficult for him as he increasingly suffered from severe stagefright. This combination of events eventually led to his decision to leave in July 1970, before their first proper album with Charisma was finished. The news came as a shock, as Mike Rutherford recalls: "I remember him telling me in the back of our Transit van which Richard MacPhail was driving at the time and being very shocked actually."[30] He also agrees to a certain point with Phillips' assessment that the band was trying too hard: "I think the trouble was in those days, we were so committed to the road, and it took so much out of us; getting to the gig, rehearsing, moving the gear, all that routine. We were like a train that couldn't slow down."[31]

Anthony Phillips' last gig was in Hayward's Heath on 18th July 1970, and although the band admit that it was the closest that they ever came to giving up altogether, the indomitable spirit which has characterised the band's career was there even at this early stage, as Mike recalls. "Before Ant's last gig at Hayward's Heath, I remember thinking that this was going to last forever. We were breaking ground with Genesis, and the next thing I drove back with Pete discussing the break-up of the band. Pete and I were in the car together and we started to have a conversation which eventually led to 'hang on a minute: maybe we should carry on?' That's how it seemed."[32]

John Silver also decided to check out of the band at roughly the same time although for very different reasons, as he himself recalls. "The reason that I left was because I'd been offered an assisted place at a university in the States. This was at the time of the film *The Graduate* which had just come out and by the end of that summer we'd already had an album and some singles out. I'd already heard myself on the radio and had the pleasure of phoning up my pals and relatives and saying, 'Listen, we're on the BBC Radio Light Programme' or it may even have been Radio One by that stage. We'd met lots of famous people and I thought that what was ahead was a pretty hard slog and so I decided to go to university rather than stick with it. The success that eventually came, accrued long after I'd left and was a result of many years of traipsing up and down the M1 in the back of a Transit van."[32a]

Looking For Someone

Genesis spent the summer months of 1970 playing a variety of gigs as a four piece, as well as completing work on their delayed album for Charisma. The difficulties still remained of who (if anyone) was going to be Phillips' full-time replacement in the band, as well as their search for another drummer following the departure of John Silver. His replacement, John Mayhew was to take up drum and percussion duties for the new album. There was also considerable discussion about the material which was to be selected for inclusion as Tony Banks recalls. "It was probably a group decision which ones went on. The songs that could have gone on included 'Twilight Alehouse' which we didn't want on the album – I can't remember why. Some songs were always going to be on the album such as 'Dusk' and 'Looking For Someone' which was always a high point for us, although 'Stagnation' was the most significant track."[33]

The album was defined by the unique sound generated by Rutherford and Phillips' combined twelve string sound which, as Mike himself admits was the dominant force on several tracks. "Having recently heard the re-mastered version of that album I listened to 'Stagnation' and I couldn't hear where Pete came in at all, it was Ant and I with the twelve string over everything else".[34]

Continuing their strategy of twin songwriting teams worked well, and the two units fed creatively off each other as Tony Banks remembers. "There was very much the two sides to the sound; one of which came from Ant and Mike in the form of the acoustic guitar sound. That was demonstrated best on tracks like 'White Mountain' and the early part of 'Stagnation'. Then there was the heavier sound which I like to think came from Peter and myself which was shown on things like 'Looking For Someone' and 'The Knife'. It's funny as things were not really planned to be that way, but that's how it happened. They were more guitar-based and we were more keyboard-based, and sometimes there were moments where we met like on 'Stagnation'. That's why it's a successful song as it was a combination of everyone's best parts."[35]

As a musical unit the band were firing on all cylinders during this period, although live performances were continually dogged by the technical difficulties that had plagued their previous tours, as Anthony Phillips remembers quite vividly. "In those days we did these big multi-instrumental changes where everybody would suddenly end up by playing different instruments. Consequently nothing would ever work and there would be long gaps between numbers where instruments would be tried out and passed across between each other. There was a thing which used to be known as the "Strat procession" where my guitar – which Tony Banks would sometimes play through his Leslie – would often go round all the amplifiers two or three times to see if it would work in different sockets. I think this is probably where Gabriel's stories started, because there was such a long time that had to be filled because various bits of gear didn't work."[36]

Trespass was recorded in July 1970, and released by Charisma in October of that year, by which time John Mayhew had departed for pastures new. Mayhew's place was taken on 24th August by a promising young drummer, Phil Collins, whose previous credentials included a stint with 1969's "flavour of the month" Flaming Youth. Collins brought a much-needed percussive edge to the band's live sound and their gigs became even more memorable. The repertoire drew heavily on their first two albums, as well as several numbers which although recorded, had not been released. Without doubt the highlight of the show was the closing number 'The Knife' which varied in length from the version we know and love on the album, to an extended version often clocking in at over nineteen minutes in length. The band's attitude to their set is perhaps best summed up by Peter Gabriel. "We talked at length about set structure. We would start with soft numbers and work up to the aggressive ones. If we kept the power in the back, we could introduce ourselves slowly like a folk band, and people would think 'OK, just another acoustic band' you could ignore us or not. And then gradually we would introduce more and more electric instruments and then we would finish off with 'The Knife', this aggressive number about this revolutionary figure on a power trip. I knew that we had the power and the balls to grab the audience and that if we hadn't got them by then, we would move them one way or the other."[37]

No one could doubt the band's dedication to their music and audiences gradually took to their particular brand of English rock. Fans now can only wonder what it must have been like to see this band of serious young musicians hunched over their instruments, fronted by a demented and frustrated drummer as Peter Gabriel kicked the living daylights out of a bass drum at the front of the stage. Working as a four piece was all very well but the band really needed a replacement for Anthony Phillips. At the suggestion of promoter David Stopps they took on board Mick Barnard, a guitarist from a local Aylesbury band Farm, who stepped into the breach for a couple of months. As far as is known Barnard was not a part of the band's recording sessions, except for one occasion when, in October 1970, the BBC invited the band to appear on their television music programme *Disco Two*. Tony Banks remembers the recording vividly: "*Disco Two* was done when Ant had left and we had this guy Mick Barnard playing guitar. It was the only appearance he ever made because he was only with us a few weeks. He was basically miming to Ant's part. The only thing that was live on *Disco Two* was Pete's voice. It was one of those awful things as they wouldn't give him any echo – the guy that did the echo had gone to tea or something!"[38]

Rutherford's reaction to the show was equally negative. "*Disco Two* was very much like Breakfast TV these days; it was live TV and it wasn't very good. I believe it has been lost and I'm not too disappointed about that actually!"[39] The broadcast performance was screened on 14th November and had the band playing "The Knife".

The year ended with Genesis playing the last of their gigs with Mick Barnard at a free concert at London's Lyceum ballroom. The final piece in the band's musical jigsaw witnessed the event and liked what he saw. Steve Hackett recalls: "I met them in 1970 and it was decided that I was going to join them at the earliest opportunity. They fulfilled contractual requirements at that moment with the existing guitarist – a chap called Mick Barnard. I think they did a further two gigs with him and then I was 'in' as it were."[40]

The band had seen Hackett's advertisement in the back pages of the illustrious *Melody Maker* asking for musicians "determined to strive beyond existing stagnant musical forms" and a meeting was arranged where Hackett had the chance to shine and prove that he wasn't just into techno flash but could also lay down moods and layers of music; a quality which definitely appealed to the other members of Genesis.

Opening The Musical Box

By the time Steve Hackett joined, Genesis had begun rehearsals for the follow up album to *Trespass* at Farnham Maltings in late 1970. *Trespass* in the meantime had received favourable coverage in the press, whilst audience reaction had bordered on the ecstatic. But this had not been translated into sales as Tony Banks recalls. "*Trespass* didn't really do a lot. The album sold something like 6,000 copies. I think we felt that was OK. Obviously we wanted it to do well but we didn't expect any fantastic sales figures. At that time we were building a live following but nothing astounding."[41]

However, the group's work ethic meant that they continued to gig up and down the country. "They would play anywhere," recalls promoter Tony Chapman. "I never had any hassles from them. They would pick up the details and be on the road even if they had to play a hundred capacity club miles away up North."[42]

Another promoter, Andrew Kilderry remembers them for different reasons: "I remember once they were the only band who forgot to ask for their money. I had them in for £75 and they did the show, and they were too scared and nervous to ask anything and off they went! The agent called me up a few days later and went mad because they hadn't been paid!"[43]

Steve Hackett, the band's new guitarist remembers his first gig with the band. "It was University College in the City or City of London University in Moorgate. It was a very shaky concert – not a pleasant experience. There were lots of mistakes. I had a fuzz box that I'd been rehearsing with all week, but suddenly on the night they gave me a different one. The fuzz box started to feedback, I played bum notes all night long and I thought; that's it the game's up – I haven't got the gig! This was followed by the Lyceum in London. There wasn't a bigger London gig at the time and although it was well received, when it was finished I was still sitting there on my stool. Finally Richard MacPhail came onstage, took my arm and said; "It's finished now, Steve" (laughter). I was that nervous after it!"[44]

The writing and rehearsing for new album took place at manager Tony Stratton-Smith's house in Crowborough. It was not an easy period for the band who were still coming to terms with the loss of Anthony Phillips. The majority of the material which was to feature on the album had already been written before Phillips left. This made it especially difficult for Steve Hackett who joined the band just as they were in the process of embellishing the pieces. Hackett recalls that, "Most of the album had been written out of rehearsals before I joined although there was still a lot of room to make improvements. No one was making the sound of a musical box; so I felt, well here's an opportunity for me for a start."[45]

In fact, "The Musical Box" holds a unique place in the band's history as Tony Banks explains: "'The Musical Box' was a hangover from the days of Ant and Mike. It was always more Mike's thing as he used a tuning on the twelve-string where the top three strings were all tuned to F# – that's where the working title came from. Ant certainly embellished those parts and I always felt that Ant should have got a credit on that song as part of the writing team. We then took it somewhere else, and the melody line at the end of the song was actually written at the time that Mick Barnard was in the group, so that was his contribution to the song. That track has the influence of all three guitarists on it."[46] This was recently reinforced when Anthony released a demo version of "F#" as part of his *Archive Collection Volume One* set.

In an effort to increase interest in their growing stable of acts, Charisma decided to package three of the best together and send them out on tour throughout the UK in January and February 1971, taking in some of the larger theatres on the gig circuit. Genesis, as the junior partners in the package opened the show for Van Der Graaf Generator and Lindisfarne who, by this time were a happening band with their massive hit "Fog on the Tyne". However, Genesis, with nothing to lose and everything to gain, in many cases stole the other groups' thunder, a view confirmed in a review by Michael Watts of *Melody Maker.* "It would be insidious to single out any one of the bands for future success, but at Sunday's concert, the beginning of Charisma's package tour, Genesis emerged with the greatest honours and audience acclaim. They are harder and more incisive than the delicacy of their album would suggest, and their vocalist, Peter Gabriel, frantic in his tambourine shaking, his voice hoarse and urgent is a focus for all the band's energy."[47]

Another witness to those memorable early gigs is the band's long-time biographer, Armando Gallo, who recalls the first time he saw Genesis, on 24th January 1971 at the Lyceum in London. "I went to see Van der Graaf Generator there with a bunch of friends because they were my favourite band. Genesis opened for Van der Graaf, and Tony Stratton-Smith was at the back at the bar with his usual drink (laughter) saying, 'have a pint Armando.' So I had the pint and then he said; 'you should check out this band, they're very good'. So I went forward and by the time they came out and did "The Knife" there must have been about fifty people in front who went crazy, but all the others just didn't care."[48]

Despite the plaudits of the critics and the fans, sales of *Trespass* did not significantly increase and Charisma focussed their promotional activities around Lindisfarne. However, the Genesis were to make gains in some unexpected places with a new audience after their first overseas gigs in Belgium in March 1971 where the band played a couple of college halls and also recorded sets for *Pop Shop,* a Belgian equivalent of *Top of the Pops*. A recording of one of these shows has recently surfaced and, despite its rough quality it nevertheless serves as a record of the energy and invention of the band at this formative stage of their development with a set comprising an early version of "Happy The Man", "Stagnation", "The Light", "Twilight Alehouse", "The Musical Box", "The Knife" and "Going Out To Get You".

The band's live following increased and they continued to perform concerts up and down the country whilst working on the follow-up album to *Trespass* although it was not plain sailing as Banks recalls. "It wasn't a particularly easy period as I remember, we were struggling a bit with some of the songs. At that point 'Musical Box' was a live success. We wrote 'The Return Of The Giant Hogweed' and that took over from 'The Knife' as being the song to close the live set and it worked pretty well. 'The Fountain Of Salmacis' worked well; it was something of a departure from the norm…"[49] Indeed this was the facet of Genesis' music that not only appealed to their audience but to the players themselves as Hackett maintains, "Things like 'The Fountain Of Salmacis' were often more of an odyssey than a song. I call them odysseys because you didn't really know where you were going to end up. The structure doesn't vary that much and this was very important; each song was an adventure – it was a journey…"[50]

Charisma finally released the album; titled *Nursery Cryme,* in November with even less promotion behind it than its predecessor. Strangely they also decided to release "The Knife" from the previous album as a single, but split into two parts, packaged in the band's first picture sleeve. However, the band line-up had changed, and the picture used omitted Anthony Phillips even though he was fundamental to "The Knife". Another Charisma Package Tour was organised in the autumn, reuniting Genesis with Lindisfarne, and the year saw both bands consolidating their position amongst Britain's most popular live acts – although with very different musical strategies. In the meantime, something was stirring in Continental Europe…

A Brave New World

Finally coming to terms with the fact that *Nursery Cryme* was, in commercial terms, no improvement on *Trespass* as Tony recalls, "I think we were considerably more depressed by the sales of *Nursery Cryme* as that again only sold about 6000 copies. By the time that the album came out the group was obviously a lot bigger. We were doing well in foreign countries at that point – Belgium and Italy – but not as well in England."[51] In fact the New Year brought more hope for Genesis – in late January the news broke that the *Trespass* album was number one on the Belgian charts. By the time they crossed the English Channel to play some more overseas gigs their new album had reached number four in the Italian charts, which astonished the band as Phil Collins recalls. "When we heard it we were amazed, it was strange that it should come from anywhere abroad, considering the amount of work that we had put in in England"[52] However, the band were not without their supporters in the UK, and a second radio session was recorded by the BBC on 9th January 1972, as part of the *Sounds Of The Seventies* series. This was followed shortly afterwards by a series of gigs in Belgium, again including the recording of what is now their earliest surviving appearance on television as part of the *Rock Of The Seventies* series, where the band performed live in a studio. Looking at this film now, the band look extremely self-conscious, but even so their music is accomplished and the choice of tracks was inspired, including highlights of their live set; "Musical Box", "The Return Of The Giant Hogweed", "Twilight Alehouse" and "Fountain Of Salmacis". It was particularly significant to see "Twilight Alehouse" because it was over a year before it was finally committed to vinyl as the b-side of the band's first minor "hit" single.

The band's touring schedule took them to Italy in April where they played a string of sell-out gigs to ecstatic audiences, and it was during this tour that songs like "Watcher Of The Skies" took shape, Tony Banks and Mike Rutherford wrote the lyrics in Naples. Also, and probably of equal significance, the band began to examine the actual performance of the songs, as Steve Hackett recalls. "On Watcher Of The Skies, I remember being the one who said, "We've got to get a Mellotron, we've got to get a light show. I remember being against doing 'Supper's Ready' live until we had all these things because I felt it wouldn't work. It was me and Peter insisting that we shouldn't do it unless we had all the sound effects of the train doors slamming and Uncle Tom Cobley and all... because we had performed a number of these type of things live and people just wandered off to the bar and we wondered why. So we had to get the whole production together before things started clicking with Genesis in those days…"[53]

The band's UK following, despite the relatively disappointing sales of *Nursery Cryme*, had increased to the point where they were given a spot on the bill for the prestigious Reading festival in August 1971. This led to invites to the next two Reading Festivals, giving them significant exposure to large audiences. Genesis made an impression and the 1972 Reading Festival is vividly recalled by longstanding fan Andy Wilkinson… "Still relatively unknown outside the club and college circuit of London and the Home Counties, this gig was to be an interesting test of their appeal in front of a very mixed bunch of festival goers, many present to see other, more prominent headlining bands. With forty-odd minutes to play, it was going to be an interesting short set… They opted to go hell-for-leather from the start and kicked off with a frenetic 'The Knife'. They sure as hell grabbed a lot of people's attention as darkness fell and Peter was, as usual, the focus of everything up there on stage. Next 'Twilight Alehouse' seemed to please the crowds with the slurred organ finale, then straight into 'Watcher Of The Skies. By now it was getting pretty dark and the majestic choral opening really did capture the atmosphere of the evening and the crowd were definitely warming to the band, who sounded totally and radically different to anything that appeared before. 'The Musical Box' followed and was to be the conclusion to their set with a short but ear and eye catching 'Return Of The Giant Hogweed' as an encore. They had stolen Friday evening musically and created a wonderful hour of festival atmosphere on a warm August evening…"[54]

The touring schedule took them the length and breadth of the UK during 1971 and into 1972 culminating with an auspicious slot at the Great Western Music Festival in Lincoln on 28th May. It was there that the longstanding bogie of Genesis and open air concerts struck. The show was a disaster by their standards although the audience and critics were blown away, especially by Peter's appearance dressed as an "an ageless Egyptian prince". Armando Gallo also remembers that particular show. "The Lincoln Festival was very good because it was a four day event; the weather was dreadful, and after they had played they thought they'd done a horrible show. But that's when I got converted to Genesis, because the atmosphere was so against them. It was two o'clock in the afternoon – it was so cold and everybody was covered in straw! As it was raining so much they gave out hundreds of bales of straw and people were sleeping under it and at the time Genesis came on people were just waking up. I wrote in my first book that this was where I stood with my wellies entrenched in the mud with twelve Italian journalists that I was taking care of and we were all just raving about it…"[55] Other memorable shows at this time included the band's show at the Olympia Theatre in Paris, where they were supported by Peter Hammill.

On their return they began the process of rehearsing and recording their new material, initially at a rehearsal room in Blackheath, although the band were not too happy with Charisma's choice of producer as Tony Banks remembers. "Charisma wanted us to have a hit, so they thought they'd bring in Bob Potter who had worked with Bob Johnson in America and people like Simon and Garfunkel and Bob Dylan. Charisma thought that he could tighten things up a bit and stop things getting too arty for their own good. He came in and we just didn't see eye to eye at all. I did the introduction to 'Watcher…' and he said it was awful, he felt it sounded just like 2001. Charisma scrambled about trying to find somebody else and they came up with Dave Hitchcock. We changed engineer during the course of the album as well as we weren't happy with the sound the guy was getting. We realised that when we got John Burns in as the engineer we could communicate with him, we were after the same sort of thing. With 'Supper's Ready' the whole thing came about by accident – for example, there were little parts like the 'Apocalypse' section where the organ solo on that started off as a very tongue in cheek sort of thing, I thought I'd play like Keith Emerson to see what it sounded like…"[56]

"Supper's Ready" was to be the backbone of the new album *Foxtrot* upon its release in October 1972. The press and fan reaction was universally favourable and "Supper's Ready" made an instant impression on concert audiences, as Andy Wilkinson, remembers. "Peter was as ever, in complete control – slim, dressed all in black with the now familiar partly shaven head and totally unique stage demeanour. He teased and taunted, providing lengthy pithy surreal stories mixed with references from Monty Python, as well as vague references to sexual innuendo and to the characters the songs portrayed. But what made the difference was that 'Supper's Ready', although only released a month before, had already become very familiar to the audience who just sat and witnessed it in awe. The song was played pretty much as it sounded on *Foxtrot*. Gabriel and the rest of the band were in top form and gave a performance of unnerving power, subtlety and precision. There were no costume changes, no props, and no zany theatrics; it was played honestly with a minimum of fuss but very intense…"[57]

The band also took an unusual step in releasing a non-album track as a single, "Happy The Man", which had been around since the very earliest days of the band, and was backed by "Seven Stones" from the previous album. It was not a success although Tony Banks remembers the song quite fondly. "I didn't have that much to do with it really, I was sort of there if you know what I mean! (laughter). Once again Mike had another tuning on the guitar where everything was tuned to a chord and he played a riff on that and that sounded good. I played guitar along with him and we built it up from there…I suppose it came as a result of being on the road just too long with Lindisfarne (laughter) we had to have one song like that!"[58]

The new show drew heavily upon the new album and their audience was such that now they were capable of playing the largest theatres in the UK as a headline act in their own right. This did little to alleviate the technical problems and appalling sound quality as Tony Banks recalls. "With the PA's in those days you could never hear the voice so we actually performed one song on stage with no lyrics, Peter was just making noises. He also introduced 'Get 'em Out By Friday' as a song called 'I've Been Travelling All Night Long' and no one noticed the difference!"[59]

Another tour with Lindisfarne took place in October to coincide with the release of the new album although this time the honours were shared. Europe had already taken the band to their hearts, now it was time to focus their attention on the USA where Genesis were very much an unknown quantity. Buddah Records, who were in charge of promotion of the Charisma catalogue in the USA, had found the band's previous album a hard one to promote in the States, but with *Foxtrot* they finally felt that they had something they could work with. A showcase gig was arranged at New York's prestigious Philharmonic Hall in aid of the United Cerebral Palsy Fund. A warm-up gig was arranged a couple of days before at Brandeis University in Boston which went off without fuss to a small audience.

The Philharmonic gig itself however, was a different matter with problems piling on problems. For instance, Leonard Bernstein showed scant regard for fellow professionals by insisting on rehearsing the orchestra on the day of the gig and there were several problems with the PA system, as Tony recalls. "The whole gig was a complete nightmare. We had an incredible hum all the way through 'Supper's Ready'. Something was really wrong with Mike's gear and I couldn't get full volume out of mine, no textures, no colours."[60] However despondent the band felt, the audience loved the show and fans started writing in to their local radio stations requesting that they play Genesis records. The stage looked set for Genesis to take the States by storm. As they were to discover though, a lot more work would have to be put in before that goal was achieved.

Conquering The New World

Having been bitten, albeit briefly, by the American bug, the band returned there in March of 1973 not before they continued their upward rise at home. They consolidated their position with a series of sell-out shows across the UK in January and February culminating at London's Rainbow Theatre – at the time about the most prestigious gig a band could get in London. It was here that they began to experiment with their stage set-up having finally perfected the musical side of things with *Foxtrot.* Rather than clutter the stage with as much gear as they could cram on it, Genesis opted for the other extreme and managed to find a way to make it appear as if there was no equipment on stage at all by the clever use of a gauze curtain (the "Sails") and ultraviolet light which also served to heighten the appearance of Peter's Day Glo makeup. This was also, as mentioned previously, Gabriel's first appearance in the full costume, comprising his head encased in a pair of bat wings, a full-flowing glittering cape covering what appeared to be a tight-fitting black body stocking. His previous dalliance with costume at Dublin's National Stadium the previous September where he had emerged during "The Musical Box" wearing a fox head and red dress had been met with stunned silence by the audience. Surviving footage of Peter's appearance at the Bataclan Club in Paris the following February where he appears in this costume gives a small sample of exactly what this theatrical element was like, although sadly it is unlikely if it will ever be released officially. The band were also filmed during their appearance at the Frankfurt Festival in January, a further indication of how far they had progressed both musically and visually. Public and press interest in this "happening" band continued to grow apace although there was no avalanche of press plaudits in the UK, Chris Welch being the sole voice in the wilderness. His review of the Rainbow gig sums up Genesis' predicament at the time: "Did not the youths and maidens dance as if possessed? And you can't blame it on rock and roll because Genesis don't play any."[61]

This was indeed the band's problem, once again the spirit of the early audiences who had wanted "something to dance to" had come back to haunt Genesis. The music press, ever ones for an easy option, categorised them in the same pigeonhole as ELP, Yes and Jethro Tull without realising that Genesis were an entity all of their own.

The art of presentation was indeed a lesson which Peter Gabriel had taken to heart as the band learned to their surprise when he opted to bring in a set of costumes for the showcase gig at London's Rainbow Theatre on 9th February 1973, as Steve Hackett recalls. "He sprang that on us that night and I was very happy he did that. He just brought them along and they were just sitting there backstage before the show. He didn't rehearse with them, he just put them all on during the numbers and I thought it was great. There was a school of thought within the band that might have said, 'I'm not too sure about that gold lamé number'. So I think he had the right sort of steamrollering approach; if he wanted to do it he just went ahead and did it. I felt the same musically, it was sometimes better to steamroller things than to try and do them by committee."[62]

Gabriel's appearance was perfectly in keeping with the surreal nature of the show as emphasised by the introductions he used, "Michael Mellotron playing the part of Tony Banks, David Drums and Sally Cymbals as Philip Collins, myself, Peter Gabriel played by Patrick Moore, Michael Rutherford by Richard Rickenbacker, and Steve Hackett by Gary Gibson himself."[63] Holding to the tenets of the old storytelling traditions, Genesis took the audience far beyond the mere artifice of rock 'n' roll into their own world. As a frontman, Gabriel was transformed and Genesis gigs were never quite the same afterwards, and neither were their audiences, who packed out show after show in the UK and subsequently in Europe. As their long-term friend and chronicler Armando Gallo was to say several years later – "Welcome to the world of Genesis"

After their brief initial foray to the USA, and the reaction to the Philharmonic Hall show, the band naturally thought that America would fall before the all-conquering heroes as the UK and Europe had already done. Upon their return to the States in March however, their illusions were to be cruelly shattered. With a massive stage production in tow there were to be very few shows where they could (even if they were willing to do so) compress their set into thirty or forty minutes as support act. Also, no self-respecting artist would want a support act that could effectively blow them off-stage with such a theatrical presentation. Consequently, apart from a few shows supporting Lou Reed and Richie Havens, the band were effectively on their own. Ironically they even used a member of what is now the longest serving road crew in rock as a support act at some shows. Dale Newman, Rutherford's guitar roadie and now long-time minder of their studio, The Farm, recalls how he first became involved with the band. "I got the phone call from Craig Schertz and agreed to do two weeks as guitar technician. My guitar skills were just enough to do what he required at the time, which was just to look after a few acoustic guitars and keep them in tune… the two weeks went well and Mike asked me if I wanted to go to Europe so I said, 'Here's my passport' and we were off!"[64] This is another facet of Genesis which marks them out from other bands; their road crew have remained with them for many years and maintain the high standards which the band set themselves.

The shows at the Free Trade Hall in Manchester on 24th February and the de Montfort Hall in Leicester on 25th February 1973 were recorded for an American radio show *The King Biscuit Flower Hour,* and manager Tony Stratton-Smith obtained the unmixed tapes from the radio station with the aim of releasing a live album. The band themselves were not too keen on this idea, although, as Stratton-Smith quite correctly pointed out, such a release would enable the band to step off the album-tour- album treadmill that they had been on since their career began. This would give them some breathing space with which to reassess their position and to begin writing for a new album. The band members capitulated and *Genesis Live* was subsequently pressed up as a double album although eventually a truncated version was released into the shops on 20th July 1973. It showcased some of the finest moments, although sadly omitting "Supper's Ready". The album was rightfully dedicated to the band's long time friend and sound engineer, Richard MacPhail whose devotion to the cause is well remembered by Phil Collins. "The sound at those early gigs around the *Foxtrot* time, in the small town halls, was probably amazing because Richard knew exactly everybody's head inside out and he was so in sympathy with what the band should sound like."[65] Test pressings of the album on the Dutch Philips label do exist although fortunately for most fans' wallets, the recent *Genesis Archive* collection has finally brought the remaining highlights of this period to us.

The band wound down live shows during the summer months in favour of work on their forthcoming album. After the success of *Foxtrot* both at home and abroad, anticipation for the band's new work was high. Perhaps, unlike previous efforts, they allowed themselves too much time to write and record, and the end result in some aspects fell between two stools. Undoubtedly the music had improved and the overall technique was immeasurably better, but there were still problems as Banks recalls. "We had a few arguments about this at the time, because really there was too much material to go on the album. I wanted to kick off 'After The Ordeal' which I actually think is the worst song we've ever recorded, I really didn't like that. I don't like the whole sort of pseudo classical thing at all…We could have got it off the album without any trouble as we shouted about it quite loudly at the time! But Pete also said that he wanted to get rid of the instrumental bit at the end of 'Cinema Show' and I said, 'We can't have that, it's great and it's got all the best bits!" So we ended up with a compromise which was to keep the whole bloody lot on and as a result the album sides were far too long, about twenty eight minutes as I recall. That was far too long for a vinyl album so it sounds pretty rough."[66]

Hackett's difficulties with the album were much more personal. By nature a quiet and rather shy individual, he had problems coming to terms with the heated and, it must be said, at times petty attitudes which was evidenced by the behaviour of the core members who had grown up with each other. As Steve maintained, it was sometimes as trivial as, "well you broke my ruler in 1963!" To which the reply was, "Ah, yes, but you pinched my sweets in 1964!"[67] The other members were used to each others foibles, but it was sometimes difficult for the new boys to find a position in which they were comfortable. Hackett eventually overcame these doubts as he remembers. "I had this with Genesis before *Foxtrot* when I didn't think I'd contributed sufficiently to the songs on that album. I always felt they were strong enough without me and I felt, 'You know, I think I ought to leave, you guys are strong enough without me.' And Tony and Mike said, 'Oh, no Steve, we really like your guitar playing and we really want you to stay with the band.'"[68] And so, freed from that nagging doubt, Hackett threw himself into the writing and recording of *Selling England By The Pound*. Without doubt it is his work which shines through, and the album is one he recalls particularly fondly. "Well, having been involved with a bunch of guys who were a songwriter's collective as they originally presented themselves, I felt I hadn't really come up with any songs for the band, and at that time I felt that it was time to express myself spontaneously as a player. I felt that this was never going to wash with the band but I said; 'I've got a few bits that go like this... (hums out tune that became 'Dancing With The Moonlit Knight') and I said, 'What I'm really all about is this, but I really don't think that you guys are in this ball park, are you?' And Phil said, 'Hold on, I think we've got something."[69] That something turned out to be the one thing that had so far eluded them: a hit single. "I Know What I Like" evolved out of a band jam session and was to prove to be the unlikely "hit" of 1973. "It was based on a riff of Steve's," Banks explains. "We used to jam on it for hours and I had the idea of playing it on fuzz piano and organ at the same time and because the piano was very out of tune with the organ, the whole thing had a nice quality about it, even when I was just playing these very simple chords. We knew we'd written something that had single potential although we were a bit embarrassed about it as we weren't supposed to be a singles band. Anyway Charisma put it out and we refused to go on *Top Of The Pops*! We thought that was enough of a stand."[70]

The single eventually reached the number nineteen slot in the UK charts and the album itself made Genesis' highest position to date reaching number three. At last Genesis had made the breakthrough to the mainstream and the ensuing tour was extremely successful and enjoyable. Hackett recalls the band's famous gigs at Los Angeles' Roxy Theatre that December. "We did three nights; two shows a night. They sold out and people were hanging from the rafters. They loved everything we did, and to my mind they were some of the greatest gigs the band ever played because it was a small room, it was very powerful and I felt very much at home. I knew what I was playing and I knew who I was, despite the fact that I was wearing a terrible jacket with strawberries all over it! I was going through my phase of looking like the guy from Spinal Tap who had the moustache! Nonetheless they loved us and I felt we were right; this was the greatest stuff this band is ever going to do, this is IT! There were things happening on stage; Pete and Phil were so loose they would start going into comedy routines. At one point they would start doing this thing where Pete would start doing an impression of Alan Whicker (laughter) and then Phil started doing the same thing, and of course, the audience didn't know what they were doing. But the band were falling about; we were in tears of laughter – we were so relaxed. We did a Christmas Eve show where, in order to sound like Mickey Mouse, Pete couldn't get his voice up that high and so he took helium. He took so much that he had hiccups for a day afterwards but he went for it. He was dressed up as Father Christmas and it was just great."[71]

The band even found time to record a concert film at Shepperton Studios outside London. Titled *Tony Stratton-Smith Presents Genesis In Concert*, it was filmed in front of an invited audience on 30th and 31st October 1973 and featured highlights from the band's new set: "Watcher Of The Skies", "Dancing With The Moonlit Knight", "Musical Box", "I Know What I Like" and "Supper's Ready" and managed to capture something of the spirit of the band at this crucial stage in their development. In fact, the live sequence from this film was to have been the promotional video for the "I Know What I Like" single, but the band rejected it at the last minute. Sadly, the plans for this film to be given a cinematic release also fell through and it remains unseen to this day, although tantalising glimpses have been shown on various television programmes and more recently, in the band's own documentary histories. Frustratingly, it is also known that earlier shows were captured for posterity on film and these too, are sadly languishing in vaults somewhere.

Also at this time, during a lull in the touring schedule, Mike Rutherford was briefly reunited with his old friend Anthony Phillips for the recording of a song which dated back to the halcyon days of 1969. "Silver Song" had been written by Phillips as a tribute to the Genesis drummer John Silver, and having enlisted Mike Rutherford to record it, they also involved Phil Collins as singer which, along with his solo spot on "More Fool Me" during the band's new show, was perhaps an early indication of what was to happen later. Phillips recalls how this elusive recording came about. "That summer Genesis had a bit of a lull writing *Selling England By The Pound.* Mike and I were talking about possible solo things. We heard about the Charisma album of modern hymns (*Beyond An Empty Dream*) and 'Silver Song' came to light at the same time. Phil came down and sang on the demo of the hymn ('Take This Heart') with a few friends. Then the 'Silver Song' idea came up – I can't remember how we played it to him, but he loved the idea. The demo is great because it has a lovely country feel to it but the sound is so wild. The drums do sound seriously 'cardboard boxey' on that. The finished version sounded a little clinical with the twelve strings; we didn't get the feel of it. Phil sang it well but he didn't sing it in the really loose way he did on the demo. He sang it correctly and brilliantly at the end with the improvised part, but it lacked the loose, summer afternoon feel the demo had. We had to do it in a day, both songs."[72] Either way, the session including the prospective B-side "Only Your Love" was recorded and proposed as a Phil Collins solo single, although this idea was subsequently shelved and the recording still lingers somewhere in the Charisma archives. The hymn which Phillips and Rutherford recorded, "Take This Heart", finally appeared on the Charisma album *Beyond An Empty Dream* in 1975 and is now one of the most collectable items for fans of both Anthony Phillips' and Mike Rutherford's work.

Such breaks were to prove a rare luxury as the band continued their gruelling concert schedule into the following year. Beginning with five sell-out shows at London's prestigious Drury Lane Theatre, the first of which is vivily recalled by Andy Wilkinson. "Mid-way through a so-far stunning and unbelievable evening, it was time to play 'Firth Of Fifth'. Tony began unaccompanied with the breezy piano intro leading into the song. Suddenly things began to go seriously wrong: one or two blindingly obvious bum notes were played, the tempo began to skew; more wrong notes. Tony had totally lost the plot!! He bravely continued, struggling heroically to get his piano back on course. Too late, the beautiful piano introduction was reduced to an unqualified disaster. Tony had no option but to stop dead. Phil rescued the situation somewhat, when he swiftly called 'two, three, four' and the band continued in unison with the rest of the song. Thankfully Tony had not lost his composure over this faux pas, and the song and the rest of the set was completed in fine style…"[73] However, this hiccup did have a long term effect, as the song has *never* been played with its introduction since! Another memorable moment from these shows occurred when Gabriel decided to avail himself of a theatrical prop common in old English theatres, a "Peter Pan Rope" with which he was hauled up to "fly" across the stage during "Supper's Ready" giving an already dramatic song even more style. The band rounded off their most successful tour to date with a string of US shows culminating in a two-night stint at New York's Academy of Music in early May 1974. The stage was now set for them to embark on another new album; one which was to take their fans and critics by surprise…

Taking The Lamb To Market

Both 1973 and 1974 were difficult years in the UK; the oil embargo placed on the West by the oil-producing States in the Middle East hit industry hard, especially the record industry. The "three day week" was one misery, but added to that, restrictions on products made from petroleum (including, of course, records) was another. Perhaps these difficulties influenced the direction the band was taking. Their previous album's title, *Selling England By The Pound,* was ostensibly a reference to the Labour Party manifesto of the time and perhaps the general frustration rubbed off on the band. What isn't in doubt is that by the summer of 1974, things in the Genesis camp were far from ideal. The restrictions that the structured approach to composition enforced were sensed most keenly by Phil Collins, who began to look for outlets for his music outside of the band. This included his own "scratch band": Zox And The Radar Boys, which included luminaries such as Bill Bruford and Peter Banks. This freedom of expression was something which Collins enjoyed, as he explained during a Radio One interview at the time. "Just keep it very loose and just have a good time… because I'm at home with the arranged things that we do, but sometimes I get a yearning to get on stage and not know what is going to happen. Occasionally we've had improvised things when equipment has broken down and they can turn out to be quite fun... The stuff on the new album… a lot of it is heading that way, towards having a very loose theme to work with and keeping a lot more of whatever happens on the night… the freer you can keep it, the better really…"[74]

Ironically, given the turn of events which was to follow, it was Collins' unrest with the band which led him initially to consider leaving, as Armando Gallo recalls. "I had moved to England and I was going back to the USA. Maybe on the Wednesday or Thursday of the week before I was due to leave, was the presentation of the gold disc for *Selling England By The Pound* and Phil came up to me and said; 'You're leaving for Los Angeles, so I better tell you before somebody else tells you; I'm leaving the band.' I said, 'Really?' He was getting this band together, which became Brand X. So I left and went back to California and then in the August there was the news that Peter had left the band, and I said; 'what do you mean, Peter's left? Phil was supposed to be leaving!"[75]

Mike Rutherford also took up work outside of the band, being reunited with his friend Anthony Phillips for what was eventually to appear as Phillips' first solo album *The Geese & The Ghost* some three years later. Meanwhile Peter Gabriel was flirting with the world of movies – an area that had always fascinated him. William Friedkin, who had gained a certain notoriety by directing the classic horror film *The Exorcist,* was taken by the story on the back of the *Genesis Live* album and thought that Gabriel might be able to work in the field of screenwriting. Naturally, he was tempted and briefly left the band to try his hand.

The "team ethic" which had guided Genesis thus far was thrown into turmoil by Gabriel's decision and Banks in particular was adamant that any individual project shouldn't be put before the interests of the group. Added to these difficulties, Gabriel's wife was expecting their first child and there were complications which placed an even greater strain on him. Steve Hackett was in a similar position with the impending breakdown of his first marriage. The band themselves, perhaps in an attempt to return to the early days, opted to record the next album out in the country and retreated to Hedley Grange, a rambling pile which had previously been the home of notorious occultist Aleister Crowley and also home to the arch hedonists of the rock world, Led Zeppelin. At an early stage it was decided to make the album into a concept, which in itself was a brave step given that the rock world was by now beginning to tire of such things, as Yes discovered when they took their "opus" *Tales From Topographic Oceans* out on the road and were soon forced to reduce the amount of new material in their set and reintroduce several old "favourites". The backlash against rock 'n' roll excess, which was some two years later to unleash the so-called "New Wave", was beginning to gather momentum and so Genesis' decision to create a concept album at this point in their career may be seen in that context as perhaps a strange one. However, Genesis are nothing if not unpredictable and the album that they were to create was the one which took everyone, fans and critics alike, totally by surprise. It remains to this day, their most talked about recording.

There were two main ideas proposed for the story, and it was the perhaps slightly more worldly-wise Gabriel who insisted that Rael, the Puerto Rican street kid, was the central figure in the new work. Perhaps Gabriel also saw the chance to indulge both his desire to create a musical story of his own and to experiment with a putative film script into the bargain. Hence, *The Lamb Lies Down On Broadway* is the band's most visual album. Having decided to write the story himself, the rest of the band threw themselves in to the task of creating the soundtrack to go with it, as Tony Banks remembers. "It was a chance to do all sorts of things like improvisations. During the writing of the album we brought in all these little bits that we had and worked on them, and for me that was such fun to do. We just set ourselves an idea and improvised on it. Some of them became more solid pieces than others. We had this sort of Chinese jam which ended up somewhere in 'The Colony Of Slippermen' I think. We had one called 'Victory At Sea' which became 'Silent Sorrow In Empty Boats'. Then there was obviously 'The Waiting Room' which was called 'Evil Jam' – we just sat there and tried to frighten ourselves!"[76]

Hackett also recalls some of these moments. "The same thing happened with the bit on *The Lamb* that we used to call 'Pharoahs', which became 'Fly On A Windshield'. It has no melody but is full of portent and has the idea of almost the "Ben Hur" rhythm; the guys in the galley. I thought, 'Oh that's good', so the guitar became this sort of screaming voice over it and I went for Egyptian phrases as we made the same modulation from E to F# that roughly parallels the modulation on Ravel's Bolero at the end."[77]

Collaborative efforts aside, however, the album was to bring its own problems. Gabriel's decision to write the story line and lyrics created some friction. Fans were already beginning to set Gabriel up on the dreaded pedestal from which it was inevitable he would either fall or be pushed. His decision to leave the band was not something entered into lightly but the problem of who did what was one which did exacerbate the problem as Banks points out. "As Peter decided it was his story he was going to write all the lyrics. It was a reasonable decision as it was his story, but I don't think it would have suffered if other people had been involved as well. A different lyric writing style has been very much a feature of Genesis over the years, although perhaps people assumed Peter wrote all the lyrics which, of course, he didn't."[78] This is particularly true even of this album where Gabriel's tardiness meant that eventually Rutherford and Banks wrote some of the lyrics for the final side of the album.

The album appeared in late November 1974, by which time the band were on tour in the USA, a tour which had been postponed due to an injury which Hackett sustained to the tendon in his thumb. Although on the face of it, this added to the delays, Banks reckons that may have been a blessing in disguise. "Well, Steve's hand was a very useful excuse! He genuinely cut his hand and couldn't play, but we were nowhere near finishing the record and we needed the time desperately, so it gave us a bit of a breathing space. A lot of people thought that we had made it up, but it was true"[79]

A further result of the injury was that Hackett had time while recovering to work on some ideas of his own which were to bear fruition a year later. The upshot for the band was that the tour began before the album had been released, which was certainly not an ideal situation, as Banks recalls, "I love the idea of playing it live and I wish it had worked better. The people that came to see us wanted to hear 'Musical Box' and 'Supper's Ready' – the things they knew. We were playing in America to an audience that hadn't even heard it as the record wasn't even out at this stage. So it was completely new music that they were hearing and it was difficult. We had so many special effects going on, which in the rehearsal room looked marvellous, but on stage they never all worked at the same time, we always had something going wrong. I hate it when something goes wrong on stage!"[80]

Nowhere was this demonstrated more fully than on the first night of the band's rescheduled European tour at the Falkoner Theatrit in Copenhagen, where at one point in the show there was supposed to be a flash. The guy mixing the flash powder got the ratio wrong so there was an enormous bang and the band stopped playing as the guy poked his head round the curtain and said; "Sorry!" to which Phil Collins' humorous riposte was: "You're fired!"

Initially the audience reaction was mixed, as Hackett's wife Kim Poor recalls. "I was a big fan of the band, although I didn't know what they looked like. A friend introduced me to them after their gig in New York which was very controversial because half of the audience loved it and half absolutely hated it and so it was a real mixture of booing and applause which caused quite a stir."[81] One can only imagine now the sheer sense of adventure that pervaded the shows supporting the album from Gabriel's introduction.. "We've written a great big lump of music and story and we'd like to play it for you, this is the story of Rael…"

Almost immediately, fans were taken aback by Gabriel's appearance – gone were the flower masks and paraphernalia of yore. Instead, he was clad in a leather jacket, jeans, T-shirt and sneakers, with his face heavily made up to reflect the swarthy complexion of street kid Rael. However, anyone mourning the loss of these costumes must surely have been compensated by the bizarre "Slipperman" costume which was to be the creative apogee of this period in the band's theatrical development and the impact that the new-look Genesis show made on the audience is recalled by Andy Wilkinson. "Out bounces our hero in a guise totally foreign – was this *really* Peter Gabriel? Short cropped hair, harsh and threatening face make-up, open leather jacket, denim and trainers… A total transformation and we were being taken to the urban streets of NY and the world of Rael… One of those rare moments when sound and visuals melt succinctly together in perfect harmony. The screens portrayed a beating crimson heart gently being shaved by a scalpel-like instrument... the band moved into a musical area never before touched or attempted by them. Like it or detest it, 'The Waiting Room', proved a fascinating insight to the band experimenting with the art of improvisation. A real cacophony of every imaginable sound from birds calling to howling synth, frantic twenty-second guitar licks and even a brief vibes solo somewhere in the middle of this."[82] Musically challenging, as it was, Andy also recalls the moment when Gabriel unleashed his most surreal costume on an unsuspecting audience. "What happened next, no one was quite ready for. The strange quirky opening phrase of 'The Arrival' reveals a long transparent plastic tunnel worming its way across the stage. Something was crawling along it. Gasps of sheer astonishment, then laughter, as the strangest, ugliest, lumpiest thing you could ever imagine emerges out of a cocoon. The beast (or Slipperman) proceeds to inflate a pair of giant testicles – surreal! Not content with this, the figure dances remarkably well, bellowing out: 'You're in the Colony of Slippermen'…"[83]

The tour was to be the band's largest to date, initially 102 shows were planned although several were cancelled due either to poor ticket sales or due to other circumstances beyond the group's control. Critical reaction was mixed but generally favourable and the fans loved the show, Genesis had managed against the odds to turn a concept album into a triumph. During the tour however, Gabriel's unease at the growing adulation heaped on him at the expense of the rest of the band became too much, and at a dinner with the others he announced his decision to formally quit at the end of the tour. This decision was kept from the public until the remaining members could decide upon their options. Gabriels's decision cast a shadow over the tour to some degree and, as Phil Collins remembers. "Everyone had prepared themselves psychologically for the last show which was in Besancon, it supposed to be in Toulouse, but due to poor ticket sales it was cancelled. We had all prepared ourselves for this last show and suddenly it was, 'Oh tonight's the last gig' which was a bit of an anti-climax. Pete played the 'Last Post' on the oboe which was strange really…"[84]

After the tour finished in Europe in late May 1975 the band took a well-earned rest before reconvening to consider their options without Gabriel. By this time Steve Hackett had almost completed work on what was to be his first solo album. *Voyage of the Acolyte* was a very apt title for the album on which both Mike Rutherford and Phil Collins played, given the circumstances surrounding it at the time. The album served to indicate that interest in the band members was still high when it achieved silver disc status upon its release later that year. This was extremely gratifying for Steve Hackett, but Genesis' fundamental problem remained: who was going to replace Peter Gabriel?

The announcement of Gabriel's departure from the band was finally made in the music press on 18th August 1975. It took fans totally by surprise, including several of the band's own inner circle, and the press took to writing obituaries and eulogies for the band almost immediately, which was to prove to be a little premature, as future events would demonstrate.

Out Of The Fire And Into The Fight…

The summer and autumn of 1975 were taken up by songwriting and rehearsals which preoccupied the band, so much so, that it could almost be said that they blocked out Gabriel's departure to concentrate on the matter in hand: the new Genesis album. Steve Hackett was already hard at work on his solo project which gave him much needed confidence in his abilities as he recalls. "The difference was that everyone had become a slightly different person. I had had some solo success in terms of being able to produce a whole album for myself, it would have been different if I'd just come up with a bunch of out-takes. So I was writing more material and it was at the point where everybody had gone off and done separate things apart from Tony, who was very disappointed that everybody hadn't been saving material, particularly for Genesis. He said, 'I'm the only one who has been writing material for this band…' and he was very disappointed about that, but as far as everyone else was concerned, no one was even sure if the band had a future."[85]

The band continued to work on the new album although they still had no idea who was to take over from Gabriel. Numerous musicians were auditioned from the hundreds that sent in tapes but none of these lucky hopefuls were deemed to be quite right for the band, although to some outside observers, the answer was patently obvious as Hackett remembers. "Well, funnily enough one of the first people to suggest that Phil should be the singer was Jon Anderson who came to Phil's wedding. At the time I said, 'I've just done a solo album and Phil sang wonderfully on it.' And Phil had sung the first song I'd ever written for Genesis, 'For Absent Friends' and I told him, 'Phil's got a wonderful range.' He said, 'Why don't you get in an extra instrumentalist and make the band stronger? Phil's got a nice voice, you seem to be aware of that already."[86]

Phil Collins' decision to take on the singer's job was motivated as much by his dissatisfaction with the quality of the people the band were auditioning as anything else, as Steve vividly remembers. "So eventually we did take somebody in to the studio and he sang a version of 'Squonk'. He had considerable trouble with the melody lines, because it was written by instrumentalists, where the melody was up and down weaving all over the place and he found it very difficult to respond to it. Phil deliberately stayed away on the day when we had the guy come in, and we'd been through a series of auditions by now and he was the best of the bunch, but he had enormous problems. The guy had a perfectly good voice, he just wasn't right for the part. And so, I remember Mike and Tony saying to Phil, 'What do you think, Phil?' and he said, 'I'll tell you what I think, I think it sounds fucking average! Let me have a go…'"[87]

The rest, as they say is history, and Collins took on the role for the rest of the rehearsals and without knowing it, the band had solved their vocalist problem. The only one who didn't seem to be at all surprised by the choice was record company manager Tony Stratton-Smith whose reaction was typically understated… "God, he sounds just like Pete. Looks like you've found your vocalist, chaps!"[88]

The resulting album, *A Trick Of The Tail* was everything that its predecessor wasn't; melodic, lush, and above all immensely accessible. The album also laid to rest any doubts that the band were not capable of writing without Gabriel, one of the most irritating assumptions that fans and the press had made. Each track was credited to the people who wrote it and revealed the collective talent that makes Genesis so special. This decision was something that the band felt strongly about as Tony Banks explains. "We'd got slightly fed up because in the very early days there was a tendency to suggest that Peter was obviously the dominant writer, as he tended to write most of the lyrics. There was an impression that he was doing all of this while the rest of us were just sitting round watching him do his creative thing. Of course, Genesis was never like that, everybody was writing and some songs were written by individuals."[89]

Collins too was quick to stress that the band were all pulling together and were perhaps finding it easier to be creative, as he related to BBC disc jockey John Peel in an interview broadcast at the time of the album's release. "It has changed in the studio because we found it very easy working with the four of us. Everything was a lot quicker, just because there were four mouths instead of five"[90]

To support the album's release and subsequent chart success, both at home and abroad, the band were about to set off on their first tour without Gabriel. One problem still remained, who was going to fill the drummer's seat while Phil was up front "wiggling his bum" and singing? At the time, there was no doubt in Collins' mind, the only drummer who was capable of the task was his long time hero, Yes alumni Bill Bruford, who was taken on board as the guest drummer for the tour. The choice was inspired, because of Bruford's credibility with the progressive rock fans who were Genesis' audience, particularly in the USA, where his influence was enormous.

Tony Banks remembers Bruford's time with the band fondly. "Well, Bill was an easy person to get along with, he's still a friend of mine in fact, and obviously he's a very versatile drummer. When we got on stage there'd be calls for 'Bruford' and I think that helped us through what was obviously quite a difficult period trying to establish ourselves without Peter as a singer…"[91]

Steve Hackett concurs. "When Phil became the singer, Bill Bruford came into the band and he gave us a big "up" because he was someone who Phil admired and we'd all admired in Yes and King Crimson. When he arrived he was immediately cracking jokes, and he dispelled any feelings of fear. He jammed along with us and said, 'Yeah, that sounds great and this will be fine…' There wasn't any kind of angst-ridden 'is this going to work out right?' So he immediately put everyone at ease with his humour which was great."[92]

The tour started at the end of March 1976 in London, Ontario, ostensibly at a low key gig originally planned for about four hundred people. In the end over two thousand fans gave Collins a hero's welcome, in spite of the odd fan or two who appeared dressed as one of Gabriel's more esoteric creations! Their new show drew upon all the strengths of both the older material and the new album and managed to leave the fans happy. In fact, Genesis' reviews flew in the face of established rock lore at the time, the "New Wave" had broken over the UK and was soon to sweep over the rest of Europe and the United States leaving many established bands and artists as casualties in its wake. To their credit, Genesis continued to plough their furrow and the fans and critics alike were more than happy with the "new" singer who had filled Gabriel's shoes so capably.

By the time the tour reached London's Hammersmith Odeon in June 1976 there could no longer be any doubt that Genesis were here to stay and they were already planning their next album when another crisis loomed.

Unquiet Slumbers For The Sleepers...

The success of 1976's album and tour must have been sweet for the band, who continued to dominate into the following year. Ironically 1977 was also to see the re-emergence of two key personnel in the Genesis story, with Peter Gabriel releasing his first solo album to critical acclaim from press and fans alike, and another founder member's first solo effort in the shape of the classic *The Geese & The Ghost* album by Anthony Phillips which was also well received. Genesis and Co, members of that most vilified of species, the "Progressive" rock group, were certainly putting up a spirited resistance to the running dogs of Punk. The music press were caught up in the hype as well, and bands which they had steadfastly championed up to this point were soon the recipients of the critical backlash which had, in some cases, been long overdue. Genesis too were to be on the receiving end of some stringent criticism when they released their new album at the beginning of the year with such headlines as "Pretentious old superstars refuse to lie down" and more tellingly still in the headline of Chris Welch's review of the band's first gig of their tour… "Cold Genesis".

The album itself *Wind & Wuthering* is, in the opinion of many fans, the last classic Genesis album: dramatic, full of character and yet also possessed of the deprecating humour which is one of Genesis' most undervalued elements. The band recorded the album at Relight Studios in Holland during the autumn of 1976, mainly to benefit from the cheaper Dutch recording costs. Although Tony Banks also recalls that it was, "Getting away from all the distractions that helped give the album quite a strong identity."[93] Certainly the album was a fine one. From the dramatic opener "Eleventh Earl of Mar" to the almost Tom and Jerry-like storyline of "All In A Mouse's Night", there was something for Genesis fans of every shade of musical persuasion. Upon its release on New Year's day 1977, the album also gave the band their first UK number one although this is disputed among fans and chart pollsters alike.

Having faced the problem of too little material available for the previous album, this time round the band were faced with the direct opposite; far too much material, as Banks recalls. "The main weakness was that we couldn't include the tracks 'Match Of The Day' and 'Pigeons'that ended up on the later EP – so none of the lighter tracks got on…"[94] It was also at this time that the crisis which had been brewing for a couple of years finally surfaced. Steve Hackett's solo success with *Voyage of the Acolyte* back in 1975 proved that he was capable of both writing and, more importantly, producing his own music. The confidence which this gave him was apparent on both *A Trick Of The*

Tail and *Wind & Wuthering* which Tony Banks recalls as being the moment when Hackett's writing really gelled with the band for the first time. "There were also things like 'Blood On The Rooftops' which I didn't have that much to do with in terms of writing, but quite a lot to do with in terms of arranging. This was the first time that Steve's writing had really fitted in to the band. It was Phil's chorus with Steve's verse and that's a really strong, great track. Also on 'Eleventh Earl Of Mar' quite a lot of the chorus parts were Steve's."[95]

However, Hackett was to experience the same difficulty that Peter Gabriel had during the writing of *The Lamb Lies Down On Broadway* and failed to get some of his best music past the "Committee Stage" of the band. This was a frustrating time for him as he remembers. "The track that became 'Please Don't Touch' was something that Genesis rehearsed originally but we didn't include it on the album. We did not develop it and I felt that was a gem so I thought, 'Hang on; here's one of my best ideas and we're not using it. Why are we including that one and not this one?' So I became aware that the intensity of playing that was important to me, was not quite as high a priority to the others and they were starting to relax a little bit more."[96]

The band's tour was to be their biggest yet, commencing with a sell out run of shows in the UK's biggest venues, beginning with three shows at London's famous Rainbow Theatre which Genesis were asked to re-open after its extensive refurbishment. For this tour, the band had to find another drummer. Bill Bruford's position with them had always been of a temporary nature and he was currently occupied with the formation of AOR supergroup UK, with Eddie Jobson and John Wetton. Eventually the band opted for their first American member in the shape of respected session player Chester Thompson, whose previous credits included stints with Alphonso Johnson and Frank Zappa. Ironically, Chris Welch's review of their opening night singled Thompson out for venomous treatment as the following extract from his review shows…

"…But for me the missing ingredient was in the percussion department. New drummer Chester Thompson has worked with Frank Zappa and is skilled and accurate. He coped with a difficult score but failed to inject personality into his playing and this became all the more marked when Phil Collins finally ceased singing and returned to his drum kit. As soon as Phil got down to work, the band took off…." His review ended with what for many was an extremely fatuous exhortation… "Bring back Bill Bruford – at least he can be relied on to help cast out demons!"[97]

The band's personal demons were still to be exorcised and Hackett's decision to leave became definite during the tour despite its enormous success – the band playing their first gigs in South America with a series of record breaking shows in Brazil during May 1977. An indication of the huge increase in popularity both at home and elsewhere was given when the band returned to the UK in June for a series of three shows at London's cavernous Earls Court Arena supported by Woodstock veteran and long time hero of the band, Richie Havens. A successful single awaited the band on the release of their first EP in May 1977. Comprising the remaining tracks from the album sessions it reached the number 18 slot in the UK charts, aided no doubt by a humorous video which included Phil Collins in a QPR top at a football match! The humour of the band was further displayed during Collins' introduction to the EP's final song which formed a part of their later tour when he referred to it as… "this next song is all about a poor unfortunate man who goes to a party where he meets a man with.. sorry meets a lady with very large knockers... and err, it depends who you know really. And unfortunately she seduces him and claims that he raped her – it's all very eternal triangle. It's off our *Spot The Pigeon EP* which is currently racing up the Indonesian charts and it's called 'Inside & Out.'"[98]

There was a further treat in store, if treat is the right word, for the band's first attempt at a concert film, which was given a gala premiere in July 1977 in the presence of Princess Anne. Tony Maylam's cinematic record of the hugely successful 1976 tour shared the billing with Rick Wakeman's *White Rock.* The film, *Genesis In Concert* was certainly not as indulgent as Led Zeppelin's cinematic effort, but it has to be admitted it came pretty close! Even Banks believes that it is not the best visual record of a Genesis concert... "We actually did it primarily as a film and Tony Maylam used to go round saying 'wonderful footage' and so on, and then used dancing girls on a beach or something during 'Entangled'. It was OK... a couple of things on it are quite nice and I suppose it's quite nice to have a record of Bill's time with the group... I think things like 'Cinema Show' were probably at their best when Bill was playing with us..."[99] Sadly this visual record of the band has never been officially released.

The last show of the tour was at Munich's enormous Olympiahalle on 3rd July 1977 and during the remaining summer months they attended to the task of whittling down the enormous amount of material for a long overdue live album. Having recorded just about every show from both the 1976 and 1977 tours, there were some difficult decisions and it was during the selection process that Steve Hackett eventually decided to leave the group. The story of how he told the band has already been well documented, but his reasoning has been the subject of debate by fans ever since. With the benefit of hindsight, Hackett's decision was a vital, if painful one, both for him personally as a musician and the group as a whole. He explained his decision to *The Waiting Room* in a recent interview ...

"I feel that it is only now that I can truly express myself in music. I think at the time I was anxious to do a string of solo albums and that was something that worried both Tony and Mike. Phil wasn't in the least bit worried; he'd been operating with Brand X for quite a while, but I think it was regarded as less of a threat because at least he wasn't pushing albums out under his own name. Perhaps if I'd come up with another group title or something it would have been less of a political hot potato, but it did seem to create waves. Nonetheless I felt that I was coming up with far too many ideas for the band to fully exploit... explore is perhaps a better word. And in order to develop I felt I had to work with other people. I was already working with great people in Genesis. I realised at this point that they were a great band and they were great at doing what they did. I felt to prove, or to attempt that level of greatness for myself, I had to do that outside the band."[100]

The live album was eventually released in October 1977, and once again displayed their fine sense of ironic humour by titling it *Second's Out.* It achieved a number two slot in the UK charts, a position that was somewhat overshadowed by the announcement in the music press of Steve Hackett's departure. As a record of both Hackett and Gabriel's time in the band, this album is hard to beat, containing most of their classic tracks from that era, as well as much of the material that was in the current live set. A line had very firmly been drawn under that period of the band's history what remained now was to consolidate on their success and to search for the one thing that had so far eluded them – a top ten single!

And Then There Were Three...

Genesis reconvened quickly in the wake of Hackett's departure, and rapidly regained the momentum created during the last two years by working again at the Relight Studios in Holland. By this time Genesis faced the harsh realities of mid-seventies England. Gone was the certainty that had ensured a new album by the group would be automatically well-received. In fact, the New Wave backlash had a healthy tonic effect upon most of the members of the "establishment" of the musical world and Genesis were well aware that something different was necessary this time round.

Hackett's departure had allowed a opportunity to re-evaluate themselves as musicians and to draw more deeply and freely upon the collective talents of the remaining members, as Mike was quick to point out, "because there's a different atmosphere with less people. People have to work harder in certain areas"[101] Nowhere was this more evident than with Mike Rutherford's role in the band, he now had to fill the vacuum left by Steve Hackett at a time when the entire band also realised that they had to change in musical terms too. The lengthy instrumental passages so revered by the fans were a millstone which had to be ditched if the band was to have any future, as Mike explained. "It was definitely a conscious effort to make songs shorter. On *Wind & Wuthering* we were definitely disappointed that we couldn't get the EP on, time-wise, because it would have made a better balance. So, we consciously cut down quite a few tracks which could have been anything from five to eight minutes long. We kept them down to about five as we felt that the strength of the track came across and there was much more variety on the album; eleven tracks for us is quite a lot. It's easy for us to elongate things and we enjoy doing that; going off and coming back to themes at the end of a song. It was quite hard for us to keep some of the songs a bit shorter."[102]

Certainly there was a greater sense of freedom about the album with the variety of songs, and the sound certainly reflected the band's change in working methods, as Phil Collins explained. "We used to go in for rehearsals for much longer and spend a shorter time in the studio, whereas now it's nearly the other way round – we leave more to chance in the studio rather than playing a song to death. I think we spent six or seven weeks with the tracks we had written; we rehearsed a couple of times so that we knew the chorus and knew the changes. The rest of the time we tried to put together several group tracks, putting someone's verse with someone else's chorus, and then with someone else's introduction – which we probably didn't do as much on *Wind & Wuthering*. We've tried to get back to group tracks a bit"[103]

The first fruits from the new album titled *And Then There Were Three* appeared in March 1978 in the shape of a single which heralded in the new look Genesis in a big way. "Follow You Follow Me" was that rarity in the Genesis canon – an instantly catchy song – one which propelled the band into the top ten of the UK charts. It ushered in their first appearance on *Top Of The Pops*, to the horror of their longstanding fans, who felt perhaps the same way as members of an exclusive gentlemen's club felt when it was opened up to women. Here at last, was a song which girlfriends could relate to and enjoy.

Once again, a mammoth world tour was undertaken by the group with no less than three separate US tours in an attempt to break up the length of time spent away from home and families. The group broke all the record books with a stage show that incorporated all the latest available technologies such as lasers and computerised mirrors, Genesis had it all. There was also another new face on stage, as the band had taken a second American into the fold for live work. Rutherford obviously knew that it was not going to be possible to play both lead guitar and bass during live performances, so he began to look at likely candidates. Like Chester Thompson, Daryl Stuermer's background was impeccable, including a time spent with Jean-Luc Ponty. Stuermer was recommended to the band by Alphonso Johnson and Daryl still recalls his audition for the band. "I met Mike and we played along to 'Squonk' and 'Down And Out'. We just did those two songs and Mike said, 'I think that will be enough', and I thought to myself, 'Is he saying that because he doesn't like my playing, or is he saying that because he knows how good I can play?'"[104] Mike was more than satisfied and Daryl's contribution to the subsequent tour was a revelation, as this writer can recall when I saw Genesis for the first time at their only UK show of the year at the enormous Knebworth Park Festival on 24th June. Having been grounded in the music of Gabriel, Hackett and Co, to finally see the band with this new guitarist was an experience never to be forgotten.

And Then There Were Three also became the band's first album to reach the number one slot officially in the UK, and also achieved a healthy position in the US *Billboard* charts, helped no doubt by the enormous efforts made during the year to break the USA in a big way. Just about every major venue in the country had the pleasure of hosting the band during one of their tours. Once again, far too much material had been written for the album and an EP was released which also contained non-album cuts; "The Day The Light Went Out" and "Vancouver". The latter was to prove to be strangely prophetic as it turned out. Everything in the Genesis camp appeared rosy – a top ten album, successful singles and above all a massively successful and entertaining live show which was drawing praise from everyone who saw it. What more could they ask?

The answer to the above question was easy to answer if you were Phil Collins' wife: a husband who spends slightly more time at home. During the year preceding the making of *And Then There Were Three*, Phil's wife Andrea had become increasingly disenchanted with her husband's peripatetic lifestyle and during the recording of the album matters came to a head. Collins was torn between his homelife and breaking the band in the USA which would, if successful, give everyone the time and the financial freedom they had been striving toward for so long. To gain that freedom however, one final push in the USA was needed and this was to prove the undoing of Phil's marriage. Andrea moved to stay with her parents in Vancouver, and Collins continued the tour. The year ended with a series of shows in Japan, Genesis' first in that territory and ones which Collins desperately wanted to avoid, although the surviving footage from these gigs shows he was the consummate showman on stage. At the end of the tour, Phil made a valiant attempt to rescue his marriage and moved to Vancouver in a last ditch effort to patch things up, but to no avail. Even this was not sufficient and his ultimatum to the band, born out of his desperation was not one which lent itself to any confidence in the group's future... "If we can record in Vancouver, then I'm still in the band, if not..."

Fortunately, the success of the album and tour meant that the much needed break from the incessant round of recording and touring could now be taken. Mike Rutherford and Tony Banks wisely decided that the time was ripe for them to have a go at solo albums of their own. This would give Collins time to try and resolve his personal problems, whilst Rutherford and Banks had a chance to extend their own creative muscles. The resulting albums, *Smallcreep's Day* and *A Curious Feeling* respectively, were released during the following year and were warmly if not ecstatically received. However, many misinterpreted the situation and saw the appearance of solo projects from the two key players as a split in the band, signalling its demise and many wondered what the new decade would bring.

Enter The Duke...

Genesis reconvened in the autumn of 1979 to begin work on their new album. The end of the decade brought new challenges for the band and the music scene in the UK had irreversibly changed with the New Wave and Disco fever taking the place of what had gone before. Challenging times indeed, and the band were to prove themselves equal to the challenge.

The relative solo successes meant that the remaining members returned to the collective fold with fresh confidence and ideas, as well as a greater appreciation of each other's roles within the band. Phil Collins too had had plenty of time in which to write and compose material of his own, once it became obvious that his attempted reconciliation with his wife was not going to work. It was the material he brought to the new album which was perhaps the first indicator of the direction which the band was to pursue increasingly throughout the coming decade. In fact, the new album *Duke* was to be very much a transitional work as Rutherford admitted. "1980 was the year we should have changed. We started to on *Duke*, to me some of the songs on that album were the end of one era and some were the start of another era..."[105]

The old era was most definitively represented by the album's closing cut, a rambling instrumental overture titled "Duke's Travels/Duke's End". At one point the "Duke Suite" as it became known, was considered as a full-blown concept tying all the tracks together, as Tony Banks remembers. "At one point we were going to join together all the group compositions on the album – they were all going to be one long song. But we decided for a variety of reasons to keep them separate. We felt that the album wouldn't be so well balanced if we had all the individual tracks on one side. The other thing was, we didn't want to repeat ourselves; you know, having done something like

'Supper's Ready' a long time ago… there would be comparisons and we didn't really want that."[106]

Rutherford however, recalls that there is some common thread between several of the songs. "There isn't really any definite concept behind the album, although there are a couple of numbers with compatible themes. The cover concept, using Koechlin's children's book character to tie things together was rather an after-thought. I suppose he just represents the little Everyman character who is a bit confused by life in the eighties. Some of the songs reflect that worry, though there is no consistent line throughout the album."[107] *Duke* certainly managed to depict the confusion felt by many as the new decade began and some of the songs were of a darker shade than those on the album's predecessor.

At the other end of the spectrum however, Phil Collins' pop sensibilities came to the fore with "Misunderstanding" which was to become the band's biggest hit single to date in the USA. It might have done as well in the UK had it been released as the opening single, but those honours went to "Turn It On Again", a song destined to become Genesis' anthem throughout the eighties. The heart of the album however, belongs to the second track, "Duchess", which was not as lyrically straightforward as it might seem. Tony Banks explains. "'Duchess' is one of my favourite tracks. It's so simple and yet it seems to capture so much atmosphere. It was at that time that girl singers were becoming popular and that's where the idea came from. Also, seen from that perspective it took it away from the group a bit because if it had been written about a man, people would have thought it was talking about the group, but talking about it that way, gave it another dimension."[108]

Duke was released in March 1980 and scored a number one in the UK, the next in a string of number one albums. So much for the doubts about their popularity expressed in the music press! The announcement of the tour itinerary for the year took many by surprise as it included a full UK tour of provincial theatres which hadn't been graced by a band of Genesis' stature since 1977. The accompanying tour of the US took in larger venues with a few smaller dates mixed in. Taking the band back to their roots was a wise decision giving them a chance to feed off their audience, and also to "dust off their twelve string guitars" and play several older pieces in the set. The 80,000 tickets for the band's UK shows were soon snapped up, with over half a million ticket applications being received. If anyone doubted the band's popularity in the UK, their appearance on *Top Of The Pops* for the single "Turn It On Again" was followed by an ITV documentary on the shows in Liverpool, and also a live broadcast of part of their show from London's Lyceum Ballroom. The last date of the tour was at the Performing Arts Centre in Saratoga Springs on 30th June, after which they all took a well-earned rest. All except for Phil Collins who, having whetted his creative appetite on *Duke*, wanted to expand his talents. Working in his own home studio he carefully created *Face Value*, an album which was to make Genesis fans and the rest of the music world sit up and take notice upon its release in February 1981.

The success of *Face Value* with its stripped down sound and strident opening single led many to believe that the demise of the group was imminent. Once again the eulogies proved to be premature, and the creative impetus which the band's solo outlets had released, inspired a new lease of life and a new direction which many fans were to find hard to take when the group's next album appeared in September 1981.

Like It Or Not

Returning to work in their own purpose-built studio, The Farm, the band opted to re-invent themselves even further as Tony Banks explained. "We'd made changes consciously in order to get away from the compulsory keyboard solo, the tambourine on the chorus and all that sort of 'wet' sound. We just wanted to go for a different approach, with a sort of very dry kind of thing: very streamlined. We were very pleased with the result. So this album, the cover and everything, was crucial – I know that many people didn't like it, but for us it was crucial. I don't think the band could have carried on if we'd done another album like *Duke*, another album in the old tradition."[109] This is also a point that Phil Collins was keen to emphasise. Having survived the "slings and arrows of outrageous press reviews" to paraphrase a certain well-known playwright, the band were equally as keen to keep on changing. "A group is a compromise and I suggested the horns on *Abacab* purely because I thought, 'Wouldn't it be interesting to see what people would think?' You know, 'Genesis and Earth, Wind and Fire – Christ! Gotta check this out.' I tried to shake people up a bit and take them off automatic pilot. A lot of people have blamed me for the change in Genesis and it's not anything that's set a precedent. If it happens on the next album, it'll be because it works for the next album. It's good for us to change."[110]

Certainly the album's opening single and title track "Abacab" was different – a hard rocking song with a sharper edge to it, sporting an abstract cover which was repeated on the album itself with the first picture of the band members on the inner cover – this was a million miles away from the pastoral Genesis which their fans had loved and which the critics had grown to despise. Once again the album charted at the number one position aided no doubt by Phil Collins' solo success earlier in the year. *Abacab* showed Genesis at their best and worst. The title track and "Me and Sarah Jane" easily fitted the conception of the traditional Genesis song. Fans were mortified however, by the inclusion of horns on "No Reply At All" and they cringed at what most have agreed since is one of Genesis' worst musical moments, "Who-dunnit?", perversely not the opinion of Tony Banks. "I listened to that album recently and one of my favourite tracks was the one that everybody hates, 'Who-dunnit?' I thought that's a great track, why don't we do more like that? I remember playing that and trying to get this sort of computer noise and Mike and Phil were listening and they thought, 'You've got something there', so we put it down on tape with some drum music that Phil was playing. We improvised on it for thirty minutes."[111]

This was the key element that Genesis needed to keep the group alive, a spontaneity to recording and writing. Gone was the shyness and self-doubt which had coloured the early band as Rutherford commented at the time. "The art of recording is to be adaptable, I would go away and spend a couple of hours with a tape recorder working on a part on the bass, developing some ideas. I'll get in the studio with a whole part worked out... and it's just not happening. So a musician reaches a certain maturity where he says, 'To hell with it', and starts again. You'll do it until it feels right. That's the sort of thing we would do in the past – no one would compromise. You have to be adaptable in the studio, you can't make ideas work."[112] The apparent simplicity of the music was deceptive however, unlike previous efforts where every musician was trying to have their voice heard over everyone else's. This time there was space for everyone as Phil Collins explained. "The music that we write together is very different from the music that everybody writes individually, because when you write on your own you fill in the gaps, but on this album you get lots of gaps but it's a very corporate unit – the gaps are there because you're listening to somebody else playing."[113]

The album certainly created a furore among Genesis fans with many bemoaning the lack of exactly the characteristics which Banks described above, while others felt that this band was now a much more acceptable proposition. The music was infinitely more agreeable to those people who were not necessarily cerebral about their music, although those who mourned the old Genesis were missing the point, as Tony explains. "There was a reaction against songs like 'Who-Dunnit?' and 'Man On The Corner' because they were simple – and yet that has always been a part of Genesis. There's this illusion that it has taken over and I don't think it has taken over at all; there's just a little more emphasis and we do it better than we used to, and therefore it gets a much higher profile because the singles are actually hits. It has always been there and it used to be things like 'For Absent Friends'"[114]

Once again, the band undertook a lengthy tour to promote the new album, beginning in Europe in late September, where the reception was mixed. The tour included two shows at the Groenoordhal in Leiden, Holland, an event which Banks remembers well. "We played Leiden in Holland and we got booed when we played 'Who-Dunnit?' So we went back and played there again."[115] Fans bemoaning the new album certainly took heart from the live set, which drew on just about every album in the band's repertoire, aided by their new-look lightshow incorporating the world's first Vari-Lites, which Genesis themselves had a hand in creating. This new computerised system of lighting could change colour and shape and was to revolutionise rock shows. It has since become a standard requirement at rock gigs. Strangely enough, one of the high points of the 1981 shows was during "Who-Dunnit?" when these lights really came into their own. The band also felt confident enough to return to the field of live films. A handful of their shows, including the last night of the tour at the NEC in Birmingham in December 1981, being recorded and released the following year under the title of *Three Sides Live*, which, with its accompanying double live album, was to continue their success into the following year.

Another indication of the creativity of this period was demonstrated when the band released the *3 x 3 EP* in May 1982, combining the remaining tracks from the *Abacab* sessions niftily housed in a sleeve which harked back to the halcyon days of the 1960's – a send-up of The Beatles' *Twist And Shout* cover. The single charted well in the UK ensuring yet another appearance on *Top Of The Pops*. The band also undertook a two month tour in August and September in support of the live album and at several shows in Europe they were supported by their heroes King Crimson. Essentially the same show as the year before, there was however, one fundamental difference in the inclusion of the entire "Supper's Ready". Phil teased the audience during his introduction,

"This next song is ten years old, so we thought we would dust off our twelve string guitars. This song has got lots of loud bits, and lots of quiet bits… this then is 'Supper's Ready'."[116]

The highlight of the year was without doubt, however, their reunion at a wet and windy Milton Keynes Concert Bowl on Saturday 2nd October with Peter Gabriel and Steve Hackett. The gig billed as *Six Of The Best* was the band's way of helping their old comrade out of the financial quagmire that had resulted from the first WOMAD festival, which Gabriel had helped to organise earlier in the year. For the fans who were there it was an actual quagmire as torrential rain hit the event, although it was an emotional evening both for fans and band members as Collins recalls. "When we did the benefit, we all laughed about it because it all came flooding back, falling over things, pulling microphone leads out of sockets, it was chaos but it was also great fun to do…"[117] For the show, the band rehearsed a special set of "oldies" which sent every one of the sixty thousand or so soaked fans away happy and left them wondering "what next?"

Just A Job To Do?

Phil's first solo tour in support of his second album *Hello, I Must Be Going* took him away from the Genesis camp for what remained of 1982 and early 1983, emphasising his growing stature as a writer and performer. The remainder of the year also saw the release of Tony Banks and Mike Rutherford's second solo projects again to mixed reactions. The summer saw the band return to collective endeavours for their first album to be entirely produced at their now completed studio The Farm. The remainder of the 1980's were to be the creative apogee of Genesis' career, both as a band and individuals, with each and every member, past and present, releasing a vast quantity of music which was, and still is, unparalleled in its diversity of styles.

However, the band's follow-up to 1981's highly successful *Abacab* was to be something of a struggle. The fact that there were no non-album b-sides to any of the singles, apart from the live version of 1980's classic "Turn It On Again", was an indication of the relative lack of material. Perhaps the growing number of solo projects had taken its toll on the group. To many, the eponymously titled album, *Genesis* was something of a disappointment. It did however, include the band's most successful single to date, the surprise hit of autumn 1983, "Mama", a song which once again re-wrote the rule books. For a start it was ostensibly about a man's obsession with a prostitute and weighed in at over six minutes in length – not ideal chart fodder in the pop-orientated 1980's. "Mama" was however, made of sterner stuff. It gained the band their highest position in the UK's charts to date, peaking at number four, helped no doubt by a *Top Of The Pops* showing of the very dramatic video for the song. Once again, the track emerged from collective endeavours in their own studio, as Tony Banks explains. "'Mama' came about because we had the studio to do it. We had this little germ of an idea Mike was playing through a fuzzbox or something like that. We thought, 'Don't worry about that' it sounded so good on its own. The drumbox sounded so good, so I put a drone on it somewhere and from that we had the skeletal idea. So we put it down – we really couldn't have done that without a studio of our own."[118]

The album also contained another Genesis classic in the shape of "Home By The Sea" with long instrumental passages that could almost have been at home on several of the band's earlier albums. The song quickly went on to become one of the favourites in live shows. It is something of a surprise to hear how the song evolved as Tony Banks recalls, "Well, it was a traditional thing but with a different approach. If you're talking about the second half rather than the first half; we were improvising. Phil was just playing in three and Mike and I were playing over the top of that. All of the little moments coalesced and it sounded fantastic… and so we came in to the studio with two thirty minute tapes of it and Mike and I just sat down and marked all the best bits, the things we thought were good. We then learned exactly what we had played and we just stuck it all together."[119] Genesis have never really been seen as an improvising band but with their own studio and a growing willingness to take musical risks their individual identities gradually emerged, more on this album than perhaps on any of their previous efforts.

However, perhaps they tried too hard to avoid the pitfalls of recycling old themes and the irresistible pressure upon the band, as Rutherford remembers. "I've always felt that we've been tied down by our history, it's often felt like a weight around our neck having to keep recording albums in a similar vein, and that's something we've tried to break away from. Each year there is a big question mark and each year it is getting bigger and bigger. This year (1983) when we started I was thinking – and I am sure the other two were too – 'am I just going through the motions?' Certainly the first couple of days were a bit slow, but then we wrote two or three things on the third day and I knew we were all hooked for an album and tour."[120]

To avoid simply re-jigging existing Genesis trademarks, the band even attempted a country-style number in the shape of "That's All" which Phil hilariously introduced during the band's subsequent live shows as, "A little country and western number where all of you boys can hitch up your pants and all of you girls can take off your dresses."[121] This single was also the subject of a humorous reunion with original producer Jonathan King when he "ambushed" the band after their performance of the song on Noel Edmonds' *Late, Late Breakfast Show* and censured them for promoting "Koala Bars". In fact this album certainly helped to increase Genesis' visual profile in the UK with numerous television interviews, and the full screening of all three promotional videos from the album.

The success of both the single and the album, which went straight to the number one slot both at home and abroad, stung the critics into even more vehement attacks, which Tony was at pains to refute. It is impossible to deny the logic of his response. "We're in the world of commercial music. Let's face it; so if a record sells, it must be relevant; that's all there is to it. It doesn't matter whether it's 'The Birdie Song' or The Sex Pistols, if it's top five music then it's relevant in some kind of way or another. All you're trying to conjure up is enjoyment for the moment, escapism through listening to a certain piece of music – that's all we're going for. It's a different world – and I think 'Mama' plays with your emotions to a far greater degree than your average pop song…"[122]

The band courted a certain degree of controversy, not only with the subject matter of the album's debut single but also with a subsequent single, "Illegal Alien" which took a slightly tongue-in-cheek look at America's immigrant problems and featured a hilarious video. That said, the song still managed to convey the glittering façade the USA presents to people from an impoverished background, and indeed the bureaucracy attached to the whole process of immigration.

However, any doubts about the quality of the band's new album were more than blown away when they embarked upon another lengthy tour in November, which, apart from the last five shows at Birmingham's cavernous National Exhibition Centre – each one benefitting a different charity – was an entirely US/Canadian affair much to the disappointment of European fans. However, the band's position in the USA was such that this tour was to be their defining moment, taking in all the largest venues, using a dramatically improved light show, taking full advantage of the Vari Lite system. The massive sound and light barrage certainly gave added impetus to several of the older pieces in the set, and anyone who witnessed the events could hardly forget the sight of the lighting gantry threatening to take off during the latter part of "Home By The Sea". The set still featured classic "oldies" like "In The Cage" and "Carpet Crawlers" alongside newer material including the hilarious routine for "Illegal Alien" and the extended homage to the Sixties that ended "Turn It On Again". The final NEC date was even attended by both the Prince and Princess of Wales. These shows were also the subject of the band's second attempt at a live video which was subsequently released in 1984 under the title, *Genesis: The Mama Tour.*

With another hugely successful album and tour under their belts, the band members went their separate ways. The intervening period prior to the next album spawned a proliferation of solo projects which again called the band's rationale for existence into question. Phil Collins' solo success continued with his third album and a mammoth world tour. Mike Rutherford finally found his solo niche with the establishment of his "part-time" band, The Mechanics, and Tony Banks devoted his time to soundtrack work. The gaps between albums began to lengthen and it was to be almost two years before the fruits of the next collective work became available – *Invisible Touch.*

Feeding The Fire

The lengthy lay off from group activity, including Phil's now legendary *Live Aid* performances, sparked concern once again that perhaps the end was nigh for Genesis. The relative dearth of material on the previous album had cast doubts about the band's longevity. Fortunately, the summer of 1986 saw those doubts swept away with the re-emergence of Genesis on television for a rare appearance on BBC's famous *Whistle Test* programme, with a behind the scenes look at the rehearsals for the forthcoming album. What was apparent was that the band members were relaxed and still creatively coming up with the goods as a collective unit.

The improvisational nature of the latest work, and the fact that at long last the stigma of the claustrophobic atmosphere of Public School appeared to have finally worn off, led to Genesis' most instantly accessible album, *Invisible Touch*. It re-defined the band as a musical unit and moved them firmly into the pop mainstream. The first single from the record was an instant hit when it was released on 15th May 1986 charting at number 15 in the UK with higher positions in Europe and the USA. The single signalled Genesis' emergence as a true pop band to rival the likes of U2, whom they easily outsold on their subsequent tour in support of the album. What made this album so special? There is no doubt that the sheer scale of the material is astounding, with everything from the pure power pop of the title track, to love ballads such as "In Too Deep". For those still reeling from the surrender to pop infection, there were traditional Genesis pieces such as "Tonight, Tonight, Tonight" and "Domino". The album brought in a whole new Genesis audience, but even so, the "new look" band continued to be the victim of the venom of the music press, who could not reconcile the band's success with the image they had in their minds. They took to savaging the band on the most personal of levels, as their manager Tony Stratton-Smith commented. "Criticism is fine, but you don't get that. Quite often in a review they don't even mention the bloody music. They go on a diatribe about the band or what Phil looks like, and that infuriates me. It's non-journalism and it hurts when they spend a lot of time making records they are very sincere about, only to have it dismissed as 'another commercial record by those millionaires'. We've never done things just for the money and we never will. OK, we earn good money. But that is a by-product. In the past we have always spent more on our shows than we've earned. Genesis have always kept their feet on the ground and stayed normal. Maybe that's what bugs some critics."[124]

Released in June 1986, the album achieved number one positions both at home and in the USA, and the somewhat bemused music press reported the resulting statistics: "Genesis remain at the top of the album chart for the second week with *Invisible Touch*. On its first week in the shops 100,000 copies were sold, of which a remarkable 10.27% were on compact disc. No other CD has sold 10,000 copies in Britain in a single week."[125]

In fact the album was another Genesis landmark, being the first rock album to have a simultaneous release on vinyl, cassette and the new compact disc format. It also ensured that the Genesis camp were well represented in the media throughout the summer of 1986, and in fact, the band were knocked off the number one spot in the USA by former member Peter Gabriel's new album, *So*. Steve Hackett's new band, GTR, also scored a chart success in the USA that summer with their debut album; *GTR* and single, "When The Heart Rules The Mind". It certainly did Genesis fans a power of good to witness how much the band's music was appreciated worldwide.

The accolades continued when the release of the second single in August 1986, "In Too Deep" almost repeated the chart success of its predecessor, reaching number 19. A demonstration of just how fruitful the recording sessions had been was indicated by the presence, on this and the subsequent three singles, of a host of non-album tracks – several of which were certainly candidates for the album itself. In the UK and USA the album spawned five hit singles between its release and the end of the summer of 1987. The third single, "Land Of Confusion" was also another first, with an award for best video. It was well deserved. The highly amusing video, designed by *Spitting Image* animators Fluck & Law laid to rest any thoughts that the band had no sense of humour! A video collection of the assembled tracks was released called *Visible Touch* including material that had not been previously available, adding to the growing collection of visual memorabilia.

All that remained for Genesis now was the ubiquitous tour in support of the album. Kicking off in Detroit on 18th September 1986 it was destined to become largest scale tour since *The Lamb Lies Down On Broadway* almost twelve years before. With over 112 scheduled dates, Genesis performed to more than one-and-a-half million fans. Once again, they utilised state-of-the-art technology, including the new MKIII Vari Lites which added emphasis to the stage show and enabled them to successfully tackle the large open air arenas and stadiums in Europe and the USA. The tour also took in several shows in Japan, only their second visit to that country, and finally included their first ever shows in New Zealand and Australia just prior to Christmas 1986. The need to comply with local Musician's Union rules necessitated the use of a four-piece string section, giving the band a chance to play a couple of numbers in a slightly different format. Rutherford also revived his 1977 classic "Your Own Special Way" which undoubtedly benefited from the addition of the string section. Without doubt, the band were 1986/87's "hottest ticket" with a string of sell-out shows at every venue they played, culminating in a record-breaking four consecutive nights at London's enormous Wembley Stadium in July 1987. These were filmed for the obligatory live video, released some two years later under the title of *Invisible Touch Tour* with the initial 5000 copies including a bonus one-track live CD single. It set standards for subsequent video presentations, being the first to be captured using Sony Hi Definition film, giving an almost cinematic appearance. A further two videos, *Genesis Videos Volume One* and *Two*, were released in 1988 punctuating the increasing hiatus before the next album. The long overdue releases were well received, comprising most (but not all) of the band's promotional videos since 1976.

This allowed some breathing space for the remainder of the 1980's and consequently saw both Phil Collins' and Mike Rutherford's solo careers take off with a vengeance. Rutherford's second album with the Mechanics, 1988's *The Living Years,* spawned one of that year's biggest hit singles and he was finally able to tour in the UK and Europe throughout the early part of 1989 to public acclaim. Collins' fourth solo album, released in November 1989, was the one which catapulted him from star to superstar status. *But Seriously* re-wrote the record books upon its release and the attendant demands on Phil's time inevitably delayed the commencement of the follow up to *Invisible Touch*, giving Rutherford a chance to consolidate his solo career with the Mechanics' third album, *Word of Mouth,* released in the spring of 1991.

All of this solo effort meant that Genesis had been effectively on hold since the end of the *Invisible Touch* tour. They did however, put in two brief but memorable appearances during this extended hiatus. Both Genesis and Phil Collins took part in the birthday celebrations for the 40th anniversary of Atlantic Records held at New York's Madison Square Gardens on 15th May 1988. The band performed a medley, incorporating solo material by both Tony and Mike with Phil singing – the only time that this is likely to happen. The band also put in an appearance at the "Silver Clef" concert at Knebworth Park on 30th June 1990 where they shared the billing with Pink Floyd,

Elton John, Paul McCartney and a host of others, on what was an extremely wet day. Genesis' performance was lacklustre and the predictable choice of songs led many fans to wonder about the future of the band. However, 1991 was to prove a pivotal year in more ways than one…

Watching The Fading Lights

Having waited such a long time for a new album, fans were not to be disappointed by the next offering from Genesis. Taking full advantage of the extra playing time on the now commonly available compact disc format, the band released the second double studio album in their history. It was preceded by a single, "No Son Of Mine", released on 21st October 1991, which signalled a new realism in the material. The song, accompanied by a dramatic monochrome video broached the taboo subject of child abuse – a million miles away from Genesis' usual lyrical fare. The single peaked at number six in the UK, announcing once again that Genesis were very much alive and kicking with plenty of musical ideas to play with. Collectively the band were as strong as ever, all the tracks being written in the studio with no material "imported" from outside projects, as Mike Rutherford commented in the album's press release. "It makes the first week a bit nerve-wracking, because you've got no songs to fall back on. We were a bit rusty, but it didn't take long to get going really. You just start jamming around, and out of chaos hopefully comes a strong moment. It's a good way for us to go, because we do a lot of work outside the band. It keeps Genesis for what it's all about; which is the chemistry of the three of us playing together…"[126]

In all, the album contained some thirteen songs and displayed a fine line in self-deprecating humour with the album title – *We Can't Dance*. Upon its release the band scored their fourth consecutive number one album in the UK, and in many other territories it achieved the same status, particularly in Germany where it was at the top of the charts for over sixteen weeks. Certainly the album was a wholly different proposition to its pop-orientated predecessor and was an entirely more satisfying prospect for the older fans whilst retaining enough of the band's growing pop sensibilities to increase their popularity, both at home and abroad. Phil Collins' writing for the band included his best work to date, and there was a reassuring return to extended format pieces as well as the shorter pieces which had dominated the last couple of albums. Rutherford had a slightly different perception of events to those expressed in increasingly vehement tones by the more die-hard fans. "A lot of people thought we'd 'Gone American' with the last album, but the fact is that in America a hit single and video can be so high profile that they can dwarf an album and people tend to forget everything that has gone before and it can overshadow an album. I certainly felt it was time for a change."[127]

And change it was, with songs dealing with subjects as diverse as dietary fads ("Living Forever"), the building of the English railways ("Driving The Last Spike"), as well as a wry dig at the obsession with fashion models ("I Can't Dance"). Tony Banks explained at the time, "*Invisible Touch* was perhaps the most direct album we've ever done. This one has a bit more mystery in it. We tried very hard to get each track so that it has an individual quality about it, but at the same time there's an atmosphere which runs through all the songs."[128] They even courted controversy in the USA with a scathing attack on the popular television Evangelists in the song "Jesus He Knows Me". It was banned in certain parts of the USA, and even here in the UK the BBC banned the video when the song was released as one of the clutch of singles.

Unusually, a television crew was given access to the recording studio during the album sessions, an act unprecedented in the history of the group. The resulting documentary, *No Admittance,* showed the members at work and at play, looking extremely relaxed apart from one moment when the frustration of trying to get the lyrics right got the better of Collins. The documentary also served to emphasise what Genesis had always maintained about their way of working, outlined by Mike Rutherford in an interview with *The Waiting Room*. "The obvious one is "I Can't Dance" which was my guitar riff coupled with Tony's keyboard part. That to me was a great little song because it just happened. We wrote it by deciding we'll try it out for the album and it will be great; or if it doesn't work, we'll throw it away. Phil had the lyrics and it just happened in the morning. That's what I like..."[129]

With the album a massive success worldwide, preparations for the obligatory supporting tour began, although this time round it was planned to be a shorter affair than previous efforts. However, no expense was to be spared in the presentation of the latest show. Having decided that the aim was to play predominantly larger venues and in particular, massive outdoor stadia in both the USA and Europe, the band invested heavily in the latest technology to enable them to bring an accessible show to the massed hordes. The technology included three of the world's first Sony "Jumbotron" video screens, to be deployed either singly or joined together, to give extra emphasis on the visual effects which have always figured so largely in Genesis' shows. It was to be the most complex show the band had ever staged as Mike admitted. "This is the most elaborate show we've ever done and the first just in stadiums. In the past we did arenas as well, which meant our hands were tied a bit. Now we've designed the show for stadiums which gives us more freedom."[130]

Technical problems were not the main worry on this tour, however personal and logistical ones were encountered from the opening night. Phil Collins' vocals were affected by a severe cold resulting in the band leaving the stage after a mere three songs almost provoking a riot from disgruntled fans. Other problems were to occur when the tour finally reached Europe with a trucker's strike affecting several gigs, then there was personal tragedy to deal with when a member of the road crew died. Even the British shows were affected. Initially they announced three UK shows, the first at Roundhay Park near Leeds, the scene of their triumph in 1987, followed by a record breaking two night stint at the massive Knebworth Park in Stevenage. Many fans were therefore both surprised and somewhat disappointed when the first of these shows scheduled for 1st August 1992 was cancelled citing logistical difficulties, although an unkind and somewhat sceptical press remarked that the band were victims of poor ticket sales.

The shows themselves were a technical triumph incorporating the visual and musical excitement expected of the band with a growing sense of fun, as evidenced by Phil

Collins' introduction to the medley of older tracks. "This goes back to the dim and slightly damp Seventies, when we wore bell bottom trousers and some of us had more hair!"[131] The new material fitted in easily with the established components of the Genesis set and they managed to take the audience by surprise with a new slant on tracks such as "Home By The Sea" and "Domino" both of which benefited enormously from the improved visuals. The tour statistics made impressive reading with Genesis playing to an average audience of 56,000 per show over the sixty or so performances on the tour. The one show at Knebworth achieved an audience of over 100,000 – not bad for a band consistently branded unpopular by the press.

Knebworth was the culmination of the summer tour and the natural expectation was that the individual members would return to the usual round of solo projects. The band, however, had other plans as Tony Banks explained. "The last time we played in England, we only played at Leeds and Wembley. This time it seemed as if maybe we would only play Leeds and Knebworth, but we didn't want to short-change any of our fans. So we decided on the Earl's Court dates – and from the point of view of the look of the show – it will probably look much better at Earl's Court. It's more controlled indoors, it's a different kind of show."[132] The dates in question were a series of six concerts which took place in early November 1992. What was surprising however, was the announcement prior to this of a series of shows at several theatre venues in the provinces, beginning with Southampton's Mayflower Theatre on 23rd October.

Genesis were looking forward to the line-up of different venues, some of which they hadn't played since the halcyon days of 1980 for a variety of reasons, as Mike commented. "I think half the time what we're looking for in our careers is variety and change. It's going to be refreshing to go back and play in some of the venues that we used to play to smaller, more intimate audiences and with no production, just some lights. That'll be very fresh for us, we haven't done it for a long time. In a way I'm surprised more bands don't do the same… and I feel we know the venues very well. In my mind I can picture Newcastle City Hall very clearly, the way the balcony goes, the way it curves at the back. Newcastle always reminds me of Lindisfarne because when we first played there Lindisfarne were like The Beatles. You felt that you wanted to tell the audience that you were friends of theirs in order to get in."[133]

The new live set was fundamentally the same for these shows as it had been for the outdoor summer tour, although as Banks remarked above, with the benefit of being indoors, the lighting effects worked much better. Perhaps the real treat was the stripped down and more intimate atmosphere of the theatres themselves and the shows were one of the hottest prospects of the year, with a £17 ticket for the gig in Edinburgh for example, changing hands for over £400!

The last show of the tour took place at Wolverhampton's Civic Hall on 17th November, the night after the prestigious gig at London's Royal Albert Hall which was broadcast on the radio. The band must have taken great satisfaction in the success of both the album and tour, but also the fact that they were still giving the "young guns" of pop a run for their money with a string of hit singles any band would be proud of. This was accompanied by an increasing round of television appearances, including a behind-the-scenes look at the gig in Nottingham by the BBC's long-running children's TV programme *Blue Peter*, and an appearance on *Top Of The Pops* in support of a live single version of "Invisible Touch" which had been released in time for the tour, although the lyrics were once again judiciously edited by the BBC so as not to offend. To capitalise on the high profile, Virgin also released a two-part live album featuring the "Short" and the "Long" tracks from the current live set. This, the band's fourth live album, demonstrated both the traditional and commercial faces of Genesis, but was the cause of some criticism from the fan base who maintained that it should have been a double album of the entire show and released as one package. Were Virgin beginning to milk the cash cow that was Genesis?

The following year was a relatively quiet one, as the individual members concentrated on solo projects. They were briefly reunited however, for a charity gig at Cowdrey Ruins in aid of the King Edward VII hospice where they were joined by such rock alumni as Pink Floyd and the remaining members of Queen.

1993 and 1994 were to be traumatic years for Phil Collins as his second marriage, to Jill, gradually came apart, and the couple and their young family became victims of the tabloid press search for a story. His 1993 album *Both Sides* went to town on the critics and was his darkest and most angry album yet. Another massive solo tour occupied Collins throughout 1994 and into 1995, and this, together with Mike Rutherford also taking advantage of the lull in Genesis activity to bring the Mechanics back to life for the highly successful *Beggar On A Beach Of Gold* album and tour, there were many doubts expressed as to whether a band with so many successful members could sustain itself as a working entity. The situation was certainly not helped by the ever-growing gap between Genesis projects. Meanwhile, Virgin kept the band's profile high with a series of releases including the long overdue re-mastering of the back catalogue from *Trespass* to *Three Sides Live*. These were released at two intervals in 1994, although not without some attendant problems, not least being the sleeves which were completely botched in some cases, a problem which has still yet to be properly rectified. The band were also captured live again on another concert video filmed over the six nights at Earl's Court, featuring just about an entire show in glorious sound and vision.

By the end of 1995, however, worries grew – four years since the band's last genuinely new album and still no sign of the long awaited return to the studio. As events would prove, there was still to be another two years before the band re-emerged – by which time fans were to be faced with their biggest challenge in twenty years: another new singer!

Across The Dividing Line

Rumours began circulating towards the end of 1995 that all was not well in the Genesis camp. Various sources maintained that Phil Collins had quit the band. In the face of these rumours, the band's record company and management maintained a stoical silence which did nothing to allay the disquiet, and it was strange to hear people begin to write the same obituaries that had been trotted out in 1975 when Gabriel made his now famous announcement.

As usual, however, the speculation and rumour were to be proven groundless. True, Collins had announced his decision to leave the band as early as 1994 at a dinner organised by manager Tony Smith. With such a lot of activity from the solo members of Genesis it was both unnecessary and possibly harmful to the band's future prospects to make any announcement prematurely as Tony Banks explained. "Well, we let it ride for a little bit because we felt that Phil was probably going to leave, but rather than forcing the issue, we thought we'd leave it until it was 100% definite. There was an official announcement between ourselves in the summer of 1995. So, we had already decided by then that Mike and I would like to try and carry on by seeing what we got out of the writing stage and seeing what was produced. I thought Mike might not be too keen because Mike & The Mechanics was going well, but he was definitely up for it."[134]

The official announcement of Phil Collins' departure was made by the Virgin Press office on Monday 29th March 1996, and even at this time of uncertainty the band displayed a great sense of humour with the headline: "Genesis end 20 year experiment, decide to replace Peter Gabriel as vocalist".[135] The decision still took many by surprise, and some were disappointed that the band hadn't had the faith to make the announcement sooner, although the remaining members presumably tried to reduce the detrimental effect of making the announcement prior to finding a replacement. However, the suspense of waiting for the announcement of who (if anybody) was to replace Phil Collins was to be even more nail-biting, as a further year of silence had to be endured before the decision was made public on 6th June 1997. I am sure the irony of the choice of day was not lost on the band – 6th June is the anniversary of the D-Day Landings in Europe during the Second World War. An apt choice because this certainly was to prove to be the D-Day for Genesis. If anything, the situation was even more precarious at this time than it had been upon Gabriel's departure back in 1975. The band's status then was that of a large cult band; in the 1990's Genesis were perceived by a large section of their audience as Phil Collins' backing band. Indeed, the music press were increasingly running advertisements for Genesis gigs in the late '80's and early '90's under the banner: "Phil Collins and Genesis".

The band's choice of new front man was almost as surprising as Phil Collins departure itself. Instead of choosing a high roller, the band, almost perversely in many people's opinion, went the other way and recruited a comparatively unknown singer. Ray Wilson was a surprise choice, his previous experience had been as singer of grunge rock outfit and one-hit wonders Stiltskin. He was a mere twenty-eight years old and, most surprisingly by Genesis standards, he was a good looking guy still possessed of a full head of hair! Initial reaction to the choice was mixed but generally favourable, although reservations were quite natural given that as yet, there was no evidence to go on. For some however, it was to be a step too far, particularly in the USA where reaction was at best lukewarm and at worst, openly hostile. Many wondered at the band's logic in their choice but it is quite simple as Tony Banks explains. "I think we always felt that we didn't want it to come out like a supergroup or something. We wanted very definitely the group to carry on having the kind of character it has, and if you can imagine any singer you care to name, whether they would or wouldn't do it is irrelevant, but if you said Steve Winwood with Genesis or whatever, you would say that it is something else entirely. So we didn't consider singers like that, we wanted somebody like Ray. He was good because he'd had enough experience so you felt he'd done it in front of a big audience and he'd proved that he had something of that. I think we were initially going for the voice and his was the voice out of all that I'd heard that personally I liked best. So it was quite lucky that the rest of it fell into place."[136]

The new album, the group's seventeenth studio recording, *Calling All Stations,* was eventually released on 2nd September 1997. It was preceded by a single "Congo" which peaked at the number 28 slot in the UK charts. The album itself peaked at number two, being kept off the top slot by the then ubiquitous Oasis. The position in the USA however, was far more daunting with the album peaking at the number 54 slot in the *Billboard* chart hindered by an extremely lacklustre promotion campaign by Atlantic. Perhaps they too had some doubts about the band's new look. Ray Wilson himself admits that Genesis' position this time round was somewhat difficult: "I think with this album we are caught somewhere between what the band has done more recently and what they've done in the past."[137] However, he also displayed a healthy sense of realism about the position as well. "I couldn't come in and replace Phil and expect to sell 11 million albums, it just doesn't make sense, and my view always was that if people who really love Genesis, if those people like the album, then I've achieved it, it has been a success."[138] Mike Rutherford also summed up the problem Genesis faced in America. "We are going to battle on, we've got to get a vibe going and at the moment things are a bit cold. The trouble is until they hear something, until they hear Ray, they can't get excited about it and it's all based on hearsay."[139] It was not all doom and gloom however, in Germany the band received silver discs for sales of 300,000 copies of the album within three weeks of it being released.

Calling All Stations as an album was, for most fans who listened to it, a welcome return to the darker more melodramatic Genesis of old. The title track itself was a genuine piece of traditional Genesis with sterling work by both Rutherford and Banks, its storyline was loosely based around events taking place on the Mir Space Station at the time, perhaps redolent of "Watcher Of The Skies". The album certainly restated Genesis' credentials as a rock band and with a lead singer who was prepared to get behind the idea of Genesis as rock rather than pop. "The idea was to establish us as a rock act, and if we'd started with one of the more obvious ballads such as 'Shipwrecked' or 'Not About Us' it would have given the wrong impression and made people think, 'More fucking middle-of-the-road Genesis, here we go.' Really the album isn't middle-of-the-road, but there are one or two songs that are. I think 'Calling All Stations', 'The Dividing Line' and 'There Must Be Some Other Way' aren't middle-of-the-road songs, these are rock songs of a Genesis type for me, and I thought it was right to start off saying 'this is a rock band' and 'this is a rock album'."[140]

Ironically, given the public apathy to the line-up in the USA, the band chose to premier *Calling All Stations* with a performance at the Kennedy Space Centre on 26th August 1997, a week before the album's release. A full range of tour dates were scheduled beginning in the USA in November, winding up in the UK and Europe the following spring. However, the situation in the USA led to a drastic realignment of the shows which were originally scheduled for major arenas and then downgraded to theatres with a capacity of between three and five thousand. The situation was certainly not one which the band relished and their reaction was characteristically feisty as Wilson explained. "The American thing is obviously very disappointing but we will play them. If we have to play smaller shows; then fuck it; we'll play smaller shows but we *will* play them. All they give a fuck about is that the places we play are busy; they don't want to play a half empty arena, stadium or anything. The way we look at it is, if we have to do theatres in America let's do *full* theatres rather than do half empty arenas."[141]

Unfortunately for Wilson, his long-held desire to play Madison Square Gardens in New York was to remain unfulfilled as the US tour was eventually cancelled entirely. As Tony Smith, the band's manager remarked to *The Waiting Room*, "The vibe simply wasn't happening in America,"[142] and the only chance the US public had to see the band was at the pre-album launch mentioned above. This naturally led to a lot of griping by US fans, although it has to be pointed out that throughout the '80s and early '90s Genesis had toured far more extensively in the US than either the UK or Europe. Reaction to the cancellation of the US tour was hostile and worrying for those who expected the same thing to happen in Europe. In fact, after some rescheduling of dates, the *Calling All Stations* tour finally got under way with a warm-up gig at Bray film studios on 23rd January 1998 in front of an invited audience of fans, followed by the first proper gig at the Sports Hall in Budapest on 28th January. This was swiftly followed by a tour of most of the major arenas in both the UK and Europe, finally winding up with a show at the brand new Hartwall Arena in Helsinki on 5th April.

For the new dates, the band also had a new guitarist replacing Daryl Stuermer whose commitments to Phil Collins' touring schedule prevented him from taking part. His replacement was almost as much of a surprise as Ray Wilson and proved that Genesis were not prepared to sacrifice anything in the music department. Anthony Drennan proved to be an inspired choice, although he may have upset purists with his interpretation of Steve's Hackett's solos during the older material but he certainly gave them a new lease of life as well. Phil's replacement in the percussion department was, if anything the most surprising of all. Nir Tzidkyahu, a thirty-year old Israeli drummer based in New York took over the rhythm section to startling effect although he admits that rehearsing for the tour did cause some problems. "'The Dividing Line' is a pain in the butt! It was just one of those experimental jam sessions in the studio and I have no idea what I played."[143]

Once again, the band utilised the "Jumbotron" screens from the *We Can't Dance* tour, although to somewhat mixed effect, primarily because they were stationary and not able to link up as they had been able to do previously. The reason for this was quite simple: money. As the band's lighting engineer Dave Hill explained, "Every time the screen moves it costs about £10,000 and besides, even The Rolling Stones didn't have the screens moving."[144] Musically however, there were no such disappointments as the band treated audiences to a show that lived up to the billing on the posters: "Genesis Through the Ages". This was, however, a somewhat misleading advertising campaign landing the band in some degree of trouble with the UK Advertising Standards Council with its depiction of the band including both Peter Gabriel and Phil Collins on the posters! However, fans who contacted the box offices at the venues in the UK were left in no doubt as to who was in the band – it was quite astonishing to be asked the following question when booking tickets: "You do realise that Phil Collins is no longer in Genesis, don't you?"

The tour in Europe and the UK was a qualified success with the combination of a rejuvenated band and a set drawing on the strengths of the Genesis catalogue. The band managed to convince their fans that there was still plenty of life in the old (or should that be not so old?) dog yet. The band even managed to headline two of the most prestigious German festivals in the summer of 1998 over such alumni as Bob Dylan and Page & Plant, rounding off the touring obligations for the album in fine style.

Soon after the tour was complete, it was announced that Virgin Records were planning to release the first of a proposed series of boxed set compilations. Covering the period from the band's inception in 1967 to the end of the Gabriel era in 1975, the first of these boxes titled *Genesis Archive 1967 -1975* was released on 22nd June 1998, charting at the number 35 position in the UK. The accompanying publicity saw an undreamed of "Reunion" between the original band members – including both Anthony Phillips and John Silver – for a series of interviews and photo opportunities at London's Heathrow airport on 11th May. The event was captured for posterity by VH1 and subsequently broadcast as part of their "Genesis Day" special narrated by Genesis "New Boy" Ray Wilson. The four CD set comprised just about everything that fans of this period – and newer ones still finding their feet in the band's enormous back catalogue – could wish for. Included were classic live recordings from both the *Selling England By The Pound* and *The Lamb Lies Down On Broadway* tours, as well as the elusive rare single b-sides and a whole disc of previously unheard material from the very beginnings of the band's story. The release of this set sparked off the usual round of speculation of a grand reunion by the classic band line-up for a tour and album. Whilst no one in the Genesis camp is either confirming or denying the prospect of such a reunion, both Steve Hackett and Anthony Phillips have maintained that it is a prospect which they wouldn't rule out or, to use Steve Hackett's words, "I would be involved but only if I can play my harmonica!"[145] The likelihood of such an event taking place whilst the band appear to still be a recording and performing entity is remote at best. I am sure that many fans would sooner see the band hit the road for a few more albums yet

Genesis' situation at present has been the subject of much speculation and it seems that certain publications have already started the process of writing the band off. We all know just how foolish that can be, particularly with Genesis, but at present all the members seem content to involve themselves in solo projects of one form or another. For the moment the stage is still set for another album by the band and it is to be hoped that they continue to rummage in their wardrobes for still more amazing music. However, one thing is for sure as we enter the new millennium, the music of Genesis stands as unique testament and has, for more than thirty years, formed the soundtrack to many of our lives.

Genesis UK Discography

Part One: 7" Vinyl singles

The Silent Sun/That's Me — DECCA F12735
A Winter's tale/One-Eyed Hound — DECCA F12775
Where The Sour Turns To Sweet/In Hiding — DECCA F12949
The Knife (Pt1)/The Knife (Pt2) — CHARISMA CB152 (PS)
Happy The Man/Seven Stones — CHARISMA CB181 (PS)
I Know What I Like/Twilight Alehouse — CHARISMA CB224
Twilight Alehouse (one-sided flexi disc issued free with October 1973 issue of "Zig Zag" magazine and subsequently re-issued as free single to first 1000 members of Genesis Information in 1976)
Counting Out Time/Riding The Scree — CHARISMA CB238
The Carpet Crawlers/The Waiting Room (Evil Jam Live) — CHARISMA CB251
A Trick Of The Tail/Ripples — CHARISMA CB277
Your Own Special Way/It's Yourself — CHARISMA CB300
Match Of The Day/Pigeons/Inside & Out — CHARISMA GEN001 (PS)
Follow You Follow Me/Ballad Of Big — CHARISMA CB309 (PS)
Many Too Many/The Day The Light Went Out/Vancouver — CHARISMA CB315 (PS)
Turn It On Again/Behind The Lines (Pt2) — CHARISMA CB356
Duchess/Open Door — CHARISMA CB363 (PS)
Misunderstanding/Evidence Of Autumn — CHARISMA CB369 (PS)
Abacab/Another Record — CHARISMA CB388 (PS)
Keep It Dark/Naminanu — CHARISMA CB391 (PS)
Man On The Corner/Submarine — CHARISMA CB393 (PS)
Paperlate/You Might Recall/Me & Virgil — CHARISMA GEN1 (PS)
The Lady Lies (Live) (one- sided flexi disc free with June 1982 issue of "Flexipop" magazine)
Firth Of Fifth (Live) (one-sided flexidisc issued free to members of "Genesis Information" in May 1983 with limited edition numbered sleeve)
Mama/It's Gonna Get Better — CHARISMA/VIRGIN MAMA1 (PS)
That's All/Taking It All Too Hard — CHARISMA/VIRGIN TATA1 (PS)
That's All/Taking It All Too Hard — CHARISMA/VIRGIN TATA-Y1 (PD)
Illegal Alien/Turn It On Again (live) — CHARISMA/VIRGIN AL1 (PS)
Illegal Alien/Turn It On Again (live) — CHARISMA/VIRGIN ALS1 (PD)
Invisible Touch/The Last Domino — VIRGIN GENS1 (PS)
Invisible Touch/The Last Domino — VIRGIN GENSY1 (PS)
(White vinyl limited edition with fold -out sleeve)
In Too Deep/Do The Neurotic (Edit) — VIRGIN GENS2 (PS)
Land Of Confusion/Feeding The Fire — VIRGIN GENS3 (PS)
Tonight, Tonight, Tonight /In The Glow Of The Night — VIRGIN GENS4 (PS)
Throwing It All Away/I'd Rather Be You — VIRGIN GENS5 (PS)
No Son Of Mine/Living Forever — VIRGIN GENS6 (PS)
I Can't Dance/On The Shoreline — VIRGIN GENS7 (PS)
Hold On My Heart/Way Of The World — VIRGIN GENS8 (PS)
Jesus He Knows Me/Hearts On Fire — VIRGIN GENS9 (PS)
Invisible Touch (Live)/Abacab (Live) — VIRGIN GENS10 (PS)
(Initially issued as a limited edition with photo booklet and numbered sleeve)

Tell Me Why (Live/Dreaming While You Sleep (Live) VIRGIN GENS11 (PS)

Part Two: 12" Vinyl Singles

Keep It Dark/Naminanu/Abacab (album version) CHARISMA CB391-12 (PS)
Mama/It's Gonna Get Better CHARISMA/VIRGIN MAMA1-2(PS)
That's all/Taking it all too hard/Firth of fifth (live) CHARISMA/VIRGIN TATA1-12(PS)
Illegal Alien/Turn It On Again (full live version) CHARISMA/VIRGIN AL1-12 (PS)
Invisible Touch (Extended) Invisible Touch/The Last Domino VIRGIN GENS1-12 (PS)
In Too Deep/Do The Neurotic (unedited) VIRGIN GENS2-12 (PS)
In Too Deep/Do The Neurotic (unedited) VIRGIN GENSY 2-12 (PD)
Land Of Confusion (remix) Land Of Confusion/Feeding The Fire VIRGIN GENS3-12 (PS)
Tonight, Tonight, Tonight (Edit)/In The Glow Of The Night/Paperlate/Tonight, tonight, tonight (Remix) VIRGIN GENS4-12 (PS)
Tonight, Tonight, Tonight (Edit)/In The Glow Of The Night/Tonight, Tonight, Tonight (12" Remix) VIRGIN GENS412 (PS)
(Limited edition with gatefold sleeve and European tour map issued in time for UK tour dates)
Throwing It All Away (live) I'd Rather Be You/Invisible Touch (Live) VIRGIN GENS5-12 (PS)
No Son Of Mine/Living Forever/Invisible Touch (live) VIRGIN GENS612 (PS)
(Limited edition with gatefold sleeve and watercolour print)

Part Three: Compact Disc Singles

Match Of The Day/Pigeons/Inside & Out VIRGIN CDT40 (PS)
Mama (Long version)/It's Gonna Get Better (Long version) VIRGIN CDT5 (PS)
Land Of Confusion/Land Of Confusion(extended version)/Feeding The Fire/Do The Neurotic VIRGIN SNEG3-12 (PS)
Tonight, Tonight, Tonight (edit)/In The Glow Of The Night/Paperlate/
Tonight, Tonight , Tonight (12" remix) VIRGIN DRAW412 (PS)
Domino (live)(Limited edition with first 5000 copies of the "Invisible Touch Tour" live video)
No Son Of Mine/Living Forever/Invisible Touch (live) VIRGIN GENDG6 (PS)*
I Can't Dance/On The Shoreline/In Too Deep(Live)/That's All (Live) VIRGIN GENDG7 (PS)*
(Limited edition with pocket biography)
I Can't Dance/On The Shoreline/I Can't Dance (Sex mix) VIRGIN GENSD7 (PS)
Hold On My Heart/Way Of The World/Your Own Special Way (live) VIRGIN GENDG8 (PS)*
(Limited edition with artwork postcard set)
Hold On My Heart/Way Of The World/Home By The Sea(Live)/Second Home By The Sea (live) VIRGIN GENSD8 (PS)*
Jesus He Knows Me (single mix)/Hearts On Fire/Land Of Confusion (Rehearsal version) VIRGIN GENDX9 (PS)*
Jesus He Knows Me (Single mix)/Hearts On Fire/I Can't Dance (The Other Mix) VIRGIN GENDG9 (PS)
(* these discs combined to form "The Invisible Series" which was housed in a slip case available with the final volume)
Invisible Touch(live)/Abacab(live)/The Brazilian (live) VIRGIN GENDX10 (PS)
(Issued as a limited edition numbered edition with box and photo booklet)
Tell Me Why/Dreaming While You Sleep(live)/Turn It On Again (1992 live) VIRGIN GENDG11 (PS)
Tell Me Why/Dreaming While You Sleep (Live)/Tonight, Tonight, Tonight (Full live version) VIRGIN GENDX11 (PS)
Congo (Edit)/Papa He Said/Banjo Man VIRGIN GENSD12 (PS)
Congo (Edit)/Second Home By The Sea (edit) VIRGIN GENSDX12 (PS)
(Limited edition with enhanced CD rom footage and promotional video for "Congo")
Shipwrecked/Phret(Instrumental)/7/8 (Instrumental) VIRGIN GENSD14 (PS)
Shipwrecked/No Son Of Mine + (live)/Lover's Leap + (Live)/Turn It On Again + (live) VIRGIN GENDX14 (PS)
Not About Us (Edit)/Anything Now/Sign Your Life Away/Run Out Of Time VIRGIN GENSD15 (PS)

Not About Us (Edit)/Dancing With The Moonlit Knight (Live)/Follow You Follow Me (Live)/Not About Us (Extended version) **VIRGIN GENDX15 (PS)**
~~The Lamb Lies Down On Broadway (live)~~/~~It (live)~~/~~Counting Out Time (live)~~/~~Carpet Crawlers (live)~~/~~Dancing With The Moonlit Knight (live)~~/I ~~Know What I Like (live)~~/~~Happy~~ The Man/~~Watcher Of The Skies (re-mixed edited version)~~/~~In The Wilderness (without strings)~~/~~Shepherd~~/Twilight Alehouse/Supper's Ready (live) **VIRGIN G BOX 98 (PS)**
(Limited edition ten track promotional sampler from the "Genesis Archive 1967 -1975" four CD set)
PS denotes singles issued with a picture sleeve. **PD** denotes singles issued with a picture disc.
+ These tracks were recorded at the bands acoustic launch for "Calling all Stations" at Cape Canaveral Space Centre 26.8.97.
# These tracks were recorded at the RTL studios Paris 17.11.97.

Part Four: Vinyl and Compact Disc Albums.

From Genesis To Revelation **DECCA SKL4990 (STEREO EDITION)**
From Genesis To Revelation **DECCA LK4990 (MONO EDITION)**
Rock Roots **DECCA ROOTS 1**
From Genesis To Revelation **MUSIC CLUB MCCD133 (CD)**
(This is only one of numerous re-issues on both vinyl and compact disc of this first album)
Trespass **CHARISMA CAS1020**
Trespass **CHARISMA/VIRGIN CASCD1020 (CD)**
Trespass **VIRGIN CASCD1020 (CD) (*)**
Trespass **VIRGIN CASCDX 1020 (RE-MASTERED CD)**
Nursery Cryme **CHARISMA CAS1052**
Nursery Cryme **CHARISMA/VIRGIN CASCD1052 (CD)**
Nursery Cryme **VIRGIN CASCD1052 (CD) (*)**
Nursery Cryme **VIRGIN CASCDX1052 (RE-MASTERED CD)**
Foxtrot **CHARISMA CAS 1058**
Foxtrot **CHARISMA/VIRGIN CASCD1058 (CD)**
Foxtrot **VIRGIN CASCD1058 (CD) (*)**
Foxtrot **VIRGIN CASCDX 1058 (RE-MASTERED CD)**
Genesis Live **CHARISMA CLASS 1**
Genesis Live **CHARISMA/VIRGIN CLACD1 (CD)**
Genesis Live **VIRGIN CLACDX 1 (RE-MASTERED CD)**
Selling England By The Pound **CHARISMA CAS1074**
Selling England By The Pound **CHARISMA/VIRGIN CASCD1074 (CD)**
Selling England By The Pound **VIRGIN CASCD1074 (CD) (*)**
Selling England By The Pound **VIRGIN CASCDX1074 (RE-MASTERED CD)**
The Lamb Lies Down On Broadway **CHARISMA CDS101**
The Lamb Lies Down On Broadway **CHARISMA/VIRGIN CGSCD101 (CD)**
The Lamb Lies Down On Broadway **VIRGIN CGSCD101 (CD) (*)**
The Lamb Lies Down On Broadway **VIRGIN CGSCDX101 (RE-MASTERED CD)**
(*) Discs marked are part of either Volume One or Two of two picture disc edition sets released by Virgin in 1991 with the catalogue numbers **TPAK1** and **TPAK17** respectively.
A Trick Of The Tail **CHARISMA CDS4001**
A Trick Of The Tail **VIRGIN CDSCD4001 (CD)**
A Trick Of The Tail **VIRGIN CDSCDX4001 (RE-MASTERED CD)**
Wind & Wuthering **CHARISMA CDS4005**
Wind & Wuthering **VIRGIN CDSCD4005 (CD)**
Wind & Wuthering **VIRGIN CDSCDX 4005 (RE-MASTERED CD)**
Seconds Out **CHARISMA GE2001**
Seconds Out **VIRGIN GECD2001 (CD)**
Seconds Out **VIRGIN GECDX2001 (RE-MASTERED CD)**
And Then There Were Three **CHARISMA CDS4010**
And Then There Were Three **VIRGIN CDSCD4010 (CD)**
And Then There Were Three **VIRGIN CDSCDX4010 (RE-MASTERED CD)**

Duke	CHARISMA CBR101
Duke	VIRGIN CBRCD101 (CD)
Duke	VIRGIN CBRCDX101 (RE-MASTERED CD)
Abacab	CHARISMA CBR102
Abacab	VIRGIN CBRCD102 (CD)
Abacab	VIRGIN CBRCDX102 (RE-MASTERED CD)
Three Sides Live	VIRGIN/CHARISMA GE2002
Three Sides Live	VIRGIN/CHARISMA GECD2002 (CD)
Three Sides Live	VIRGIN GECDX2002 (RE-MASTERED CD)
Genesis	CHARISMA/VIRGIN GENLP1
Genesis	CHARISMA/VIRGIN GENCD1 (CD)
Invisible Touch	VIRGIN GENLP2
Invisible Touch	VIRGIN GENCD2 (CD)
We Can't Dance	VIRGIN GENLP3
We Can't Dance	VIRGIN GENCD3 (CD)
The Way We Walk Volume One: The Shorts	VIRGIN GENLP4
The Way We Walk Volume One: The Shorts	VIRGIN GENCD4 (CD)
The Way We Walk Volume Two: The Longs	VIRGIN GENLP5
The Way We Walk Volume Two: The Longs	VIRGIN GENCD5 (CD)
Calling All Stations	VIRGIN GENLP6

(Released as limited edition with three sided record and a fourth vinyl side etched with a picture of the band)

Calling All Stations	VIRGIN GENCD6 (CD)
Genesis Archive 1967-1975	VIRGIN GENBOX6 (CD)
Trespass	VIRGIN VJCP -68091 (CD) +
Nursery Cryne	VIRGIN VJCP-68092 (CD) +
Foxtrot	VIRGIN VJCP-68093 (CD) +
Genesis Live	VIRGIN VJCP-68094 (CD) +
Selling England By The Pound	VIRGIN VJCP-68095 (CD) +
The Lamb Lies Down On Broadway	VIRGIN VJCP-68096-97 (CD) +
A Trick Of The Tail	VIRGIN VJCP-68098 (CD) +
Wind & Wuthering	VIRGIN VJCP-68099 (CD) +
Seconds Out	VIRGIN VJCP-68100-01 (CD) +
And Then There Were Three	VIRGIN VJCP-68102 (CD) +
Duke	VIRGIN VJCP-68103 (CD) +
Abacab	VIRGIN VJCP-68104 (CD) +
Three Sides Live	VIRGIN VJCP-68105-06 (CD) +
Genesis	VIRGIN VJCP-68107 (CD) +
Invisible Touch	VIRGIN VJCP-68108 (CD) +
We Can't Dance	VIRGIN VJCP-68109 (CD) +
The Way We Walk Volume One: The Shorts	VIRGIN VJCP-68110 (CD) +
The Way We Walk Volume Two: The Longs	VIRGIN VJCP-68111 (CD) +
Calling All Stations	VIRGIN VJCP-68112 (CD) +

(+) These are the recently issued Japanese limited editions of the Genesis catalogue complete with fully restored artwork and centre labels as on the original vinyl albums.

Exploring The Musical Box

A look at some of the more collectable recordings by the band

Genesis' recording history begins with the release on February 2nd 1968 of their first single, "The Silent Sun" issued by Decca records. This recording was released in a variety of versions in different territories, with perhaps two of the most interesting ones being the US promotional version issued by Parrot Records and the New Zealand pressing. Having gained no success with this initial release, the band released a second single on 10th May 1968, this time the choice of material is much more interesting to collectors, featuring two non-album tracks, "A Winter's Tale"/ "One-Eyed Hound". Once again, the single was met with bland indifference by the public and stock or promotional copies of either this single or its predecessor are now becoming very difficult to find.

The first album appeared in March 1969. Titled *From Genesis To Revelation,* it achieved minimal sales upon its release – 649 copies of the stereo edition and approximately half that number of sales for the mono version. The mono copy is particularly sought-after and commands a high price to collectors. The final release from this album appeared on 27th June 1969 and once again included two album tracks, "Where The Sour Turns To Sweet"/"In Hiding" to no avail, making this another much prized item for collectors. Re-issues of this album, some containing the non-album tracks from the second single, have been many, and add little if anything to the album itself, although on occasion, there have been interesting, if not to say controversial, sleeve notes accompanying them. The most recent re-issues on compact disc have had the added bonus of a set of picture postcards of the band from the period, with one or two previously unreleased tracks, "Image Blown Out" and "She Is Beautiful", both of which have since appeared (and in better recorded quality it must be added) on the band's *Genesis Archive 1967 – 75* four CD set.

By the middle of 1970, the relationship with Jonathan King and Decca was now at an end, and the band signed up to the fledgling Charisma Records. This was to be a fruitful relationship for both record company and artists, initiated by the release in October 1970 of the band's first proper album, *Trespass*. It appeared on the company's "Pink Scroll" label, before being re-issued in 1972 on the more familiar "Mad Hatter's Tea Party" label. Copies on the original label are consequently more valuable than later variants. A promotional single was prepared for various radio stations in the UK which coupled "Looking For Someone"/"Visions Of Angels". These singles are now extremely hard to find and without doubt constitute one of the most collectable items from this period. Charisma also issued a stock single from the album in September 1971, strangely enough almost a year after the album was released. An odd decision, the single featured the band's stand-out live track, "The Knife" split into two parts and accompanied by a picture sleeve which included "new boys" Steve Hackett and Phil Collins.

Genesis' next album for Charisma, *Nursery Cryme,* appeared in late 1971 and once again was released on the "Pink Scroll" label, packaged in a gatefold sleeve designed by Paul Whitehead, who had also executed the artwork for the band's first album on the label. An interesting variant of this, is the version with an advertisement for the "Charisma Package Tour" which featured Genesis, Van Der Graaf Generator and Lindisfarne. By now, Genesis were beginning to gain attention in the UK and elsewhere, although not sufficient to persuade Charisma to issue a single to help promote the album, although promotional EPs were issued in other territories.

The band's next choice of single was equally bizarre. In May 1972, they issued "Happy The Man", a song which dated back to the very earliest incarnation of the band. Coupled with "Seven Stones" from the *Nursury Cryme* album, this was to be the band's last picture sleeve single in the UK until 1978's "Follow You, Follow Me" and a copy of the single in its original sleeve (a live shot of the band) commands a very high price to collectors.

1972 also saw the release in October, of the classic *Foxtrot* album which saw Genesis reach their highest point to date, finally achieving headline status in the UK and Europe. Strangely no single was issued in the UK from the album (perhaps at the time, Charisma still viewed Genesis as an album band?), although "Watcher Of The Skies" was issued in many territories coupled with "Willow Farm".

That view was to change the following year with the release of the next studio album, preceded by the long awaited live album, *Genesis Live,* comprising several of the strongest tracks from their current live show, at a bargain price which enabled it to be put out in large chain stores like Woolworths and WH Smiths. A double test pressing album produced for the Philips label in Holland is reputed to exist and would certainly be a very expensive item to add to your collection should you be able to find one. *Genesis Live* was also the first to be issued on what has since become one of the best loved record labels; the "Mad Hatter's Tea Party" label and subsequent re-pressings of the previous albums appeared on this label as well.

October 1973 saw the next single from the as yet, unreleased new album. This single was to give Genesis their long awaited hit. "I Know What I Like" was the chosen track, coupled with another golden oldie "Twilight Alehouse" which, like "Happy The Man" before it, was a hangover from the early days of the band. The single achieved a position of number 19 in the UK charts and there was even a flexidisc edition of its B-side given away with the October edition of *ZigZag* magazine. This flexidisc was also part of the compendium package given away at the shows in support of the album, and was also re-issued as a free single with an early edition of the band's official fan club magazine *Genesis Information* in 1976.

The new album *Selling England By The Pound* also achieved a healthy chart position upon its release in late October 1973, and was the first studio album by the band to be issued on the "Mad Hatter's Tea Party" label. An interesting variation appeared in Italy, where it was issued in a gatefold sleeve encompassing a live photograph on the back cover, with the lyrics on the inside instead of on an insert as in the UK.

Late 1974 would herald the most controversial work to date. *The Lamb Lies Down On Broadway*, a double album opus, although one hesitates to call it a "Rock Opera". It was preceded by a single, "Counting Out Time"/"Riding The Scree", both taken from the album, and gave an appropriate flavour of the band's new work. Genesis had already taken to the road to promote the new album before it was released in late November 1974. A second single was issued on 21st April 1975 coupling one of the more accessible tracks from the album "The Carpet Crawlers" with a live version of the instrumental jam session, "The Waiting Room (Evil Jam)". This was to be Genesis' last release with Peter Gabriel as their front man – his departure was announced officially in August 1975.

1976 saw not only a change of personnel in the band but also a change in record labels. Charisma decided to change their single label from the familiar "Mad Hatter..." to a plain silver centre, although the former label was retained for albums. First recipient of this change in styles was the new single, "A Trick Of The Tail", title track of the new album, coupled with another album track, "Ripples". More surprising than the return to melodic music, was their new singer: Phil Collins. The drummer stepped bravely into the limelight as the band's fortunes took another dramatic leap forward. *A Trick Of The Tail* itself meanwhile, outsold its predecessors and achieved a number 3 position in the UK album charts.

Consolidating their success, yet another new album was complete by the end of 1976. *Wind & Wuthering* was to be the last studio album to feature Steve Hackett, who had decided to leave at the end of their highly successful world tour in July 1977. Released on New Year's Day 1977, the album was everything that was anathema to the music industry at the time. Melodic and dramatic instead of brash and dissonant, *Wind & Wuthering* features several of Genesis' finest musical moments. A single was issued in February 1977, coupling album track "Your Own Special Way" with "It's Yourself", an out-take from the previous album. The single achieved the position of number 43 in the charts.

Prior to the release of their long overdue second live album, the band issued their first EP of songs which had been left over from the recording sessions. Comprising three tracks; "Match Of The Day"/"Pigeons"/"Inside & Out", the single surprised even the band themselves becoming their highest chart entry with a position of number 14 aided no doubt by the band's recent UK tour and a hilarious video made for the opening track. This was also to be the band's first single issued in a picture sleeve since the heady days of 1972.

Steve's Hackett's announcement of his departure in August 1977 overshadowed the release in October of *Seconds Out*, the second live offering packaged in double album format, which encapsulated the best moments from their live shows and achieved a number two position in the charts. Original editions of this album on vinyl had inner record labels depicting the live show which were subsequently removed when Virgin took over the Charisma catalogue in 1982/83.

Continuing to demonstrate a sense of humour, the remaining Genesis members opted to call their new album, *And Then There Were Three*, a reflection on their current status as a three-piece recording band following Hackett's departure. If 1975's *The Lamb Lies Down On Broadway* took fans by surprise by its brashness, then this album had the same effect by providing the band with a massive chart hit when the first single from it, "Follow You Follow Me" attained the number 7 position in March of 1978. The single appeared with another album track as its B-side, "Ballad Of Big" and was issued in the customary picture sleeve, which varied from territory to territory usually incorporating the year's tour dates in each region. The USA produced the most interesting variant of the single with a re-mixed version, longer than its UK counterpart, and an edited B-side version of "Inside & Out". As was the norm with US singles, this edition did not come with a picture sleeve. The album itself was issued in April 1978 and went straight to the number three position in the UK charts. Original editions of the UK album are easy to spot because they contained an advertisement for the band's only UK show that year, at Knebworth Park. June saw the release of another EP of material from the album comprising "Many Too Many", a further track from the album, and two non-album cuts, "The Day The Light Went Out" and "Vancouver", both of which make this single much sought after by collectors. Once again it was issued in a picture sleeve which varied from territory to territory.

1979 saw the band on hiatus with solo projects to the fore, so only one notable item appeared in the UK that year. Attendees at the Reading Festival in August could, if they wished, avail themselves of a free flexidisc of "The Silent Sun" given away by Decca Records. No doubt the fact that Peter Gabriel was one of the headline artists that year may have had something to do with this.

1980 saw the band members return to the fold after their solo efforts. The resulting album saw a new look Genesis characterised by a new sound, leading to what was to become the first of a series of successful chart singles. "Turn It On Again" backed with "Behind The Lines" almost repeated the success of "Follow You Follow Me" yielding a number 8 position in the UK charts. The new album, *Duke*, released in March 1980 became the bands' first number 1 album in the UK. The original vinyl edition has become a collectable item as it features a cartoon-style centre label designed by album cover artist, Lionel Koechlin, which was subsequently removed when Virgin Records took over Charisma.

Duke broke the mould in more ways than one, with the issue of no less than three singles in the UK. The second, "Duchess", released in May 1980, didn't repeat the success of its predecessor reaching only the number 46 position in the UK charts. It did, however, give UK fans another collectable item in the shape of its B-side, the Mike Rutherford penned "Open Door". Charisma had seen another track from the album give the band its first real breakthrough in the USA. "Misunderstanding", a Phil Collins composition, had achieved a healthy position in the US charts and Charisma hoped it would repeat that position here in the UK. The single, when released in August 1980, didn't quite live up to expectations attaining the number 42 slot in the UK. However, UK fans were rewarded with another collectable B-side, Tony Banks' "Evidence of Autumn".

Riding high on the back of an enormously successful series of theatre shows, both in the UK and USA, the band were soon back at work in their own studio which had been purchased and renovated in 1980. The next album was quite a surprise to many fans. Gone was the hyperbole and excess that many felt was the Genesis trademark, and in its place was a leaner, meaner sound, no doubt helped by the band engaging Hugh Padgham as producer, in place of Genesis stalwart David Hentschel. Padgham's previous credits included The Police, XTC and more interestingly; Phil Collins' first solo effort, *Face Value* released earlier in 1981.The first single from the album was the title cut, "Abacab" a pure rock track which caught many fans off guard. In fact, the entire album was a surprising departure from the norm, including several out-and-out pop songs such as "No Reply At All", which even featured the Earth Wind & Fire horn section, and the ghastly "Who-Dunnit?" which was even considered for single release at one point. The "Abacab" single itself was issued in an abstract artwork sleeve which was reproduced on the label of initial copies of the 7" version, before the now usual silver logo was reinstated on later issues. The b-side was another album track "Another Record" and the single peaked at the number 9 position in the charts.

Abacab was issued in September and immediately charted again at the number one slot. The vinyl album was issued with five variants of artwork for reasons best known to the band themselves. Two subsequent singles were issued, the first being "Keep It Dark" released in October 1981 backed with a non-album track, "Naminanu". The 12" edition had the album-length "Abacab" as an added bonus. The final single from the album in the UK has since become one of the most collectable to be released by the band during the eighties. Initial copies of this 7" only single, "Man On The Corner" issued in March 1982, were packaged in a white picture sleeve with an illustration of a man standing on a corner. It has been very difficult to ascertain exactly how limited these editions were, because many stores received both this version and the standard black and green sleeve, but, since its release, copies of this edition have become even scarcer and the blue vinyl edition is even more highly prized. The single is also of interest to completists because it featured another non-album b-side, "Submarine".

Not ones to keep their fans waiting long for new material, the band returned to the long obsolete EP format for their next release in May 1982. The 3x3 EP used up the three remaining complete tracks from the *Abacab* sessions and packaged them neatly into a picture sleeve which parodied The Beatles' Twist & Shout EP of almost twenty years earlier. The single comprised the following tracks; "Paperlate"/"You Might Recall"/"Me & Virgil" and charted at the number 8 position. It was also Genesis' first picture disc single which is another of the more collectable items from this period.

Independent of the band, two flexidiscs were released in this period. The June 1982 edition of *Flexipop* came complete with a green vinyl flexi of the band's performance of "The Lady Lies" from their concert at Knebworth in 1978, and in May 1983 the band's fan club, *Genesis Information,* issued a black vinyl flexi with a live version of the classic "Firth Of Fifth" recorded during the 1981 tour. The single itself was free to members of the club but to obtain the limited numbered sleeve you had to pay the princely sum of 50p! Needless to say, both of these items are extremely collectable.

Following the success of the 3x3 EP, the band embarked upon a tour of the USA and Europe in August 1982 to promote their new live album *Three Sides Live* which had been released in June 1982 reaching the number two position in the chart. The album was issued in two different formats, in the UK it was really "Four Sides Live" because the fourth side was comprised of a further selection of live recordings dating back as far as 1976. The US version contained the three tracks from the recently issued EP, as well as the two non-album b-sides from *Duke,* a nice gesture to fans who had previously been unable to pick these items up on the relevant singles. Both versions of the album are essential to any Genesis collection from this period.

Having seen Phil Collins enjoy a hugely successful first solo tour in November 1982 to February 1983, the band were soon hard at work on their sixth studio album in only eight years. The initial release from the new album was a song about a prostitute of over six minutes duration, which many deem suicidally long for a single. "Mama" became on its release in August 1983 the band's highest-ever chart success, peaking at number four. As usual, the single was backed by another album track, "It's Gonna Get Better" and on the 12" edition both tracks were the full length versions. The 12" also had an initial sleeve with cut-out stencilled lettering on hard card. Interestingly, over four years later this single was reissued on CD by Virgin as part of their "Virgin Classics" series, along with 1977's "Spot The Pigeon" EP, which also came in a nice reproduction of the original sleeve.

It was also the band's first album to be released on the new compact disc format, and they also re-issued both *A Trick Of The Tail* and *And Then There Were Three* in this format that year. The latter appeared twice, with two different catalogue numbers, the former edition now being highly collectable. The remainder of the band's back catalogue was gradually re-issued on CD format over the next few years.

The album that followed, was called *Genesis* and is to many fans, a somewhat lacklustre effort by previous standards. It did however see the band stretch out and embrace even more musical styles, including "That's All" which became the second single in October 1983. This release generated three collectable items, the 7" version was available in a limited picture sleeve, although the b-side was another album track "Taking It All Too Hard". There was also a shaped 7" picture disc and a 12" vinyl version that had the added bonus of the live version of "Firth Of Fifth" released earlier in the year by the band's fan club. The final single from *Genesis* appeared almost a year after the album's release. "Illegal Alien" was an anarchic look at America's illegal immigrant problem accompanied by a hilarious video which had the band dressed up as fugitives from justice. This was another single which appeared in 7", 12" and picture disc versions – the only real difference being the inclusion on the 12" single of the complete live version of "Turn It On Again" with the now famous (or should that be infamous?) "Sixties Medley" which was missing from the other 12" version.

There was almost a two year wait before Genesis reappeared, in which time Phil Collins had enjoyed further massive success with his third solo album, *No Jacket Required,* and Mike Rutherford had taken his "Mechanics" out for their first test drive. Upon their return, the band demonstrated that they were not simply out to recreate the tried and trusted formulae but were eager to branch out still further. May 1986 saw the first evidence of this with the release of "Invisible Touch", the title track from the band's thirteenth studio album. A loud, brash up-tempo pop tune, this track was backed by an album cut "The Last Domino", originally part of a longer track which, along with the other opus on the album, "Tonight, Tonight, Tonight" was to serve as some reassurance to the fans of the band's lengthier epics. The single was issued in both 7" and 12" versions, the former also being issued as a limited edition clear vinyl single with fold out sleeve, and the 12" containing an extended version of the A-side. The album itself also became the first to gain a simultaneous release on vinyl, cassette and compact disc.

Invisible Touch became the high water mark for Genesis. During the twelve or so months after the release of the first single from the album, it spawned no less than five hit singles in both the UK and USA. The album placed Genesis firmly out in front as the major British band of 1986/87, and their massive ten month tour later that year made them the biggest grossing concert act in the USA. The second single from the album appeared in August 1986 coupling "In Too Deep" with a further non-album cut "Do The Neurotic" which appeared on the four different versions of the single. The 12" picture disc version was the band's first (and last) to be issued in this format and is quite collectable.

"Land of Confusion" was the third single from the album and also the first to be issued in compact disc format. In addition to the standard version of the track it contained a remix, as well as "Feeding The Fire", another non-album track. The CD also included the previous single's b-side as a bonus. "Tonight ,Tonight, Tonight", a track which had courted some controversy in the USA where it was used as part of the advertising campaign for Michelob beer, became the fourth single issued in January 1987. This threw up one of the more unusual releases from the album. When issued, the single came in all the usual formats; CD, 7" and 12" vinyl with variations on the 7" vinyl for b-sides and the unusual inclusion of "Paperlate" from the band's EP of several years before. Unusually, it was also re-issued on a limited edition 12" single in a gatefold sleeve shortly before the band began the European leg of their tour. Also the label on this record states that "Paperlate" was once again included and yet it is missing from the record itself! The final single from the album appeared after the UK tour and coupled "Throwing It All Away" with another non-album track, the irresistibly catchy "I'd Rather Be You". On the 12" version there was the added bonus of a live "Invisible Touch". Strangely enough, given the band's recent embrace of new technology, this single was not issued as a compact disc edition.

With the growing success of all the individual members of the band it was to be some four years before another Genesis album appeared. In the meantime, Virgin Records opted for a clever marketing ploy to keep interest in the back catalogue ticking over: they re-issued all the albums from the Peter Gabriel era as budget priced picture disc editions. Despite the fact that the discs themselves were delightfully packaged and came in slipcases, many fans bemoaned the wasted opportunity of not including the single b-sides and other material from this period on these editions, thereby taking full advantage of the extra recording time available in CD format.

The wait for the new album was well worth it. Genesis rewarded their fans with *We Can't Dance*, one of their most convincing albums in years in terms of combining both the more commercial elements of the band's music with more traditionally orientated pieces. It was the first studio double album in almost twenty years, and the sheer volume of material was reflected in the array of additional items for the collector on the b-sides of the singles from it.

The initial single from the album, "No Son Of Mine" was released on 8th November 1991 backed with another album track, "Living Forever" on the 7" version. The 12" version was initially issued with a limited edition watercolour print and the additional bonus of another live version of "Invisible Touch". This was also to feature on the CD version which was the first of what became an entire collection of singles titled "The Invisible Series".

We Can't Dance was released on 21st November 1991 and immediately claimed its place at the top of the UK album charts, aided by a healthy number six position for the single which was to be the band's last 12" vinyl single release. Once again, five singles were issued from the album, all of which gained respectable chart success and created a whole new range of Genesis collectables. *We Can't Dance* itself was issued in various limited edition packages, often accompanied by press material, making these promotional editions much sought after. With their tongues firmly in their cheeks, "I Can't Dance", the band's second single, poked fun at the Levi jeans adverts and added another track to the growing list of non-album b-sides in the shape of "On The Shoreline" which appeared on the cassette, CD and vinyl editions. Making up for the loss of the 12" format, scrapped due to changes in the number of formats eligible for chart inclusion, a two-part CD single was issued including not only the b-side mentioned above, but also a remix of the a-side; the "Sex Mix", and two live tracks; "In Too Deep" and "That's All".

The flow of new material continued with the third single from the album, "Hold On My Heart" which appeared on 6th April 1992, including another album track as the b-side on the vinyl edition. However, the two CDs made for some very interesting listening as they included live versions of "Home By The Sea" and "Your Own Special Way" – the latter being of most interest as it was taken from the band's Australian shows featuring a string section. This edition also came with a set of colour artwork postcards.

Controversy dogged the next single. "Jesus He Knows Me" was a savage indictment of American TV evangelists and was banned in certain parts of the USA. In the UK the BBC banned the video which didn't hamper the single's progress to the number twenty slot after its release on 21st August 1992. A further non-album b-side graced the vinyl edition, and this track, "Hearts On Fire" also appeared on both CDs in addition to a live rehearsal version of "Land Of Confusion" and the "other" mix of "I Can't Dance".

The single also came with a limited edition box in which you could house all the other singles in the "Invisible Series". All of these editions are now deleted and becoming increasingly difficult to find, making them a worthwhile addition to any collection. To promote their forthcoming live album, the band opted to release a live single which appeared the day after their last show at London's Earl's Court Arena. Coupling live versions of "Invisible Touch" with "Abacab" on the vinyl edition, and adding "The Brazilian" to the CD, the single was released as a limited edition with a numbered sleeve and photo booklet. The CD version was housed in an individually numbered card box and with only 50,000 of these made, it is easily one of the most collectable items from the more recent material. The vinyl single was subsequently issued in a standard picture sleeve. The single also to charted giving the band their third appearance on *Top Of The Pops* to promote the album.

The band opted to release the live album in two parts. The first edition, comprising the shorter more "commercial" material was humorously titled, *The Way We Walk – Volume One: The Shorts,* and was issued a few days after the end of the autumn UK tour. The final single from the *We Can't Dance* album appeared on 9th February and coupled another album track, "Tell Me Why" with a further selection of live material including live versions of "Dreaming While You Sleep", "Turn It On Again" and "Tonight, Tonight, Tonight". Once again the single appeared as a two-part CD and was also available on vinyl and cassette with all royalties from the sales going to *Save The Children, Bosnia* and *Red Cross Bosnia.* This was followed a week later by the release of the second part of the live album, *The Way We Walk Volume Two: The Longs* which unbeknownst to Genesis fans was to be Phil Collins' swansong with the band.

Keeping the profile high, Virgin Records decided to issue the entire Genesis back catalogue from the first Charisma album up to and including *Three Sides Live* as re-mastered editions. The craze for re-mastering had begun a few years before and there was a genuine argument for doing so in Genesis' case, as even the band themselves admitted many of the earlier albums suffered from poor production. However, with this project taking place only a couple of years after the picture disc re-issues, fans could be forgiven for thinking that Virgin were taking liberties. The finished albums were issued in two batches, the albums from *Trespass* to *The Lamb Lies Down On Broadway* were issued in April 1994, and the remaining catalogue appeared in October of that year. Once again, criticism was levelled at these releases for not including any additional material, although by then it had been rumoured that the band were to put this right with the compilation of a series of archival boxed sets – the first of which has only recently seen the light of day.

It was to be a further four years before another Genesis album appeared, and before that fans had to recover from the shock announcement made on 29th March 1996 that Phil Collins had quit the band. Ray Wilson, formerly of Stiltskin, was Collins' replacement, and the band's new album, *Calling All Stations,* was finally released on 1st September, entering the charts at the number two position. Unusually for these days, the album was still issued on vinyl, as well as cassette and CD. The LP edition was spread over three sides of the vinyl, the fourth side being etched with a picture of the band – unusual to say the least! The initial single from the album appeared on 15th August and comprised an edited version of "Congo", accompanied on the first of the now obligatory two part CD by two non-album cuts, "Papa He Said" and "Banjo Man". The other CD included an edited version of "Home By The Sea" and enhanced CD-ROM images for those fans with the requisite technology.

As ever, Genesis have done things slightly differently and by releasing the single after the album they were, perhaps, harking back to the old days when such things were the norm. Since its appearance, there have been a further two singles from *Calling All Stations*; the second of which was, in my opinion at least, a much more suitable candidate. "Shipwrecked" appeared in the now-normal two-CD set format including two new non-album instrumentals, "Phret" and "7/8", the first instrumental B-sides since 1981. The other CD contained live versions of "No Son Of Mine", "Lover's Leap" and "Turn It On Again" from the Cape Canaveral launch in August 1997. In the USA, an edited version of "The Dividing Line" was issued as a promotional single containing both the full length album version and a live version of "Turn It On Again" recorded at the Cape Canaveral set. The edit, and the fact that it is a promotional edition, makes this one of the most sought after items from the latest album. The final single appeared two days prior to the first UK show on the *Calling All Stations* tour on 23rd February 1998. The track selected was "Not About Us", a glorious acoustic song which should have done well in the charts but mysteriously didn't. The extra tracks spread over the two CDs proved beyond doubt that despite the new line-up's possible teething problems, there was nothing wrong in the writing department. The non-album tracks, "Run Out Of Time", "Anything Now", "And Sign Your Life Away" served notice that Genesis were still a potent songwriting team. The additional acoustic tracks taken from the TV show in France were a nice reminder of one of the highlights of the tour and comprised delightful versions of the classic "Dancing With The Moonlit Knight", "Follow You Follow Me" and an extended version of the single itself.

Fans might have thought that after all this activity, Genesis were about to retire for the usual lengthy break but far from it. 22nd June 1998 saw the release of the long awaited first boxed set, under the title of *Genesis Archive 1967 – 75*. This eagerly awaited item comprised a four CD set packaged with an eighty page booklet and text written by a varied collection of people connected to the band. In addition, there was a ten track CD sampler taken from the set, limited to 4000 copies, which is now a highly sought after item. The discs themselves catalogue the band's development in reverse order from the heady days of *The Lamb Lies Down On Broadway* – which is captured here in all its live glory by a complete archival recording of the show at Los Angeles' Shrine Auditorium on 20th January 1975. Working gradually backwards through another classic live show from 1974 at London's Rainbow Theatre, including the long overdue "Supper's Ready" with Peter on vocals, and the remaining B-sides to the band's singles from this period. Finally, the fourth disc reveals some hidden gems from the very earliest days of the band's story including out-takes and demo versions of tracks from their first studio album.

The most recent items added to the Genesis catalogue have been issued by Virgin Japan. These are limited edition versions of the entire Genesis album back-catalogue (*Trespass* to *Calling All Stations*) with fully restored artwork, gatefold sleeves (where these appeared originally) inner sleeves, picture bags and even the original record labels in most cases (apart from the band's first two albums for Charisma). All in all, just the thing to tide fans over until the band themselves return to the studio to create another album.

Collector's Corner

A look at some of the more collectable memorabilia

Being a fan of Genesis, or any other band for that matter, can be an expensive business, especially in the current commercially minded world of music. The revenue generated by the sales of a single or album by any established group or solo artist is frequently outstripped by sales of 'merchandise' at concerts and by other items released by record companies. The most frequently seen are tour programmes, T-shirts and badges, all of which have their own horde of fans dedicated to collecting them.

In addition, there are those dedicated souls who spend their time trying to collect video and audio material by their favourite artists. As long as there has been recorded music, there have been those willing to bootleg these items and it would probably merit a book in its own right. Genesis and its various offshoots have to be one of the most frequently bootlegged groups of musicians in the world and the amount of material is, quite frankly, staggering. It is far easier to offer an outline of the material which is commercially available from the field of official merchandise, and to document the TV and video material which is available to begin a collection. Hence in this chapter I will deal with two or three specific areas which include tour programmes, books, fan magazines, official videos, TV appearances and performances, along with an outline of a selection of the bootlegs currently available to those interested in such things

One: Tour Programmes 1972 – 1998

In these days when rock memorabilia is fast becoming an area considered to be a "worthwhile investment", anyone who possesses an assortment of tour programmes, handbills and other material from concerts would do well to ensure that their collection is well taken care of. Genesis and the individual members of the band have generated a great deal of material in this field, enough to satisfy even the most dedicated collector. Tour programmes have been in existence for over a hundred years and they have always been collected.

For Genesis the story really starts in 1972 with the first of a batch of increasingly intricately designed programmes. Prior to this period, Genesis were usually relegated to the role of support slot on a show by another artist and, as such, did not merit any special mention in the main artists' programme, if they had one.

This changed with their show at the 1972 Lincoln Festival, for which there was a programme costing the princely sum of ten pence! This was a 44 page booklet designed by David Wills and, as the artists included on the bill included Roxy Music, The Faces, Rory Gallagher and Status Quo, is a highly sought after item by collectors. Genesis are mentioned on page 18 with a brief text by Geoff Ward and a small black and white photo of Peter Gabriel.

The second programme of the year to feature Genesis in any depth was produced for the *Melody Maker* "Poll Concert" featuring the bands and artists who had won the varying categories in the annual reader's poll. The concert took place at the Kennington Oval London on 30th September 1972 and this time Genesis were in the company of Focus and ELP. The sixteen-page booklet included articles on the main bands and Genesis's appearance is restricted to a photo on the last page. However, by now Genesis were beginning to draw attention as a major attraction themselves and to merit more space in tour programmes.

In early 1971 Genesis had been on the bill of the first of the Charisma package tours, later titled the "Six Bob" tours because as a ploy to attract people to the shows, ticket prices were pegged at 6 shillings (about 30 pence in current money). In October 1972, Genesis were again touring with Charisma stablemates Lindisfarne, the current flavour of the month who were promoting their hit album and single "Fog on the Tyne". The Lindisfarne autumn tour featured a programme which was the first to include the name "Genesis" on the cover. The sixteen-page booklet also included a two-page spread on the band with two black and white photos and full page advertisement for both the new Lindisfarne album and Genesis latest album *Foxtrot* accompanied by a text by Jerry Gilbert from the music paper *Sounds*. Even at this time, it was obvious that Genesis were an act to look out for, and all of these programmes are extremely difficult to find now representing a sound investment to any collector lucky enough to have them in their possession.

1973 began with the first headlining tour by Genesis in the UK, and the first programme dedicated entirely to the band. Frankly it is not much to look at, being a simple eight-page booklet with a rather garish yellow cover incorporating a photo of the band outside the Bottom Line Club in New York. Inside, there is a brief biographical outline of Genesis and its members together with details of their equipment and a list of the UK tour dates.

A rather unusual item also appeared at this time, a four-page booklet which announced "John and Tony Smith in conjunction with Charisma present: Genesis On Tour." The cover features a photograph of the band in Central Park, New York. It also announces that the special guests on the tour are String Driven Thing, another Charisma act from the period. The booklet seems to have been given out at gigs on the February 1973 tour, mine is accompanied by a handbill for the band's show at Exeter University on 14th February. The interior of the booklet is given over to the full lyrics of "Supper's Ready" accompanied by a rather fascinating explanation of the lyrics to each section.

Perhaps the most intriguing programme ever produced by the band is that which accompanied their UK tour in October 1973. The entire package was enclosed in an envelope which, once opened had the following contents a "Genesis Compendium" including cut-out dice and revolver, a page of programme notes by Michael Wale, a poster and a flexidisc copy of 'Twilight Alehouse', the b-side from the band's first 'hit' single 'I know what I like'. A complete copy of this particular package will fetch a considerable amount of money these days.

1974 saw the band consolidate its position both at home and in Europe, beginning with a series of sell-out shows at the Theatre Royal, Drury Lane, accompanied by a twenty-four page booklet issued by the Charisma Press Office. It is complete with full biographical notes on the band and reproductions of several features from the music press. This appears to be the only programme from the UK for the year.

Before the end of 1974 the band had released what, to many fans, was to be their finest album, *The Lamb Lies Down On Broadway*. As usual, a tour brochure was published and this one is one of the most satisfying. The cover features a design supposed to look like a tree, with the knots in the wood making it appear to smile on the front cover, and frown on the back. Inside there is a full colour series of photographs taken by Armando Gallo, as well as a full text and reproduction of the story from the album cover. The programme was issued in both the USA and Europe/UK with the former containing a different version of the album story and US tour dates.

Strangely for a band of their stature, Genesis did not issue a commemorative programme for the *A Trick Of The Tail* tour in 1976. Instead, a brochure was issued to commemorate the release in early 1977 of the film *Genesis In Concert,* which was available at its premiere on 31st January 1977. The next year's tour for *Wind & Wuthering* saw a welcome return to form, with the release of two brochures, of which the first is undoubtedly the best Genesis programme ever issued. The "World Tour '77" programme has it all, excellent photography by Robert Ellis, an inspired text by journalist Barbara Charone, even an advertisement for ex-member Anthony Phillips's first solo album *The Geese & The Ghost*. This programme is quite common and should be an essential purchase for collectors. Later in the year another brochure was issued, "Genesis European Tour '77 Picture Book". This was exactly what its title proclaimed it to be, a 24 page collection of pictures by Robert Ellis. I must admit that this is my least favourite programme, mainly because the photography included is, compared to its predecessor, very poor.

1978 was the best year for Genesis tour programmes. No fewer than four were produced, beginning with the US tour postergramme accompanying the massive tour that the band undertook in April 1978. This folds out into a full-colour Genesis poster, while on the other side there is a mixture of information about the band, their stage equipment and brief extracts from the first book by Armando Gallo, *Genesis The Evolution Of A Rock Band,* published in the UK that year. The band only played one show in the UK during their mammoth trip around the world in 1978. This was the prestigious headlining appearance at the Knebworth Festival on Saturday 24th June and a special programme was produced for the event. Titled: "Knebworth A Midsummer Night's Dream", the cover was a delightful cartoon-style image of a couple of characters, one of whom looks suspiciously like Tony Banks! The text includes items on all of the major acts appearing at the show including Tom Petty, Jefferson Starship and Brand X, as well as a list of the available food and refreshments at the show (30p for a pork pie, those were the days!). The band continued on tour throughout the summer, headlining numerous festivals in Germany for which a special programme was produced. This has to be one of the nicest programmes in the collection, including a beautiful artwork front cover and great live shot of Genesis on the back. More interestingly, however, it is the only programme to be written in more than one language; the text describing Genesis and the other artists on the bill is written in both English and German, a nice touch for fans whose first language isn't English. The band also travelled to Japan for the first time at the end of November 1978 and a special programme was issued to commemorate the historic event. Text is, of course, in Japanese but the excellent photographs included make this a worthwhile addition if you can find a copy.

After the surfeit of programmes in 1978, the brochure produced for the band's 1980 UK/US tour was something of a disappointment. Sporting a black cover with "Genesis In Concert 1980" on the front, the interior 28 pages are a mix of advertisements and extracts from Armando Gallo's second book on the band, *Genesis: I Know What I Like,* which had been published in the UK that year. Copies of this particular programme are plentiful and should pose no problem to anyone trying to find a copy.

The worrying trend towards rather poor programmes continued with the 1981 *Abacab* programme. Maybe the band had just run out of things to say or didn't want to produce an elaborate, and therefore, more expensive brochure. Either way, the programme for the tour was particularly disappointing. The booklet bore a white "*Abacab*-style" cover with colour live shot, and the interior pages were another mixture of live and backstage shots with no text, apart from a letter reproduced from a fan who had applied for tickets for the shows without enclosing payment! Fortunately, the trend did not last and the following year's effort for the *Three Sides Live* tour of Europe, the USA and the UK was a much better production. Again the brochure mixed live photos with an informative text written by Andy Mackrill who was Genesis's tour manager at the time. This was coupled with a full tour itinerary and advertisements for the tour merchandise.

1982 was also the year which witnessed the event Genesis fans had been dreaming of since 1975, a reunion between the band and former frontman, Peter Gabriel. A one-off concert was organised as a benefit to pay off the debts Gabriel had incurred as one of the organisers of the ill-fated WOMAD Festival earlier in the year. Titled "Six of the Best: A Benefit for WOMAD" the programme had a black and white cover incorporating a live shot of Peter Gabriel with the band rehearsing for the show in London's Hammersmith Odeon a few weeks before. Inside there was a mix of colour photos as well as a series of quotes by members of the band about the event and brief biographies about the other acts on the bill; John Martyn, Talk Talk and The Blues Band. This is a MUST for any collection.

The "Mama Tour" of the USA in 1983/84 also encompassed the five dates at the National Exhibition Centre in Birmingham, England and produced another rather lacklustre programme. Sporting a grey cover with the album logo on the front, the interior was taken up by a rather uninspired series of photos, some of which were taken from the "Illegal Alien" video shoot and tour rehearsals. The five UK shows saw some slight variation because each night was dedicated to a different charity and as such, each night's programmes bore a different cover.

The 1987 tour is Genesis's biggest to date with over 112 dates played, taking in Europe, the USA and Canada, Australia and New Zealand, as well as a second visit to Japan. There are two variants on the tour programme for this series of concerts. The first is the US/Australian programme which bore a beige cover with a stylised 'Domino' on it. Inside again is the usual mix of live and studio photos. The European programme differs from this in several aspects. Most noticeable is the black 'Domino' cover. Inside there is, in addition to the mix of photos and adverts, a two page spread about support act on the European leg; Paul Young, and a page dedicated to Tony Stratton-Smith the founder of Charisma Records, Genesis's record label of so many years, who had died of cancer in March 1987, halfway through the tour. Either version of these programmes can be easily found at record fairs and are very common.

Genesis' tour for the *We Can't Dance* album in 1992 produced another two programmes. First was a large format edition with a white cover with the band in their famous "I Can't Dance" dance routine. Inside is a mix of photos of the new stage show and biographical text. The second programme was produced solely for the UK shows in October and November and was, like the venues the band played, a smaller affair which apart from a different cover a-la *The Way We Walk Volume Two: The Longs* album cover, is exactly the same as its larger predecessor.

Genesis's latest tour programme appeared in 1998 and was produced for their *Calling All Stations* European/UK tour. It was a glossy affair once again. The cover featured the new album artwork, while inside was a brief text outlining some of the band's thoughts on the album and their past history. It had an interesting selection of photographs, although somewhat marred by the "sci fi" artwork design and graphics. This programme will be of particular interest to US fans because of the cancellation of the band's US tour.

Two: Solo Tour Programmes 1977-1997

The first to venture out as a solo artist was Peter Gabriel who toured the USA, Europe and UK to promote his March 1977 eponymous album. The booklet designed for this outing set the trend for all of Gabriel's subsequent programmes, and is bizarre to put it mildly. Sporting a grey cover featuring a picture of London's Waterloo Bridge with one of the passers by circled in red it has no titles to indicate what the booklet is. The interior twelve pages are just as unusual, featuring demographic details of Europe, a medical report on Gabriel and reprints of the album lyrics. It also came with a promotional poster for the 'Modern Love' single.

As far as I have been able to find out, Gabriel did not release a programme for his 1978 tour and his next booklet was issued to coincide with the UK tour in 1980. Another unusual production this booklet was titled "Peter Gabriel Tour of China 1984" a sly dig at the fondness of artists at the time who were falling over themselves to be the first to play in China and the kudos that they sought to attract from doing so. Modelled on Chairman Mao's famous "Little Red Book", the booklet incorporated a series of advertisements culled from Chinese newspapers along with the UK tour dates. This is one of the more difficult items to find and is a worthwhile, if strange, item in any collection.

The UK tour in 1983 also yielded another tour brochure. This one was a little bit more traditional with details about Gabriel's band and the WOMAD festivals but still incorporated unusual features including a centre page dedicated to a cut out and keep Peter Gabriel mask!

The *This Way Up* tour in 1987 produced what to many is the best of Peter Gabriel's programmes. The 48-page brochure incorporated a mix of information about Gabriel and his band, as well as details about Amnesty International and a three page spread about American poet Anne Sexton whose poetry had inspired the song "Mercy Street". Gabriel had collaborated with Sting and U2 in the US-only *Conspiracy Of Hope* tour in 1986, and this was followed by the more ambitious *Human Rights Now!* world tour in 1988, a celebration of the fortieth anniversary of the signing of the International Declaration of Human Rights by the United Nations. The tour featured Sting, Bruce Springsteen, Youssou N'Dour, Tracy Chapman and Peter Gabriel and the tour brochure incorporated details on each artist, as well as the full text of the Declaration itself. Gabriel's involvement with humanitarian causes continues to this day and an interesting brochure was released to commemorate his involvement in the three day "WOMADELAIDE" Festival held in Adelaide, Australia, in February 1993 as part of the United Nations' *International Year for the World's Indigenous Peoples*. The fifty-six page brochure gives full details of the festival and its participating artists who were drawn from all over the world, including brief biographical notes and black and white photography.

Gabriel's *Secret World* tour was a truly global one, lasting over a year and reaching almost every conceivable part of the world. The tour brochure, in stark contrast with his stage presentation, was extremely disappointing and also very expensive. The thirty eight page booklet is housed in a black and white cover with a padlock on the front, and a suitcase on the back. The interior has photos of the band and some information on a couple of humanitarian projects which Gabriel was giving his support to, but was otherwise extremely uninspired.

The most recent programme in which Gabriel has appeared was issued for the recent concert in aid of "Amnesty International" which was held at the cavernous Palais Omnisports de Bercy in Paris on 10th December. Gabriel was one of numerous guests at this gig and the programme itself is a rather lacklustre large format programme with accompanying text in French.

Steve Hackett's solo touring career began in 1978, but his first proper tour programme didn't appear until 1981. The *Cured* tour brochure set the standard by which all of his subsequent programmes can be judged. The cover incorporated a live shot and advertisement for the new album. Inside the text gave a brief and informative synopsis of Hackett's career, as well as biographical details and equipment lists on the other members of his band and a full tour itinerary.

1983 produced two tour programmes. The first was the brochure accompanying the *Highly Strung* UK tour in April/May. Again it contained a good mix of information on Hackett's career and his band within its sixteen pages and is a worthwhile addition to your collection, if you can find a copy. He was out on the road again in October 1983 promoting his new acoustic album *Bay of Kings* with a tour of UK university halls. For these shows, a small fold-out brochure was designed, featuring a colour photo of Steve Hackett on the cover with the title "Bay Of Kings: An evening of solo acoustic guitar with Steve Hackett". The interior had basic information including the venues on the tour and colour photos of the live show from earlier in the year, and it folded out to a small colour poster of Steve on stage. This is certainly one of the hardest programmes to find and although small, is a lovely addition to a collection.

His most recent tour programme is that produced for the *Momentum* UK tour in 1988. This is a very stylish affair with full colour album artwork cover and sixteen pages of text and photographs. There was no programme produced for the 1993 *Guitar Noir* tour and so this represents all of Steve Hackett's output in this area to date.

Phil Collins' solo career began with a vengeance in 1981 and his first tour as a solo artist was in support of his *Hello, I Must Be Going* album in 1982. A tour brochure was issued which featured the album artwork to *Hello, I Must Be Going* on the cover, and inside there was the usual mix of photos and text including amusing spoof school reports on all the other band members. Phil Collins' school report included the comment, "Tries hard and is quite short." which, I suppose is still a fair reflection of Phil's career, he is still trying *very* hard!

His next solo outing was in support of his *No Jacket Required* album in 1985, a truly global affair taking in Europe, the USA and Canada, Australia and Japan. The twenty four page brochure was the usual mix of photos and background information – although no actual text was included which was quite surprising given Phil's rapidly growing status both at home and abroad.

By 1990, the trend toward photo booklets rather than tour programmes in the old manner had really taken hold. In the main these were frequently overpriced and only of interest to collectors. Phil's 1990 tour brochure fell into this category. The booklet itself was a large format design featuring a picture of Phil on the cover dressed as a circus ringmaster, in keeping with the stage design for the tour. Inside was a rather motley collection of photos of the band attired in the costumes of several circus acts. No text accompanied the photos and the entire packaging was rather disappointing.

The programme for the 1994/95 *Both Sides* world tour is a far superior effort and probably the best of his programmes to date. Another large format design incorporating a picture of Phil's drum kit disguised as oil drums, once again in keeping with the idea behind the stage design. Inside again there are photos of the various members of the ever-growing orchestra that Phil takes on the road with him and the text accompanying them is both informative and amusing.

The latest tour programme, produced for his *Dance Into The Light* US and European tour of 1997, continued the above trend with a large format glossy brochure packed with (not altogether flattering) photos of his ever-expanding band and a very tongue-in-cheek text, no doubt written by Phil himself. Strangely enough, the recent Big Band jazz tour was not accompanied by a programme although I am sure this will be rectified next time.

The most recent member of Genesis to venture out on to the road is Mike Rutherford who, with his other band, Mike & The Mechanics, has done four tours so far. The first in 1986 was a solely US affair and, as far as I am aware, provided no tour programme.

His second tour in 1989, in support of the highly successful *Living Years* album, brought forth a postergramme, which, apart from a tour itinerary, provided little more than a series of live shots that included a large full group portrait. I suppose the band still had to fully establish a reputation, hence the lack of supporting text within this effort.

Rutherford's next tour in support of the equally successful *A Beggar On A Beach Of Gold* album surprisingly produced no tour programme at all, much to the disappointment of collectors. However, the most recent *Greatest Hits* tour was provided with the "Hits Tour Manual 1996", a twenty-page colour booklet containing a selection of photos from the 1995 tour, including some from the band's shows in South Africa, along with informative and amusing text. It was also unusual as it included the addresses of the various fan clubs that have sprung up in recent years. To fans of the Mechanics outside of the UK this programme will be extremely collectible because the 1996 tour only took in the UK.

Rutherford's most recent tour in support of the M6 album took place in May/June of 1999 and the tour programme was sadly another lacklustre affair with a selection of very mediocre photographs and basic text, but again was an essential item for the avid collector, especially for the US fans who didn't have the opportunity to see the band this time around.

Biographies and Fanzines

For a band the size of Genesis, it is surprising to find that there have been less than a handful of books about the band. The same can be said of fanzines, official or otherwise which have appeared in droves about acts with less than half of Genesis's staying power. However, what has been lacking in quantity has more than been made up for in the quality as documented below.

GENESIS – THE EVOLUTION OF A ROCK BAND - ARMANDO GALLO.
SIDGWICK & JACKSON ISBN 0 283 98439 2 (CLOTH)/0 283 98440 6 (PAPER) 1978.
The first book of any note, first published in the UK by Sidgwick and Jackson in 1978 and worth its weight in gold, was *Genesis: The Evolution Of A Rock Band* by respected journalist Armando Gallo. Gallo had followed the band since 1971 and he managed to blend his own superb photographs with an informed, intelligent and at times, amusing text in a way which has set the trend for rock biographies since. Sadly, this edition is no longer in print.

GENESIS – I KNOW WHAT I LIKE - ARMANDO GALLO
DIY BOOKS DISTRIBUTED BY SIGWICK & JACKSON ISBN 0 283 98703 0 1980.
It was, however, updated two years later under the title *Genesis I Know What I Like*, which brought the band's story up to the beginnings of work on the *Duke* album, and added sections on each member as well as a useful discography. The book was also issued as a limited edition hardback in calfskin with embossed autographs by the band and, as only 1000 copies were made, these are now much sought after. Gallo has in fact re-issued this book recently as a limited edition hardback with a new cover although surprisingly with no additional text.

GENESIS ILLUSTRATED LYRICS - KIM POOR
Published at about the same time as Armando's first book, there also appeared an interesting artwork book on the band: *Genesis Lyrics*. This was designed by Steve Hackett's wife, Kim Poor, a longstanding fan of the band (she must be, she married a band member, after all!). The book drew upon Kim's designs for lyrics to published Genesis songs, and makes an interesting contrast to the other biographical works available as well as showcasing some of Kim's artwork.

THE BOOK OF GENESIS - HUGH FIELDER.
SIDGWICK & JACKSON ISBN 0283 99074 0 1984.
There was a four-year gap before anything else of note was published, but 1983/84 saw a plethora of books on the subject of Genesis. Hugh Fielder, a stalwart follower of the band, and music correspondent for *Sounds* in the UK set the ball rolling with his book, *The Book Of Genesis* which took the form of an extended interview with the various members, accompanied by numerous photographs.

Genesis – From One Fan To Another - Armando Gallo
Omnibus Press ISBN 0-7119-0515-0 (Paperback)/ 0-7119-0514-2 (Hardback)

This was soon followed by another book by Armando Gallo. This one took a slightly different approach and drew exclusively upon his amazing photographic archive of the band, with supporting text kept to a minimum, enabling the photographs to more or less tell the band's story for him. Titled *Genesis: From One Fan To Another* this forms another highly recommended addition to the growing canon of books available.

Genesis - Janis Schacht.
Proteus Books Limited ISBN 0 86276 257 X 1984.

Another example of the "Genesis Mania" which was sweeping the music press during 1983/84 appeared in the shape of Janis Schacht's book *Genesis* published by Proteus books in 1984. Textually, the book was certainly well-informed and was also blessed with several photographs which had not previously seen the light of day.

Genesis – Peter Gabriel, Phil Collins And Beyond - Kamin & Goddard
Sidgwick & Jackson ISBN 0-283-99093-7 1984.

The final book to appear in 1984 was another interesting peek into the world of the band by photo journalists Philip Kamin and Peter Goddard titled, *Genesis: Peter Gabriel, Phil Collins And Beyond*, a somewhat prophetic title given developments within the Genesis camp. The writers took another different tack opening the book with a chapter about the now legendary reunion concert in 1982, before looking back fondly on the individual members and their careers with a great selection of photographs, making this book a perfect foil to the others published at this time.

Genesis: The Illustrated Discography - Geoff Parkin
1981

Initially released in 1981 and republished in 1984, this book was a goldmine of information to collectors of Genesis records and gave full details of most of their worldwide releases both as Genesis and as individual solo artists. The re-issue in 1984, titled: *Genesis: Turn It On Again,* brought even more detail to light and both editions were to remain indispensable to fans until very recently.

Genesis – A Biography - Dave Bowler and Bryan Dray
Sidgwick & Jackson ISBN 0 283 061324 1992.

After the deluge of printed word about the band in 1984, those fans left still wanting more were to be in for a long wait with the next book on the band appearing in 1992. It was published as a spin off from the *Genesis: A History* video project that was released in 1991. The authors, Dave Bowler and Bryan Dray were supposedly consultants on the band's *Genesis: A History* video project and their book: *Genesis An Authorised Biography* was released in 1991. It comes across as rather studious in its approach to the band's lengthy history and incredibly patronising toward their prospective audience, although in their favour, it has to be said that this was the first book to deal with the solo careers in any depth. The book has also been re-issued in paperback with a slightly updated text and some different photographs.

Genesis Discografia 1968 – 1993 - Mario Giammetti / Genesis Counting Out Time: The Worldwide Singles Discography - Max Demont

1994 saw the issue of a book by long time fan and editor of the Italian Genesis fanzine, *Dusk*, Mario Giammetti. As its title suggests, this publication examined the recorded output of the band and its solo members and is little more than a list of their recordings (official and otherwise!) which will prove useful to collectors for the detail it provides. This was in turn followed in 1995 by another book outlining Genesis' recorded output. This time the detail is outstanding, and Max Demont's book, *Genesis Counting Out Time: The World Wide Singles Discography* certainly lives up to its name with a tremendous amount of information on its subject and is indispensable for collectors.

Fortunately for fans of the band's formative period, Armando Gallo was finally persuaded to re-issue his magnificent tome, *Genesis I Know What I Like* earlier that year. Fundamentally, this is the same book as the 1980 edition but in view of the fact that that edition and its predecessor, "*Genesis The Evolution of a Rock Band*" are now long out of print, this is an essential purchase for Genesis collectors. The book is published in hardback with a magnificent new cover designed by Paul Whitehead and with an introduction by that artist. As Mike Rutherford said in his original introduction to this book: "It would be easy if we could just say to people; here – read this…" and those words are still true today. This is without doubt the most indispensable biography of the band and the yardstick by which all others are still measured. The book is available direct from Armando at his address: Armando Gallo PO Box 198, 12405 Venice Boulevard, LOS ANGELES, California 90066 USA.

Genesis – The Complete Guide To The Music Of… - Chris Welch
Omnibus Press ISBN 0-7119-5428-3 1995.

The final book to appear about the band to date is long time rock critic Chris Welch's pocket sized volume *The Complete Guide to the Music of Genesis* which sadly does not live up to its title and is full of glaring mistakes which is disappointing given Welch's long time championing of the band's cause, although there are some insights to be gained from the text.

In terms of individual solo member's biographies, only Peter Gabriel and Phil Collins receiving anywhere near the attention that their careers deserve.

The Phil Collins Story - Johnny Waller
Zomba Books ISBN 0-946391-78-5 1985

Collins was the first to receive a biographical treatment with Johnny Waller's book, *The Phil Collins Story* published by Zomba Books in 1985. This took Phil's career from the beginning up to and including the release of his third solo album, *No Jacket Required.*

Phil Collins The definitive Biography - Ray Coleman
Simon & Schuster ISBN 0-684-81784-5 1997.

The next publication was Ray Coleman's *Phil Collins – The Definitive Biography* published posthumously in 1997 after the author's death. Sadly this is another volume which does not live up to its title and instead concentrates an inordinate amount of its time on Phil's marriage break up in 1993/94.

Peter Gabriel - Armando Gallo
Omnibus Press ISBN 0-7119-0783-8 1986.
Armando Gallo turned his attentions to Peter Gabriel's career with the release of another of his excellent photo books which covers up to and including the *So* album in 1986. As you would expect, the book is an excellent photographic chronicle of Peter's career to date and is an essential addition to any collection, although Armando's introductory comments are likely to surprise many Genesis fans!

Peter Gabriel An Authorized Biography - Spencer Bright
Sidgwick & Jackson ISBN 0-283-99498-3 1988.
Gabriel's next appearance in print was two years later in 1988, with the publication of Spencer Bright's worthy tome: *Peter Gabriel – An Authorised Biography*. Dealing in graphic detail with Gabriel's career, both in and out of Genesis, up to the release of *So* and the subsequent tour, it is an insightful look behind the personality who many Genesis fans still see as the artistic heart of the band. Bright updated the book in 1990 upon its release in paperback, and further updated it for a new fully revised hardback edition in 1999.

Human Rights Now! - James Henke
Bloomsbury Press ISBN 0-7475-0318-4 1988.
With the completion of the *Human Rights Now!* tour in 1988, Gabriel was a contributor to the book which chronicled this milestone in musical political awareness. It documents the entire tour and gives a useful background to the United Nations' Declaration of Human Rights itself and the accompanying photographs are worth the price alone.

Peter Gabriel In His Own Words - Chris Welch
Chris Welch has rejoined the fray with another book which appeared in 1997, and which is little more than a collection of extracts from interviews which Peter has given over his career and is rather more of an insight into the mind of a rock journalist than into the artist himself.

From Genesis To Revelation Biografia Oficial De Anthony Phillips: Co-Fundador De Genesis - Sara Cavalle
Antropovision ISBN B-22.618/ 96.
Surprisingly enough, given their solo successes, neither Mike Rutherford, Tony Banks or Steve Hackett have been the subjects of a biography yet, and the final work of any note to date has that other Genesis Founding Father, Anthony Phillips as its subject. The author, Sara Cavalle is a colleague of Anthony's friend and fellow musician Guillermo Cazenave and the book *From Genesis To Revelation Biografia Official De Anthony Phillips Co-Fundador De Genesis* was written in Spanish for the Spanish record company Astral who market several of Guillermo and Anthony's albums.

Bootleg Recordings

Bootleg or illegal recordings of music have been around for a very long time. In fact, before the advent of recorded sound the bootleggers were plying their trade in the shape of unauthorised transcripts of existing sheet music and orchestral scores. The argument still rages over the validity of bootlegs. The record companies quite correctly maintain that such recordings deprive them of revenues that may be spent on nurturing new talent and of course, depriving the artists themselves of royalties on their work. At least one member of Genesis, when asked about the vexed issue of bootlegs, answered that he "wasn't concerned by them because the fans who buy them, buy all the official stuff anyway…" and indeed several members of the band are reputed to collect their own "bootlegs" so who is right and who is wrong?

To fans and collectors, however, the bootleg is sometimes seen as an essential part of any collection, be it as a memento of a favourite gig that they attended, or as historical documents detailing live output. Often it is the only method of obtaining unusual or otherwise unheard studio material, or live versions of songs no longer in the band's repertoire. Whatever the relative merits of the arguments, Genesis and its solo members are without doubt, extremely well represented by bootlegs. Initially pressed on vinyl, many of these are ironically enough, now highly sought-after collector's items in their own right and, more recently on compact disc where a veritable explosion of "new" titles has occurred over the last few years. What follows is by no means a comprehensive list, but will give fans a flavour of exactly what you can expect should you decide to embark on this particular avenue of the Genesis "collection". Of course, I have no knowledge where such items can be obtained so, in the words of the song: "Please don't ask!"

The Hiding Place comprises the now famous tracks from the BBC *Night Ride* Session of 1970: Shepherd/Pacidy/Let Us Now Make Love/Stagnation along with Looking For Someone taken strangely enough from the *Trespass* album itself. GNV1000.

This particular combination of tracks is also duplicated on the appropriately titled *The Shepherd* compact disc (Flashback 09.90.0126.33) which ruins the recording however by including dubbed in applause! This disc also contains Twilight Alehouse/ Watcher Of The Skies/Get 'Em Out By Friday and The Musical Box from various BBC sessions making it an interesting addition to a collection as many of the BBC sessions have yet to be released officially.

For live recordings the earliest of any known show appeared last year. Titled *Beside The Silent Mirror* (ARC012) this recording is ostensibly from the band's first overseas gig in Belgium on 7th March 1971 and as such, is of historical interest alone for the formative set which comprises: Happy The Man/Stagnation/The Light/Twilight Alehouse/The Musical Box/The Knife/Going Out To Get You. Sound quality is not of the best but that is more than compensated for by the unusual set including the as yet unofficially released *The Light* parts of which were later used in *Lilywhite Lilith.*

From 1972 onwards the band's live shows are increasingly well represented beginning with *The Musical Fox* (Wild Bird Records WBR 9016) from the Charleroi Festival 16th January 1972 comprising the following tracks: Happy The Man /Stagnation/The Fountain Of Salmacis/Twilight Alehouse/The Musical Box/The Return Of The Giant Hogweed.

Another interesting recording from this period is *Genesis Rome 18 Aprile 1972* (Tintagel TICD009) which documents the band's first Italian tour in good sound quality and comprising the band's set from that period: Happy The Man/ Stagnation/ The Fountain Of Salmacis/Twilight Alehouse/Improvisation/The Musical Box/The Return Of The Giant Hogweed/The Knife/Going Out To Get You. This set is complimented by Old Man's Tale (GNV004) which is taken from the band's shows at Naples (19.4.720 and Pavia (14.4.72) including an unusual version of "Can-Utility & The Coastliners" under the title of "Bye, Bye, Johhny!" as well as a rare version of "Seven Stones". More recently still a recording of the band's show in Ravenna (15.4.72) has been released on Lizard records (LZCD010) comprising the same set as Rome '72.

Other recordings from this period include:
Come Ancient Children (ARC/GNV 015) Reading Festival 1.8.72.
Through The Looking Glass (ARC/GNV017) Genoa Teatro Alcione 22.8.72.
Sharpened To The Hilt (ARC/GNV016) Lugo 15.4.72 and Verona 9.4.72.
Imperial College (Night Sun 001) Imperial College London 18.11.72.

The following year saw the band's popularity grow and with it the number of recordings representing the various tours with perhaps the best ones being from the band's later tours in support of the *Selling England by the Pound* album. Recordings from this period include:

Fantasia (Exposure EX002) which is a recording of the show at Los Angeles' Roxy Theatre 19.12.73 comprising the following: Watcher Of The Skies/Dancing With The Moonlit Knight/The Cinema Show/I Know What I Like/Firth Of Fifth/The Musical Box/Horizons/Supper's Ready.
Welcome To Epping Forest (Rus Foley RFCD8) Rainbow Theatre 20.10.73
This Planet's Soil (NEWOX 73) Ostensibly a recording of the band's filmed performance at Shepperton Studios on 30th November 1973.
First We Were Five (Rock Calendar Records RC2113) Tufts university 7.11.73.
Romeo Show (Highland HL072/73 2 cd set) Felt Forum NYC 22.11.73
Selling England By The Session (Highland HL032/33 2 cd set). This set is extremely interesting because as its title suggests, it is comprised entirely of out-takes and demos from the *Selling England...* album.
In The Beginning (Volumes 1-6) (Extremely Rare EXR005/006/013/014/018/022) This ever expanding series of discs chronicles the band's 1973/74 studio out-takes in great detail with more demos than you could shake a stick at!
More Fool Me (Highland HL029/30 2 cd set) Orpheum Theatre Boston 24.4.74.
Moonlit Queen (Highland HL101/02 2 cd set) Massey Hall Toronto 2.5.74.

Live in Montreal (The Swingin' Pig TSPCD-040-2) Perhaps one of the most famous (or should that be "Infamous"?) bootlegs of all time, originally issued as a single LP vinyl release titled *L'Ange Gabriel* (and under several other guises as well), this one captures the band at their peak with an excellent radio broadcast of the Montreal University show and tracks from one of the later BBC sessions 20.4.74.

The band's *The Lamb Lies Down On Broadway* shows are also well documented on bootleg including the following...
The Lamb Descends On Waterbury (OXY 089-090 2 cd set) comprising the entire show from the Palace Theatre Waterbury 12.12.74 as well as a delightful series of studio demos and out-takes from the rehearsals.
Rael Imperial (Highland HL059/60 2 cd set) West Palm Beach 10.1.75 (plus studio demos)
Supper's Ready With A Little Lost Lamb (Coloseum records 97-C-025 2 cd set) Lakeland Arena 11.1.75/Rainbow Theatre London 20.10.73
Rael Live in Manhattan (Suite 2) Madison Square Gardens NYC 28.1.75.
The Lamb Lies Down On Dusseldorf Philipshalle Dusseldorf 6.4.75.
Tales Of Ordinary Madness (Dream Weaver Records DWR396078-2) Birmingham Hippodrome 2.5.75. (Another well known bootleg when originally released on vinyl as *Swelled and Spent*).
The Waiting Room (Flashback Records) Wembley Empire Pool 15.4.75.

1976's *Trick Of The Tail* tour has also been documented by a handful of bootlegs of which the most complete recording to surface is that of the band's show at the Syria Mosque in Pittsburgh on 13th April. Titled *A Trick Of The Show* (Highland HL010/11 2 cd set) this contains the almost complete radio broadcast of the show. Other recordings from this year include:
Melody of 1976 (Highland HL061) Hammersmith Odeon London 11.6.76.
Dance on a Berkeley (Highland HL094/95) Berkeley Community Theatre 29.4.76.
There were also several earlier vinyl editions of shows from this tour all of which are now long since deleted and would form the basis of a collection in themselves.
A Trick Of The Takes (Highland HL198 CD) This is compiled from the studio sessions for the *Trick* album.
1977 and 1978's tours are documented by a fine series of recordings mainly taken from either soundboard or radio recordings and the following are among the most easily located....
Genesis – Chicago On The Air (LaXious 03-04 2 cd set) combines some of the "best bits" from two shows: Chicago Transit Auditorium 16.2.77 and The Uptown Theatre Chicago 13.10.78.
Water & Wrecking (Highland HL117 CD) Kiel Open House 6.2.77.
Before Riches (Silver Rarities SIRA 124/125 2 cd set) captures the band's show at London's Earls Court Arena 24.6.77 which is also captured on *Simply Follow* (Highland HL062/63 2 cd set).
Second Nature (Highland HL042/43 2 cd set) Fox Theatre Atlanta 13.3.77.

Genesis – Tour Rehearsal (Highland HL037/38 2 cd set) comprises a soundboard recording of the band's rehearsals for their massive 1978 tour and as such is interesting to listen to in order to see what tracks they finally omitted from their set.
Once In A While (Highland HL106/07 2 cd set) Gothenburg Scandinavium 7.6.78.
Knebworth Show (Highland HL078/79 2 cd set) Comprises almost the entire show from Knebworth Park 24.6.78.
Follow You Follow Me (Great Dane GDRCD 8918 2 cd set) comprises the entire show from Chicago's Uptown Theatre 13.10.78 and has been released under various other titles including the famous vinyl album, *From The Mouth Of The Monster.*

The tours which spanned 1980 through to 1982 are also well represented by recordings including the following:
Genesis – Duke Side Live (Highland HL019/20 2 cd set) Lyceum Ballroom London 7.5.80. This is also available under the title: *Musica* (Stonehenge STCD 2110/11 2 cd set).
Steeltown Revelations (Record company unknown 2 cd set) Sheffield City hall 17.4.80.
Perfect Three Sides Live (Highland HL081/82 2 cd set) Nassau Coliseum 29.11.81.
Small Club at Marquee (Highland HL104/05) Marquee Club London 27.9.82.
Apocalypse (Ghost Records Ghost 0101/0102 2 cd set) Palasport Rome 7.9.82.

Strangely enough, the 1983/84 tour seems to be very poorly represented by recordings with only a couple easily available, including…
Genesis – Los Cage (Highland HL171) Los Angeles Forum 14.1.84.

This dearth of material has been more than compensated for by the plethora of recordings from the band's last three tours with an increasingly varied range of recordings appearing on the market…..
Invisible Touch World Tour (Gen69191/2 2 lp set) Joe Louis Arena Detroit 19.9.86
Illegal Alien (Beech Martin Records CD005) Los Angeles Forum 1986.
Triangle On Domino (Highland HL108/09 2 cd set) Berlin Reichstagsgelande 8.6.87.
Touch To Supper's Ready (Highland HL127/28 2 cd set) Los Angeles Forum 17.10.86
Astrodome (Red Line – Postscript PSCD2198 2 cd set) Houston Astrodome 9.5.92.
Live At The Skydome (Flashback flash 08.92.0180 2 cd set) Toronto Skydome 9.6.92.
Luxury (BB 692) Three Rivers Stadium Pittsburgh 26.5.92.
Live In The Big Apple (Red Phantom 2093/94 2 cd set) Giants Stadium east Rutherford New Jersey 3.6.92.
Vienna (BKCD003/04 2 cd set) Vienna Wiener Prater Stadion 16.7.92.
Legend (Men at Work – Vox Populi 5554 2/1 2 cd set) St Jakob Football Stadium Basle 25.7.92.
Live – L'Espace Grammont Montpellier (WN- EG3 PC12 1-2 2 cd set) L'Espace Grammont Montpellier 20.7.92.
There are also a whole batch of discs representing the band's final show at Knebworth Park on 2nd August with the following being a representative selection…

Summer Nights (Kiss the Stone KTS 106-107 2 cd set).
Sincerely Yours (Why not records WOT 2006 2 cd set).

Hold On My Heart (On stage ON2234 2 cd set).
World Dance (HM Digital Recording OHM 4-A 2 cd set).

Strictly Mechanic (RFCD 13A/B 2 cd set) Stuttgart Schleyerhalle 12.2.98 (also available under the title *Through The Ages*)
A New Beginning (Gentle Three 001 CD) NEC Birmingham 25.2.98.
Live In Dublin (No Record company 2 cd set) The Point Theatre Dublin 9.3.98. (Also available under the title of *A Single Lonely Voice*).

The Solo Artists

As you may expect, the varied solo outings by the band members have also been well documented and the following is a concise outline of some of the material which has appeared for collectors…

Phil Collins/Brand X
Nightmore Patrol (Highland HL158) Glass Union Rochester NY 28.9.77 and Stockholm 30.8.78.
Phil's Masques (Highland HL031) A Brand X show from Park West Chicago 25.9.79.
Phil Collins – The Fabulous Jacuzzis and One Neat Guy (Oh Boy 2-9096) Perkins Palace Pasadena 23.1.83.
Live in Utrecht (?) Prins van Oranje Hal Utrecht 10.4.94.
Both Sides Tour (Twilight Music TMCD 003/04 2 cd set) Wembley Arena 13.12.94.
Mr Nice Guy (Oxygen OXY021) Fukuoka The Dome 7.5.95.
Phil Collins – Man of the Year (Optimum 05 CD) New York 28.10.96/ Paris 3.2.97 .
Don't You Know? I'm Mad (Gizmo Dick GDR 9801/02 2 cd set) Palais Omnisports de Bercy Paris 13.12.97.

Peter Gabriel
A Whiter Shade Of Pale (Highland HL015/16 2 cd set) Chateau Neuf Oslo 31.8.78/Bottom Line Club NYC 4.10.78.
Stonybrook (ML 9621) Stonybrook University 28.10.78.
Meeting at the Reading (Ghost Records Ghost 0103) Reading Fesival 26.8.79.
Chinatour (Lizard records LZCD011/12 2 cd set) Palasport Genoa 29.9.80.
So Alive (Manic Monster Music MMM 003) Giants Stadium New Jersey 15.6.86.
Laguna Beach (German Records GR031) Grand Slam Club 3.4.93.
Live from a Secret World (Pluto records PLRCD 9318) Le Zenith Paris 24.4.93.
Secret World (PG-001/002 2 cd set) Tokio Nippon Budokan Hall 8.3.94.
Glastonbury Festival (Festival Music FMCD-001/002 2 cd set) Glastonbury Festival 26.6.94.
Woodstock (Wood 99410) Saugerties New York "Woodstock II Festival" 25.8.94.

Steve Hackett/GTR

Star of Sirius (Highland HL050/51 2 cd set) Stockholm Gota Lejon 5.10.78.
Spectral Horizon (Neo Digital NDAL 1003) Chicago 10.10.80
Steve Hackett – In Concert (Evening Star Records ES-001) Reading Festivals 26.8.79/28.8.81
I Know What I Like (Heart Breakers HB807-1/2 2 cd set) Guildford Civic Centre 29.1.83.
GTR-Nerotrend (Elements of Crime Elements-083) Demos and out-takes from the second GTR album.
Full Moon And Empty Spaces (Alternative Record Company ARC009-10 2 CD set) Villa Torlonia Frascati 5.7.93 and several tracks from earlier shows from 1978 and 1980.

Mike & The Mechanics

Miracle Mania (Elements of Crime Elements-041) Tower Theatre Philadelphia 19.6.86.
All I Need Is A Miracle (Viva CD7539) Tower Theatre Philadelphia 30.3.89.

In addition to the above, most shows by Genesis since the early 1970's have been audio recorded on varying kinds of equipment and exist in collectors' archives all over the world so the task of collecting them all is, I would say an impossible one, but if you like a challenge – good luck!

Private Video Recordings.

Since the advent of hand-held video recording equipment in the early 1980's, many fans have taken to recording shows visually and these recordings are an additional source of material for die-hard fans. Prior to this, hand-held Super 8mm cameras recorded snippets of shows without benefit of a soundtrack. The following is a selection of material that is known to exist in video format.

Genesis

Castle Hall Osaka Japan 30.11.78 (Excerpts).
Toronto CNE Grandstand 28.8.82 (Entire concert).
Montreal Forum 21.11.84 (Entire concert).
Joe Louis Arena Detroit 17.9.86 (Entire concert).
Madison Square gardens NYC 3.10.86 (Entire concert).
Bernabeu stadium Barcelona 13.5.87 (Entire concert).
L'Hippodrome de Vincennes Paris 3.6.87 (Excerpts).
Wiener Prater Stadion Vienna 16.6.87 (Entire concert).
Oakland Coliseum 20.6.92 (Entire concert).
Parkstadion Gelsenkirchen 3.7.92 (Entire concert).
Niedersachsenstadion Hanover 10.7.92 (Entire concert).
Roundhay Park Leeds 31.7.92 (Entire concert).
Budapest Sporthall 28.1.98 (Entire rehearsal concert).
Hallenstadion Zurich 13.2.98 (Entire concert)
Bologna Palasport 17.2.98 (Excerpts).
Palasport Rome 18.2.98 (Entire concert).

Milan Filaforum 19.2.98 (Entire concert).
Earls Court Arena London 27.2.98 (Entire concert).
NYNEX Arena Manchester 6.3.98 (Entire concert).

Peter Gabriel

Roxy Theatre Los Angeles 1977 (Super 8mm silent footage).
Toronto CNE Grandstand 8.11.82 (Excerpts)
Kemper Arena Kansas City 4.12.82 (Entire concert).
Berkeley UOC 1982/83 (Excerpts from two shows).
Empire Theatre Liverpool 18.9.83 (Entire concert).
Falkoner Theatrit Copenhagen 1.10.83 (Entire concert).
United Nations Building New York 16.9.86 (Entire concert).
Rochester NY War Memorial 7.11.86 (Entire concert).
Joe Louis Arena Detroit 17.11.86 (Entire concert).
Houston Astrodome 7.12.86 (Entire concert).
Cologne Muengersdorfer Sportstadion 19.6.87 (Entire concert).
Palatrussardi Milan 10.7.87 (Entire concert).
Philadelphia Spectrum 27.7.87 (Entire concert).
Palau St Jordi Barcelona 30.9.87 (Entire concert).
Offenbach Ruhrstadion 13.9.87 (Entire concert).
Berlin Eisporthalle 11.11.87 (Entire concert).
Wembley Stadium 2..9.88 (Entire concert).
Palais Omnisports de Bercy Paris 4.9.88 (Entire concert).
Nou Camp Stadium Barcelona 10.9.88 (Entire concert).
Academy of Music NYC 6.4.93 (Entire concert).
Frankfurt Festhalle 21.4.93 (Entire concert).
Palagiacchio Marino Rome 18.5.93 (Entire concert).
Stuttgart Schleyerhalle 20.5.93 (Entire concert).
Munich Olympiahalle 21.5.93 (Entire concert).
Sheffield Arena 24.5.93 (Entire concert).
Montreal Forum 29.6.93 (Entire concert).
Philadelphia Spectrum 6.7.93 (Entire concert)
Philadelphia Spectrum 8.7.93 (Entire concert).
Los Angeles Great Western Forum 22.7.93 (Entire concert).
Glastonbury Festival 26.6.94 (Entire concert).

Steve Hackett

Teatro Orfeo Milan 20.5.88 (Entire concert).
Het Noorderlight Tilburg 28.5.88 (Entire concert).
Stadio Plebiscito Selvazzano Padua 6.7.93 (Entire concert).
Palermo "Sonny Boy" 1.12.94 (Excerpts).

Mike & The Mechanics

Philipshalle Dusseldorf 27.2.89 (Entire concert).
Mainz Rheingoldhalle 10.3.89 (Entire concert).

Phil Collins

Palau St Jordi Barcelona 17.5.90 (Approximately half of the concert)
Frankfurt Festhalle 11.5.90 (Entire concert)
Toronto Skydome 17.7.94 (Entire concert)
Oslo Spektrum 4.4.94 (Entire concert)
Frankfurt Festhalle 27.9.94 (Entire concert)
Wembley Arena 7.12.94 (Entire concert)
Toronto Skydome 20.3.97 (Entire concert)
Philadelphia Spectrum 29.3.97 (Entire concert)
Pori Fest Jazz Festival ?.6.98 (Entire concert)

Genesis On Video

As you would expect with a band of Genesis's stature there is no shortage of material on film by the band. Over the last few years in particular, TV appearances, interviews and so on have become increasingly common and form yet another area for fans to begin a collection. Here I have divided the available footage into two distinct sections, first, the commercially released and recorded videos/films of the band, and second, television appearances. In both cases I have referred solely to appearances on UK TV and videos which are (or have been) available in the UK with one or two exceptions which are worthy of note for reasons which will become apparent.

Part One: Commercial Films & Videos

Tony Stratton-Smith Presents: Genesis in Concert

As its title suggests, this is a live performance of the band's set from the time of the *Selling England By The Pound* tour. Unfortunately this film has never been domestically released although it was available recently on laser disc in Japan. Whether this was officially sanctioned however, is open to debate! The film was recorded at the Shepperton Film Studios on 30th and 31st October 1973, and features the following songs: Watcher Of The Skies/Dancing With The Moonlit Knight/I Know What I Like/Musical Box/Supper's Ready. The film is complete with all of Gabriel's costumes and between song stories and is sixty-three minutes in length. This was the first Genesis film which Paul Flattery and Jim Yukich directed for the band.

Genesis In Concert.

Another film sadly unavailable in this country. It was shot at Glasgow and Stafford during the *A Trick Of The Tail* tour and as such, is the only visual record of the band with Bill Bruford on drums. The film was shown in UK cinemas in 1977 and has gained several showings since, although no domestic video release has been planned. The film features the following songs: I Know What I Like/Fly On A Windshield/

Carpet Crawlers/Cinema Show (Pt2)/Entangled/Supper's Ready (Pt2)/Los Endos. Filming was by Tony Maylam and the entire film lasts some forty minutes. Although this has not been released in the UK, those of you with the latest technology (and money to burn) can obtain it on laser disc from Japan; NTSC VPLR70468.

The 1977 tour was also filmed although so far only a small segment of it has surfaced. This is from the shows at the Palais des Sports Paris and once again the project was organised by Yukich and Flattery. The tracks broadcast comprise a twenty-five minute compilation including, Dance On A Volcano/Los Endos/The Lamb Lies Down On Broadway and Musical Box (closing section).There is rumoured to exist a complete film of one of the band's Paris shows from this tour although I have been unable to confirm this.

Sadly no complete film from the 1978 tour has appeared in this country, apart from the BBC's *Nationwide* documentary from the European tour which features some footage from Mannheim, Leiden and Knebworth, including a complete performance of "The Lady Lies". Japanese fans were luckier with a television screening of highlights the band's show at the Sun Plaza Hall in Tokyo on 3rd December which comprised the following tracks: 11th Earl Of Mar/Dance On A Volcano/Los Endos/I Know What I Like. There is also supposed to be a fuller version of this footage although it has not been shown since 1978.

The *Duke* tour in 1980 was featured in two different television programmes which were screened in the UK during the tour. First of these was the *Live in Liverpool* documentary filmed at the Empire Theatre on 2nd May and screened on Granada TV on 3rd. This was a film about the tour and featured live and interview footage lasting for fifty minutes. The BBC also made their contribution to the Genesis archive during this tour by filming the show at the Lyceum Ballrooms in London on May 7th. It later featured as an edited special on their popular *Whistle Test* programme including the following tracks: Duchess/Guide Vocal/In The Cage/ Cinema Show/ Ravine-Raven/Afterglow/Dance On A Volcano/Los Endos.

Strangely enough, there also exists an almost complete film in the BBC archive, and yet not from the Lyceum show. It features a different concert from the *Duke* tour possibly from the Drury Lane Theatre Royal shows earlier in May. The film lasts for 132 minutes and comprises the following songs: Deep In The Motherlode/Dancing With The Moonlit Knight/Carpet Crawlers/Squonk/One For The Vine/Behind The Lines/ Duchess/Guide Vocal/Turn It On Again/Duke's Travels/Duke's End/Ripples (Instrumental End Section Only)/The Lady Lies/In The Cage – Medley/Afterglow/Follow You Follow Me/Dance On A Volcano/Los Endos/I Know What I Like. The main reason for suspecting that this is not the same show as shown on the *Whistle Test* lies in the fact that the Lyceum show from 7th May was also broadcast on BBC Radio One and ended with a performance of "The Knife" whereas on this film, after "I Know What I Like" the backing music is played as the house lights go up – any ideas anyone?

From 1981 onwards, Genesis fans have been fortunate enough to have a video release to commemorate each successive tour by the band begining with *Three Sides Live* recorded during the *Abacab* US/UK tour in 1981. This video was released by Wienerworld Video in 1982 and featured the following tracks: Behind The Lines/ Duchess/Misunderstanding/Dodo-Lurker/Abacab/No Reply At All/Who-Dunit?/In The Cage-Cinema Show-Colony Of Slippermen-Ravine Medley/Afterglow/Me And

Sarah Jane/Man On The Corner/Turn It On Again. The video also featured backstage and interview footage with Hugh Fielder and lasts for approximately ninety minutes. Wienerworld TVE 90 0982 2.

The *Mama* tour lasted several months and was recorded for posterity in the form of the *Mama Tour* video which comprised an almost complete live set compiled from the shows at the National Exhibition Centre in Birmingham between 25th to 29th February 1984. The full set listing on the video was; Abacab/That's All/Mama/Illegal Alien/Home By The Sea/Second Home By The Sea/Keep It Dark/It's Gonna Get Better/In The Cage: Cinema Show-Raven Medley/Afterglow/Turn It On Again – Sixties Medley. The running time of the video was 102 minutes and it sadly omitted what for many fans was the highlight of the show: the first of the two medleys which incorporated 11th Earl Of Mar/Firth Of Fifth/The Lamb Lies Down On Broadway/Musical Box. However, the video does capture the essential drama of the show. This was also the first video by the group to be released by Virgin Video. VVD090.

To coincide with the European leg of the *Invisible Touch* tour the band released the *Visible Touch* video which compiled the promotional videos released for singles from that album. The tracks included were: Anything She Does/Throwing It All Away/Tonight Tonight Tonight/Land Of Confusion/In Too Deep/Invisible Touch. There was also a small documentary on the tour and the entire video lasts 48 minutes. Virgin Video VVD 204.

The extended hiatus which occurred after the end of the 1986/87 tour gave the band time to compile and release two video collections which tied up the loose ends of the promotional videos released for singles by the band over the years. Titled *Genesis The Videos Volume One* and *Genesis The Videos Volume Two,* they are an indispensable part of any Genesis collection. The tracks on volume one were: Mama/No Reply At All/Land Of Confusion/That's All/Tonight Tonight Tonight/Duchess/Anything She Does/Robbery, Assault And Battery/In Too Deep/Abacab/Follow You Follow Me. This collection has a running time of 55 minutes. *Volume Two* comprised the following tracks; Illegal Alien/Throwing It All Away/Misunderstanding/Ripples/Keep It Dark/Trick Of The Tail/Home By The Sea/Second Home By The Sea/Man On The Corner/Turn It On Again/Many Too Many/Invisible Touch. This collection runs for 57 minutes. The confusing thing about these two collections is that the videos are not in chronological order and there are several omissions; "Turn It On Again" and "Man On The Corner" are live films, which is surprising because there were promotional videos made for these two tracks. It is also something of a surprise that the videos for both "I Know What I Like" and "Match Of The Day" are missing. The other complaint frequently voiced by fans is that they had already purchased the videos to "Invisible Touch" on the *Visible Touch* compilation. However, to new fans both videos serve as a great introduction to the band's career. Virgin Video VVD329/330.

As if the release of the two video compilations wasn't enough, the band also released a visual record of their *Invisible Touch* tour in the form of the *Invisible Touch Tour* video filmed at the band's record breaking four night stint at Wembley Stadium in July 1987. The video captured the show in its entirety with the exception of the "In The Cage Medley" which was already available on previous videos, and the full track listing is as follows: Mama/Abacab/Domino/That's All/The Brazilian/Land Of Confusion/Tonight Tonight Tonight/Throwing It All Away/Home By The Sea/ Second Home By

The Sea/Invisible Touch/Drum Duet/Los Endos/Turn It On Again – Sixties Medley. This was the first music video to be filmed in high definition and marks the beginning of the group's association with Sony that was to culminate in the stage show for their next tour. The film also came with a limited edition CD of the live track 'Domino'. Virgin Video VVD358.

Genesis – A History appeared in 1991 and was a long overdue look at the band's career including interviews with all band members and also with brief interviews with ex-members Anthony Phillips, Steve Hackett and Peter Gabriel. This is another must for collectors featuring previously unseen live footage, and has a running time of 90 minutes. The band's appearance at the 1990 Knebworth Festival was also recorded and released in 1991 as part of the two video package; *Knebworth – The Event* which also features appearances by all the other acts on the bill. The videos were released by Castle Music Pictures in May 1991. CMP 2058.

Genesis' most recent video release, *The Way We Walk In Concert*, captured their 1992 *We Can't Dance* tour, filmed at their six night residence at London's Earl's Court Arena. The video managed to bring all the visual excitment of the show to the small screen and features the following tracks; Land Of Confusion/No Son Of Mine/Driving The Last Spike/Old Medley (inc Dance On A Volcano-The Lamb Lies Down On Broadway-Musical Box-That's All-Follow You Follow Me)/ Fading Lights/Jesus He Knows Me/Dreaming While You Sleep/Home By The Sea/Second Home By The Sea/Hold On My Heart/Domino/I Can't Dance/Tonight Tonight Tonight/Invisible Touch/Turn It On Again. 135 minutes. 0864963.

As far as is known at the moment, there is no plan to release any live visual record of the band's *Calling All Stations* tour, although at least two shows were recorded by local television crews. These were the gigs at the Spodek Arena, Katowice, Poland on 31st January 1998 and at the Stadthalle, Vienna, Austria on 15th February 1998. There are, of course, various extracts from other concerts that were broadcast on the relevant television networks in the respective territories.

Genesis UK Television Appearances

It is difficult to imagine nowadays with the coverage of the band on TV and film that this wasn't always the case. Film of any kind from the period prior to 1976 is very hard to find and much sought after. The following represents as full a visual record of the band from this period and beyond as I have been able to piece together. Where no footage from the UK is known to exist, I have included details of foreign footage for the sake of completeness.

BBC Training film 1968 (Unreleased) features a performance of 'In Hiding' (the only known footage of original line-up). According to recent information this was done in a similar way to later *Top of the Pops* recordings with the singer 'live' and the band miming to a backing track of the song.

"Stagnation" and "The Knife" 8mm film shot at the band's gig supporting David Bowie at London's Roundhouse on 11th March 1970. As far as is known, this is the only live concert footage of the band from this period including both Anthony Phillips and John Mayhew in the line-up.

Disco Two BBC TV November 1970 performance of 'The Knife' with Mick Barnard (Anthony Phillips's replacement).

Rock Of The Seventies Belgian TV special broadcast in the UK and filmed in 1972. Includes studio performances of Musical Box/Fountain Of Salmacis/Twilight Alehouse/The Return Of The Giant Hogweed.

Bataclan Club Paris 10.2.73. A recent addition this film was shot by French TV and includes footage of Gabriel in his various costumes including the legendary "Fox's head" and also includes the only Gabriel period visual performance of "The Knife" currently available to fans although there are reports of a further two complete concerts from this period available in the television company archives

Montreal University 20th April 1974. Filmed by the students at the University, this film captures the band at the height of their powers. A 45-minute extract compiled from both live and still photography is currently available although the entire concert is believed to exist possibly in the University's archives.

Melody 1973/74. This is a recently released addition to the coverage of the band at a crucial period in their development. It was first seen when a clip from it of the band performing "Willow Farm" was used as part of a French TV documentary *Les Enfants Du Rock* back in 1986, this is the first time that the entire footage has become more widely available. Broadcast in France some time during the *Selling England By The Pound* tour, this film features an entire performance of "Supper's Ready" and "I Know What I Like". My copy is time coded which would suggets that this video was considered for commercial release at some point.

Trefpunkte A very highly sought after item this, being the only acknowledged visual record of *The Lamb*. Filmed at the Shrine Auditorium on 20th January 1975 it includes footage of "The Slipperman" as well as "In The Cage" and "Musical Box".

Your Own Special Way Tyne Tees TV 1977.

"Follow You Follow Me" *Top Of The Pops* BBC TV 1978.

"Turn It On Again" *Top Of The Pops* BBC TV 1980.

Tiswas ITV includes promo video for 'Misunderstanding' 1980.

Tiswas ITV includes promo video for 'Abacab' 19.09.81.

'Abacab' *Top Of The Pops* BBC TV 27.08.81.

'Paperlate' *Top Of The Pops* BBC TV 27.05.82.

Three Sides Live In America (Shortened version of official video) broadcast on ITV 1983.

'That's All' *Late Late Breakfast Show* ITV 22.10.83.

TV AM interview 17.11.83.

Midlands News 26.2.84.

TV AM interview 04.08.84 includes 'Illegal Alien' promo.

Freezeframe ITV Documentary 1985.

Whistle Test BBC TV 17.12.85.

Whistle Test BBC TV 10.6.86.

Whistle Test Extra BBC TV 20.9.86

Montreux Festival BBC TV 1986
Fast Copy interview 1986.
Music Box interview 1986.
Montreux Festival BBC TV 1987.
Look North News Roundhay Park Leeds 28.6.87.
Coca Cola Live Report Wembley Stadium 3.7.87.
The Rock of Europe Wembley Stadium 4.7.87.
"Throwing It All Away" *Wogan Show* BBC TV 29.6.87.
Atlantic At Forty Madison Square Gardens NYC 15.5.88
The Story So Far BBC documentary 31.3.91.
We Can't Dance (Electronic Press kit) 1991.
"No Son Of Mine" *Top Of The Pops* BBC TV 31.10.91.
"Hold On My Heart" *Top Of The Pops* BBC TV 9.4.92.
Children's BBC 17.4.92.
TV AM interview 21.7.92.
TV AM interview 22.7.92.
TV AM interview 23.7.92.
No Admittance Yorkshire TV documentary 24.7.92.
"Jesus He Knows Me" Countdown studios 29.7.92.
Channel 4 daily news 31.7.92.
Calendar Yorkshire TV news 1.8.92.
Knebworth Park Concert 1.8.92.
Anglia TV News ?.7.92.
Granada Weekend Manchester Apollo 30.10.92.
The O-Zone BBC TV 8.11.92
Blue Peter BBC TV 26.11.92
TVS interview 20.11.92.
Calling All Stations (Electronic Press kit) 1997
Congo (Promotional video) 1997
Berlin acoustic concert 22nd August 1997. Performed as part of the band's promotional duties for their new album *Calling All Stations* this includes performances of No son of mine/Lover's leap/Invisible touch.
Cape Canaveral Launch 26/8/97 (Virgin Records Electronic Press Kit).
Shipwrecked (Promotional video) 1997.
Talking Music VH1 interview at the Bray Studios tour rehearsals 23.1.98.
"Not About Us" (Promotional video) 1998.
VH1 interview about first "Boxed Set" 13.5.98.
VH1 "Genesis Archive" Special 6/7/98.
The Story So Far... Network (RTE Ireland) 6/7/98.
Behind The Music. VH1 (USA) This is a US documentary broadcast on 18.12.98 and interestingly contains interviews with all key membersof the band including the elusive Anthony Phillips. It was in part researched by myself and Jack Beerman whose name will no doubt be familliar to some of you.

Needless to say, the above is only a representative selection of the television footage available by the band and it does not cover material from other countries where there is a phenomenal amount of material (Official and otherwise) available on the band, but it may serve as an indication of exactly how much material there is to be collected in this area.

The Solo Artists On Video

Fans of the various solo members of the band have been quite well served with video material either on TV or commercially available product, especially if you happen to be a fan of either Phil Collins or Peter Gabriel. The following is a break down of the material available in the UK to collectors.

Tony Banks On Video:

Banks has yet to release a compilation of the promotional videos to the singles he has released and many of these are highly sought after items.

The Waters Of Lethe (Promotional film) 1979. This Is Love (Promotional video) 1983. Short Cut To Somewhere (Promotional video) 1986. Throwback (Promotional video) 1989.

'I'll Be Waiting' *This Morning Show* ITV 1.11.89. "*Rock School*" BBC TV 27.3.88. "*Rock School*" BBC TV 17.4.88. "*Rock School*" BBC TV 8.5.88. "*Rock School*" BBC TV 15.5.88. *I Wanna Change The Score* (Promotional video) 1991. *The Gift* (Promotional video) 1991. *Only Seventeen* (Promotional video) 1995. Pebble Mill BBC TV '*Walls Of Sound*', 'Only seventeen' 1996. Tony's music also appears in the soundtracks to the following films all of which are available on commercial video. *The Shout* (with Mike Rutherford) 1979. *The Wicked Lady* 1983. *Lorca and the Outlaws* 1985. *Quicksilver* 1985.

Phil Collins On Video

Phil Collins' solo success has been such that he has appeared on just about every TV show in the UK that you could possible think of as well as several you wouldn't! He has also released a series of highly successful commercial video collections all of which are part and parcel of any collection of his material.

Part One: Commercial Videos

Phil's first video release was a video E.P. featuring the tracks released as singles from his highly successful first album: *Face Value* and its successor*; Hello, I Must Be Going* The tracks included were; In The Air Tonight/I Missed Again/Thru These Walls/You Can't Hurry Love. Originally issued by PMI it was subsequently re-issued by Castle Music Video CMVG 5017.

Collins also released a live video from his 1983 US tour. Titled *Live At Perkins Palace* it featured sixty minutes of live concert footage from one of his US shows including the following tracks: I Don't Care Anymore/I Cannot Believe Its True/Thru These Walls/I Missed Again/Behind The Lines/The Roof Is Leaking/The West Side/In The

Air Tonight/You Can't Hurry Love/It Don't Matter To Me/People Get Ready. Picture Music International MC2059.

The E.P. format was repeated in 1985 with the release of the *No Jacket Required* EP. combining the videos from the album again and comprising the following tracks; Sussudio/One More Night/Who Said I Would/Don't Lose My Number/Take Me Home. Virgin VVC 095.

Another live video followed the completion of the tour and this release is an excellent example of how live videos should be made featuring as it does, almost an entire live show with little over all editing. The 89 minute video includes the following tracks; Only You And I Know/Against All Odds/Who Said I Would?/Sussudio/Behind The Lines/The West Side/One More Night/In The Air Tonight/Like China/You Can't Hurry Love/It Don't Matter To Me/Hand In Hand/Take Me Home/It's Alright. WEA Music Video 2 52411-3.

Phil Collins is 'Buster' was the film of the making of the *Buster* movie. Released in 1989 by Vestron video VA 17253. The film itself is also now available on commercial video.

The Singles Collection released in December 1989 re-issued the earlier promotional videos which had been deleted along with the two promotional videos from the "*Buster*" soundtrack. The full track listing is: Don't Lose My Number/I Missed Again/A Groovy Kind Of Love/Who Said I Would?/You Can't Hurry Love/Thrue These Walls/Sussudio/One More Night/Two Hearts/In The Air Tonight/Easy Lover/Against All Odds/Take Me Home. Virgin Video VVD 594. The 1990 "*But Seriously*" tour produced another live video to add to Phil's growing collection. This one is a complete show recorded at the Berlin Waldebuehne in July and contains the following songs: Hand In Hand/Hang In Long Enough/Against All Odds/Don't Lose My Number/Inside Out/Do You Remember?/Who Said I Would?/Another Day In Paradise/Separate Lives/Saturday Night Sunday Morning/The West Side/That's Just The Way It Is/Something Happened On The Way To Heaven/Doesn't Anybody Stay Together Anymore?/One More Night/Colours/In The Air Tonight/You Can't Hurry Love/Two Hearts/Sussudio/A Groovy Kind Of Love/Easy Lover/Always/Take Me Home. Virgin Video VVD783.

Phil took the video E.P format to extremes with the 1992 "*But Seriously – The Videos*" collection which featured film of every track from the album including live footage to make a rather nice compilation including the following tracks; Hang In Long Enough/Another Day In Paradise/Do You Remember?/Colours/Something Happened On The Way To Heaven/All Of My Life/I Wish It Would Rain Down/Heat On The Street/That's Just The Way It Is/Saturday Night Sunday Morning/Father To Son/Find A Way To My Heart. Virgin Video VVD1010 77 minutes.

Phil's only video from his concerts on the 1994/95 world tour was titled *A Closer Look* this video is a backstage look at the preparations for the tour and was sold at gigs to raise money for the homeless charities in each city on the tour. So far it has not gained a full commercial release although it was shown in the UK the day before Phil's shows at the Manchester G-Mex!

Phil's most recent video *Live And Loose In Paris* was released on 20th July 1998 and featured edited highlights of Phil's show from Paris during the *Dance Into The Light* tour and captures the show brilliantly. It is strange however, that this show has been edited, after all; Phil's fans have always been treated to a full performance on video but nevertheless this is an essential addition to collections. Tracks are: Hand In Hand/ Hang In Long Enough/Don't Lose My Number/Another Day In Paradise/Against All Odds/Lorenzo/Separate Lives/Long Long Way To Go/In The Air Tonight/ Timbantiocha/Easy Lover/Dance Into The Light/Wear My Hat/Something Happened On The Way To Heaven/Sussudio. Warner Music Vision 3984 23466-3

PART TWO: UK FILM & TELEVISION APPEARANCES

From humble beginnings to the superstardom he now so rightly enjoys, Phil's rise to fame has been well documented by film and TV and the following charts that rise through the medium of film and video in the UK.

Calamity The Cow Children's Film Foundation film 1967.
And so to F. with Brand X *Old Grey Whistle Test* BBC TV 1979.
Pop Quest BBC TV 1979.
"In The Air Tonight" *Top Of The Pops* BBC TV 1981.
"I Missed Again" *Top Of The Pops* BBC TV 18.3.81.
"In The Air Tonight" *Prince's Trust Gala Concert* 1981.
"In The Air Tonight" *Secret Policeman's Ball* (Film) 1981.
"If Leaving Me Is Easy" *Top Of The Pops* BBC TV ?.5.81.
Wogan Show BBC TV 1982.
"In The Air Tonight" *Prince's Trust Gala Concert* 1982.
"*Freezeframe*" ITV Documentary 1982.
"You Can't Hurry Love" *Wogan Show* BBC TV 1982.
"Why Can't It Wait Til Morning"/"You Don't Know Like I Know" (Duet with Leo Sayer) *Leo Sayer Show* BBC TV 1982.
"I Don't Care Anymore" *Three Of A Kind Show* BBC TV 1982.
The Other Side Of The Tracks Channel 4 Documentary 1983.
The Making Of 'There's Something Going On' Documentary about Phil's involvement with Anni Frid's solo album ITV 1984.
The Tube Channel 4 TV interview 11.2.85.
"Sussudio" *Top Of The Pops* BBC TV 1985.
"Take Me Home" *Top Of The Pops* BBC TV 1985.
Live Aid Wembley Stadium/JFK Stadium Philadelphia ITV 13.6.85.
"We Said Hello Goodbye" *Joan Rivers Show* BBC TV 1985.
"Against All Odds" *The Two Ronnies Show* BBC TV 25.12.85.
"One More Night" *The Two Ronnies Show* BBC TV 31.12.85.
"Sussudio"/"One More Night" *BPI Awards Ceremony* ITV 20.2.86.Birmingham NEC (Eric Clapton concert featuring Phil drumming in Eric's band) ITV 1986.
Earsay Channel 4 interview 1986.
Prince's Trust Rock Gala ITV 26.6.86.
Film '87 interview BBC TV 1987
Prince's Trust Rock Gala ITV 1987.
Prince's Trust Rock Gala ITV 15.5.88.
Parkinson: One on One interview BBC TV 16.7.88.
"A Groovy Kind Of Love" *Top Of The Pops* BBC TV 8.9.88.

Aspel & Company Interview ITV 10.9.88.
"A Groovy Kind Of Love" *Top Of The Pops* BBC TV 15.9.88.
The Last Resort ITV 15.9.88.
This Is Your Life ITV 16.10.88. *BBC Variety Club Awards* 1988.
Wired interview Channel 4 TV 23.10.88.
Donahue interview Channel 4 TV 1988.
"Two Hearts" *Top Of The Pops* BBC TV 25.12.88.
The "Brit" Awards Ceremony ITV 13.2.89.
Entertainment USA BBC TV 1989.
"Another Day In Paradise" *Top Of The Pops* BBC TV 1989.
Rapido Channel 4 TV 1989.
Tommy Philadelphia 12.5.89 (Phil appearing as "Wicked Uncle Ernie") ITV.
Jonathan Ross Show ITV 1989.
Going Live BBC TV 1989.
Big World Cafe Channel 4 TV 1989.
Off The Wall interview 1989.
Big World Cafe Channel 4 TV 30.10.89.
Wogan Show BBC TV 13.1.90.
BPI Awards Ceremony ITV 20.2.90.
Rock Steady Channel 4 TV 30.4.90.
"I Wish It Would Rain Down" *Top Of The Pops* BBC TV 1990.
TV AM interviews 1990.
BSB Hit Studio 1990.
What's That Noise? BBC TV 15.10.90.
MTV Music Awards ITV 27.10.90.
Billboard Awards ITV 1992.
Symphony For The Spire BBC TV 15.8.92.
"Both Sides Of The Story" *Top Of The Pops* BBC TV 21.10.93.
"Both Sides Of The Story" *Top Of The Pops* BBC TV 28.10.93.
Prince's Trust Gala Concert 25.12.94.
Prince's Trust Gala Concert Royal Albert Hall London 11.7.96.
"Dance Into The Light" (Promotional video) 1996.
"Dance Into The Light" *TOTP* BBC TV 1996.
"Dance Into The Light"/ "It's In Your Eyes" *Des O'Connor Show* ITV 1996.
The Noise ITV 1996.
Live & Kicking BBC TV 1996.
"It's In Your Eyes" (Promotional video) 1996.
"It's In Your Eyes" *TOTP* BBC TV 1996.
The Phil Collins Big Band Tour Documentary BBC TV 23/12/96.
Granada TV Interview 11.11.97.
"Wear My Hat" (Promotional video) 1997.
Parkinson BBC TV 06.02.98.
Live By Request LWT 1.10.98,
National Lottery Live BBC TV 24.10.98.
True Colours (Promotional video) 1998.
Big Screen ITV 1999. "You'll Be In My Heart" (Promotional Video) 1999.

Peter Gabriel On Video

Gabriel's record on the video front is not quite as prolific as Phil's but what material is available more than makes up for the gaps between releases.

Part One Commercial Videos

The first commercial release was 1987's *CV* a compilation of Gabriel's promotional videos going back as far as 1982 and serves as a great compilation of these often hard-to-find items, several of which gained limited if any airing on TV. The track listing includes: Big Time/Don't Give Up(2)/Shock The Monkey/Mercy Street/ Sledgehammer/I Don't Remember/Red Rain/Don't Give Up(1). Virgin Music Video VVD241. 40 minutes.

Gabriel's second commercially released video *POV* appeared in 1988 and features footage shot at the last of Peter's shows on the *This Way Up* 1987 tour at the Lykabettus Hill Theatre in Athens. The video is an inventive mix of live footage interspersed with old super 8mm footage and even the odd snippet of Genesis although you have to be quick to spot them. The track listing is as follows: This Is The Picture/San Jacinto/ Shock The Monkey/Games Without Frontiers/No Self Control/Mercy Street/ Sledgehammer/Solsbury Hill/Lay Your Hands On Me/Don't Give Up/In Your Eyes/ Biko. Virgin Video VVD626. 85 minutes

Gabriel's concerts for the University of Peace at the Jingu Stadium in Tokyo on 20th and 21st December 1986 were also released in 1987 under the title "Hurricane Irene" and the video included Peter's performance of the following songs at the concert: Red Rain/Sledgehammer/No Self Control/Biko/Red Rain(Reprise). 30 minutes.

All About US was issued in 1993 and included an interesting background to the making of the album as well as the complete promotional videos to Digging In The Dirt/Steam/Blood Of Eden/Solsbury Hill/Zaar/Come Talk To Me/Kiss That Frog. Sadly the version of Solsbury Hill was not the original 1977 version but one made for the 1991 *Shaking The Tree* album. It is intriguing to speculate why this video and those to 'Modern Love' and 'Games Without Frontiers' were not included in this compilation

Secret World Live is Peter's latest foray into video and as its title suggests, it is a live concert video filmed at the Palasport Nuovo Modena Italy on 16th and 17th November 1993.The film manages to capture the drama and hi technology which made the shows on this tour so remarkable and contains the following live tracks: Come Talk To Me/Steam/Across The River/Slow Marimbas/Shaking The Tree/Blood Of Eden/San Jacinto/Kiss That Frog/Washing Of The Water/Solsbury Hill/Digging In The Dirt/ Sledgehammer/Secret World/Don't Give Up/In Your Eyes. Picture Music International PM898. 103 minutes.

Part Two: UK Film & Television Appearances

Peter's television and film appearances in the UK have increased steadily over the last few years. Always one to shy away from interviews he nonetheless has been the subject of an increasing number and they have frequently been insightful and on occasions amusing.

"Solsbury Hill" (Promotional video) 1977.
"Modern Love" (Promotional video) 1978.
Kate Bush Special ITV 28.12.79.
"No Self Control" *Top of the Pops* BBC TV 1980.
Tour rehearsals and interview 1980.
"Games Without Frontiers" (Promotional video) 1980.
Whistle Test interview BBC TV 9.10.82.
The Southbank Show documentary ITV 31.10.82.
This Is The Picture (Promotional video) 1984.
Whistle Test BBC TV in studio 1986.
Breakfast Time interview ITV 18.07.86.
Entertainment USA BBC TV 08.01.87.
BPI Awards Ceremony ITV 09.02.87.
"Here Comes The Flood" *First Five Billion Show* ITV 1987.
Whistle Test BBC TV 1987.
Wogan Show interview BBC TV 29.11.87.
Off The Wall interview 12.03.88.
Prince's Trust Gala Concert 23.06.88.
Rapido Channel 4 TV 15.04.89.
Rapido Channel 4 TV 21.06.89.
Rhythms Of The World BBC TV 1989.
Rock Profile ITV 1989.
One To One interview 1989.
Rock Of Europe Cable TV 31.10.89.
Star Test Channel 4 TV 30.11.89.
Mandela Day Concert Wembley Stadium 16.04.90.
Blue Night Channel 4 TV 1990.
Abrazo de Esperanza Concert for Chile BBC TV 1990.
Rapido Channel 4 TV 19.03.91.
What's That Noise? BBC TV 1992.
Entertainment Express 22.01.93.
"Be Still" (Promotional video) 1994.
GMTV News 28.06.93.
Saturday Night Live 1992.
Late Night With Letterman 1995.

Steve Hackett On Video

So far Steve has only appeared on three commercial videos although he has made numerous television appearances over the years.

The Making Of GTR appeared in 1987 to tie in with the recent tour by Hackett's group which also featured former Yes guitarist Steve Howe. It is an interesting look at the making of the one and only GTR album, and includes interviews with all the band members and rehearsal footage making it a worthwhile addition to any Hackett collection. BMG Video 1987 30 Minutes.

Steve Hackett – Live, a long overdue live video from the guitar maestro appeared in 1991. Initially recorded for the Central TV, "Bedrock" series and screened on UK TV this video was eventually issued on Castle Music Pictures in 1991. The video contained the following tracks; Camino Royale/Please Don't Touch/Everyday/In That Quiet Earth/Depth Charge/Wonderpatch/In The Heart Of The City/Black Light/ Horizons/Jacuzzi/Theatre Of Sleep/Jazz Jam/Spectral Mornings/Clocks. 60 minutes CMP6064.

Steve's performances in Tokyo for the *Genesis Revisited* album were captured on video and released by his own record company, Camino Records, in 1997. The video captures the entire show as performed by Steve and his band of intrepid musos and contains the following tracks: Watcher Of The Skies/Riding The Colossus/Firth Of Fifth/Battle Lines/ Camino Royale/In The Court Of The Crimson King/Horizons/ Walking Away From Rainbows/Heat Of The Moment/In That Quiet Earth/A Vampyre With A Healthy Appetite/I Talk To The Wind/Shadow Of The Hierophant/ Los Endos/Black Light/The Steppes/I Know What I Like. Camino Records CAMVT15.

Part Two: UK Film & Television Appearances

Beat Club Bremen October 17th 1978. Originally broadcast in Europe this show eventually was screened in the UK a year later. It is the only live concert footage from Steve's first tour and lasts for sixty minutes.

How Can I? (Promotional video) 1978. Shadow of the Hierophant Circus TV 1979.

Everyday/Clocks (Promotional film by Polygram Records) one track was shown on the BBC *Old Grey Whistle Test* 1979.

The Show (promotional video) 1980. Nottingham Theatre Royal 27th August 1981. Shown as part of the *Videosounds* TV series in the UK.

Gas Tank Channel 4 TV. Music and chat show hosted by Rick Wakeman on which Steve featured playing 'Camino Royale' and 'Hackett's Boogie' 1983.

"Cell 151" (Promotional video) 1983.

"When The Heart Rules The Mind" (Promotional video) 1986.

First Run Steve & Steve Howe as resident vj's (!) Sky TV 1986.

"Sailing" (Promotional video) 1990.
"All Is Mended"/ "By A Paved Fountain" *The Bridge* VH1 performance 04.97.

Mike Rutherford On Video

Mike has become increasingly well known as a solo artist since he instigated the Mechanics in 1985 and there are numerous TV shows on which he and the band have appeared. So far only two commercial videos have appeared, the first contains the promotional videos to the singles from the first two Mechanics albums along with amusing interviews with the band members.

Mike And The Mechanics – A Closer Look was released in the UK in 1991 and contained the videos to the following tracks: Silent Running/All I Need Is A Miracle/ Taken In/Nobody's Perfect/Nobody Knows/Seeing Is Believing/The Living Years. Warner Music Vision 9031 72543-3.

To tie in with the 1996 UK *Hits* tour, a further video compilation was released. In addition to the tracks contained on the above mentioned video, which has long since been deleted, the new video also contained all the promotional videos from the band's third and fourth albums, *Word Of Mouth* and *Beggar On A Beach Of Gold* along with the remixed version of their classic track, "All I Need Is A Miracle" which had been released as a promotional device for the album. To collectors, this compilation is most useful because of the inclusion of the tracks from *Word of Mouth* which gained little, if any, screening on terrestrial TV in the UK and so, this video represents the chance to complete video collections. The full track listing is as follows. All I Need Is A Miracle (96 Version)/Another Cup Of Coffee/A Beggar On A Beach Of Gold/Over My Shoulder/Word Of Mouth/The Living Years/A Time And Place/Everybody Gets A Second Chance/Stop Baby/Seeing Is Believing/Nobody Knows/Nobody's Perfect/ Silent Running/All I Need Is A Miracle/Taken In. The video was issued by Warner Music Vision and had the following catalogue number: 0630-13851-3.

Part Two: UK Film & Television Appearances

"Working In Line" (Promotional video) 1980.
"Half Way There" (Promotional video) 1982.
"Silent Running" *Top of the Pops* BBC TV 1985.
Sky Channel interview 05.04.86.
TV AM interview 08.11.88.
"Living Years" *Wogan Show* BBC TV 13.01.89.
TV AM interview 15.01.89.
Night Network ITV 1989.
Motormouth ITV 1989.
Prince's Trust Rock Gala ITV 26.08.89.
In Profile 07.04.89.
"Living Years" *Grammy Awards Ceremony* 1990.

The Making Of Word Of Mouth Official film 1991.
TV AM interview 13.03.91.
Word Of Mouth (Promotional video) 1991.
A Time And Place (Promotional video) 1991.
Victory Club London (Album launch) 18.01.95
"Over My Shoulder" (Promotional video) 1995
"Over My Shoulder" Des O'Connor Show 1995.
The Bridge VH-1 13.02.95.
"Over My Shoulder" GMTV 15.02.95.
"Over My Shoulder" *David Letterman Show* 07.03.95.
Ellis Park South Africa (Rugby World Cup Programme ITV) 1995.
"Beggar On A Beach Of Gold" (Promotional video)
"Beggar On A Beach of Gold" *Top Of The Pops* BBC TV 22.06.95.
"Beggar On A Beach Of Gold" VH-1 1995.
"Another Cup Of Coffee" (Promotional video) 1995.
VH1 interview and live performance 1996.
"All I Need Is A Miracle '96" (Promotional video) 1996.
"All I Need Is A Miracle" *Des O'Connor Show* ITV 1996.
Uncut VH1 1999. "Whenever I Stop" (Promotional Video) 1999. "Ordinary Girl" (Promotional Video) 1999.

Anthony Phillips
Film & Television Appearances

Strangely enough, the most prolific recording member of the group past or present has been conspicuously absent from television with only a handful of appearances I am aware of and not one of them from the UK, his home country!

VH1 *New Visions* US TV 12.1.88 Anthony as guest VJ on two hour programme promoting his new album *Slow Waves Soft Stars* and playing two tracks from it; "Elevenses" and "Sospirando". TV AM interview with Simon MacCorkindale about the *Tarka* album including footage of the famous whale rescue from the Alaskan pack ice including "The Anthem From Tarka" as its background music. ?.10.88.

Hidrogen A Spanish TV programme promoting "New Age" music on which Anthony and Guillermo Cazenave appeared in July 1997. Featured tracks are; Lucy An Illusion, Sortilege, Peggy In The Sky Without Diamonds. Needless to say, there is an enormous archive of material from overseas as well as the multitude of "private" recordings (both audio and video) from concerts etc which in many cases form an altogether endless supply of additional material for the devoted collector. In some cases, sadly, these items may be the only surviving record of a particular line-up or performance and the documenting of all such material could form the subject of another book in its own right.

The Meadows of Englewood and *From Genesis to Revelation* are the first attempts to bring Anthony's music to the visual arena. Both were produced and released in early 1998 by the Spanish company; Astral, and are also distributed by his UK record company, Blueprint. Both videos contain footage of Anthony at work in his studio as well as tantalising snippets of him playing live and talking about his career to date and as such are essential additions to any collection of his work.

The Meadows of Englewood Astral GVA30 1997.

From Genesis to Revelation Astral GVA30 1997

Fans & Fan Clubs

Complementary to any band's activities, it now seems increasingly necessary for the artist to be served by a fan club. In the thirty or so years of the career of Genesis they have had several official and unofficial ones which have chronicled their careers with varying degrees of success and longevity. The first 'Official' fan club was run by Amanda Gardner and called *The Hogweed Youth Movement* and consisted of regular newsletters on the band's activities. The club ran from 1971 until 1974 when Amanda was forced to give it up due to other commitments.

The gauntlet of running an information service on the band was taken up in October 1976 with the first issue of the *Genesis Information* newsletter written and published by Geoff Parkin. Throughout the late seventies and eighties this was to be the mainspring of information on the band with quarterly newsletters and magazines. In all, from its inception to its downfall in 1992, fifty-three magazines were published, in addition to the two books Geoff wrote of which details are mentioned elsewhere in this text. *Genesis Information* also had a US branch run by Brad Lentz which was basically just a US distributor for the magazine. In addition to the Genesis magazine, Geoff also instigated *Phil Collins News*, an A5 sized publication dedicated to Phil and his solo career. In all some three issues were published between 1983 and 1984.

The next magazine to appear was published in Australia and was to become Australia's Official fan club magazine. Titled *Ripples,* the first issue appeared in early 1987 and was written and published by David Birtwell and Richard Harms. This was a well-produced and designed magazine which set a standard for its successors. Unfortunately, due to a variety of problems, the magazine folded in 1991 having printed twenty-one issues in all.

August 1987 saw the inaugural issue of *The Waiting Room* which is now the longest established Genesis magazine in the world. Originally written and produced by Ted Sayers, Peter Morton, Iain Buckle and Alan Hewitt, the magazine is still published and is now approaching its fortieth issue.

Two noteworthy foreign language magazines appeared within a few months of each other in 1991, beginning with *Dusk* the Italian Genesis magazine written and produced by Mario Giammetti. This was followed in December 1991 by the German magazine *Invisible Touch* (now called *IT*) written and produced by Helmut Janisch, Bernd Zindler and Peter Schutz. Both of these magazines continue to write about the band and its solo members and have taken to issuing English language editions of their publications.

Peter Gabriel is now served by his own official fan club, *The Box,* which apart from Peter's work also acts as an information service for the numerous "World Music" artists who are housed under Peter's "Real World" record label. There is also an unofficial magazine dedicated to Peter's music called *Kontakt.*

The most recent addition to the world of fan clubs is that of Genesis founder member, Anthony Phillips. *The Pavilion* covers all of Anthony's activities past and present and is written and produced by *The Waiting Room* editor, Alan Hewitt.

The increasing use of technology has led to a proliferation of fan sites on the Internet with Genesis finally establishing their own official site in 1997. In addition to this, both Steve Hackett and Anthony Phillips have their own web sites the addresses for which can be found below.

Fan Club Addresses

All of the following are part of the International Genesis Fanclub Network.

The Waiting Room c/o Peter Morton, 97 Oldfield Road Sheffield, S6 6DU UK.

Dusk c/o Mario Giammetti, Casella Postale 10, 82100 Benevento, Italy

IT c/o Helmut Janisch, Postfach 261 36002 Fulda, Germany

Peter Gabriel has his own Official fan club at the following address.
The Box c/o Real World P O Box 35 BATH, Avon BA1 1YJ UK

Kontakt (Unofficial Peter Gabriel magazine).
Mic Smith, 23 Redshank Avenue,
Winsford, Cheshire. CW7 1SP, UK.

Anthony Phillips's Official fan club can be contacted at the following address.
The Pavilion, c/o Alan Hewitt,
174 Salisbury Road, Everton Liverpool, L5 6RQ
UK

Genesis Official Web Site:
www.genesis-web.com

Steve Hackett Official Web Site:
www.stevehackett.com

Anthony Phillips Official Web Site:
http://www.argonet.co.uk/users/jeremyb/index.html

The Waiting Room Web Site:
http://www.genesis-path.com/twr/twr/html
E- Mail: Alan@twr.aol.com

The Path Web Site:
http://www.uio.no/~tholter/genesis.html

Dusk Web Site:
http://space.tin.it/musica/smazzill/dusk/htm.
E-mail: lorasismo@tin.it

Tony Banks

The Fugitive From Fame

"If people only knew how much Tony Banks brought to Genesis they would give his solo records a second chance." The words of Phil Collins in a recent interview accurately assessed the current position of the Genesis keyboards man. His solo albums have reflected the heart of the Genesis sound, as well as a varied array of other musical styles and personas, and yet the success which he has achieved with Genesis has, as yet eluded Tony as a solo artist. However, many may ask why, if he is so successful with the group, does he need a solo career at all? The answer is quite simple; without an outlet for the variety of material that they produce, the band would have long since ceased to exist. In recent years Tony, Mike, Phil and before them Peter, Anthony and Steve have all generated a massive catalogue of material, certainly too much for any band to cope with, hence the solo outings. This has not only served to keep the band fresh, but has also given each individual a chance to flex their creative muscles in ways which have certainly kept the band's output both intriguing and inspired.

Banks' first solo album appeared in 1979 during the group's hiatus at the end of their mammoth 1978 world tour for the *And Then There Were Three* album. Titled *A Curious Feeling* it was very dark and dramatic, reminiscent in many ways of *Wind & Wuthering*. To some extent Tony agrees with that assessment. "I looked at it as an excuse to go a little further down the road we pursued on *Wind & Wuthering*. That was one of the most extreme Genesis albums – I think it was the most musical and the most grandiose album we ever did. With 'One For The Vine' I was confined to ten or so minutes and I wanted to try and expand that same sort of feeling over a whole album, which was the intention on *A Curious Feeling*. I wanted to be able to use all the little differences of soft and loud and contrasting them, both within the same song and with another, but still to tell one story effectively throughout."[1] The timing of the album came about due to Phil Collins desire to take some time off from the Genesis tour/record/tour schedule. "When Phil was having problems with his marriage, in order to give him a bit of breathing space, Mike and I said, 'Well we want to do our solo albums, why don't we do them now?' That would give us time and we could get back together afterwards."[2]

Some of the material which ended up on the album originated from the earlier *A Trick Of The Tail* period was considered by Banks for a solo album at that time, especially after the success of Steve Hackett's first solo effort, *Voyage of the Acolyte*. However, Tony did not consider the time to be right to release a solo project of his own, and his commendable patience resulted in the finished product being a more rounded effort. The album also expanded Tony's musical skills, he played lead guitar on it for the first time in many years. Many people forget that Banks frequently played guitar in Genesis, especially in the period after Anthony Phillips' departure, and even on the epic "Supper's Ready". However, Tony recalled the problems he had during the album sessions playing an instrument that he was not naturally at home with. "When I did 'A Curious Feeling' I actually played the lead guitar and bass as well and I had to stick bits of foam under the strings to stop them vibrating. I could never work out how to stop the strings vibrating after you played them!"[3]

With the trend in music at the time being still geared very much toward the New Wave element, Banks' decision to make the album a conceptual piece based around the idea of a man consciously losing his mind was an intriguing (and brave!) one. "I liked the idea of the songs, the way in which they reflect the idea of this person going through this terrible sense of loss and knowing that he's going downhill and to see what he's feeling at the time. In terms of a concept album, I always felt that Genesis were so out of tune with what was considered mainstream, I really didn't think twice about it."[4] The record was originally inspired by the science fiction story *Flowers For Algernon*, but when Banks contacted the author to ask if it was OK to base the album around the premise in the book, he was told there was a musical coming out written around it. Another case of a missed opportunity.

At this time, Banks and Rutherford both became involved in the world of sountracks when they were asked to contribute music to the film *The Shout* although in the end, their work was overlooked when the film came out. "I liked the film, I thought it was quite good and we were involved with it quite closely. But the day they decided to do the main credits, which was where I thought the music would be the main thing, they did it without us, and we were really depressed by that."[5] The track eventually surfaced as the opener on the album as "From The Undertow" and, as its title suggests, it was originally written as an introduction to the Genesis track "Undertow" and Banks thought it was too good not to use. "I thought the piece of music was good, and as it hadn't really been used in the film, I thought why not use it as a starting point for the album. It sets a certain kind of atmosphere I think because it has a slightly uneasy quality about it."[6]

Banks used a singer with a Genesis connection for his debut solo LP, Kim Beacon former lead vocalist with the final incarnation of Charisma band String Driven Thing who had supported Genesis on their first headlining tour of the UK in 1973. Banks also placed the current Genesis producer, David Hentschel in control, however due to his commitments with Rutherford's solo album, Hentschel declined and opted to work with Mike. Banks engaged the services of David Bascombe, a tape operator at the time, who has since gone on to produce many albums by established artists, including Tears For Fears.

Banks' main problem was how to project the album. "Everyone seemed to be saying 'well, you're using another singer, it's your solo album, but it's not you singing' and it was a slight problem."[7] Ironically, *A Curious Feeling* was to give Banks his highest chart position coupled with his best sales, and overall he still thinks fondly of the album.

"For me, of all the music that I've ever been involved with – including the stuff with Genesis – *A Curious Feeling* is perhaps the most satisfying 45 minutes of music I've ever done."[8]

If Banks' first solo album was laden with the orchestral trappings of Genesis, his next effort, 1983's *The Fugitive* was to be a much sparser affair. Overcoming the dilemma of who to have singing on the record, Banks opted to do the job himself, and surprised and delighted fans with an album of songs which should have improved his commercial position, and even provoked one critic to remark, "*The Fugitive* features some bright, catchy pop tunes which would surprise a few of the cynics if only they'd bother to listen."[9] The album's initial single "This Is Love" achieved a lot of airplay and yet still failed to make any dent on the more pop-orientated charts. Banks was resigned to this state of affairs. "As I'm sure you're aware, this business is so wrapped up in people's perceptions of what they think, and what they want, and it all tends to be based on image."[10] If image was what was lacking, it was more than made up for by the music – an exciting mix of experimentation, especially on the album's two jazzy instrumentals "Thirty Threes" and "Charm". Banks however admits to some reservations about the latter track. "I'm not so sure about 'Charm', as I did it as a bit of a joke with the silly noises and things. It needed heavy drumming in the middle, but the drummer I used on that, Andy Duncan, really wasn't up to it. At one point I thought I would play the drums myself as it was so simple even I could do it!"[11]

The other significant difference from Banks' previous album was the predominance of the drum machine in the area of writing, a technique perfected on the previous Genesis album, *Abacab,* which he embraced wholeheartedly on this project. "I guess at that point things like drum machines and so on were starting to come in more and more and the change in Genesis as a whole happened as well. Those machines do tend to tie you a little bit in certain ways. They give you a lot of freedom in the sense that there's so much you can do with them, but they do tend to lock you into a particular tempo; if it's in 4/4 then it's in 4/4 for ten minutes!"[12]

Concurrent with the production of this album, Banks was also at work on his first proper film soundtrack for Michael Winner's re-make of the 1943 classic, *The Wicked Lady*. The film gained a certain degree of notoriety with the British Board of Film Censors who wanted to remove one scene in which the central protagonists try to whip each other to death with much displaying of cleavage into the bargain! The album divides nicely into two halves with side one featuring the music as composed by Banks, and side two the orchestral variations which comprised the film's soundtrack. It was interesting to hear both sides and it gave an insight into how such projects can change from the initial idea to a finished score. The completed film convinced Banks to try for more work in this field, and this search was to lead to the music that appeared on his next album. Surprisingly, this project also spawned a single comprising one side of themes played by Banks and the other of the orchestral variations on those themes. The single was very low key and now forms one of the most collectable items in Tony Banks' catalogue.

There was to be almost a three year wait before Banks re-appeared as a solo artist with 1986's *Soundtracks* album. As its title suggests, the music on this project was drawn from two films that Banks had become involved with. Ironically, neither of the films represented on the album were in the running when Tony had been approached to create the score for the follow-up to the science fiction extravaganza, *2001: A Space Odyssey*. Banks recalled. "The guy chose me because he really loved the theme from *The Shout*, he could even sing it!"[13] Banks tried several pieces, even writing one with the producer in attendance, but to no avail as he reflects wryly on the whole experience. "The whole thing wasted about six months and it really was a setback for me. There were quite a few film offers coming in. I was actually sent the script to *Terminator*, and although I doubt that I'd ever have ended up doing the film, it was something that I was in the running for. So, the whole *2010* thing meant that I had to turn down other offers, and the film writing side of things took a setback. It was obviously a big blow to my self-confidence as well."[14]

Banks was eventually approached to write the soundtrack to a low budget sci fi film, *Lorca And The Outlaws* which had a budget of £200,000, and agreed to do the soundtrack for free just for the experience. The film was appalling and failed to gain a general release in the UK, even video copies are hard to find! However, the project wasn't entirely futile, as during the course of it Banks had the chance to work with Jim Diamond and Toyah Wilcox, and the resulting two songs from the film featuring their vocals appeared on an EP later in the year. Tony was particularly pleased to be able to work with a female singer after all his time with Genesis. "The idea of a female voice on what is essentially a traditional Genesis song was an interesting idea, it just changed the whole character of it completely." Tony also worked with Marillion vocalist, Fish, on the opening track of the album *Short Cut To Somewhere* written for another low key film, *Quicksilver.* Ironically it was never used in the finished movie. "I wrote some demo pieces for them, which they liked, and it went from there. It was a weird situation actually, as I was writing for committees. I ended up being involved in conference calls with about six people in Los Angeles, and it was a complete nightmare. I survived that, but the problem was that I had a song to write for the film, it was crucial. I wrote three pieces for one section – the first they liked but didn't feel that it was appropriate, and the second ended up as 'A House Needs A Roof' on *Bankstatement* although it was just an instrumental at that point."[16]

Eventually the producers engaged Giorgio Moroder to compose a track with Roger Daltrey which achieved nothing upon its release as a single. The album perhaps serves best as an example of how not to do things, and although Banks was certainly badly served by those involved with the two films, at least he did gain experience in this field including essential knowledge of the notorious vagaries of Hollywood. The contrast between this album and Genesis' next album, *Invisible Touch,* which hit the number one spot both in the UK and USA and went on to spawn a massive five hit singles, could not have been greater. It seems that Phil Collins' remarks about Genesis fans not realising Tony Banks' contribution to Genesis and therefore giving his solo projects more of a chance, was still true and that long sought after solo success was still as far away as ever. Compounding that sense of frustration, Banks' other compatriot in Genesis, Mike Rutherford, after an initially shaky start with his first two solo albums, had finally struck pay dirt with his "other band". Mike and the Mechanics scored a hit with "Silent Running" from their self-titled debut album and went on to achieve even greater success in 1988, leaving Banks wondering what he had to do to get a hit!

Taking a leaf out of Rutherford's book, Banks' next effort was an attempt at a band persona, *Bankstatement* submerged Tony within a group. "The theory was that having tried all these different combinations, a group might be a better idea. Obviously Mike tried it with The Mechanics and it worked really well, so I thought I would try the group thing."[17] The group was based around Banks with vocalists Janey Klimek (formerly of 'The Other Ones') and Alistair Gordon, with production duties taken on by Steve Hillage. The album contained a surprising mix of material, from the straight pop of 'Diamonds Aren't So Hard', to lovely ballads such as 'I'll Be Waiting' and 'That Night' as well as the musically excellent 'The Border'. 'I'll Be Waiting' was actually to feature as Banks' first appearance on British TV as a solo artist when he appeared on the *This Morning* show on 1st November 1989. The album was not very well received by fans or critics. Many saw it as a diminution of his talents although as Banks himself explained, the success or lack of success of a record is down to a great many features, most of which are not under the control of the artist. "Now in the record business, it's almost impossible to put out an album and expect it to do something without the hit single as well, the shops just won't take it, which is the problem. I don't think it's a very healthy situation at all."[19]

Banks' solo efforts were to continue with the release in 1991 of *Still,* his sixth solo recording. Deciding to run through the whole gamut of possibilities, Tony engaged the services of no less than five singers on this album, a decision which has been discussed and argued over by his fans ever since. To many the album represents a great step forward in Tony's oeuvre, to others it represented a diminution of his own persona. Certainly, the choice of Fish again as one of the singers raised more than a few eyebrows! Equally surprising to some was the use of former teen pop idol Nik Kershaw whose impressive writing credits include numerous hits in his own right, as well as penning the hit song 'The One And Only' for Chesney Hawkes, among others. Tony's explanation for the plethora of singers is quite simple. "Well, this was the chance to go through the whole catalogue of possibilities! The problem was that I'd decided it didn't matter what I did in terms of commercial success, and so I decided to do an album and use whatever singer I want to use including those I knew and those who might be interested."[20] The album contained over an hour's worth of music, in a variety of styles, and fully utilised the dynamics of the chosen singers and musicians. The first single "I Wanna Change The Score" should have been a massive hit. Its catchy hook and melody would have gained it a chart position if released by anybody else, but again, Banks' lack of image ensured that this was not to be the case. However, additional complications hindered the song's chances. "I think the thing we didn't realise was that there are two factors here. Nik Kershaw as a singer seems to have become very unfashionable. People seem to have put him down as an ex-weenybopper! The other thing was that he himself didn't want to get back into the limelight, and he realised after he'd agreed to do the singing that it might also involve him in the video and promotional side of things and he didn't want to do that."[21]

Two further singles from the album, 'The Gift' and 'Still It Takes Me By Surprise' also failed to make any lasting impression on the charts. Tony himself, remains singularly unimpressed by the situation and still maintains that this album is one of his favourites. "For me personally, from where I stand, and it's a totally undetached viewpoint I know, but of all my albums the two I am most satisfied with are *A Curious Feeling* and *Still* in terms of what I wanted to do."[22] Certainly the choice of musicians helped give the album a more evenly rounded feel and sound to it, including amongst others, Steve Gadd, Vinnie Colaiuta on drums, Daryl Stuermer on guitars and Martin Robertson on saxophone. Musically it contains several of Banks' finest moments, including the hauntingly beautiful 'Water Out Of Wine' featuring a soulful vocal performance by Janey Klimek.

Tony Banks' fans would have a long time to wait for another album. Indeed, after *Still,* Banks went on record as saying that he would not release any further solo projects. Thankfully, this has proven not to be the case and his latest effort, *Strictly Inc* was released in September 1995. Continuing the idea of a band, the album bears no mention of Tony Banks on the cover, instead simply bearing a computer animation from the video from the first single, "Only Seventeen". Even the video for the single does not feature either Tony or any musician, instead relying on a mixture of hand drawn and computer generated animation to tell the story of a young girl who becomes involved in a shady underworld far away from her comfortable upbringing. For this album, Tony relied on one singer throughout the project, Jack Hues, former front man of '80s band Huang Chung. This gave the album something that had maybe been lacking on previous outings, consistency of vocals, and Jack's voice is certainly impressive. "His voice is actually a bit like mine only better and he can do all the things I want to be able to do."[23]

The album contains a vast array of music in its sixty three minutes and manages to pull out several surprises including the beautiful "A Piece Of You" and the bitterly ironic "Strictly Incognito" where Jack Hues' slightly manic vocals give an added dimension to the track. There is also a degree of social comment, from the political sleaze detailed on "Charity Balls", to the temptations of money on "The Serpent Said". The album culminated in a seventeen minute opus titled, "An Island In The Darkness". "With all of the other tracks I kept myself pretty much well in check, but with this one I just went for it really."[24] Banks also experimented more with computers and programming on this album than ever before. "The great thing about a computer is that you can get various ideas and slot them together and see how they sound."[25] Several of the tracks hark back to the most recent Genesis album although Banks also admits that he has dug a little further into his past for some pieces too, especially on the last track. "It was a chance to introduce a bit of what I hadn't had on the last couple of albums; the big drama, the vocals are intense and it has a kind of moody feel to it. Going into the guitar solo which relates to early songs such as 'Firth of Fifth' because the theme is repeated; soft and loud. It's a definite Genesis kind of thing, but a lot of the stuff in between is non-repetitive and some of the piano improvisations, I just took as I played them, actually."[26]

Banks has continued his partnership with Nick Davis, who produced his last two solo albums as well as the last Genesis album. It certainly seems to be a fruitful collaboration, although Tony admits that, "He occasionally steals a chord from me!"[27] The album failed to dent the charts. However, as far as the fans are concerned, it certainly has the power to move and satisfy. All that remains now is for that elusive hit! Apart from his solo activities Banks is also the major mover in the organisation and co-ordination of material for the series of Boxed Sets, outlining Genesis's career from the hazy days of 1967 right up to the present.

Tony Banks UK Solo Discography.

7" and 12" Vinyl Singles

For A While/From The Undertow **CB344 (7")**
For A While/A Curious Feeling **CB365 (7" PS)**
This Is Love/Charm **BANKS1 (7" PS)**
This Is Love (Extended version)/Charm (Extended version) **BANKS12 (12" PS)**
And The Wheels Keep Turning/Man Of Spells **BANKS2 (7"PS)**
The Wicked Lady(Banks/The Wicked Lady (NPO) **A 9825 (7")**
Short Cut To Somewhere/Smilin' Jack Casey **CB426 (7" PS)**
You Call This Victory/Redwing/Lion Of Symmetry **CBEP415 (7" PS)**
Shortcut To Somewhere/Smilin' Jack Casey/K2 **CB426-12 (12" PS)**
Throwback/Thursday The Twelfth **VS1200 (7" PS)**
Throwback/Thursday The Twelfth/This Is Love **VST1200 (12" PS)**
I'll Be Waiting/Diamonds Aren't So Hard **VS1208 (7" PS)**
I'll Be Waiting/Diamonds Aren't So Hard/And The Wheels Keep Turning **VST1208 (12" PS)**
I Wanna Change The Score/Hero For An Hour **VS1347 (7" PS)**
I Wanna Change The Score/Hero For An Hour/Big Man **VST1347 (12" PS)**
The Gift/Back To Back **VS1362 (7" PS)**
The Gift/Back To Back/A House Needs A Roof **VST1362 (12" PS)**
Still It Takes Me By Surprise (Edit) The Final Curtain **VS1406 (7" PS)**

Compact Disc Singles

Throwback/Thursday The Twelfth/This Is Love **VSCD1200 (PS)**
Throwback (Remix)/I'll Be Waiting/Queen Of Darkness/Big Man **BANKSCD1 (PROMO CD)**
I'll Be Waiting/Diamonds Aren't So Hard/And The Wheels Keep Turning **VSCD1208 (PS)**
I Wanna Change The Score/Hero For An Hour/Big Man/The Waters Of Lethe **VSCDT1347 (PS)**
The Gift/I Wanna Change The Score/A House Needs A Roof/Redwing **VSCDT1362 (PS)**
Still It Takes Me By Surprise(Edit)/The Final Curtain/Still It Takes Me By Surprise **VSCDT1406 (PS)**
Only Seventeen/Only Seventeen(A Saabson/ Svenson remix)/The Serpent Said/Only Seventeen (House mix by Andy Falconer) **VSCDG1553 (PS)**
Only Seventeen (Radio edit)/Only Seventeen (Full length version)/The Serpent Said/Only Seventeen (House mix by Andy Falconer) **VSCDJ1553 (PROMOTIONAL VERSION PS)**
Walls Of Sound (Remix)/Back To You/Only Seventeen (Instrumental) **VSCDT1575 (PS)**
PS denotes a single issued in a picture sleeve.

Vinyl and Compact Disc albums

A Curious Feeling **CHARISMA RECORDS CAS1148/CASCD1148 (CD)**
The Fugitive **CHARISMA RECORDS TB1/TBCD1 (CD)**
The Wicked Lady **ATLANTIC RECORDS 78-0073-1**
Soundtracks **CHARISMA RECORDS CAS1173/CASCD1173 (CD)**
Bankstatement **VIRGIN RECORDS V2600/CDV2600 (CD)**
Still **VIRGIN RECORDS V2658/CDV2658 (CD)**
Strictly Inc **VIRGIN RECORDS CDV2790 (CD)**

Top: "Rock Of The Seventies" Genesis, 1972. (l-r) Mike Rutherford, Phil Collins, Peter Gabriel, Tony Banks, Steve Hackett.
Photo: Unknown - Courtesy of IT Magazine

Middle: "Watcher Of The Skies" (l-r) Mike Rutherford, Peter Gabriel in batwing shock, and Phil Collins.
Photo: Unknown - Courtesy of Bill Brink.

Bottom: Mike Rutherford in classic double-neck pose, Liverpool Empire Theatre, 9th January 1977.
Photo: Alan Perry / TWR

Top left: Steve Hackett in a big girl's blouse, Earl's Court 1977. *Photo: Author's Collection.*
Top right: Rael revisited. Gabriel at Knebworth, 1978. *Photo: Alan Perry / TWR*
Bottom left: "A Flower?" Gabriel, Milton Keynes Bowl, 2nd October 1982. *Photo: Alan Perry / TWR*
Bottom right: Hackett "On Safari", Reading Festival, 26th August 1981. *Photo: Alan Perry / TWR*

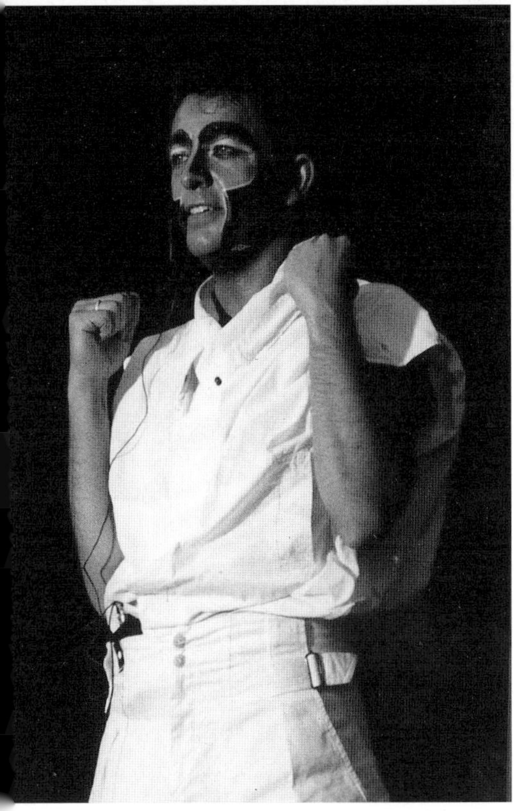

Above left: Peter Gabriel, Crystal Palace Football Ground, 9th July 1983.
Above right and below: Phil Collins, Tony Banks and Mike Rutherford at the record-breaking Wembley Stadium series of shows, July 1987.
All photos: Alan Perry / TWR

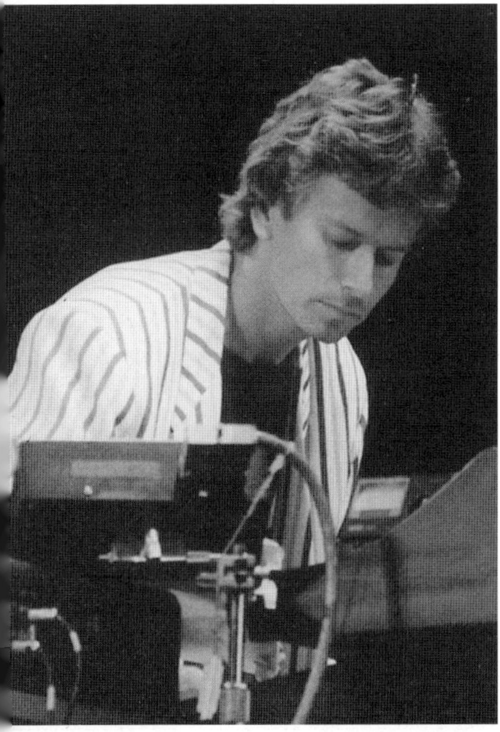

Above left: Anthony Phillips, "Now which way did that song go...?" *Photo: E. Sayers / TWR*
Above right: Anthony Phillips. *Photo: C. Willis (courtesy of A. Phillips)*
Below: Steve Hackett and Gandalf in Vienna, 10th March, 1990.
Photo: Unknown

Above left: Mike Rutherford, Zurich Volkshaus, 25th February 1989. *Photo: Guido Truffer / TWR*
Above right: "Any tabloid reporters in the house... kindly leave NOW!" Phil Collins, Zurich Hallenstadion, 15th May 1990. *Photo: Guido Truffer / TWR*
Below: Genesis, Earl's Court Arena, 3rd November 1992. *Photo: Stephanie Stratton / TWR*

Top left: Paul Carrack with Mike & The Mechanics at Nottingham Royal Centre, 1995. *Photo: Alan Perry / TWR*

Above: Tony Banks at The Farm, 1995. *Photo: Richard Nagy / TWR*

Left: Phil Collins, NEC Birmingham, 7th November 1997. *Photo: Jon "Armando" Guntrip / TWR*

Top Right: Steve Hackett and Friends, Tokyo, 17th December 1996. (l-r) Chester Thompson, Julian Colbeck, Steve Hackett, John Wetton, Ian MacDonald. *Photo: Kudos*

Bottom right: "Congo" video shoot, Malta, 3rd August 1997. (l-r) Nir Zidkyahu, Ray Wilson, Tony Banks, Mike Rutherford.
Photo: A Gouder / TWR

Above: The long-suffering Dale Newman at The Farm Studios.
Below: "Time to dust off those trusty twelve strings..."
Genesis in rehearsal at Bray Film Studios Windsor, 23rd January 1998.
Photos: Ian Jones / TWR

Phil Collins

No Drum Kit Required

Where do you begin to describe Phil Collins' solo career? Perhaps it might be as well to remind ourselves of his humble beginnings. His youth was spent at stage school and through a variety of guises including a stint in the hit musical *Oliver!* and a less auspicious appearance in the Children's Film Theatre production of *Calamity The Cow* but, despite his grounding in acting, Phil's first love was (and still is) drumming. His uncles were persuaded to organise the purchase of his first drum kit when Phil was five years of age and, as the saying goes, he never looked back!

Collins' earliest exposure to "performance" came when his mother, an agent for a West End Theatrical School, found him his first leading role as *Humpty Dumpty* when he was only six years old. From there it was a short step to the tortuous world of child modelling and by his mid-teens Collins had done it all. He played extra parts in such famous films as The Beatles' *A Hard Days' Night* and *Chitty Chitty Bang Bang*. At the age of fourteen, Collins joined the Barbara Speake Stage School and a role in the hit musical *Oliver!* followed, which was to lead to some concerns by his school when the production's needs overran the needs of his education. Fortunately for all concerned, this problem soon resolved itself when Phil's voice broke. During 1967 Phil also appeared in the now famous Children's Film Foundation movie, *Calamity The Cow,* mentioned above. It gave him a brief and inauspicious introduction to the film industry; his precocious nature led to several disputes with the film's director which led eventually to his being almost completely written out of the script.

Shortly after this, Collins joined another stage school where, along with a friend, he formed The Real Thing, the first of a number of groups in which he was to appear. In addition to playing the drums, Collins also sang, an early indication of what was to come. The first big break came in 1969 when a young keyboard player named Brian Chatto had been approached by composers Ken Howard and Alan Blaikley with regard to putting together a band. Since Chatto was friendly with the staff at London's Speakeasy club, which was practically Collins' second home by this point, it was easy for him to recommend a drummer. After an initial rehearsal at the Marquee, Collins and his guitarist friend, Ronnie Caryl, joined the band, Flaming Youth.

Howard and Blaikley had already made their names as the songwriters for Dave Dee, Dozy, Beaky, Mick and Titch and The Herd. Ever with an eye to the main chance, they looked toward an event that had already captured the imagination of the world, the first moon landing. They steered the band, giving them their imaginative interpretation of what would happen if the human race had to abandon Mother Earth. This was to be encompassed in a set of eight pop songs, and strikes us now as pretentious in the extreme, but this was the sixties, and people's perceptions were different then. The band moved into de Lane Lea Studios, then one of the top recording studios in the capital, and with a two week deadline, set to work. They eventually took the grand total of forty hours to record the album – an enormous amount of expensive studio time for the period.

The result, titled *Ark Two* was issued by Fontana in October 1969 and drew mainly favourable comments from the music press, especially *Melody Maker* which deemed it "pop album of the month" even in the august company of new releases by Stevie Wonder, The Band and The Small Faces. The band got off to a good start with a showcase at London's Planetarium and at a party at Blaikley's home but sadly, neither the album nor its accompanying two singles were destined to make any headway in the charts. To be fair, however, 1969 was a heavyweight year, with albums by King Crimson, Led Zeppelin, Pink Floyd and of course, a fledgling release by a little known band called Genesis.

Flaming Youth continued to play gigs throughout what remained of 1969 and into the early part of 1970, but by the time that it came to work on the follow-up album, it was plain to Collins and Caryl that the writing was on the wall for the band. Howard and Blaikley's new material was esoteric to say the least, and not at all to Collins' taste. By the end, the band had evolved into a free-form jazz combo featuring John Mayall's brother Rod on organ.

During the summer of 1970, an advertisement in the back pages of *Melody Maker* caught Collins eye. "Tony Stratton-Smith requires drummer sensitive to acoustic music and acoustic twelve-string guitarist..." Phil decided to attend the auditions but not before he buttonholed Stratton-Smith at one of his usual haunts, London's Marquee Club. Having ascertained that the group were a worthwhile proposition, he took Ronnie Caryl to the auditions at the lead singer's parents home. The group of course, was Genesis. However, Collins had other irons in the fire, and apart from playing on several well-known albums in the summer of 1970, he also considered joining Yes when Bill Bruford let it be known that he was leaving. However, the audition for Genesis was to be the making of a star, and Peter Gabriel still recalls the initial impression that Phil Collins made on the fledgling group.

"I remember noticing him as he sat down on the stool. Before he even picked up the sticks, I thought, this guy can play. Because he had a confidence, a self-assurance I could feel. It was like watching a jockey getting into the saddle, and instinctively knowing, from body language that here is someone who knows what he's doing."[1]

His restless nature meant that even during his tenure with the band his session work was capacious, including undertakings with several heavyweights of the music industry. His growing dissatisfaction with the formalised music in Genesis around 1973, led to the foundation of his own band, Zox and the Radar Boys. This gave Collins a chance to scratch the itch of improvisation which had been growing for a while, as he recalled during an interview with Radio One prior to the *Lamb* tour.

"Well, I mentioned it to Bill Bruford and he said he wouldn't mind having a bash, Steve (Hackett) had mentioned it to John Lord and he said he wouldn't mind having a bash too, so people are from different kinds of bands. It's a very loose thing and the idea behind it is to just go on stage and basically start from scratch, not knowing what you're going to play… it isn't a formal band… we've stopped playing pubs and clubs and if I can get anybody that's in the same frame of mind to just keep it very loose and just have a good time. Don't get me wrong, because I'm at home with the arranged things that Genesis do, but sometimes I get a yearning to get on stage and not know what's going to happen. Even a lot of the stuff on the new album is heading that way, towards having a very loose theme to work with, and keeping a lot more for whatever happens on the night. This is especially true when you're touring night after night with very dense passages, nine weeks in America and playing every night, the freer you can keep it, the better really."[2]

Collins was also involved during this period in a small project with Mike Rutherford and Anthony Phillips, who were at the time working on what was to eventually become Phillips' first solo album, *The Geese & The Ghost* in 1977. Phillips had unearthed a song he had written as a tribute to Genesis' first full-time drummer, John Silver, and had decided to record it and asked Phil Collins to sing on the session. "Silver Song" was duly recorded on a day off between gigs on the band's hectic UK tour for their *Selling England by the Pound* album in October 1973.

During the hiatus caused by Peter Gabriel's departure from Genesis in the summer of 1975, Collins decided to become involved in another "scratch" band, although this one turned into a beast with a slightly longer pedigree. Brand X became Phil's mainstay between Genesis projects throughout the late seventies and early eighties, before demands on his time and talents led him into other fields of endeavour.

The first inkling of Collins' future solo career occurred following the end of Genesis' huge tour in support of their *And Then There Were Three* album, which was to be their most successful to date. Success with the band was paid for in Phil's case by the failure of his first marriage. Andrea Bertorelli, his childhood sweetheart, was simply unable to cope with the enforced isolation which was part and parcel of life on the road with a successful rock band at this time. Initially, Phil tried to compromise by agreeing to move to Vancouver in Canada where Andrea's family lived, but to no avail.

Ironically as his marriage collapsed, Collins' confidence as a songwriter increased and the Genesis album of the time, *Duke* released in March 1980, featured the first songs he had written for the band. The subject matter of "Misunderstanding" and "Please Don't Ask" was part of Collins' exorcism of his personal problems.

Having so much time on his hands while Banks and Rutherford worked on their solo projects meant that Collins was finally able to commit his ideas to record in his own home studio. The first results of these efforts appeared in December 1980 in the shape of the dramatic "In The Air Tonight" single that became an instant success, reaching the number two position in the UK.

Collins made the surprising decision to release his first solo work on the Virgin Records label instead of Charisma, which at that time housed every member of Genesis past and present. His reasoning was to encourage people who would not normally look twice at a Genesis project, and his decision was proven to be correct when his debut album, *Face Value* released in February 1981, achieved number one status both in the UK and in many other territories.

The album was an angst-ridden exploration of the failure of Phil's marriage. The use of the first person in his lyrics gave the album an almost "Dear Diary" feel, which appealed to a wider audience than Genesis' much more impersonal lyrics could, although Phil himself was still taken aback by the instant success of the record. "It was just a complete shock – a solo album that was done under those circumstances, so lazily. I was very intense obviously when I was doing it, it wasn't 'OK I want to make a record' it was just suddenly there was a record and suddenly people liked it."[3]

With success in both the album and single charts Collins chose not to tour in support of *Face Value.* However, his commitments to Genesis meant that the hard working multi-instrumentalist was soon ensconced in Genesis' newly acquired studio, The Farm. Work had begun on the album that would finally bring Genesis and their fans kicking and screaming into the 1980's, *Abacab*, although its reception was to prove almost as divisive as *The Lamb Lies Down On Broadway* almost ten years previously.

Phil Collins' solo follow up was recorded and ready to go by the end of 1982, and with a determination of character the first single from the album took everyone by surprise by its subject matter. The song was written about a "Peeping Tom", of all things, although Phil was quick to emphasise the lightweight intent behind the lyrics. "I don't know why I always go for these seedy characters but it's all very lightweight. 'Thru These Walls' just came from a line I heard somewhere else."[4] The album *Hello, I Must Be Going* was, by comparison to its predecessor, a somewhat lacklustre affair which fell between the two stools of continuing the examination of the marriage break up, with several songs being hangovers from the first album, and the more up tempo numbers which signalled Collins' emerging rehabilitation. Without doubt however, the track that was the album's saviour was the homage to The Supremes' Motown sound – always one of Collins' biggest influences – in his cover of their classic "You Can't Hurry Love" which became his first UK number one single and was to propel him to superstardom.

Collins finally toured in his own right for the first time in November and December 1982 and into the spring of 1983 with a show that drew on both his albums. The band included Genesis stalwarts Chester Thompson and Daryl Stuermer, as well as his Brand X cohort Peter Robinson on keyboards. Success was compounded by success as Collins became a highly sought after producer including work with Anni Frid of Abba whose album *There's Something Going On* was to be one of his first production tasks. He also managed to get back behind his beloved drum kit again when Robert Plant asked him to guest on the recording and tour for his *Principle of Moments* album in 1983. Collins returned to duties with Genesis for the self-titled album released in October 1983 and even during the subsequent enormous US tour, he managed to find time to contribute the title song to the soundtrack of Taylor Hackford's film *Against All Odds* which was another huge success.

Continuing the upward momentum, Collins was soon at work on that all-important third solo album. With *No Jacket Required* he really hit the big time. The promotion began with the catchy first single "Sussudio", a hit in January 1985, which paved the way for the album to become a huge hit around the world. The accompanying tour took Collins to every continent. Probably the key factor with this album was that some of the material was speedily constructed, rather than thought about and pondered over. "I wrote the songs very quickly this time", Collins pointed out in an interview in *Genesis Information* magazine. "In about three weeks I had ten or eleven."[5] Maybe that spontaneity appealed to the fans who quickly sent the album to the top of the UK charts. The album was a fortunate mix of the classic pop now refined to a new height, and several more introspective songs including the thought provoking "Long, Long Way To Go".

Phil had also worked as the producer on his friend and Earth Wind & Fire member, Philip Bailey's album *Chinese Walls* which yeilded yet another pop classic in the shape of "Easy Lover". The single dominated the UK charts throughout March and April 1985 helped no doubt by an excellent promotional video. Both Collins and Bailey experienced problems with the inherent racism still present within the record industry, when the black music department executive at Bailey's record company, Columbia – who amazingly hadn't heard of Phil Collins – told Bailey that if he made a pretty album, black radio might not play it. This in itself was a reiteration of Collins' own experience at the time of his first solo album, when he suggested that his record company send a sampler to several black radio stations the retort was, "They're gonna know you ain't black".[6]

Phil Collins' entry to the "Big League" was confirmed by his appearance at June 1985's "Live Aid" concert organised by the then plain Bob Geldof, in aid of famine relief in Ethiopia. The resultant global extravaganza saw two synchronised concerts in London and Philadelphia on Saturday 13th July televised live around the world. What made Collins' performance out of the ordinary however, was the fact that, courtesy of Concorde, he managed to play at both events, as well as squeezing in percussion duties for Eric Clapton and the reformed Led Zeppelin.

Further soundtrack work also kept him busy, including another hit with the single "Separate Lives" which formed part of the *White Nights* soundtrack in 1986. Phil also turned producer for his long-time friend Eric Clapton for the guitar hero's *August* and *Behind The Sun* LPs. He also took the time to sit in as drummer for several of Eric's shows, a duty which he has sporadically fulfilled ever since.

Having seen Collins' rise to stardom, many Genesis fans were beginning to predict his exit from the band, although Phil himself was at great pains to explain his rationale for staying. "The solo stuff is more important to me because it's me, but I never differentiate between what's more important; it's all important to me. I enjoy playing with the band, we all enjoy writing with each other, and we do it all infrequently enough for it to be fun. We do an album every couple of years, that's what it boils down to. By the time I've done what I want to do and they've done what they want to do, it always ends up being every couple of years. There's no legal or binding thing between us except that we actually enjoy doing it."[7]

This enjoyment was to shine through in 1986 and most of 1987 when he, and the other band members were occupied with the writing, recording and performing of Genesis' hugely successful *Invisible Touch* album. Collins then returned to his acting work with a starring role alongside Julie Walters in the controversial life story of Great Train Robber "Buster" Edwards. Phil's acting talents, whilst not of the Lawrence Olivier school, were nonetheless sufficient to gain critical acclaim for his part, although the self-styled moral majority took exception to the film's apparent "glorification" of crime, a charge which is easily refuted if you actually watch it. Not content with merely acting in the film, Collins was also persuaded to contribute to its soundtrack. The resulting two singles, a cover of Wayne Fontana & The Mindbenders' classic "A Groovy Kind Of Love", and Phil's own "Two Hearts" achieved further chart success keeping his profile high while he worked on what was to become his most successful album to date.

Always the workaholic, the quality of Collins' output has never suffered by his constant effort, as was clearly demonstrated by his fourth album, *But Seriously.* Its November 1989 release was preceded by a single "Another Day In Paradise" which clearly emphasised, as if there was any doubt, that Collins was more than capable of writing songs which said more than the average pop fare. The single's story of a homeless person's plight was so effective that the US Senate Commission on homelessness used it as part of their campaign on the issue. The album, in the meantime, became his first to be issued with extra tracks in compact disc format, although the "extras" were released to vinyl collectors as single b-sides. Demand for the live shows reached fever pitch with the Collins band undertaking an eight month tour in support of the album that had now gone several shades of precious metal. These shows were recorded and a subsequent live album, *Serious Hits Live* was released to yet more acclaim in the autumn of 1990.

The years that followed have seen many highs and lows for Collins. Success continued with Genesis' 1991 hit album *We Can't Dance* and subsequent groundbreaking tour, while his work as producer, session musician and actor could each fill a book on their own. 1993 was however, to prove to be a pivotal year, both in the fortunes of Genesis and Phil Collins. His second marriage to Jill Tavelman ran into problems at this time, much to the obvious delight of the tabloid press, who hounded the couple at every opportunity. Collins' growing disaffection with Genesis eventually led to him announcing his decision to leave to the band in 1994. His subsequent album, *Both Sides,* released in late 1993 was by far his darkest and angriest. Collins vented his frustrations out in a rant against the press, his wife and social injustice all in one go. His decision to play all the instruments himself led to some criticism that the tracks are a little "one-dimensional", but nevertheless the album charted at the number one position and the corresponding tour was his most successful to date. It was divided into two parts, the "Both Sides" tour of Europe and the USA which ran from April to December 1994, and the "Far Side" tour which took in more exotic locations including the first solo shows in South America and South Africa among others.

Collins' subsequent decision to leave Genesis was kept secret until they found a replacement and the news was eventually broken on 29th March 1996. Many wondered what Genesis would do next and of course, what Collins' next project would be. His answer was to go out that summer with a jazz combo and play at several of the most prestigious European jazz festivals. The BBC screened a documentary of the tour at Christmas 1996.

By that time, Phil had already begun work on his fifth solo album that eventually appeared late in the year, and once again contained a mix of upbeat and conscience songs. Titled *Dance Into The Light* it took Phil's pop sensibilities and merged them with his uncanny knack of writing lyrics which can talk at several levels, making the album one of his most satisfying efforts – although the public didn't think so. This album was the first not to gain automatic entry to the number one spot in the UK. The tour had no such problems however, and the resulting spectacular received rave reviews and played to enthusiastic crowds both in the USA and Europe.

The jazz experiment of 1996 had whetted Phil's appetite, and it was no surprise when he returned to this format for his next outing in the summer of 1998, with a string of shows in Europe and the USA, giving Collins a chance to stay behind the drum kit and perform a set drawn from his own material and that of Genesis, along with many staples from the jazz repertoire all lovingly presented to an enthusiastic audience.

So, what does the future hold for Mr Collins? After the recent release of Disney's animated movie *Tarzan,* featuring several tracks from Phil's pen, and the consequent prize of an Oscar for best song, it is also likely that he will have a new solo album ready in the near future.

Phil Collins Solo UK Discography

7" and 12" Vinyl Singles

With Flaming Youth

Guide Me Orion/From Now On (Immortal, Invisible) **FONTANA TF1057. (7")**
Man Woman And Child/Drifting **FONTANA 6001 002 (7")**
From Now On (Immortal, Invisible/Space Child **FONTANA 6001 003. (7")**

With Brand X

Sun In The Night/Disco Suicide **CHARISMA BRAND 1 (7")**
Soho/Dance Of The Illegal Aliens **CHARISMA CB340 (7")**
(The B-Side to this single was in fact: "Noddy Goes To Sweden")
Soho/Noddy Goes To Sweden/Pool Room Blues **CHARISMA CB340-12 (12")**
Modern; Noisy And Effective/Swan Song **CBS XPS155 (7")**

As Phil Collins

In The Air Tonight/The Roof Is Leaking **VIRGIN VS102 (7" PS)**
In The Air Tonight/The Roof Is Leaking **VIRGIN VSK102 (7"PS)**
(This edition came with cartoon booklet created by Phil's brother: Clive)
I Missed Again/I'm Not Moving **VIRGIN VS402 (7" PS)**
I Missed Again/I'm Not Moving **VIRGIN VS402-12 (12" PS)**
If Leaving Me Is Easy/Board Drawing Demos **VIRGIN VS423 (7" PS)**
If Leaving Me Is Easy/Drawing Board Demos **VIRGIN VS423**
(7" Limited Poster sleeve) (The demos were: In The Air Tonight/I Missed Again/If Leaving Me Is Easy)
Thru These Walls/Do You Know, Do You Care? **VIRGIN VS524 (PS)**
Thru These Walls/Do You Know, Do You Care? **VIRGIN VSY524 (7" PICTURE DISC)**
You Can't Hurry Love/I Cannot Believe Its True **VIRGIN VS531 (7" PS)**
You Can't Hurry Love/I Cannot Believe Its True **VIRGIN VSY531 (7" PICTURE DISC)**
You Can't Hurry Love/I Cannot Believe Its True/Oddball **VIRGIN VS531-12 (12" PS)**
Don't Let Him Steal Your Heart Away/Thunder & Lightning **VIRGIN VS572 (7" PS)**
Don't Let Him Steal Your Heart Away And so To F… (Live) **VIRGIN VS572-12 (12" PS)**
Why Can't It Wait Til Morning?/Like China **VIRGIN VS603 (7" PS)**
Against All Odds/Making A Big Mistake (M Rutherford) **VIRGIN VS674 (7" PS)**

Against All Odds/Making A Big Mistake (M Rutherford) **VIRGIN VSY674 (7" PICTURE DISC)**
Sussudio/The Man With The Horn **VIRGIN VS736 (7" PS)**
Sussudio (Extended remix)/The Man With The Horn **VIRGIN VS736-12 (12" PS)**
Sussudio (Extended remix)/The Man With The Horn **VIRGIN VSY736-12 (12" PICTURE DISC)**
One More Night/I Like The Way **VIRGIN VS755 (7" PS)**
One More Night/I Like The Way **VIRGIN VSS755 (7" PICTURE DISC)**
One More Night (Extended mix) I Like The Way **VIRGIN VS75512 (12" PS)**
Take Me Home/We Said Hello, Goodbye **VIRGIN VS777 (7" PS)**
Take Me Home (Remix)/Take Me Home/We Said, Hello Goodbye **VIRGIN VS777-12 (12" PS)**
Separate Lives/Only You & I Know **VIRGIN VS818 (7" PS)**
Separate Lives/Only You & I Know (Extended mix) **VIRGIN VS818-12 (12" PS)**
Separate Lives/Only You & I Know **VIRGIN VSY818 (7" PICTURE DISC)**
In The Air Tonight ('88 Remix)/I Missed Again **VIRGIN VS102 (7" PS)**
In The Air Tonight ('88 Remix)/I Missed Again **VIRGIN VST102 (12" PS)**
A Groovy Kind Of Love/Big Noise (Instrumental) **VIRGIN VS1117 (7" PS)**
A Groovy Kind Of Love/Big Noise (Instrumental) **VIRGIN VST1117 (12" PS)**
A Groovy Kind Of Love/Big Noise (Instrumental) **VIRGIN VSTG1117 (12" PS)**
(This edition appeared in a gatefold sleeve)
Two Hearts/The Robbery (Excerpt) (Anne Dudley) **VIRGIN VS1141 (7" PS)**
Two Hearts/The Robbery (Full length) (Anne Dudley) **VIRGIN VST1141 (12" PS)**
(This edition appeared with a limited edition set of four postcards)
Another day in paradise/Heat on the street **VIRGIN VS1234 (7" PS)**
Another day in paradise/Saturday night, Sunday morning/Heat on The street
VIRGIN VST1234 (12" PS)
I Wish It Would Rain Down/Homeless (Another Day In Paradise Demo) **VIRGIN VS1240 (7"PS)**
I Wish It Would Rain Down/Homeless/You've Been In Love (That Little Bit Too Long)
VIRGIN VST1240 (12" PS)
Something Happened On The Way To Heaven/I Wish It Would Rain Down (demo) **VIRGIN VS1251 (7" PS)** (Also issued as limited edition with photo booklet same tracks different catalogue number : **VSP1251**)
Something Happened On The Way To Heaven (One World Remix Something Happened…(7" version)/I Wish It Would Rain Down (demo) **VIRGIN VST1251 (12" PS)**
That's Just The Way It Is/Broadway Chorus (Demo Of Something Happened On The Way To heaven) **VIRGIN VS1277 (7" PS)**
That's Just The Way It Is/Broadway Chorus/In The Air Tonight (Extended version)
VIRGIN VST1277 (12" PS)
Hang In Long Enough/Around Whe World In 80 Presets **VIRGIN VS1300 (7" PS)**
Hang In Long Enough (Pettibone 12" mix) Hang In Long Enough/Hang In Long Enough (Pettibone Dub Mix) **VIRGIN VST1300 (12" PS)**
Do You Remember? (Live)/Against All Odds (Live) **VIRGIN VS1305 (7" PS)**
Do You Remember? (Live)/Against All Odds (Live)/Doesn't Anybody/Stay Together Anymore? (Live) **VIRGIN VST1305 (12" PS)**
Both Sides Of The Story/Always (Live) **VIRGIN VS1500 (7" PS)**
Everyday/Don't Call Me Ashley **VIRGIN VS1505 (7" PS)**
We Wait & We wonder (Edit)/Hero (Demo version) **VIRGIN VS1510 (7" PS)**
Dance Into The Light/Take Me Down/ Face Value **EW066 (7")**

Compact Disc Singles

You Can't Hurry Love/I Cannot Believe Its True/Oddball **VIRGIN CDT1 (PS)**
In The Air Tonight (extended version)/In The Air Tonight ('88 remix)/I Missed Again
VIRGIN VSCD102 (PS)
A Groovy Kind Of Love/Big Noise(Instrumental)/Will You Still Be Waiting?
VIRGIN VSCD1117 (PS)
Two Hearts/The Robbery (full length version) **VIRGIN VSCD1141 (PS)**
(Issued as a limited edition in heart-shaped box)
Another Day In Paradise/Saturday Night, Sunday Morning/Heat On The Street
VIRGIN VSCD1234 (PS)

I Wish It Would Rain Down/Homeless (Another Day In Paradise demo)/You've Been In Love (That Little Bit Too Long) **VIRGIN VSCD1240 (PS)**
Something Happened On The Way To Heaven (7" version)/Something Happened On The Way To Heaven (one world remix)/I Wish It Would Rain Down (Demo) **VIRGIN VSCD1251 (PS)**
That's Just The Way It Is/Broadway Chorus/In The Air Tonight (extended version) **VIRGIN VSCD1277 (PS)**
That's Just The Way It Is/Broadway Chorus/In The Air Tonight (extended version) **VIRGIN VSCDX 1277 (PS)** (Limited edition in shaped box)
Hang in Long Enough/Around The World In 80 Presets/Hang In Long Enough (Pettibone 12" Mix) **VIRGIN VCSDT1300 (PS)**
Hang In Long Enough/That's How I Feel/Hang In Long Enough (Pettibone Dub Mix) **VIRGIN VSCDX1300 (PS)** (Limited edition numbered disc)
Do You Remember?(Live)/Against All Odds (Live)/Doesn't Anybody Stay Together Anymore (Live)/Inside Out (live) **VIRGIN VSCDT1305 (PS)**
Do You Remember? (Live)/Doesn't Anybody Stay Together Anymore? (Live)/The Roof Is Leaking (live) **VIRGIN VSCDX1305 (PS)** (Limited edition in shaped "Carousel" style box)
Doesn't Anybody Stay Together Anymore? (Live) (One track single free with initial copies of the video: "But Seriously: The Videos" in Woolworths stores only)
Both Sides Of The Story/Always (Live)/Both Sides Of The Demo **VIRGIN VSCDT 1500 (PS)**
Both Sides Of The Story/Always (live)/Both Sides Of The Demo/Rad Dudeski **VIRGIN VSCDG1500 (PS)**
Everyday/Don't Call Me Ashley/Everyday (early demo) **VIRGIN VSCDT1505 (PS)**
Everyday/Don't Call Me Ashley/Everyday (early demo)/Doesn't Anybody Stay Together Anymore? (Live) **VIRGIN VSCDG 1505 (PS)** (Limited edition with 1994 "Phil Collins" Calendar)
We Wait And We Wonder (Edit)/Take Me With You/Stevie's Blues (There's A Place For Us Demo) **VIRGIN VSCG 1510 (PS)**
We Wait And We Wonder/For A Friend/Hero (home demo) **VIRGIN VSCDX1510 (PS)**
Dance In To The Light/Take Me Down/It's Over (home demo) **FACE VALUE EWO66CD (PS)**
It's In Iour Eyes/Always(live)/I Don't Want To Go **FACE VALUE EWO76CD (PS)**
It's In Your Eyes/Easy Lover (live)/Separate Lives (live) **FACE VALUE EWO76CD (PS)**
Wear My Hat/ Wear My Hat (edited hat dance mix)/Wear My Hat (hat dance mix)/Wear My Hat (Wear My Dub) **FACE VALUE 0630 19073-2 (PS)**
True Colours/I Missed Again/In The Air Tonight **VIRGIN/FACE VALUE VSCDT1715 (PS)**
True Colours/Don't Lose My Number/Take Me Home **VIRGIN/FACE VALUE VSCDG 1715 (PS)**
You'll Be In My Heart (Phil version) / You'll Be In My Heart / Trashin The Camp **EDEL0100735DNY (PS)**

PS denotes an edition with a picture sleeve.

Phil Collins Vinyl and Compact Disc Albums.

As Flaming Youth

Ark 2 **FONTANA STL5533**

As Brand X

Unorthodox Behaviour **CHARISMA CAS1117**
Moroccan Roll **CHARISMA CAS1126**
Livestock **CHARISMA CLASS 5**
Masques **CHARISMA CAS1138**
Product **CHARISMA CAS1147**
Do They Hurt? **CHARISMA CAS1151**
Is There Anything About? **CBS 85967**
X Communications **OZONE RECORDS (USA) OZ-001**
Xtrax (Compilation) **PASSPORT RECORDS PB6054 (USA)**
The Plot Thins – A History Of Brand X **VIRGIN CDVM 9005**
Live At The Roxy **ZOK RECORDS**

As Phil Collins

Face Value **VIRGIN V2185/CDV2185 (CD)**

Hello, I Must Be Going	VIRGIN V2252/CDV2252 (CD)
No Jacket Required	VIRGIN V2345/CDV2345 (CD)
But Seriously	VIRGIN V2620/CDV2620 (CD)
Serious Hits – Live!	VIRGIN PCLP1/PCCD1 (CD)

(Initial copies were issued as limited edition with slip case and photo booklet)

Both Sides	VIRGIN CDV2800 (CD)

(Australian import copies were accompanied by a live four-track single: "Live From The Board" featuring the following tracks: Sussudio/Easy Lover/Separate Lives/My Girl)

Dance Into The Light	FACE VALUE 0630-1600-2 (CD)
Greatest Hits	FACE VALUE/VIRGIN
A Hot Night In Paris	WARNER 3984 27221-2 (CD)

Promotional interview discs and samplers

Phil Collins.... Profiled!	ATLANTIC RECORDS PR3092-2
Phil Collins.... The Story – The Interview Disc	ATLANTIC RECORDS PRCD5370-2
Phil Collins – Dance Into The Light Interview Disc	WARNER RECORDS PC008
You Ought To Know (Toyota cars promotional sampler) Solo	
The Phil Collins Big Band Big Hits Sampler	GREENWOOD TRUST COMPANY

Peter Gabriel

From the Cocoon to the Secret World

Peter Gabriel's decision to leave Genesis, announced officially in August 1975 caught many off guard. The question, with hindsight, is: should we have been so surprised? The answer is perhaps as misleading as the question. Of course, any long-term observers of Gabriel's career would not have been shocked by his decision to leave the band – the two were no longer mutually inclusive; Gabriel's sense of a "Real World" did not equate with the slightly phantasmagorical world of Genesis circa 1976.

With no definite "career" to follow, Gabriel's decision appeared bizarre on an epic scale, but was it really so? The answer is, in my opinion, "No". He always knew that he could return to music for a living, so what makes his decision to leave so much more of a shock than the previous departures from the band, was the element of pragmatism. Peter decided to concentrate primarily on his family and as such, he was the first member of Genesis to do so. This was perhaps the element which neither the band nor Peter himself were ready for – realism. Although *The Lamb Lies Down On Broadway* can be described as a "Modern Fairy Tale" perhaps the real world had not injected itself enough into the cosseted Genesis scene and so, Gabriel's departure was the best thing for everyone, although, of course, not everyone thought so at the time and not everyone agrees now.

Whatever the ramifications of his decision on those around him, after his departure Gabriel could not long resist the attraction of writing his own music, and the summer of 1976 saw him begin work on what would appear in early 1977 as his first solo album. Intriguingly enough, he enlisted both Mike Rutherford and Anthony Phillips to help with the initial demos for this project, and although none of that material was used on the finished record, it would no doubt make for interesting listening (Since work began on this biography, a Charisma tape reel featuring some of these demos has emerged from Anthony Phillips' tape archive, although it is unlikely that any of this material will ever be released).

Gabriel's search for a new musical style initially led him into working with Bob Ezrin, who had produced albums by Alice Cooper as well as Lou Reed's *Berlin* and Kiss' *Destroyer* albums. The new album was recorded at Nimbus Studios in Toronto during the autumn of 1976. In many ways it can be seen as a transitional work, in which Gabriel was searching for his own musical voice and, as such, several of the tracks were a surprise including the delightful barbershop harmonies of "Excuse Me" and the melodrama of "Moribund The Burgermeister". The album was released in the UK in February of 1977 on Charisma Records to widespread critical acclaim and a twenty date tour of North America was set up to promote it in March and April.

Perhaps the most surprising aspect of the tour was Peter's appearance, without any of the usual costumery associated with his time in Genesis. Instead, he relied solely on the music and a simple but effective light show. Even more surprising perhaps, was the inclusion in the set of several classics in the shape of "Ain't That Peculiar?" and "All Day And All Of The Night", as well as the resurrection of Gabriel's alter-ego "Rael" for "Back In NYC". The shows brought him an entirely new audience in the USA, as well as the stalwart Genesis fans who welcomed their hero's return to the fray. This success was confirmed when the first single from the album, "Solsbury Hill", was a hit on both sides of the Atlantic. A further surprise in the shows came with the previously unheard material from the as yet unrecorded second album, still almost a year away. Peter's first UK shows took place in April 1977 and were a warm-up exercise for a full European tour scheduled for September and October 1977. For these shows, Gabriel was joined by the same musicians as on the earlier US tour: Tony Levin (bass), Larry Fast (synthesisers), Steve Hunter (guitars). Both Fast and Levin were to become long time members of Gabriel's band and Levin is still with him over twenty years on. The tour was another hit with audiences, although it wasn't quite as successful with the Swiss police during the final leg of the tour when the band were arrested on their way from Besancon to St Gallen for a gig. The police mistook them for members of the German terrorist group Baader-Meinhof. Even an a-capella version of "Excuse Me" wasn't enough to convince them that the guys weren't "fugitives from justice" and it was left to tour promoter, Richard MacPhail to convince them. As you can imagine, the music press had a field day with this story sparking off such headlines as *New Musical Express'* "Gabriel Gang Freed".

Despite a successful tour, album and single, Gabriel was in debt to the tune of £200,000 at the end of 1977, and still not satisfied with his endeavours so far. In an effort to resolve this he decided to involve Robert Fripp – whose work with King Crimson had so inspired the early Genesis – in the production of his second album. Fripp himself was a very reluctant collaborator and wanted to give Gabriel the complete freedom of expression that was in some ways missing from his first record. However, this approach was not without problems, as Gabriel was a very slow worker.

For the new album, Gabriel enlisted the help of Bruce Springsteen's keyboard player, Roy Bittan along with Levin and Fast and extra help from respected session musos, Sid McGinnis on guitar and Timmy Capello on saxophones. A single was released in advance containing two tracks from the forthcoming album: "DIY" and "Perspective", but it made no impression on the charts. Later in the year it was re-issued with a remixed A-side and an unreleased track on the flip side but also to no avail. The album itself, also titled *Peter Gabriel* like its predecessor, was released in June 1978 with far less critical comment than the first album, and its lack of a high profile single caused problems later when his contract with Atlantic Records in the USA was up for renewal.

The album itself was a lyrically darker affair than its predecessor and songs like "Home Sweet Home" with its description of someone on the edge of a nervous breakdown really challenged the listener. Once again, Gabriel undertook an extensive tour of the USA and Europe to promote the album and the shows continued to place the emphasis firmly upon the music, with improvisation playing a large part of the show, especially with the debut of further new pieces which in many cases were far from finished. On this tour Gabriel changed his appearance once again, with a closely cropped head and what can best be described as a bin liner for clothing he was rapidly putting clear blue water between his days as the "Caped Crusader" in Genesis. In particular, his appearance at 1978'1

Battersea and Knebworth Park festivals, amidst the rise of the "New Wave" in British music which was enjoying its first flush of major league success, was enough to give several music critics serious cause for concern.

"Peter Gabriel was the first of the day to get the audience off its collective ass," one journalist commented, "but his recent surge to credibility is perplexing; to me he is as anonymous today as he ever was with Genesis. But the rest of the audience endorsed Gabriel's oddly-arranged music and went quite wild over his Punk parody of 'A Whiter Shade of Pale' which I found both unfunny and unspectacular."

Not all critics found the new album such a daunting or confusing prospect and he drew several plaudits from the press, and his fans continued to be as loyal as ever. Gabriel rounded off the year with a series of sell-out shows at the prestigious Hammersmith Odeon in London including an extra special event on 24th December which, thanks to an oversight on promoter Harvey Goldsmith's part, led to a double booking of the venue by both Gabriel and Tom Robinson. The resulting show billed as "Rob & Gab Christmas '78" was one of the highlights of the musical calendar with guest appearances by Elton John, Paul Jones, Phil Collins and Andy McKay for what turned into the Rock & Roll party of the year.

1979 saw Gabriel taking stock of his position whilst working on material for his third solo album, although he did put in a couple of appearances at the Reading and Glastonbury festivals during August, at which several new pieces were again given a pre-album airing and anyone who heard him perform "Biko" for the first time will, I am sure never forget it! The remainder of the year was taken up in the studio where his mode of writing was undergoing a fundamental change with the emphasis being placed more on rhythm rather than melodies. To help him, Peter acquired the services of producer Steve Lillywhite whose previous credits included Siouxsie And The Banshees' "Hong Kong Garden" and XTC's "Making Plans For Nigel". Gabriel was striving to break out of the constraints of traditional rock music. In addition to Lillywhite, he had also enlisted the help of Phil Collins on percussion who brought with him a novel effect; the now famous "gated reverb" which was to become one of the features of Gabriel's new sound. Collins created the effect through a gate compressor unit, a device that both shut off sound and squashed it. "Intruder" was the first beneficiary, and Collins later used it to great effect on his own first solo album, *Face Value.*

This new rhythmic approach gave Gabriel the opportunity to explore an idea that had been with him since 1977 when he first heard of the death of South African political activist, Stephen Biko. At the time he was writing the track which was destined to become "Biko", Gabriel came across a recording of the music played at Biko's funeral and he was intrigued by its rhythmic, uplifting quality. Gabriel also used the marimba, an African instrument similar to a large xylophone on the album, as well as the vocal talents of Kate Bush.

This new-found artistic freedom was one thing, but the adventurous (and some might say controversial) subject matter of some of the new work was to prove too much for his American record company Atlantic, and A&R man John Kolodner in particular, who is reputed to have remarked upon hearing the new record that it was "commercial suicide". A meeting with the heads of the record company was far from successful; they objected to "Biko" on the grounds that no one in the US was aware of what was happening in South Africa (a crass indictment of the US music scene). They also thought that "Family Snapshot" (a song based on the thoughts of an assassin as he stalked his prey) was too controversial. Atlantic's decision to drop Gabriel from their roster of artists was referred to in Gabriel's own words as "an example of the short-sighted, bigoted attitude commonly found in the hierarchy of the American record industry. It will be ironic if this album turns out to be more successful."

Peter's prediction about the album was well-founded. The first single from it "Games Without Frontiers" reached the number four spot in the UK charts in April 1980. The video for the single was censored by the BBC because of its use of children's dolls(?), and the line "we piss on the goons in the jungle" was also edited out. The album once again titled *Peter Gabriel*, was eventually released in May 1980, by which time Gabriel had already had the satisfaction of an enormously satisfactory tour of the UK. The album became Gabriel's highest chart entry to date when it went straight into the UK charts at the number one position. In all, three singles were released from the album although none of them equalled the success of "Games Without Frontiers". Without doubt, however, it was "Biko" which must have brought Gabriel most satisfaction as it went on to create a life of its own, becoming the anthem for all of those striving to bring an end to South Africa's repressive Apartheid system. It must have also been extremely satisfying for him to watch the frantic efforts of Atlantic records to re-sign him to their label for an advance of $750,000 – an enormous sum of money in1980. Gabriel however, opted to join David Geffen's newly established label, whose promise of artistic freedom and record company support were much more important.

The two-year hiatus between third and fourth albums was not, as some have supposed, an indication that Gabriel was out of ideas, far from it. The success of the third album gave him a much needed respite to recharge his creative batteries. Gabriel's influences and inspirations were taking him even further afield, and it was during this period that he started gathering tapes of music from all over the world convinced that a new and powerful force was soon to be unleashed upon music.

"I feel that an important influence on music over the next few years will be ethnic in origin and I can hear it being combined with electronics and more expressive, emotive use of synthesiser."

This fascination led to a desire to promote a festival to bring this music to a wider audience which would eventually result in the staging of the first World of Music Arts and Dance (WOMAD) festival in the summer of 1982. The event was originally planned for the summer of 1981 but experienced long delays due to the lack of a major financial backer. This in turn, led to delays on Gabriel's already behind schedule album.

The new record deal with Geffen gave Gabriel artistic freedom and a certain degree of financial security, although there was some concern expressed by the traditional lack of a title for the new album. After three issues of what Gabriel saw as his periodic "Music Magazine" the new record company felt that a title was needed for this effort. The untitled album was filled with new sounds that Gabriel had been acquiring, Ethiopian pipes formed the harmonies around which "The Family & The Fishing Net" was written, while the Brazilian surdo drum was the rhythmic basis for "Kiss Of Life".

The first single "Shock The Monkey" was an early indicator of the new direction that Gabriel was taking. However, it failed to make any impression on the charts. With the new album following hot on its heels in September 1982, it was all too much for one reviewer in the UK music paper, *Sounds.*

"Forget Heavy Metal; Punk; The Rolling Stones; forget the most horrendous musical niche you can think of – because the most horrendous of the lot is this: the Comfortably Middle Aged Set at which Genesis and associates sit at the head of the (leather-bound) table…"

Not all of the reviews were quite as extreme as that and indeed, in many areas Gabriel was praised for breaking down musical barriers – he even received noteworthy reviews in several black music papers. As in 1979, Gabriel opted to premier the album live, in this instance at the event which he had spent so much time (and money) helping to organise; the WOMAD Festival which took place at the Showering Pavilion in Shepton Mallet over the weekend of 16th to 18th July 1982. Unfortunately one of the major problems was the fact that the authorities had restricted the performances by Gabriel and the other headliners, Echo & The Bunnymen, to the four thousand seater Showering Pavilion. This rather reduced the appeal of the festival proper for fans of the two most popular acts. Gabriel's performance that day was amazing as one fan recalls…

"Coming on stage dressed in the usual black uniform, he began singing over a backing tape, until the rest of the band joined in and the song built up to a crescendo. In fact this is how most of the songs from the first half of the set developed, beginning sparsely with just piano and drums. Particularly effective were "I Have The Touch", "Lay Your Hands On Me" and "Shock The Monkey". However after "Shock..." a new dimension was added when Ekome, the Bristol-based drummers from Ghana, joined the stage for "Rhythm Of The Heat" which Gabriel described as being about a white man who finds himself surrounded by blacks and is consequently shit-scared. This was particularly apt since Gabriel and his band were outnumbered by Ekone. For this song, Gabriel seemed to get himself into a trance-like state and performed a strange kind of ritual dance. By the end of this intense song Gabriel seemed visibly exhausted." The second set was even more challenging than the first, where he was joined on stage by long-time friend and hero Peter Hammill and Indian violin master, Shankar for an improvised set which drew warm applause from the crowd.

Gabriel's new work had also been the subject of a documentary by ITV's *South Bank Show* which was broadcast on Sunday 31st October 1982 and captured the artist at work in the studio spliced with some of the magical moments from the WOMAD Festival. During the programme, Gabriel was keen to reply to the detractors of his new work. "One of the real satisfactions for me with this record is that I'm played on black stations in America, and even though in the white press I had some fair slagging this time, I had some very good reviews in black magazines… there are definitely elements of this hybrid between electronic non-European influences. I think a lot more musicians are now working in this area and there will be a style of music to emerge in the eighties which I think will be very important and influential…"

A second single from the album failed to make any impression on the charts even though its B-side should have attracted interest, co-written by Gabriel, Shankar, David Rhodes and Stewart Copeland. The album, despite critics' reservations reached the number ten spot in the UK charts and Gabriel embarked on his lengthiest tour to promote it. Opening in Boston USA on 28th October 1982, the new tour lived up to everyone's expectations as the band played a set high on drama and comedy with Gabriel taking everyone by surprise again by appearing with his face adorned with make-up for the first time since his days with Genesis.

The surreal element was taken to even greater heights (or should that be depths?) in 1983 when Peter was invited to appear at the San Remo festival in Italy for which a special performance was required. Gabriel had to appear as an alien visitor to the festival, asking questions of the presenter about the festival itself before finally appearing on stage with an appallingly under-rehearsed studio band to perform "Shock The Monkey". On the second night he failed to amuse the highly reserved TV studio audience by swinging out over them on a rope half way through the song only to fall off!

Gabriel had also taken to performing songs in the language of the country he was playing in, and having previously issued his third album as a German language edition back in 1980, he did the same for the fourth album titling it originally enough *Deutsches Album*. It was particularly interesting for the alternative versions of several of the songs, many of which were noticeably longer than their UK counterparts.

By the end of 1983, a long overdue live album had also finally been issued, *Peter Gabriel Plays Live,* contained most of the highlights of his current set. The success of the album and tour were somewhat marred by a series of family problems. This, and his increasing desire to branch out into other areas of endeavour, meant that after the completion of the 1982/83 tours, he devoted a large amount of time pursuing a project which he had initially contemplated during the mid 1970's – the creation of an adventure theme park – "Real World". It is an idea which he is still struggling with now. He also submerged himself in his work and ideas for his fifth album that was still three years away. A lot of other events were to influence him before that however.

In 1984, Gabriel and his wife Jill had a trial separation. During this trying time Gabriel made two visits to Brazil and Senegal which exposed him to even more of the rhythmic influences which were so evident on his fourth album. He began preparing rhythm tracks for the as-yet untitled fifth album early in 1984 but made slow progress. The main reason for the delay came through his involvement in the soundtrack for the *Gremlins* film to which he contributed "Out, Out", hardly his best recording ever. He made another much more successful contribution to the *Against All Odds* soundtrack where he was in the company of tracks by both Phil Collins and Mike Rutherford. His contribution, "Walk Through The Fire", was an old track left over from the third album to which he added lyrics and re-recorded. It was eventually released as the second single from the soundtrack later in 1984.

Also that year, Gabriel became heavily involved with the soundtrack to Alan Parker's controversial film *Birdy*. This was an intriguing project utilising both existing music and newly recorded pieces, which succeeded in capturing the state of shock experienced by the film's central character upon his return to "society" at the end of the Vietnam War. Unlike many rock stars, Gabriel took the precaution of warning his fans that not all of the music on the soundtrack album was new, with the equivalent of a Government health warning on the sleeve. It sold less well than his previous albums but the sales of 150,000 copies world-wide made a respectable total for a film soundtrack.

Another vital component to emerge from this period was Gabriel's involvement with another producer. In the past, he had not always been happy with the production on his records, but in Daniel Lanois, he had found the perfect foil to his own maverick creativity. Lanois' production credits included Martha & The Muffins and he had also co-produced U2's *Unforgettable Fire* album with Brian Eno (another hero of Gabriel's who had helped on Genesis' *The Lamb Lies Down On Broadway*). As usual, the slowly, slowly work ethic meant that the album was a very long time in the making, One deadline, 31st July 1985 passed and so did another on 14th December 1985. Lanois was so frustrated that he resorted to what was supposed to be a playful action: he locked Gabriel in a back room in the studio and said he wouldn't release him until some lyrics had been completed.

Finally, the finishing touches to Peter's fifth solo album were in place by January 1986 and on 8th February the executives arrived to hear the album. On Tuesday 11th the pressing of the album started and on 24th April 1986 the first single, *Sledgehammer,* was released.

It was certainly a departure for Gabriel, upbeat, up mood and rude! If the single was a surprise, then the accompanying video was even more so. Produced by Stephen Johnson, it involved a technique called "pixellation" which was a method of shooting movement frame by frame to give the illusion of human animation, first used on the Talking Heads' video for "Road To Nowhere". The final cost of the video, which took over three weeks to make, was to be some £120,000, but it was money well spent. The single went into the UK charts at number four, and number one in the USA in July, where it ironically knocked Genesis' "Invisible Touch" single from the top spot!

The album topped the charts on both sides of the Atlantic, going straight to the number one slot on its release in the UK on 19th May 1986. By the summer of 1987 it had sold over five million copies world-wide, going double platinum in the USA with sales of over two million, and double platinum in the UK with sales of over 600,000. The album was a re-affirmation of what Gabriel's fans had known for years – here was an artist who was able to lay bare the very soul of his subjects. Not all his fans were pleased, however, and in fact many maintained that the album's title, *So,* actually stood for *"Sell Out"*. They couldn't handle the fact that their hero was actually having a commercial success on his hands. As usual, the critical reaction to the album was mixed – dividing between the enthusiastic and openly hostile. "Brilliant," said *The Guardian.* "Universal message that hope springs eternal," ran *The Times.* "The music which Peter Gabriel makes is terrifically uninteresting. It says nothing, being merely an ordering of sounds mostly artificial," said John McKenna of Eire's *Hot Press.*

Following on from the success of the first single from the *So* album, Peter wasted no time on releasing a second in September 1986. This time it was be the anthem against unemployment "Don't Give Up" a plaintive and evocative song running the entire gamut of emotions connected to its subject matter. The single caught the imagination of the public both at home and abroad and was rewarded with another healthy chart position eventually peaking at number nine in the UK. This was no doubt helped by the video which showed Peter in a clinch with his vocal co-star on the song, Kate Bush and this appearance no doubt raised a few eyebrows and started a few rumours as well! Interestingly enough, there was also a second version of the video made, which, to this writer's mind would have made a more appropriate accompaniment to the song, including as it did footage of unemployment queues, the Twenties Great Depression and other relevant material. This song was destined to become a highlight of Peter's forthcoming shows and none more so than at the show at London's Earl's Court Arena on 29th June when Kate Bush appeared on stage with him to a rapturous welcome.

Having contributed an anthem to the growing movement for human rights in the form of "Biko", it was only a matter of time before Gabriel became involved in that movement. So, to the probable despair of his record company, he interrupted his promotional tour of Europe to take part in the *A Conspiracy Of Hope* tour of the USA in the summer of 1986, to help raise membership of Amnesty International. Gabriel was in good company as the Amnesty rock & roll circus also included The Police, Lou Reed, Bryan Adams and U2. The shows were a huge success and recruited an additional 100,000 new members for Amnesty in the USA. Gabriel was not the headline artist, but there is no doubt that he stole the show, as footage from a couple of the gigs proves, turning in stunning performances of a mixture of both old and new material.

The tour for the new album proper began in November, but not before one more special performance outside the United Nations Building in New York on 16th September 1986, where he was joined by Shankar, Little Stephen and Youssou N'Dour whose plaintive vocals were such a high point on the new record. From the first show of the tour in Rochester NY on 7th November, Gabriel took audiences on a trip filled with drama and humour with a new look stage show astonishing in its simplicity. Gabriel had ditched the facial make-up from the previous tour and the stage set included a series of moveable lighting gantries which attacked Gabriel mantis-like at several points during the show. He interrupted his tour schedule again in December to fit in two gigs at Tokyo's Jingu Stadium in aid of the University for Peace, with appearances again by Little Stephen, Youssou N'Dour and Nona Hendryx who had previously been the support act on his first solo tour back in 1977.

The tour continued well into 1987 with growing plaudits from fans and critics alike, and to demonstrate that the success of "Sledgehammer" had not been a mere fluke, the album's third single, "Big Time" released in March 1987 proved to be made of equally stern stuff. It was a totally different song, quirky, with wryly humorous lyrics accompanied by another brilliant video where the lyrics were quite literally translated visually with Gabriel appearing in a loud evening jacket and tie with his big head being superimposed on a small body. The tour continued across Europe and the UK finally ending in Athens in October, with the shows captured for a long overdue live video *PoV*, to be released over a year later. Gabriel also contributed a live version of "Biko" to Richard Attenborough's Oscar nominated Biko biopic *Cry Freedom*.

The success of the tour, and the financial security which it brought, meant that Gabriel was finally able to invest in his own recording studio: Real World. The facility has the dual purpose of enabling Gabriel to record in his own time, but also to give other artists facilities which they might never otherwise have. It has since led to the creation of the Real World record label which has dealt with Gabriel's recorded output since 1989. During the respite after the end of the *So* tour he was able to return to writing for another soundtrack, one which was to cause considerable controversy. Having been approached by Martin Scorsese to write music for his film *The Last Temptation Of Christ* Gabriel had the chance to explore a whole gamut of musical ideas and soundscapes which resulted in the soundtrack titled *Passion*, his new record label's first release in 1989.

Gabriel did not long remain a stranger to the concert stage however, and became involved in the *Prince's Trust Gala* performing two shows for them in June 1988 where he played "Sledgehammer" accompanied by Phil Collins amongst others. The second benefit concert was far more in keeping with Gabriel's ethnic involvements, being the 70th birthday celebrations for the imprisoned South African, Nelson Mandela, held at Wembley Stadium. He appeared with Sly and Robbie's posse to sing "Set Them Free" and then later to perform "Biko" in his own right backed by Simple Minds, along with versions of "Sun City" and "Free Nelson Mandela." This was Gabriel's first ever appearance at the stadium, and many people were surprised to see him back there a mere three months later as part of the *Human Rights Now!* entourage. In order to prepare for this, Gabriel and his band had spent a week rehearsing, and surprised everyone by appearing unannounced at the WOMAD festival (now an established part of the UK rock circuit) in August.

Gabriel's involvement with the *Human Rights Now!* tour was a concomitant effect of the success of the 1986 *A Conspiracy Of Hope* tour of the USA, and comprised nineteen dates taking in every continent apart from Australia. Accompanying Gabriel on the tour were Bruce Springsteen, Sting, Youssou N'Dour and Tracy Chapman along with other guests who appeared at various concerts. Once again, Gabriel was not the headliner, that honour being shared by Springsteen and Sting. However, his energy and genuine commitment to the cause of Human Rights gave his performances a special edge and it was wholly appropriate that he should be involved in this landmark tour commemorating the 40th anniversary of the signing of the United Nations Declaration of Human Rights. The tour ended in October in Buenos Aires.

In early 1989, Gabriel travelled to Moscow to promote the Greenpeace movement's *Breakthrough* album, and the year also saw the release of the *Passion* soundtrack, undoubtedly one of Gabriel's most dramatic and moving works. He also found time to help out on fellow Real World artist and friend Youssou N'Dour's album and to appear on the *Shaking The Tree* single and video. In 1990, Gabriel also joined in the celebrations at Wembley Stadium following the release of Nelson Mandela from prison and also took part in a special concert from Chile *Embrazo de Esperanza* where he duetted with Sinead O'Connor. 1990 also saw the delayed release of the *PoV* video which gained good reviews, as well as a compilation album of some of his greatest "hits", which though not really appropriately titled, did contain some interesting alternative versions of some of his classic songs.

Gabriel spent most of 1991 in the studio trying to nail down ideas for the long overdue new studio album, although he managed to fit in a trip to Dakar to play a short set in honour of Nelson Mandela's visit there, and also to appear at the *Simple Truth* concert held in aid of Kurdish refugees. Gabriel also organised the first Real World recording week, captured for posterity by BBC TV cameras, involving artists from all over the world ending with a gala concert at the studios.

September 1992 saw the release of the long awaited follow up to 1986's *So*. In marked contrast to its predecessor's up beat mood, *Us* was a rather introspective affair, influenced no doubt by Gabriel's marriage break up. It was nevertheless a powerful album and contained some of his strongest work, courting controversy again with the video for the first single, "Digging In The Dirt",which was banned by the BBC for its overtly violent nature. The album failed to reach the number one spot, but sold well both here and abroad supported by the mammoth *Secret World* tour in April 1993, the lengthiest and most inventive embarked upon to date. Beginning with a series of warm-up shows at the Grand Slam Club in the USA, Gabriel had enlisted the help of set designer Robert LePage who created the new look stage based round the "Male" and "Female" or "Yin" and "Yang" signs. Also featuring a telephone box and a tree, the stage set was without doubt one of the most visually stimulating, and with the band now including both Shankar and female singer Joy Askew, the tour was a huge world-wide success. It encompassed more than a year of shows and included numerous WOMAD events both in the US and elsewhere, as well as a guest appearance at the "Woodstock" anniversary in August 1994. Gabriel's involvement with technology also led to the release in late 1994 of his first interactive CD ROM called *Xplora 1* as well as a couple of additional music video compilations and a second live album and video from the *Secret World* tour.

Since the end of the tour Gabriel has submerged himself in a variety of projects, many of which are still ongoing. His most recent appearance being for the release of the *Genesis Archive 1967-1975* four CD set which he helped to compile, including a VH1 video special about the early years. December 1998 saw Gabriel emerge from his seclusion to perform at an Amnesty International gig in Paris and with the new *Up* album nearing completion, the year 2000 could see the "Angel Gabriel" returning to the spotlight again.

Peter Gabriel UK Solo Discography

7" and 12" Vinyl Singles

Solsbury Hill/Moribund The Burgermeister	**CB301 (7" PS)**
Modern Love/Slowburn	**CB302 (7")**
DIY/Perspective	**CB311 (7" PS)**
DIY/Mother Of Violence/Teddy Bear	**CB319 (7")**
Solsbury Hill (Live)	**SFI 381 (7")**
(This was a one-sided flexi disc given away to attendees at the Christmas '78 shows in the UK)	
Games Without Frontiers/The Start/I Don't Remember	**CB354 (7" PS)**
No Self Control/Lead A Normal Life	**CB360 (7" PS)**
Biko/Shosholosa/Jetzt Kommt Die Flut	**CB370 (7" PS)**
Biko/Shosholosa/Jetzt Kommt Die Flut	**CB370-12 (12" PS)**
Shock The Monkey/Soft Dog	**SHOCK 1 (7" PS)**

Shock The Monkey/Soft Dog SHOCK 122 (7" PICTURE DISC)
Shock The Monkey/Soft Dog SHOCK 12 (12" PS)
I Have The Touch/Across The River CB405 (7" PS)
I Don't Remember (Live)/Solsbury Hill (Live) GAB1 (7" PS)
I Don't Remember (Live)/Solsbury Hill (Live)/Kiss Of Life (live) GAB12 (12" PS)
(This edition appeared with limited edition "white label" copy of Games Without Frontiers/ Schnapschuss: Family Snapshot)
Walk Through The Fire/The Race (Larry Carlton) VS689 (7" PS)
Walk Through The Fire/The Race (Larry Carlton)/I Have The Touch VS689-12 (12" PS)
Sledgehammer/Don't Break This Rhythm PGS1 (7" PS)
Sledgehammer/Don't Break This Rhythm/I Have The Touch ('85 remix) PGS112 (12" PS)
Sledgehammer (Dance mix)/Don't Break This Rhythm/Biko (12" Extended version)/I Have The Touch ('85 remix) **PGS113 (12" PS)** (limited edition re-issue of single)
Don't Give Up/In Your Eyes (special mix) PGS2 (7" PS)
(also issued as limited edition with video still poster sleeve)
Don't Give Up/In Your Eyes (special mix)/This Is The Picture PGS212 (12" PS)
Big Time/Curtains PGS3(7" PS)
Big Time (extended version)/Big Time (7" version)/Curtains PGS312 (12" PS)
Red Rain/Ga-Ga (I Go Swimming instrumental) PGS4 (7" PS)
Red Rain/Ga-Ga (I Go Swimming instrumental)/Walk Through The Fire PGS412 (12" PS)
Biko (Live)/No More Apartheid PGS6 (7" PS)
Biko (Live)/No More Apartheid PGS612 (12" PS)
Shakin'The Tree/Old Tucson VS1167 (7" PS)
Shakin' The Tree/Old Tucson/Sweeping The Leaves VST1167 (12" PS)
Solsbury Hill/Shakin' The Tree VS1322 (7" PS)
Solsbury Hill/Shakin' The Tree/Games Without Frontiers (live version) VST1322 (12" PS)
Digging In The Dirt/Quiet Steam PGS7 (7" PS)
Steam/Games Without Frontiers (Massive DB Mix) PGS8 (7" PS)
Blood of Eden/Mercy Street PGS9 (7" PS)
Kiss That Frog (album edit)/Kiss That Frog (Mindblender mix edit) PGS10 (7" PS)
Lovetown/Love To Be Loved 660480-7 (7" PS)

PS denotes single issued in a picture sleeve.

Compact Disc Singles

Solsbury Hill/Moribund The Burgermeister/Solsbury Hill (Live) CDT33 (PS)
Sledgehammer/Don't Break This Rhythm/I Have The Touch ('85 remix) CDT4 (PS)
Big time (Extended)/Curtains/No Self Control/Across The River/Big Time GAIL3 12 (PS)
Biko(Live)/No More Apartheid/I Have The Touch ('85 remix) CDPGS 612 (PS)
Shakin' The Tree/Old Tucson/Sweeping The Leaves VSCD1167 (PS)
Solsbury Hill/Shakin' The Tree/Games Without Frontiers (live) VSCDT1322 (PS)
Digging In The Dirt/Digging In The Dirt (Instrumental)/Quiet Steam/Bashi-Bazouk **PGSDX 7** (PS) (This edition appeared in a limited edition box with fold out lyric sheet)
Digging In The Dirt/Digging In The Dirt (Instrumental)/Quiet Steam/Bashi-Bazouk PGD7 (PS)
Steam/Games Without Frontiers (Massive DB Mix)/Steam (Oh, Oh Let Off Steam Mix)/Games Without Frontiers (live) **PGSDX8 (PS)** (Limited edition in shaped case the standard edition contained the same tracks with the catalogue number **PGSDG8)**
Blood Of Eden/Mercy Street/Blood Of Eden (special mix) PGSDG9 (PS)
Blood Of Eden/Mercy Street/Sledgehammer PGSDX9 (PS)
Kiss That Frog (Edit)/Digging In The Dirt (Rich E mix)/Kiss That Frog (Mindblender mix) PGSDG10 (PS)
Kiss That Frog (Edit)/Across The River/Kiss That Frog (Mindblender mix edit)/Shaking The Tree (Bottrill remix) **PGSDX10 (PS)** (Limited edition with postcard set)
Red Rain (Live)/San Jacinto (Live)/Mercy Street (Live) PGSCD11 (PS)
(Limited edition numbered cd ep from "Secret World Live" album)
Lovetown/Love To Be Loved/A Different Drum 660480-2 (PS)

Vinyl and Compact Disc albums

Peter Gabriel	CHARISMA CDS4006/PGCD1 (CD)
Peter Gabriel	CHARISMA CDS4013/PGCD2 (CD)
Peter Gabriel	CHARISMA CDS4019/PGCD3 (CD)
Peter Gabriel	CHARISMA PG4/PGCD4(CD)
Peter Gabriel Plays Live	CHARISMA PGDL1/ CDPGD100 (CD)
Birdy (Film soundtrack)	CHARISMA CAS1167/CASCD1167 (CD)
So	VIRGIN PG5/PGCD5 (CD)
Passion (Film soundtrack)	REAL WORLD RWLP1RWCD1 (CD)
Shaking the tree (Twelve Golden Greats)	VIRGIN PGTV6 (VINYL)
Shaking the tree (Sixteen Golden Greats)	VIRGIN PGTVD6 (COMPACT DISC)
Us	PG7/PGCD7 (CD)
Secret World Live	PG8/PGCD8 (CD)

Steve Hackett

The Acolyte's Voyage To A Dark Part Of Town

Steve Hackett's career began before he joined Genesis with session stints in bands such as Canterbury Glass, Steel Pier and Sarabande to name but a few. His first foray into the world of recording came when he joined the band Quiet World in 1970. In a recent interview with *The Waiting Room* magazine, Hackett remembered the circumstances in which their album came to be recorded. "It was three South African brothers, the Heathers, who wrote the stuff. Their father was a medium, they had lived in England and then moved back to South Africa only to return to England later. Their father stayed behind in Africa and he used to send them tapes of various characters speaking through him. It was very strange as we used to sit down and listen to these tapes. One of these characters was called Kitumbi, who claimed to be the 'Spirit of Music'. He described the way in which music could be written and he described it in very visual terms. He said what was going to happen; there was going to be a kind of hybrid and modern music would include the sounds of the street. I still use that as an influence; some of the things he said."[1]

The album, *The Road,* was released in 1970 by Dawn records and has more recently still, been re-issued on compact disc by Tashiko records in Japan. It is certainly an interesting period piece although there is little indication of the musical direction which Hackett was later to take. As Hackett himself says, "It depends on whether you like that album. I think of it more as a product of its time, rather than a great album."

Hackett's first proper solo effort actually appeared while he was still a member of Genesis, and was released in 1975 whilst the band were still in the recess created by the recent departure of Peter Gabriel. The album, called *Voyage Of The Acolyte* gave vital reassurance to the members of Genesis that interest was still high in the band when it achieved a silver disc in the album charts. Hackett remembers the album fondly. "Casting my mind back, I think it was during 1974 that there was a slight lull after touring. Anyway, at one point I had the Mellotron at home and I seemed to spend hours doodling on it. I put one or two ideas together. Following on from that I began to wonder what I could come up with without the restriction of the band. I came up with one or two things that I was convinced that they would hate and that seemed to goad me even further on in that direction and try things that I felt they would avoid."[2]

The album would eventually feature both Mike Rutherford and Phil Collins, and it was an extremely enjoyable outing, with a wide variety of music on it. Several tracks were destined to become favourites in Hackett's live set, including the maniacal, "A Tower Struck Down", and the lyrically gorgeous, "Shadow Of The Hierophant". Hackett's commitments to Genesis' live and recording schedules meant however, that he was unable to tour with this album, and it was to be a further three years before the Steve Hackett road show would wend its way to a venue near you.

Steve's decision to leave Genesis after the conclusion of their highly successful *Wind & Wuthering* world tour in July 1977 was a very brave but necessary step if he was to develop his own musical identity without the constraints of Genesis' committee writing modus operandi. Although quoted with some venom at the time of the split, Steve is anxious to correct the misinterpretations that have been given to his position at this time…

"I did an interview in the States and I didn't realise that they were going to sell it to a British newspaper but I was particularly fiery that day and it came out sounding as if I hated their guts which is far from the truth. I had a lot of good times with the band and I consider that to be my formative period really."[3]

Hackett was now free to concentrate on developing his own identity, and the first fruits of this search for a musical "soul" came about with the album *Please Don't Touch*. This was a heavily guested project including appearances by Woodstock veteran, Richie Havens, and the first appearance in the UK by soul singer Randy Crawford who lent her delightful vocals to the track "Hoping Love Will Last". A lot of the material for the album was written while Hackett was still in Genesis.

"During that period I kept coming up with ideas, and none of them, or less and less of them I should say, seemed to fit the band. I knew with a song like 'Hoping Love Will Last' there was no way that Genesis were in a position to do that. Obviously it was for a female singer, and with the greatest respect to Phil, I couldn't imagine him singing that."[4]

Steve finally set off on his first solo tour and it was amazing to hear the introduction to "Please Don't Touch" as a set opener. The shows drew from this album, its predecessor, and the as yet unrecorded third album. Steve's first solo gig was at the Chateau Neuf in Oslo Norway on 4th October 1978 and his first UK show took place at Cardiff University on 23rd October. Both the shows and the new album were favourably received by the fans and critics alike.

For touring purposes it was impossible to use the musicians who had appeared on the album itself, so Steve assembled his own band which included several players who were to become firm favourites over the next few years including Pete Hicks on vocals, John Shearer on drums and, of course, Steve's brother John on flute and bass pedals. Together they formed an impressive array of talents on stage and the build up was now under way for what many fans still credit as being Hackett's finest musical moment.

After the success of the *Please Don't Touch* tour, Hackett was soon back in the studio recording the tracks, some of which had already been aired live and arranged during that tour. He remembers, "The tour was a marvellous thrill and *Spectral Mornings* was recorded off the back of that, so everyone was on a high really."[5] He took the band to

Hilversum Studios in Holland to record the album and that studio is still a place that Steve has fond memories of. "*Spectral* was recorded at the beginning of '79. It was very, very cold: sixteen degrees below zero and very little sleep! I used to come in at 3am and the maids used to start making the rooms. I swear they used to start at four! It was a very big studio and the whole experience was absolutely wonderful."[6] The album was a massive success both at home and across Europe where it was ecstatically received by the fans who packed out the theatres on the first full length tour of the UK and Europe including a headline spot at one of the three days of the Reading Festival in August 1979.

The album had everything: lyrical ballads such as "The Virgin & The Gypsy" and even an anti-drug song in the shape of "Everyday". The variety of the musical influences was apparent too, from the delicate beauty of "The Red Flower of Taichi Blooms Everywhere" to the heavy rock of "Clocks: The Angel of Mons". Hackett also included another of those anarchic, left-of-centre pieces like "Carry On Up The Vicarage" for the previous album in the bizarre "Ballad Of The Decomposing Man" which many interpreted, quite wrongly, to be an anti-Union song influenced by current events in the UK. Hackett, however, tells it quite differently.

"It was really a straight George Formby parody; probably a very bad impression of George Formby, but nonetheless it was meant to be humorous"[7]. That sense of humour was evident during the stage show with the antics of the members of his band, but it was the sheer talent of those players which really captivated this viewer at several shows on the tour. The set also included a couple of unreleased tracks in the shape of the dramatic "The Steppes" which appeared on the next album and has retained its position as a highlight of the live set, and the camp humour of "Hercules Unchained" ultimately issued as a single B side.

Once again, there was only a short wait for Hackett's next album. *Defector* was released a little under a year after *Spectral Mornings.* It seems he was taking the words of the spirit Kitumbi from his Quiet World days quite literally in trying to explain in music the fable of a defector from the Eastern Bloc who, arrives in the West and is amazed to find that everyone dreams in colour. The idea is a very striking one and Hackett explained part of the rationale behind it. "Yes, in fact, we found that when we toured later and went to Estonia in what was then the Soviet Union, there was a limitation of colours. There were two colours that the buildings were painted, and the rest was concrete. I found that the insides of churches were the only places where there was any imagination and colour."[8]

Musically the album was far heavier than the previous efforts and Hackett admitted the change in an interview with Hugh Fielder for *Sounds* in July 1980. "I've felt more involved in every aspect of this tour than I've ever done, the music, the organisation and the audience. I want to get closer to them and to be more expansive. With Genesis it wasn't done to come offstage and cry 'Oh yeah' or anything like that. It was always more analytical. Perhaps it's that I'm reacting against now. I've moved to the centre of the stage now both mentally and physically."[9] The change certainly showed in the stage presentation for which Hackett dressed in anonymous black jeans and T-shirt finally discarded the gypsy player look which had become his trademark in Genesis. The album itself drew favourable reviews and contained the mix of music which always makes his albums a pleasure to listen to, including yet another masterpiece of eccentricity, "Sentimental Institution", for which he utilised a device he had discovered in Holland during the *Spectral Mornings* sessions. "I found this machine which was designed for lounge use in Holland at a place called Relight Studios, where we did *Wind & Wuthering*. It was an amazing machine – on one side of the keyboard it would give you pre-recorded riffs with discs that you used in order to achieve them. I used it on "Defector" on *Sentimental Institution* doing the 'Big Band' sound which was produced to sound like an old 78 record. In fact it's one of my favourites because it is a parody of something traditional and you have to listen closely to it to realise that the lyrics are a total send up."[10]

The tour also saw Hackett's first solo visit to the USA where his show drew upon all of his albums, as well as a playful rendition of the operatic standard "Oh Sole Mio" which, apparently was not too well received in Turin where it was booed by several members of the audience!

The next musical outing was to signal "All Change!" with a completely revamped band and musical style. The *Cured* album in 1981 has to be the one which has divided followers the most, marking Hackett's first outright flirtation with the world of "commercial" records. This, combined with the conspicuous absence from the record of most of his regular touring band, many of whom were almost regarded as members of the family by the fans who had grown used to the more melodic side of his music, left some suspicious as to the future direction. Hackett stripped things down to basics, and was accompanied on it solely by his brother and keyboard player Nick Magnus who also co-wrote a couple of tracks. The result was a more commercial sounding album, although Hackett was quick to explain his reasons behind such a career change. "Well, at the time I was learning to sing and trying to develop a musical personality which at times ran contrary to my musical leanings. It wasn't a conscious decision to start writing commercial songs. I think it was an album of finding my way."[11]

Whatever the reasons, *Cured* was to be a turning point in Hackett's career. The reasons for not employing the talents of his existing band were many, but sadly the main one was financial – although there were concerns when band members wanted a greater responsibility for the music. "On the second album I wrote the occasional track with the band and they wanted to have more and more of a creative input and they wanted to write songs. So there was a resistance to some of the ideas that they had on one level. On the other level it was impossible to maintain weekly wages."[12] Hackett again took to the road in order to promote the album with his largest European tour to date, including several shows in the Eastern Bloc where, as he was quick to point out in an interview with Rick Wakeman on the *Gastank* series a year or so later, he was actually a bigger draw than his peers in Genesis. The tour also saw Hackett incorporate into his live set-up two players who were later to feature heavily in other bands: Chas Cronk who played bass and later also played for Rick Wakeman before forming Cry No More and Ian Mosley who took over John Shearer's drum stool before going on to find more success with Marillion.

1982 was a relatively quiet year, and apart from writing material for his next album, Hackett also took time to become involved in a couple of charitable projects. These included the organisation of a special concert for the *Poland Aid* charity, and another in aid of the Tadworth Children's Home where he was joined on stage by his old cohorts from Genesis, Mike Rutherford and Peter Gabriel. Hackett, of course, on Saturday 2nd October 1982, also took part in the Genesis benefit concert to help bail out Peter Gabriel's cash-starved WOMAD project.

Early in 1983 the first indication of a new direction was given by the appearance of a single from the as yet unreleased album. "Cell 151" was probably one of the most unlikely hits of the year and gave Hackett his highest chart placing for a single in the UK. It was backed by a marvellous live version of "The Air-Conditioned Nightmare". The irony of it all was that at this time, things were not going too well with the record company. Charisma Records were at this time in the throes of a take-over by Virgin Records and Hackett was one of the artists caught in the middle. "A&R were starting to make comments that didn't fit the MD's ideas and so it left me in the middle trying to steer a sensible course"[13] Sadly, the end result for Hackett was an album, *Highly Strung* which, with the right amount of promotion, could have been extremely successful. However, disagreements were not just over A&R decisions, as Steve points out. "There were two things that I disagreed with Charisma at the time. Firstly, so many fans were asking for a live album, and I wanted to deliver one but they were firmly against that. I felt it was the right move and I still think it would have been the best thing to do. The other was the idea of an all-acoustic album that I started doing in my own spare time and with my own money as it were, which was the album that became *Bay of Kings*. I started recording that in 1980 but it wasn't released until much later."[14]

Not so much later after *Highly Strung* as it turned out. Having failed to resolve the problems with Charisma, Steve sought an independent release for the *Bay of Kings* album which was released in October 1983 on the Lamborghini Records label, itself a subsidiary of PRT. Yet another new album and another UK tour, this time taking in the smaller clubs and university halls which was very much a "back to basics" approach, but one which definitely suited the more intimate nature of the music itself. The shows themselves however, didn't pass off smoothly. At Ashton-under-Lyne the show had to be cancelled due to poor ticket sales and an appalling lack of publicity, Poor publicity had also led to a previous show being booed when the audience who had been led to believe it was to be an appearance by Hackett *and* his band were not too appreciative of a solely acoustic show! He drew not only upon the material from the acoustic album itself, but also threw in some older favourites treating them to an acoustic setting.

That small hiccup aside, the tour was a great success and so was the album. It received its finest accolade from the virtuoso violinist Sir Yehudi Menuhin who used a track from it as part of the soundtrack to the television programme about his Music Foundation: *From Kew to the Findhorn Foundation*. Hackett was also one of only two artists to sell out concerts at London's prestigious Barbican Centre so, obviously not everyone felt the same way as those who booed his show! Hackett's own view of the album was simple and honest. "I viewed it as music without props that pre-dates New Age and Unplugged. The derivations from the Classical, Flamenco and Folk and all of those kinds of traditions are still there. There's also the influence of the nylon guitar, because with Genesis we had specialised in twelve string extravaganzas, so I felt that nylon was the area I was most interested in, because it had the widest range of dynamics in all acoustic areas. I think it was a reaction against dependency… the pyrotechnics of rock; the smoke and lasers; and dancing girls in the wings!"[15]

If Hackett's view of *Bay of Kings* was that it was a reaction against rock and roll excess, his next project took off down a path which few musicians had explored successfully at that time: the area of "World Music". The new album, *Till We Have Faces,* was a rhythmically charged exploration of the percussion and samba music of Brazil, where most of it was recorded. It came as a surprise to both fans and critics who, in the main, loathed it, although Hackett explains it in the following terms. "I thought of it as a learning experience, being involved with that number of rhythmic percussion players. I would meet them in the street where they would demonstrate their skills and we would put them in the studio. The situation in Brazil was that I could only get recording studios that started at midnight, and so I got home at eight in the morning and as these things often conspire they were doing renovations upstairs and so I did that album on very little sleep! Then I brought it back to England and mixed it again. It's an album that falls into two halves. I think of it as the cohesive song element and the more improvised, the more rhythmic side."[16] As he pointed out in the sleeve notes to the re-issue of the album, it was impossible to take a Samba School on the road and so it remains the only Steve Hackett album which has never been played in a live context. However, he still thinks he didn't go far enough with the project. "I think, with hindsight, I should have gone even further with it and made it even more a World Music album, if that's the term, and abandon all Western civilisation whatsoever."[17]

He still has material from this period which was not released at the time, although I suspect that several pieces may have appeared on projects since, and it is certain that had the project been released now, its reception would have been much better – perhaps another example of how often Hackett is ahead of the game as an innovative artist. His outlook on producing work of this type is typical of the attitude that has shaped his entire career. "I've usually found that the best thing to do is exactly what you wanted, and then you've got a much better chance of pleasing the fans, but then you've usually got a good chance of upsetting record companies, so it's very difficult to please both the business and the public."[18]

He made his first live appearance for two and a half years at a charity gig staged by Marillion at the Hammersmith Odeon in February 1986, where he joined in on a performance of the early Genesis classic "I Know What I Like". At this time rumours had started to abound that Steve had joined an AOR Supergroup with ex-Yes man, Steve Howe. Many fans were naturally sceptical, especially after his disenchantment of his time in Genesis but, lo-and-behold, in March 1986 the debut single from the aptly titled *GTR* arrived in the shape of the track "When The Heart Rules The Mind".

Steve's involvement in this project came about via a chance meeting with Brian Lane. "Brian was manager of Yes and had offices in the same area as where I was living at the time and we bumped into each other. Funnily enough, years earlier in Los Angeles when I'd done the *Please Don't Touch* album, he wanted to work with me in a group, and I didn't really want that. We were talking one day and he said, 'Steve Howe's not doing anything at the moment; he's out of Asia.' He became very excited about forming a group with two guitarists, and over lunch one day he mentioned it to Kim and she said to me, 'Why don't you do something like that?' I said I would meet Steve (Howe) and it very quickly became the basis for forming a group, because we felt that if we just made an album and didn't tour it, we wouldn't give the album the best chance. The group really grew up to facilitate the liaison between the two of us. Brian's association with Geffen Records was in the ascendant and consequently they became very interested in the band, which I had always seen as a project. They were on the boil and then they went off and Arista got involved. It was something that initially was going to take three months to record and ended up taking nine months to record in a top studio. It became a big success in the States, but was not as well received over here… I don't think of it as the best record I've ever made and that's putting it diplomatically!"[19]

The creative output between the two guitarists was evident on the first single, which had been written on the very first day of recording. It went on to be a huge success in the USA and also achieved a respectable chart position here and in Europe during that remarkable summer of 1986 when Genesis & Co seemed to be sweeping all before them. A follow up single, "The Hunter", was issued in the USA and in several European territories as well, but failed to make any impact on the charts. A lengthy tour was also undertaken to promote the album, culminating with sell-out shows at the Hammersmith Odeon. The concerts themselves were divided into three sections with the two guitarists playing separate solo sets, before being joined by the band for the main event, prompting one reviewer to remark, "Three bands for the price of one".

The other musicians in the band were well-known if not actually famous: Max Bacon the lead singer had formerly fronted Heavy Metal act Bronz; Phil Spalding had played bass for Mike Oldfield amongst others, and drummer Jonathan Mover had played numerous sessions. So it was a coherent band unit and in the main, the shows were well received.

Almost two years were to elapse before Hackett appeared with a new album in his own right. Once again he opted for the "back-to-basics" approach and released another acoustic album, *Momentum*, a further demonstration of Hackett's skills with the "Small Orchestra" as he calls the acoustic guitar. He was determined to, "Just simply go out and play in front of people, without any fuss, and again to show that I could do it without the props, without the conglomerate, without the big budget. So I started doing acoustic shows, and again it was different pressures, because what appears simpler on paper is actually complex when you have to go out and play it yourself. In many ways there are much more pressures because you don't have a band."[20] The tour in the UK was extensive, taking in university halls and several theatres where the show would be well received. Hackett also toured Europe and gained further acclaim from the audiences. The album also reached a respectable position in the New Age and Classical charts and received generous plaudits from the normally hostile British Press.

Concurrent with this album, Hackett was also at work on another rock album. In fact it was almost ready for release at the same time as *Momentum.* It was to have been another star studded project featuring amongst others, Brian May, Chris Thompson, Bonnie Tyler and Marillion's Steve Rothery. However, due to various contractual problems, the project, under its working title of *Feedback* was never released, although a few pieces from it have since sneaked out on other albums – especially some of the re-issues of Hackett's albums on compact disc. Hackett himself admits to stealing from this mysterious project. "I'm plundering ideas from that album which I'm using on some things now. At the time it wasn't contractually possible to release it, although with the production we are capable of now, it doesn't feel contemporary enough. So the production we have now on the *Guitar Noir* album is superior to that."[21]

The years between 1989 and 1992 were frustratingly quiet as far as the outside world was concerned but far from quiet for Hackett himself as he was occupied with a variety of projects, including the building of his own recording facility, Crown Studios. Another activity was the setting up of his own record label, Camino Records, which now covers all of his releases and is a highly respected independent record label in the UK. Once again he became involved in a charitable project when he heard about the forced repatriation of the Vietnamese "Boat People" from Hong Kong against their will, "A lot of artists were involved in making yet another version of 'Sailing' … we were looking for an emblem for the cause, and it seemed perfect for it."[22] The single was released as part of the *Rock Against Repatriation* project, which was also accompanied by a charity auction of rock star memorabilia. 1992 saw the tying up of contractual loose ends with Virgin Records, who were the inheritors of his catalogue when they took the ailing Charisma Records over in 1982. The resulting compilation album *The Unauthorised Biography* contained a selection of Hackett's finest moments from his back catalogue as well as two new tracks, one of which, "Don't Fall Away From Me" was another hangover from the *Feedback* project. Although very much a stop gap measure it was nonetheless a chance to give newer fans a pocket introduction to Hackett's work as he himself explained. "It was a respite. I think that again, Billy (Budis) and I sat down and decided that we would include tracks which hadn't received as much attention as others. So, instead of doing an album of stage favourites, we decided to include stuff like the Randy Crawford track, 'Hoping Love Will Last'."[24]

That album was followed by the long overdue live album, *Timelapse*, initially released by the Dutch Crisis record label, and subsequently by Camino Records as part of their re-issue project in 1994. The album drew together two concerts with ten years separating them; the first was performed in New York in 1981 and the second was a television broadcast in the UK in 1990. As such, it was a clever way of representing the way in which Hackett's live sound and style had changed over the years. Live shows became very much a part of Hackett's life again later in that year when he embarked on a US tour primarily to promote *Timelapse*, but also using the opportunity as a springboard for material from the new album which he was finishing off at the time.

This new record, *Guitar Noir* was finally released in 1993 and was Hackett's first rock album for almost ten years, and his twelfth studio album to date. *Guitar Noir* managed to capture his early blues influences as well as combining both acoustic and electric elements more successfully than ever before. "I tried to marry the acoustic influences, in other words, the acoustic guitar was incorporated into electric songs which I hadn't done before – it was either electric or acoustic. Now I see all music as terribly similar – I see opposites as similar."[25] His schedule took in his first comprehensive UK tour for over five years, combined with return visits to North America and his first shows in South America. The tour finished with a handful of shows in Italy later in the summer. The album received less than complimentary press in some quarters, although at the shows themselves, Hackett and his new band received a rapturous reception. The new stage show drew heavily upon the new material although there were a few oldies too.

The tour itinerary took Hackett back to Italy in the summer of 1994 for a series of acoustic concerts with Julian Colbeck, as well as a couple of shows as part of David Palmer's orchestral ensemble playing orchestral variations on the music of Genesis, Yes, Pink Floyd, Queen and Jethro Tull. 1994 also saw Hackett revisit his Blues roots in a big way with an album mixing standards from the Blues repertoire with new tracks written in that vein. This came as a surprise to many, although exactly why is a mystery, because he has never made any secret of his love of the Blues. In fact, several of his earliest musical ventures were on the Blues harmonica, and he recalled auditioning for Genesis with parts of his Blues repertoire. "When I was auditioning for them I ran through a number of things I was able to do, one of which was the Blues harp, consequently I'd wanted to do something in a Blues style as far back as the Sixties and never really had the chance. After years of doing very carefully crafted albums, and meanwhile in my bedroom I would still be practising my blues vibratos, and thinking, 'when can I use this?'"[26] *Blues With A Feeling* also included newly written tracks among the Blues standards he covered, and Hackett's reason for doing this was quite admirable. "I noticed that Blues could be falling into the same trap as Classical music where a certain amount of writers perform wondrous works and we just repeat them endlessly. In the period of the Sixties Blues revival, with bands like Fleetwood Mac doing originals, people didn't seem to mind as much. Maybe the word 'Purist' wasn't bandied about in the same way then, it can be very limiting."[27] Certainly that is not an accusation that can be levelled at Hackett's music, and the album was a wonderful romp and not at all politically correct.

While out on the 1994 Italian tour, or as he likes to put it, "The Italian Job", he got the inspiration for another live album, but this one was certainly different. *There Are Many Sides To The Night* was a faithful rendering of the acoustic shows which he and Julian Colbeck played in Italy in November and December of 1994. The idea behind the album was as ironic as the title. "Well, every time I play Italy there's normally a bootleg album (laughter). There's at least one that gets made from the concerts and I don't think the quality of bootleg recordings is that great so, if you like you can look at this as the Official Bootleg."[28] As an introduction to Hackett's acoustic material and to give a different slant to several of the established rock tracks, this album is hard to beat.

The remainder of 1995 and the early part of 1996 were spent working on a project that surprised Genesis fans on its release. The very idea of Steve Hackett recording an album of Genesis "covers" would have seemed ridiculous to most at the time. He however, sees things quite differently. "I'm always gonna be remembered for those Genesis albums above all, no matter what I do. There's still that, but plainly I also feel that certain things have changed over the years; my own experiences, my own techniques, ability to play. All these techniques have changed so much and I often wondered what those numbers would sound like if they were re-recorded with the technology of now?"[29] Having taken that idea on board, Hackett set about obtaining the services of a band of musicians, many of whom had been associated with Genesis, including Bill Bruford, Chester Thompson and Paul Carrack to name but three. Throughout the project Hackett was very careful not to meddle with anything if it wasn't broken. "I took the philosophy that there was no point in changing everything just for the sake of it, if something was wonderful in the first place I wouldn't rework it, so to some extent some things have been extended."[30]

With his previous involvement in David Palmer's orchestral treatment of the Genesis catalogue on the *We Know What We Like* album in the mid-eighties, Hackett has treated the established Genesis repertoire with great respect, love and above all, humour, and this return visit to his heyday with the band is a delight. He also took to the road for a handful of shows in Japan where the album was initially issued prior to its subsequent release in the UK on 22nd September 1997 with a different running order to its Japanese counterpart. The shows in Japan included both Julian Colbeck, by now no stranger to Steve's live band, along with Chester Thompson and John Wetton. Hackett thoroughly enjoyed himself on the tour, as he explained to *The Waiting Room* Magazine. "It was a very interesting line-up, chock full of pals. We had ten days' rehearsals which was less than I would have liked."[31] The shows from Tokyo on 16th and 17th December 1996 were recorded and subsequently issued as a double live album and initially the show was also broadcast on a "Pay Per View" channel in Japan. Its success continued when Camino released it under the title of *The Tokyo Tapes* in early 1998. As if that wasn't enough living in the past, the long-running US radio show *The King Biscuit Flower Hour* delved into its archives and aired a recording of GTR's concert from the Wiltern Theatre Los Angeles in 1986, itself another welcome addition to the collectors' archives.

Late 1997 and early 1998 saw the re-issue of most of Hackett's back catalogue on his own Camino Records label, which thankfully allowed fans to complete their collections, as his manager, Billy Budis, explained. "With the difficulties we've had with various independent companies we've decided to take control of them ourselves and use them as a launch base for our own record label."[32] In the meantime, Hackett had another unconventional project underway in the form of an acoustic album, accompanied by orchestra, based around the Shakespeare play *A Midsummer Night's Dream.* It was released by the Classics Division of EMI records on 2nd March 1997. Hackett explained how the album came about in an interview given to *The Waiting Room* Magazine in August 1997. "*The Midsummer Night's Dream* came about as a result of a number of acoustic pieces which I'd recorded and had on the back burner, thinking this will probably go out on some small independent label, probably our own, at some point. There won't be any interest from any major record labels. And I found out that, on the contrary, EMI were very interested in my musical activities."[33] The album incorporated several older pieces within the weave of newer pieces written specifically for the project, and the result was one of Hackett's most satisfying albums to date. Amazingly it was also a successful one, the album actually reached the top of the Classical charts in the UK upon its release.

1999 saw Hackett just as busy on a multitude of projects, the most recent of which is his *Darktown* album released by Camino Records on 26th April. A startling album, it certainly makes the listener look hard at themselves and several taboo subject areas, as well as serving as the closest thing to a Hackett autobiography in music yet. It certainly lives up to the description given in the Press Release accompanying the album. "A nightmare theme park of an album from a man truly possessed."[34] It is certainly not for the fainthearted, and gives added weight to the assertion that Hackett is among the most challenging and talented of artists still to be working in the field of rock music in the UK and, with a further two albums planned, one the long-awaited collaborative effort with his brother John, and an album of "standards" featuring Jim Diamond on vocals who also graces Hackett's latest effort. His fans need not worry – this Acolyte's Voyage is far from over!

Steve Hackett UK Solo Discography.

7" & 12" Vinyl Singles.

Children Of The World/Love Is Walking **DAWN DNS100 (7")**
How Can I?/Kim **CHARISMA CB312 (7")**
Narnia (Remixed)/Please Don't Touch **CHARISMA CB318 (7")**
Everyday/Lost Time In Cordoba **CHARISMA CB334 (7")**
Clocks -The Angel Of Mons/Acoustic Set (live) **CHARISMA CB341 (7")**
Clocks -The Angel of Mons/Acoustic Set(live)/Tigermoth (live) **CHARISMA CB341 12 (12") (PS)**
The Show/Hercules Unchained **CHARISMA CB357 (7") (PS)**
Hope I Don't Wake/Tales Of The Riverbank **CHARISMA CB385 (7") (PS)**
Picture Postcard/Theme from "Second /Chance" **CHARISMA CB390 (7") (PS)**
Cell 151/Time-lapse At Milton Keynes **CHARISMA CELL 1 (7") (PS)**
Cell 151/The Air-Conditioned Nightmare (Live)/Time Lapse At Milton Keynes **CHARISMA CELL 12 (12") (PS)**
(This was also a limited edition with a bonus free "white label" copy of the "Clocks" 12" single).
A Doll That's Made In Japan/A Doll That's Made In Japan (instrumental) **LAMBORGHINI LMG16 (7") (PS)**
A Doll That's Made In Japan/Just The Bones **LAMBORGHINI 12MHG16 (12") (PS)**
When The Heart Rules The Mind/Reach Out (Never Say No) **ARISTA GTR1 (7") (PS)** (This edition also appeared as a limited edition with poster "Family Tree" sleeve)
When The Heart Rules The Mind/Reach Out (Never Say No) **ARISTA RECORDS GTRSD1 (7" PICTURE DISC)**
When The Heart Rules The Mind/Reach Out (Never Say No)/Sketches In The Sun/Hackett To Bits **ARISTA RECORDS GTR121 (12") (PS)**
Sailing/Sailing (Instrumental) **EPIC RECORDS EIRS 139 (7") (PS)**
(This was the charity recording made for the "Rock Against Repatriation" project and includes Steve and a host of other celebrities)

PS Denotes a picture sleeved edition.

Vinyl and Compact Disc Albums

Voyage Of The Acolyte **CHARISMA CAS111 1975.**
Voyage Of The Acolyte **VIRGIN CASCD111 1991.**
Please Don't Touch **CHARISMA CDS4012 1978.**
Please Don't Touch **VIRGIN CDSCD4012**
Spectral Mornings **CHARISMA CDS4017**
Spectral Mornings **VIRGIN CDSCD4017**
(Initial copies of the compact disc of "Spectral..." had a bonus spoof track as a run out at the end of the disc).
Defector **CHARISMA CDS4018**
Defector **VIRGIN CDSCD4018**
Cured **CHARISMA CDS4021**
Cured **VIRGIN CDSCD4021**
Highly Strung **CHARISMA HACK**
Highly Strung **VIRGIN HACKCD1**

Bay of Kings	LAMBORGHINI LMGLP3000
Bay of Kings	START SCD10
Bay of Kings	PERMANENT PERMCDL20(*)
Till We Have Faces	LAMBORGHINI LMGLP4000
Till We Have Faces	START SCD11
Till We Have Faces	PERMANENT PERMCDL19(*)
GTR	ARISTA GTR1
GTR	ARISTA ARCD8400
Momentum	START STLP15
Momentum	START SCD15
Momentum	PERMANENT PERMCDL21 *)
Timelapse – Steve Hackett Live	CRISIS 500 001-2
Timelapse – Steve Hackett Live	CAMINO CAMCD11
The Unauthorised Biography	VIRGIN CDVM9014
Guitar Noir	PERMANENT PERMCD13
Guitar Noir	CAMINO CAMCD12(*)
There Are Many Sides To The Night	KUDOS KUDOSCD2.
Blues With A Feeling	PERMANENT PERMCD27
Genesis Revisited	MERCURY PHCR -1454
A Midsummer Night's Dream	EMI 5 56348 2
GTR	KING BISCUIT FLOWER HOUR 70710-88021-2
Genesis Revisited	REEF SRECD704
The Tokyo Tapes	CAMINO CAMCD15
Darktown	CAMINO CAMCD17

(*) Albums marked thus were originally issued on the Lamborghini Records label and subsequent compact disc editions appeared on the START Records label and later on, on Steve's own labels: Permanent, Kudos and Camino. These albums have also subsequently had additional tracks added to them and have been re-mastered.

Mike Rutherford

The Genesis of a Mechanic

Mike Rutherford began his career hoping to be able to play London's Marquee club. Well, he has certainly come a long way since that particular aspiration was fulfilled.

Rutherford's solo recording career began during the respite which followed the end of Genesis' massive *And Then There Were Three* world tour in 1978. With Phil Collins resident in Vancouver both Banks and Rutherford opted to begin writing and recording material for their own solo albums. Previously such events had been very much frowned upon, as Steve Hackett and Peter Gabriel can testify, being perceived as threats to the stability of the band. By this time, however, Genesis was a well established unit both at home and elsewhere and the opportunity to stretch their individual legs, so to speak, appealed to both musicians as Rutherford explained. "I think the feeling was that it was about the right time to do it. Steve Hackett was a little bit unlucky, he left before we reached the stage where the band was successful enough for us to take a year or so off, and it just felt right to have a break from each other and do some solo stuff."[1]

Rutherford's solo effort was the first to be released in 1979. Titled *Smallcreep's Day*, it took its title from a book by Peter Currell-Brown, and was in part a concept album, outlining the fascination of the character Smallcreep with what the end result of his day to day work in a factory might be. Half of the album was given over to this concept and the other half was dedicated to more straightforward songs, although Mike was somewhat worried about the division as he recalls, "I was thinking about writing some shorter songs as well, as I was worried that a whole concept album might be too stodgy – too heavy in a sense."[2] Critically well received, the album also marked a brief reunion with Rutherford's long-time friend and fellow Genesis founder, Anthony Phillips, who contributed keyboard parts to the album. Rutherford, "I hadn't planned to use Ant actually, but by then he was also a very good keyboard player and I thought this was something new, having Ant on keyboards and I was looking to try new and different things."

There were two singles from the album, although neither of these achieved chart success. The B-side of one, "Compression", has a long history, being one of Rutherford's leftovers from a much earlier Genesis recording session. With the return to the punishing schedules of Genesis' subsequent return to action it was to be a further three years before his next solo release.

With a break in Genesis' recording duties after the *Abacab* album and tour, Rutherford returned to the studio to record his second solo album. Once again displaying a fine line in irony, Rutherford called it *Acting Very Strange* and surprised many by taking on the vocal duties himself which certainly gave the album a harder edge than its predecessor. It gained grudging critical acclaim, including these comments from Hugh Fielder of *Sounds*. "If Mike Rutherford's first album dropped too easily into the 'solo-contribution-from-a-member-of-a-famous-band' category, the second makes no such mistake and contains virtually no references to his day job. Instead it contains more references and clues to Mike's own character and musical tastes than he's ever revealed on one piece of vinyl before. The self confidence this requires is there in abundance and suddenly he's not hiding behind the songs anymore."[3]

The album displayed the heavier side of Rutherford's character, as evidenced by such numbers as "Maxine" and "Acting Very Strange", as well as a great sense of humour in "Couldn't Get Arrested". Unusually, he opted to release the album on WEA records rather than Charisma, and the decision to sing himself was driven by a desire to "get it out of his system", as he explains. "I look at it as something that you have to do once in your career. Looking back at the album, bits weren't great but probably what made me realise after that album became a struggle, was that as a songwriter, if you want the best voice in the world to sing you can get someone to do it. So I thought, 'I've probably got it out of my system'. I did it once and it made me decide I'd never do it again. I can't really sing that well."[4]

The album also spawned his first solo promotional video for the song "Halfway There" which included Rutherford in a dream whilst on an aeroplane. It also featured amongst other props, a gigantic saxophone, a bar of chocolate and ten pence piece whose significance is still best known to either Rutherford or the video director. On his return to recording commitments with Genesis, the public were once again deprived of the chance of seeing Rutherford in a solo context, although that would be addressed with his next solo project.

Having decided that the traditional solo album was not the direction to take, Rutherford opted to submerge his identity within a group format and his 1985 project bore the name Mike + The Mechanics. Rutherford's credentials had always been established in the songwriting department, it was what he was good at, and to that end he decided to build a songwriting co-operative around himself – shades of the formative Genesis again. He enlisted the help of BA Robertson and Chris Neil. It was a fortunate pairing; Robertson's ear for a tune and Neil's production abilities enabled Rutherford to enhance his own creativity. Rutherford recalls the process. "Looking back on it, it was a bit like Genesis. I wanted to be a songwriter, so I got together with Chris Neil and BA and we tried to get other people to do our songs. I always believed in that but it didn't really happen. I suppose making a version of 'Silent Running' didn't seem a good song to cover, so once again history was repeating itself."[5]

History was definitely repeating itself in the choice of the other personnel in the band, with Paul Carrack returning to the fold having initially been in the frame as the singer on *Smallcreep's Day*, although Rutherford's method of auditioning people does not match normal expectations. Carrack explained. "I didn't actually audition for that… I bumped into BA Robertson who asked me to sing on a demo for him; he tracked me down. I did that for him and he mentioned that he was writing with Mike for a solo album he was doing, and would I be interested in coming down? So, BA drove me down there one day and they were working on 'Silent Running' and they didn't even have any lyrics so I just sort of la la'd and made it up. I guess that was an audition!"[6]

The album was eventually put together and released after the initial single had achieved some chart success in the USA, and subsequently it achieved a healthy chart position in the UK. A further single from the album, the highly catchy "All I Need Is A Miracle" served notice that Mike + The Mechanics were no flash in the pan. Once again Rutherford recycled some of the abandoned ideas for this album. For example for one part of the track "A Call To Arms" Rutherford recalls, "It was a Genesis bit. The main sequence had been discarded from the Genesis album before (*Genesis*) and I always liked it, so I tried to do it and it didn't come out right. I had a couple of people play on it from a band I'd produced."[7]

The rest of the personnel for the band were selected including veteran singer Paul Young from the sadly defunct Sad Café, who together with Paul Carrack was to form the vocal heart of the new band. Young's introduction was equally as accidental as Carrack's as he recalls. "I got a phone call from Chris Neil and he said, 'I'm doing a solo album for Mike Rutherford, do you want to come down and sing?' So I went down and the first track I tried was 'All I Need Is A Miracle', and they seemed pretty pleased with it and said it was cool for me to do a couple more. So I did, and I got a nice cheque thinking that was the end of it! (laughter). Then I got a call about three months later saying that 'Silent Running' and 'Miracle' had been top and five respectively in America, and we had another one on the boil and did I want to go over there and tour with them. So we became the Mike + The Mechanics touring band almost by default really."[8]

Rutherford had finally found his songwriting collective and the success of the first album and US-only tour of June/July 1986, enabled him to finally establish himself as a bona fide songwriter with a wider range of styles than ever displayed within Genesis. The album appealed to traditional Genesis fans, as well as those who were blissfully unaware of Rutherford's pedigree, making the album one of the great success stories of 1986. All this happened just prior to Genesis' massive *Invisible Touch* tour, making it an incredibly successful year for the band and their offshoots. However the activities surrounding this success precluded Rutherford even contemplating a follow-up to the Mike + The Mechanics album for some two years. Nonetheless, during the spring and summer of 1988, Rutherford and the band returned to the studio to prove that the success of the first album had not been a fluke.

The initial single "Nobody's Perfect" was released in November 1988, and charted in the UK top ten. Its rockier nature established Rutherford's talents as a rock guitarist, but it was to be the second single, released early in 1989 which was once and for all, to establish Mike + The Mechanics as a force to be reckoned with. The single "The Living Years", a personal exorcism of Rutherford's grief at the recent loss of his father, took the UK charts by storm – reaching the number two slot and similar positions elsewhere around the world. The success of the single took even Rutherford by surprise. "I don't think that we thought it was going to be a big hit. At the time of doing it, I was working with Brian and we'd both lost our fathers, so it was a very emotional time. That song was so emotional that we thought it might not work. So BA and I said we'll try it and if it comes out sugary and sickly, we'll forget it."[9]

The album displayed a wider range of material than its predecessor, including several out and out rock tracks which, when combined with the more traditionally melodic songs on it, gained the band a huge audience across the UK and Europe. The resulting *Living Years* tour of 1989 took in most of the major theatre venues in Europe, as well as the band's first handful of gigs in the UK to a rapturous welcome from audiences. A further single was released later in 1989 to round off the year nicely for the band.

Strangely enough, Rutherford did not fully capitalise on the increasingly long gaps between Genesis records to produce a further album. Work on the next Mike + The Mechanics album did not begin until late 1990 and it proved a difficult one for the band, for Rutherford and for producer Russ Titelman, who was not the right man for the job. Mike remembers, "I decided to make a change in the choice of producer. Russ was originally producing it and although I like his work very much, it just didn't seem to work. On the second day I said to everyone in the band, 'I don't think this is going to work' and they all said, 'Oh, give it a try'. Sometimes things would go great but after about two and a half months, I wasn't enjoying it and found myself driving to work slowly! (laughter)"[10]

The resultant album *Word Of Mouth* was a lacklustre affair compared to its predecessor, and although there were certain sparks of magic on it, on the whole it is an album which falls between two stools, as Mike himself admits. "Chris Neil came back, and we weeded out some songs, but by then the whole thing had become a bit of a problem. I'd lost interest and it was laboured. I'm sure that was reflected on the album, but having said that, some stuff was very good. 'Get Up' I like very much, and 'Word Of Mouth' as well. There's a bit more drive to it, but the Mechanics are more about moods and atmospheres and somehow I think that was missing from this album."[11]

In all, there were three singles although none of them emulated the success of the previous record, and with no tour, due in large part to Rutherford's return to Genesis, *Word of Mouth* was to be very much an undervalued album.

Late 1991 and 1992 saw Rutherford fully occupied with writing and touring commitments for Genesis' hugely successful *We Can't Dance*. He finally returned to his own recording studio to begin work on the next Mechanics album in early 1994 with high expectations for this project and, as it proved, those expectations were to be correct.

First indications of the nature of the new album appeared upon the release of the first single, the infectiously catchy "Over My Shoulder" which stormed up the UK charts upon its release in February 1995. The album *Beggar On A Beach Of Gold* was in hot pursuit and soon reached the top five in the UK charts. If the previous album was a strain, the problems attached to this one were much more palatable as Mike recalls. "I was very pleased with this album. As I said before, to me the Mechanics are more about moods and atmospheres, and this album is more like that. I had great difficulty selecting the tracks for this one; there were six that I thought were definite and seven that could be there and I could chop and choose."[12]

Without doubt this album was the band's "coming of age". There was not a duff track on it, and the writing team was now expanded to included both Paul Young and Paul Carrack, something which brought an even wider range of styles into the pot and made for a much more satisfying album. Promotion in the UK began with a massive tour of provincial theatres in June/July 1995. In all, three singles were released with each one achieving a respectable position in the charts. The band were also invited to play a handful of shows in South Africa, which happened to coincide with the Rugby Union World Cup. For a band as sport mad as the Mechanics this was an added bonus as Paul Young recalls: "I was very pleased to be there while the rugby was on. They just booed us forever when we wore the rugby shirts. We all got into rugby last year and went to all the matches, and sat surrounded by thousands of green shirts and there was one thin line of white shirts, it was great."[13]

To consolidate upon this hard won success, the Mechanics released a compilation album of their greatest hits in March of 1996, accompanying it by another massive UK tour and the promotional blurb on the album I think sums up the attitude of the band and their fans. "For a part-time band, the Mechanics have enjoyed huge success around the globe. It's not just the wrinklies who like a good tune ya know."[14]

Mike and the Mechanics have certainly proven that point with audiences that span the entire gamut of age ranges, and refreshingly their audience is not exclusively Genesis fans, indeed many still have no idea that the tall guy on bass and guitar has a full time day job!

Mike Rutherford/ Mike + The Mechanics UK Discography

7" and 12" Vinyl Singles

Working In Line/Compression	**CB353 (7")**
At The End Of The Day/Overnight Job	**CB364 (7" PS)**
Halfway there/A day to remember	**K79331 (7" PS)**
Acting Very Strange/Couldn't Get Arrested (nix mix)	**RUTH1 (7" PS)**
Acting Very Strange (Extended) Couldn't Get Arrested (extended nix mix)	**RUTH1T (12" PS)**
Hideaway/Calypso	**U9967 (7")**
Silent running/I get the feeling	**U8908 (7" PS)**
Silent running/I get the feeling/Too far gone	**U8908T (12" PS)**
Silent running/I get the feeling	**U8908P (7" PICTURE DISC)**
All I Need Is A Miracle/You Are The One	**U8765 (7" PS)**
All I Need Is A Miracle(remix) You Are The One/A Call To Arms	**U8765T (12" PS)**
All I Need Is A Miracle (Remix) You Are The One/A Call To Arms	**U8765P (12" PICTURE DISC)**
Nobody's Perfect/Nobody Knows	**U7789 (7" PS)**
Nobody's Perfect/Nobody Knows/All I Need Is A Miracle	**U7789T (12" PS)**
The Living Years/Too Many Friends	**U7717 (7" PS)**
The Living Years/Too Many Friends/I Get The Feeling (live)	**U7717T (12" PS)**
Nobody Knows/Why Me?	**U7602 (7" PS)**

Nobody Knows/Why Me?/Nobody's Perfect **U7602T (12" PS)**
Word Of Mouth/Let's Pretend It Didn't Happen **VS1345 (7" PS)**
Word Of Mouth/Let's Pretend It Didn't Happen **VST1345 (12" PS)**
A Time And Place/Yesterday, Today, Tomorrow **VS1351 (7" PS)**
A Time And Place/Yesterday, Today, Tomorrow/Word Of Mouth (East West Mix)/**VST1351 (12" PS)**
Get Up/I Think I've Got The Message **VS1359 (7" PS)+**
Stop Baby/Get Up **VS1376 (7" PS)**
Everybody Gets A Second Chance/The Way You Look At Me **VS1396 (7" PS)**
Over My Shoulder/Something To Believe In **VS1526 (7" PS) #**

+ This single was withdrawn from the stores and its b-side used on the CD of "Stop baby".
# This single was a limited edition numbered edition.

Compact Disc Singles

The Living Years/Too Many Friends/I Get The Feeling (Live) **U7717 CD (PS)**
Nobody's Perfect/Nobody's Perfect(extended)/Nobody Knows **U7789 CD (PS)**
Nobody Knows/Why Me/Nobody Knows **U7602 CD (PS)**
Word Of Mouth/Let's Pretend It Didn't Happen **VSCD1345 (PS)**
Word Of Mouth/Taken In(live)/Let's Pretend It Didn't Happen **VSCDX1345** (Limited edition numbered sleeve)
A Time And Place/Yesterday, Today, Tomorrow/Word Of Mouth (East West Mix) **VSCD1351 (PS)**
A Time And Place/Yesterday, Today, Tomorrow/Word Of Mouth (East West Mix) VSCDX 1351 (Limited edition photo wallet edition)
Get Up/I Think I've Got The Message/Before The Next Heartache Falls **VSCDG1359 (PS)** (withdrawn from stores)
Stop Baby/Get Up/Before The Next Heartache Falls **VSCDG1376 (PS)** (Part 1 of 2 part digipak)
Stop Baby/I Think I've Got The Message/My Crime Of Passion (Acoustic version) **VSCDT1376 (PS)** (Part 2 of 2 part digipak)
Everybody Gets A Second Chance/The Way You Look At Me/At The End Of The Day **VSCD 1396 (PS)**
Everybody Gets A Second Chance/The Way You Look At Me/At The End Of The Day **VSCDX1396 (PS)** (Limited edition with sheet music)
Over My Shoulder/Something To Believe In/Always The Last To Know **VSCDG1526 (PS)** (Part 1 of 2 part digipak)
Over My Shoulder/Something To Believe In/Word Of Mouth/Over My Shoulder (Live) **VSCDX1526 (PS)** (Part 2 of 2 part digipak)
Beggar On A Beach Of Gold(Edit)/Help Me/Nobody Told Me **VSCDT1535 (PS)** (Part 1 of 2 part digipak)
Beggar On A Beach Of Gold/Boys At The Front/Little Boy/Beggar On A Beach Of Gold (acoustic version) **VSCDX1535 (PS)** (Part 2 of 2 part digipak)
Another Cup Of Coffee/You Never Change/You Don't Know What Love Is **VSCDG1554 (PS)** (Part 1 of 2 part digipak)
Another Cup Of Coffee/The Living Years/Everyday Hurts/How Long? **VSCDX1554 (PS)** (Part 2 of 2 part digipak) (Limited edition in embossed box with set of postcards tracks 2-4 are from the Simon Mayo Radio Session)
All I Need Is A Miracle '96/The Way You Look At Me/Don't **VSCDT1576 (PS)**
All I Need Is A Miracle '96/Get Up(live)/Over My Shoulder (live)/All I Need Is A Miracle'96 (radio edit) **VSCDG576 (PS)**
Silent Running/Stop Baby/Plain & Simple **VSCDT 1585 (PS)**
Now That You've Gone (radio edit)/A Beggar On A Beach Of Gold (live)/Silent running (live) **VSCDT1732 (PS)** (Part 1 of 2 part digipak)
Now That You've Gone/I Believe (When I Fall In Love It Will Be Forever) (live)/Word Of Mouth (live) **VSCDX1732 (PS)** (Part 2 of 2 part digipak)

Now That You've Gone / A Beggar On A Beach Of Gold (live) / Silent Running (live) **VIRGIN VSCDT1732 (PS)**

Now That You've Gone / I believe (When I Fall In Love It Will Be Forever) (live) / Word Of Mouth (live) **VIRGIN VSCDX 1732 (PS)**

Whenever I Stop / Now That You've Gone (live) / Whenever I Stop (unplugged) **VIRGIN VSCDX1743 (PS)**

Whenever I Stop / Ordinary Girl (unplugged) / My Little Island (live) **VIRGIN VSCDX1743 (PS)**

PS denotes a picture sleeve edition.

Vinyl and Compact Disc albums

Smallcreep's Day	**CHARISMA**	**CAS1149/CASCD1149 (CD)**
Acting Very Strange	**WEA**	**WEA K 99249/80015-2 (CD)**
Mike + The Mechanics	**WEA**	**252 496-1/252496-2 (CD)**
Living Years	**WEA**	**WX 203 256004-1/256 004-2 (CD)**
Word Of Mouth	**VIRGIN**	**V2662/CDV2662 (CD)**
Beggar On A Beach Of Gold	**VIRGIN**	**CDV2772 (CD)**
Hits	**VIRGIN**	**CDV2797 (CD)**
Mike & The Mechanics	**VIRGIN**	**CDV2885 (CD)/(MD)**

ASSOCIATED ARTISTS AND TRIBUTE ALBUMS.

Over the years there have been a few recordings issued by musicians associated with the band especially the longstanding "live band" members, Daryl Stuermer and Chester Thompson. There have also been an increasing number of "Tribute" albums to the band and their work. The following are details of the most easily available albums in both category.

DALE NEWMAN SOLO ALBUM.

Dale has been in the service of the band since he was enlisted as Mike's guitar technician way back in 1973. Since then he has not only continued in that position but is now responsible for the day to day administration of the group's recording studio: The Farm. Dale's first recorded work was as one of the vocalists on Anthony Phillips' Sides album in 1978 and he has only recently decided to "go solo" himself initially with a CD EP of songs and currently with a full blown album in progress.

The Eyes Have It **DECISION PRODUCTS DP1306206-2 1998.**

DARYL STUERMER SOLO ALBUMS.

Daryl is no stranger to Genesis fans being the guy who bravely stepped into Steve Hackett's shoes in 1977 and continued as the band's live guitarist until 1992. In addition of course, he has also been in all of Phil Collins' live bands since Phil went solo in 1982. Initially Daryl released a series of albums with his brother in the mid Seventies under the generic title of Sweetbottom – the only album for which details are readily available is as follows:

Sweetbottom **ELEKTRA RECORDS K52110 1978.**

Daryl has more recently released two albums of his own music and although these are not commercially available here in the UK, they are nonetheless, well worth trying to track down.

Steppin' Out	**GRP RECORDS A-9573 (LP)**
Steppin' Out	**GRP RECORDS D-9573 (CD)**
Daryl Stuermer Urban Island Music	**(NO CATALOGUE NUMBER)**

CHESTER THOMPSON SOLO ALBUMS.

Chester has long been regarded as the "backbone" of Genesis' live sound and fans have often wondered what a solo album by this genius of the percussion would sound like. In 1991 they got their wish when Chester finally released his first and so far only solo album; *A Joyful*

Noise. Initially only available in the USA it was released in the UK and Europe in May of this year by Steve Hackett's Camino Records.

A Joyful Noise — MOO RECORDS RZ 79341 (CD)
A Joyful Noise — CAMINO RECORDS CAMCD16

RAY WILSON SOLO ALBUMS/SINGLES.

As "Guaranteed Pure"

Guaranteed Pure — RECORD COMPANY/CATALOGUE NUMBER UNKNOWN
Outpatients '93 — DICK BROTHERS D DICK 1 CD

(This was a compilation album of tracks from artists who had recorded at the Funny Farm recording Studios for former Marillion front man – Fish's record company. Guaranteed Pure's contribution to the album was the track; "Swing your bag").

As Stiltskin

The Mind's Eye — WHITE WATER RECORDS/VIRGIN 7243 8399522-6-PM527 (CD) (UK)
The Mind's Eye — EASTWEST RECORDS 61785-2 (CD) (US) 1994.

(Both versions of this album contained a different running order and differing tracks)

Inside/America/Inside (Extended version) White Water Records CD Single LEV1CD 1994 (PS)

Footsteps/Sunshine & Butterflies(Live)/Footsteps (Extended Version)
White Water Records CD Single — WWR D2 1994 (PS)

Rest In Peace/The Poltroon/Inside (Acoustic Version) WHITE WATER RECORDS CD SINGLE WWR D3 1995 (PS)

All of the above singles were also released as vinyl and cassette editions.

As Cut

Another Day/I Hear You Calling/Adolescent Breakdown (Monitor Mix) Virgin Germany CD Single 8 95634 2 8/2/99 (PS)

Millionairhead — VIRGIN GERMANY (CD) 8 47060 8/3/99

GENESIS "TRIBUTE" ALBUMS

Over the past few years the growth of the "Tribute" band has inspired a cottage industry of bands recreating the music of their heroes live on stage and Genesis have been well served by their own tributes both at home and further afield.

Various Artists "The River Of Constant Change" (Double CD) MELLOW RECORDS MMP270
Various Artists "Supper's Ready" — MAGNA CARTA RECORDS MA 9004-2
ReGenesis "ReGenesis Live" — MYSTIC RECORDS MYSCD112 1997.
Various Artists "The Fox Lies Down" — EAGLE RECORDS EAGCD057 1998.
ReGenesis "Here it comes again" — MYSTIC RECORDS MYSCD126 1999.

Anthony Phillips

Putting Together the Parts and Pieces

Just when Genesis seemed to be gaining some critical respect, Anthony Phillips chose to leave, a decision that almost finished the band. In fact, as both Mike Rutherford and Tony Banks admit, his departure was the only time when the remaining members felt that they could not continue. Phillips' contribution to the *Trespass* album was considerable, and it remains one of Genesis' finest efforts. Phillips' reasons for leaving the band were both artistic and temperamental, but he still remains certain that he made the correct decision.

Immediately after his departure, Phillips resolved to continue to study music, a decision influenced by several classical pieces he had been listening to at the time. "I suddenly had this feeling that I must be able to control an orchestra, and learn to orchestrate. Therefore it was a question of learning to write music down."[1] He spent the years after his departure gaining a licentiate degree from the Royal College of Music in London, initially drawing his income from teaching music – something he may yet return to in later life. His first foray into the world of commercial music after his departure from Genesis, was to be the much vaunted but sadly unreleased composition 'Silver Song', written in 1969 as a tribute to the original Genesis drummer, John Silver. This putative single featured Phillips along with Mike Rutherford and Phil Collins, and was to have been released under Phil Collins name, but was shelved by Charisma and has yet to see the light of day. Many other pieces of music and songs were co-written by Phillips and Rutherford during the early seventies, and a couple of these have recently seen the light of day on the re-issues of Phillips' albums. The collaboration also produced the hymn "Take This Heart", released on a Charisma album of religious songs in 1975, now one of the most collectable items in Phillips' catalogue. "I just asked the music master at Charterhouse if he'd entertain the idea and he said yes. I took down a rough score as I didn't know how to write down the vocal parts. Brian Roberts did the live recording in the Chapel at Charterhouse. I loved it, to us it was very thrilling, it reminded us of our school days in a way. It was very much co-written lyrically."[2]

Creative collaboration with Mike Rutherford was eventually to lead to the first proper Anthony Phillips solo album in 1977. *The Geese And The Ghost* began life in the mid-seventies, however trends and tour schedules were to conspire against it, as

Anthony explained. "It began as a partnership between Mike and myself. It was when Genesis did *The Lamb*, and as that became a double album, Mike couldn't afford the time, so it just became impractical to continue working that way. He felt more comfortable making it and calling it my solo album, which was probably fair enough."[3] With no interest from any record companies to speak of, it was recorded under quite primitive conditions on board Tom Newman's floating studio on a canal at Little Venice, in London. The process was not entirely without incident as Anthony remembers. "It had to be done on the cheap, and Tom's barge was going through teething problems, and so was the studio on it! We kept having breakdowns all the time, and the barge also kept on being rammed by other barges."[4]

Despite the problems, the album was finally released in March 1977 on Charisma's subsidiary Hit & Run Records, in fact it was their first release. The album also appeared on Passport Records in the USA, the first of a long-standing record deal that served Phillips well until the late 1980's. As a first effort the album was a great surprise to original Genesis fans, and drew upon all of Phillips' musical influences to create a many-layered soundscape that was totally unique. Perhaps the most interesting aspect of this album is the history of some of the pieces. "I think one can divide the material on it mainly between two eras. Some of it represents bits and pieces from what I used to call 'the 1969 era' of writing with Mike Rutherford – stuff we used to do on twelve strings. 'Collections' was from that period, from '69 on piano and a lot of the stuff from *The Geese and the Ghost* itself also dates from that period, but not all of it. The next bulk of material was from just after I left the band, because in the final four or five months nobody seemed to be writing anything or if they were it was in secret. So after I left, after having done very little creative work, there was a great outpouring of material. All of the stuff like 'God If I Saw Her Now', 'Which Way The Wind Blows' and most of 'Henry' all came steaming out."[5]

However, the delay in releasing the album meant that when it finally emerged it was into the new dawn of the Punk era. As such, it was crucified by the press eager to jump on the new bandwagon that labelled any recording artist of Anthony's ilk as being at best redundant and at worst pretentious. This was an accusation which cannot be levelled at Anthony's music by anyone who has really listened to it, and many observers contest that the album still represents one of Phillips' finest moments, although at the time he had his reservations about recording more material. "After putting all that effort into *The Geese & The Ghost* there didn't seem to be much point. I found that if I stopped to think about it I couldn't face the fact that I'd put all this effort into the album and nothing had happened. So I just had to keep working to not think about it..."[6] The creative effort expended during this period was to result in several later projects.

"During the first part of 1976 I recorded things like 'Tregenna Afternoons', I did all of the 'Macbeth' project which ended up as 'Reaper', and parts of the 'Scottish Suite', loads and loads of things, we did all the first demos of 'Tarka'".[7] The proliferation of material banked by Phillips from this period was to serve him well over the next few years. His US record company, Passport Records who had the initial faith to release his first album, continued although they made it clear that ideally they required something more commercial than *The Geese & the Ghost*. "Anyway, it was songs that they wanted, and I was able to draw upon quite a lot from this period. Like 'Birdsong', for example, which was from just after I left Genesis – especially the verse. 'Regrets' was from a couple of years before. 'Squirrel' was from straight after Genesis, 'Paperchase' was written in 1976. Some of the songs I wrote were completely new stuff, 'We're All As We Lie', 'Moonshooter', 'Pulling Faces' was another new one. Also 'Wise After The Event' had that guitar riff which was very much a new Rickenbacker big sound with funny sorts of pedals and things. 'Now What (Are They Doing To My Little Friends?)' was inspired by an awful TV programme about blokes culling seals, and so the album was a mix of old, middling and new."[8]

The new album, titled *Wise After The Event* drew upon a wider range of material than its more pastorally tinged predecessor, even spawning Phillips' first UK single' "We're All As We Lie". It was coupled with two non-album tracks, "Squirrel" and "Sitars & Nebulous", which were omitted due to lack of space, making the single another major collector's item. The album also included an impressive array of additional talents including Mike Giles (King Crimson), John Perry and orchestrator Jeremy Gilbert. Production was by Rupert Hine, already making a name for himself in that field and no mean musician in his own right. He remembers the album fondly. "I was always interested in pushing Anthony to do the singing himself and some days he'd feel good about that, some days he'd feel that other people could be doing it better. There were pressures from the record company and management side but on this album we tried very much to pursue the course of Anthony's character being his voice as much as his guitar."[9] John Perry also remembers *Wise After The Event.* "Well, basically it hurt! I must admit it took me a little while, probably half a day to understand where Anthony was coming from. When somebody like Anthony comes along it's not like painting by numbers, it's not something that falls into a pattern. Anthony has a very personalised style and you're trying to contribute to that, it's a case of stopping and putting your thinking cap on."[10]

Certainly the fans had to put their thinking caps on, even when looking at the album sleeve which, once again, bore a staggeringly original piece of artwork by Phillips' friend Peter Cross. It included an amazing array of zany characters over its gatefold sleeve. However, by now the fierce detractors in the British music press had little time for the progressive music that they themselves had lauded so fiercely only three years previously, and reviews tended to vary from totally antagonistic to deprecating at best. To his fans, however, *Wise After The Event* was a fine follow up to his opening salvo but with commercial success still elusive in an increasingly hostile marketplace, the question remained "What do I do next?"

1979 was to prove a memorable year for the British public in many ways. Margaret Thatcher became our first woman Prime Minister, and a winter of discontent blew through the country. Meanwhile, musically the UK was in the grip of the "New Wave". Into this atmosphere of aggression and frustration Phillips released what were to prove to be two of his finest albums, *Sides*, and the first of what is now a series of albums all bearing the generic title, *Private Parts & Pieces.* Far from being an inhabitant of some remote ivory tower, he too, was clearly affected by the ongoing mood of frustration and anger in the UK music business at this time, and this shines through on several of the tracks on the *Sides* album. The opening track 'Um and Aargh' a clear reference to record company pressures and the hypocrisy of the music press. "Coming back into the scene and trying to make my name, being at the mercy of the press was pretty tough actually... you heard these stories about A&R men who really didn't have a clue – they were very posey."[11]

The album includes several of Phillips' finest tracks, including the lyrically gorgeous "I Want Your Love" and "Bleak House" but this was not enough to save the album from the surgery of the record company. "There were two completely instrumental pieces, one twelve string which could have been a *Geese And The Ghost* thing, and another synth-based piece which would have preceded 'Slow Dance' by about ten years. Rupert Hine was very keen to go with those, being an instrumental composer himself. But he was getting his instructions from the record company."[12] Rupert confirms this view himself. "I don't think *Sides* gained a lot by the attempts at more commercial songwriting; outside singers and so on. You can hear these attempts to make the music more widely appealing for better or worse."[13] Other problems beset the album, including pressure to complete the recording process which had the knock-on effect of squeezing the amount of time available for rehearsal and preparation. "The thing that was iffy about the album was the fact that my overdubbing time got really squeezed. We started off in style if you like, and ended in style mixing at Trident but the middle part was dodgy. We did the overdubs at this place called Matrix which was dreadful! I wanted to spend more time on 'Nightmare' on the overdubs, but it all had to be done extremely quickly – it was almost a case of getting all the overdubs done in a day."[14]

With the added help of such excellent musicians as Mike Giles and John Perry, the album managed to rise above these problems. It presented a truer picture of Phillips talents, both as a songwriter and instrumentalist capable of writing material of more worth than the pop culture into which the album was born. At the same time as this album, another appeared which displayed the rich legacy of Phillips' instrumental talents. *Private Parts and Pieces* was to serve as the template for a whole series of albums encompassing all the facets of music which Phillips has explored. Initially released in the USA, in the UK the album was subsequently included as a limited edition free with the first five thousand copies of the *Sides* album, a generous gesture towards his fans. The album includes archival material from the mid '70's, mainly acoustic guitar and piano pieces. "Home recording studios didn't really stretch to doing anything with much scope or a great number of tracks on it. So, I just used to record acoustic guitar and piano pieces".[15] The mixture of elements on the album served as a useful indicator of the influences which have guided his music, and a couple of the tracks have a lengthy pedigree. "'Field Of Eternity' was an early long instrumental which I took the guitar piece out."[16] Phillips freely admits that he was lucky in having an abundance of music from which he could select a "best of" so-to-speak. The exigencies of the music business did not make for plain sailing with the album, however. "When I took the tapes to Trident studios to master it, Ray Staff had to do a lot of work on it as there were so many problems."[17] Phillips had done most of the recording in his home studio that was not as well equipped as a commercial studio. "There's all sorts of weird and wonderful things going on if you listen to the album closely. In fact, some of the instruments themselves are quite surprising on an album by a supposed "rock" artist, including a harmonium, and a "pin" piano which in fact was an ordinary piano with drawing pins under the hammers to create a harpsichord effect!"[18] The album was never intended to break into the mass commercial market and by now the situation for "serious" musicians was practically untenable in the UK, unless you were already an established name. Into this atmosphere was born the second of the *Private Parts & Pieces* albums, subtitled, *Back To The Pavilion*. Indicative of Phillips' increasing frustration with the music scene in the UK was the dedication on the back cover: "This album is dedicated to all those who still champion the 'Old Fashioned' ideals of beauty, lyricism and grandeur in art against the tide of cynical intellectualism and dissonance." He was not prepared to meekly collaborate with the ongoing butchery of the music that had been his mainspring and inspiration currently going on in Britain, and particularly the cynical attitude of the music press against whom he had already fired a salvo on *Sides*. His attitude has become even harder since then. "That was really cynical with the turncoats that one day had been praising bands and the next day, when the new thing was in, started rubbishing them."[19]

The album was the first of a whole batch that only appeared in the USA, because of the contractual situation (or lack of it) in the UK. "Following the so-called commercial albums, *Wise After The Event* hadn't done anything, and when *Sides* hadn't been the great commercial top ten hit that they thought it would be, that contract went. This was before RCA, but I had an existing contract with Passport and so the only outlet for this album was through them."[20] Once again, Phillips found himself having to draw on existing material for the album. "There were no advances coming from them so the music that could be used had to be available, hence the use of guitar and piano."[21] Included in this list was the "Scottish Suite" ostensibly written for an ambitious project based around Shakespeare's play *Macbeth*, to set the dialogue to music composed by rock musicians. Sponsored initially by Genesis' publishers Fuse Music, the project never really got off the ground. However, the album itself was another intriguing mixture of music including several further pieces dating back to the early Seventies, including "I Saw You Today", and "Back To The Pavilion". Finally the missing "links" from *Wise After The Event* were also included, and the eventual CD re-issue of the album also included another delightful classic, "Lucy An Illusion".

Late 1980 saw Phillips without a record deal in the UK and with the wind set fair against his style of music, his only avenue was his existing deal with American record company Passport Records who were to remain his champions throughout most of the decade until their eventual demise in 1988. With the relative lack of success of both previous attempts at song-oriented records, the question was even more "What do I do now?" as Anthony himself recalls. "It was a question of trying to look for a different angle that didn't require a lot of money, but wasn't an acoustic album."[22] Phillips had been contacted earlier in the year to write the theme and incidental music for a TV series called *Rule Britannia*. Having been given far greater leeway on the composition he decided to use his recently acquired synthesisers on the project and with a certain amount of cross-referencing the music began to take on an extra dimension. "During the summer of 1980 I did actually record what became the Prelude separately to the whole plan. That was done out of the blue; I just had an idea and I recorded it very quickly in about three or four hours. The Anthem was done in a similar way."[23]

At last Phillips was being paid to be inventive in the studio, and the resulting music was startlingly original in both its style and its use in the six programmes of the series. It was during this period that he began to pick up TV and jingle work, very much a composer's stock in trade, and it is this area of endeavour that has increasingly featured in Phillips' work schedule. At the outset of the *Rule Britannia* project he was intending to use a Polymoog piece which he had left over from *Sides* which encouraged him to explore further in this area aided by his friend Richard Scott who worked with him on the album. "I started working on this extra keyboard piece, which I wanted to be a more modern, short five-minute piece – and that ended up as the whole album."[24] Recording was no easy process, only having access to 8-track facilities and all the percussion tracks having to be individually recorded and then the whole thing transferred on to 16-track which involved a multitude of sub-edits. "It was a complete nightmare for the engineer, Chris David, because it was all in sections as there were a lot of cuts and changes. I'd put some edits into pieces to lay the guide synth parts down, so he had to take the edits apart and then put them back together again at the sixteen track stage."[25] Nor was composing the music for the TV series a piece of cake either, as Anthony recalls. "I was handed a list of words like 'Greed' and 'Irony'. I had to sit and write ideas to 'Greed'! The *Rule Britannia* team was quite exceptional – they were all very interested not just to listen to the title music but to listen to all the music I'd done. I think I was lucky, I think television work isn't normally like that."[26]

Intriguingly, Phillips also wrote a symphony at the same time, and the *Rule Britannia* signature tune was one of the major themes from it. Sadly the symphony itself has yet to see the light of day. RCA Records signed Phillips on the strength of the album and even went as far to release a single coupling "Prelude '84" with "Anthem 1984" which was awarded "Single of the Week" status by *Record Mirror* in July 1981. The album itself also garnered a complimentary press, although an instrumental album was never going to give Phillips his big break, unless attached to a major film or TV series. Nevertheless, the album was a refreshing change, and the idea of longer conceptual pieces of music linked by a common theme or story was to be further investigated, as both Anthony and Richard Scott continued their partnership. Next they embarked upon a foray into the world of musicals – so often fraught with pitfalls.

As if the prospect of being involved full-time in a musical wasn't enough, Phillips also found time during late 1981/82 to compile another of the generic *Private Parts & Pieces* albums. *Antiques* was to be the third in the series to date. Unlike its predecessors however, this album was more of a collaborative effort between Phillips and his Argentine friend Henrique Berro Garcia. "I got together with Quique and played some music informally. I took round some of my duets which I'd actually scored, such as 'Old Wives Tale' and some parts of the 'Hurlingham Suite'. It was a great time that summer (1981). I remember about the time that '1984' came out I did the 'Masquerade' stuff with Richard at Send, I also did a lot of stuff with Dennis Quinn; I helped him record his first lot of demos about that time as well."[27] Musically the album was purely driven by the informal 'jams' that the two musicians performed often in the evening after dinner, and the relaxed atmosphere of these shines through in the music. With one or two exceptions, the music also broke with the tradition of the series by using new music rather than archival material. "It was all pretty much new stuff. We started off saying that we should keep it simple, and then we got one or two ideas for slight variations like at the end of 'Old Wives Tale' where all those extra guitars come in and we started dubbing up a bit."[28] The entire process of recording took a little over a month, although listening to the music gives no indication of the brevity of the project and it is to the enduring credit of both musicians that this is the case.

Unusually for an album in this series, *Antiques* was also released in the UK as well as the USA, although this was more down to good luck than planning. "RCA still had me on board, although '1984' didn't do what they wanted it to do. This wasn't the next proper album as far as they were concerned and they weren't interested in it. Tony Smith managed to persuade them to put it out over here. He had to insist that they put it out for an advance of £1! The pressure was already building up for what eventually became *Invisible Men*. The usual thing happened with Passport, it just drifted out in the States without any great fanfare."[29] The album's relaxed aura gives no indication of the trials and tribulations that lay in wait over the next two or so years, mainly concerning a young lady by the name of *Alice*.

Rock musicians and musicals have had a somewhat chequered history originating with Pete Townshend's opus *Tommy* in the mid 1960's. Very few, if any, musicians have made the transition successfully. So what exactly motivated Anthony to try his hand at something so radically different to the fields in which he had been working? The *Alice* project evolved out of another musical effort, a putative attempt to transfer Kit Williams' book *Masquerade* onto the musical stage. Phillips' involvement was supposed to be very much on the sidelines and stemmed from his association with producer Rupert Hine and his manager Tony Smith. However, Rupert's schedule with many of the then "in" musicians of the current New Wave of the English music scene, meant that Phillips gradually became more involved. "I wrote lots and lots of stuff. We eventually got three or four demos out, which were OK, but it never felt cohesive at all."[30] Rumours abounded that Kate Bush and big names were to take part, but sadly none of these high flown ideas ever came about, and Phillips was left with a plethora of material which he was determined to develop further. In order to progress that goal, he turned to his friend Richard Scott with whom he developed several pieces. "With encouragement from Tony Smith we demoed four or five songs which worked out pretty well. The funny thing is that not much in *Alice* came through from *Masquerade* but some pieces were influenced and inspired by it."[31] A suggestion was made that the pair contact Leeds Playhouse, an innovative theatre company on the lookout for something more adventurous. As Phillips recalls. "There was the idea that a new dream team comprising Richard's ideas, coupled with Nicholas Hytner's theatrical experience and know-how, would manage to carve a brilliant product."[32] Nicholas Hytner has since gone on to achieve major musical success with *Miss Saigon* and also the recent Oscar nominated film *The Madness of King George* and so, even back then, it was an enthralling prospect.

Not quite so enthralling was the prospect of spending a wintry March in Leeds, especially with a Germanic landlady who, if Phillips is to be believed resembled one of Wagner's Valkyries! Phillips and Scott spent most of 1983 working on full demos for the musical after Leeds Playhouse commissioned them, and by the end of that year there were about eight songs shaped up. The discipline of a musical however, does not rely solely on the music. Drama is the most important aspect and if the music doesn't fit, the music must be changed, as Phillips recalls. "The great discipline I learned was that in most of the songs the action has to flow through them. You can't have frozen moments where you are talking about an emotion – except for the odd ballad."[33] If nothing else he gained a far wider experience of musical styles, having to write pieces from quadrilles to boogie woogie for the project. "There were a couple of set pieces with three washerwomen-type characters doing a silly sort of dance, and I had to learn boogie woogie for one track called 'Duck and Dive'. It was a million miles away from working with Genesis, and that was quite good actually. However, I'd have to sit in a rehearsal room learning how to do it – so much for the great composer!"[34]

The musical had a budget of £80,000, which sounds an enormous amount of money, but compared to the £2,000,000 spent on *Starlight Express* at the same time, it is amazing to think that the show was ever completed at all. Budgetary constraints were not the only problems. Rehearsals were conducted in a fragmentary way and Phillips was prevailed upon to write the arrangements for the show with only a few weeks to go. "I have never worked as hard in my life. I would have three hours' sleep a night, and I'd wake up in a state of complete panic and start work again."[35] The entire project was finally completed and ran for six weeks in March – April 1984. It was deemed a success, playing to packed houses every night and Phillips looks upon it as a worthwhile experience for any musician. Sadly the musical has not been staged since its debut, and the music, in the main, remains unheard although a couple of pieces have been released elsewhere. The lovely song "Walls And Bridges" was given the instrumental treatment on Phillips' fourth *Private Parts & Pieces* album under the title of "Lights On The Hill".

Useful experience or not, the musical left Phillips with some serious decisions to make. During this period he had finally moved to London into his first house, an arduous process for anyone, but especially so for a musician faced with limited income from royalties and deprived of the opportunity of earning money from sessions due to commitment to the musical. "I actually lost money over those six months. It was a ludicrous thing to do at the time, because I'd just moved into a new house and had a mortgage and a house full of lodgers. I was really up against the wall when it came down to it."[36] Faced with no prospect of a big advance from a record company, and the need to recoup some lost momentum (and money), Phillips and Scott decided to develop some of the music they had been writing over the past year or so and record an album of more blatantly commercial songs.

Consequently, the pair began work on what was, almost a year later, to emerge as Phillips' next album. The exigencies of the time have to be borne in mind when considering this project; the lupine pest of household bills and other nasties made frequent and unwelcome appearances. To try and alleviate the situation he considered a variety of options. "As far as the direction was concerned, I'd done *Private Parts & Pieces* albums, I'd done all sorts of things which were all ticking over and making bits of money. But nothing was pulling in a lot, therefore the attitude from Tony Smith and the Genesis office was, 'these are the demands of the time; this is the era Post Punk, New Romantic whatever you want to call it, this is what you need to do."[37] The very idea of Phillips being cast in the same mould as the likes of Duran Duran and Spandau Ballet may seem very far-fetched now, but there was the clear understanding that in order to gain a wider acceptance in a marketplace that was becoming increasingly polarised, a mainstream album was what was required. Always a fan of rock he set about the task with a vengeance, taking on board the fact that his Genesis cohorts, Rutherford and Banks were currently recording albums on which they had decided to sing, Phillips took the plunge himself and had some singing lessons. "Mike Rutherford and Tony Banks were both doing solo albums (*Acting Very Strange* and *The Fugitive* respectively) and they were doing their own vocals and I think there was a feeling that in the absence of knowing anybody particularly well, I'll have a crack at it myself."[38] Listening to the album now it is difficult to imagine the problems as the work progressed.

From a promising beginning with four or five songs, it became increasingly difficult to sustain interest in a project which, after all, had been dictated more at the behest of the record company than by any genuine desire of Phillips to become a "pop" star. "Early in 1983 there was all this stuff about 'looking the part' and trying to make an image out of it, and being the Anthony Phillips Band and all that stuff."[39] Musically however, despite the problems, the album did contain many fine moments, including the emotion of "Women Were Watching" and "Exocet" which caught the frustration of the time with the political situation in the UK over the Falklands War. If either track had been promoted better each could have been a success, but as it was "Exocet" was dropped from the UK version of the album. It finally turned up almost ten years later on the Virgin CD re-issue in 1991. As an exercise in compromise however, the album perhaps took Phillips as far as anyone could reasonably expect him to go, although even the American record label were not completely happy, rejecting several cuts. "We took the rough mixes to RCA who had been quite keen on *1984* and the guy was quite complimentary but said 'there's no single here'."[40] Eventually the album surfaced in the UK on a small independent label, Street Tunes, who actually picked it up while Phillips was occupied with the *Alice* musical in Leeds.

Writing and recording were no problem however and over thirty tracks were laid down, many in quick fire succession. "We used to work incredibly fast, and we didn't even work evenings. Richard would arrive at about 10.30am and we'd have a backing track done by lunchtime! I remember I wrote 'Bouncer' one morning before he arrived, literally that was it; pick up a twelve string 'right, he's not here yet, let's record this.'"[41] Many of the tracks were tried in different permutations by both collaborators, and a few found a place on other projects, most notably the compilation album *Harvest Of The Heart* released by Street Tunes in 1985, as well as a couple of others which surfaced on the CD re-issue. Of the remainder, they still exist and who knows, some may find their way on to a future compilation?

Having flirted with the risk-laden world of the charts and musicals, Phillips returned to what he considers himself to be best at; a new instrumental album, the fourth in the *Private Parts and Pieces* series, subtitled *A Catch At The Tables*. In fact, the years 1984 – 87 were to be dominated by volumes in this series with no less than four appearing in that time. Of these, *A Catch At The Tables* is perhaps the most rounded representing most of the facets of Phillips's music, from beautiful acoustic pieces and keyboard works as well as a new song, "Sistine".

Private Parts & Pieces V and *VI* were quite radically different from previous offerings. *Private Parts & Pieces V*, (subtitled *Twelve*) was an album of spartan elegance, utilising solely acoustic guitars to develop themes based around the twelve months of the year. This album can almost be seen as Phillips' *Four Seasons*. The music is tightly developed and lacks the usual warmth associated with his work but nonetheless demonstrated admirably his command of form and style. 1986's *Ivory Moon*, the sixth album in the series, demonstrated a similar notion only this time the instrument used was piano, not synthesiser. The result was another elegant, charming but somewhat characterless album, although there were brief snatches of the old humour among some of the titles. Interestingly enough, it also included a couple of the pieces from the abortive *Masquerade* project for which much material had been written, as he recalls. "I wrote stacks for it and it sort of petered out. So I had some experience of writing things in that sort of declamatory style where you have to project songs. So there were two things on *Ivory Moon* which were, if you like, my attempts at songs for *Masquerade.*"[42] These pieces served to give his fans a brief look at what might have been.

The eighteen months or so that followed the release of the sixth *Private Parts & Pieces* album saw radical changes in Phillips' career. 1987 started well enough, with the release once again in the USA only, of the seventh of the *Private Parts & Pieces* albums subtitled *Slow Waves Soft Stars.* This was a return to the mixed format which characterised most of its predecessors and was, in a way, a reaction against the rather purist feel of the previous two albums in the series. "*Private Parts & Pieces V* and *VI* had to be done. It was great to do albums like that but I felt I couldn't do another. Purity is fine but too much purity becomes spartan, and I think it is quite taxing to listen to an album of only one sound."[43] Certainly Phillips could not be accused of too much purity with this offering, which had all the usual trademarks on it, delightfully whimsical acoustic guitar pieces and some intriguing synthesiser parts which had many wondering whether Phillips had succumbed to current "New Age" trends. "When I came to do *Private Parts & Pieces VII* the upturn hadn't really happened in the New Age thing. I had a few synth pieces from library albums that I'd done which were dreamy, because a lot of the things they want for library albums have to have some kind of pulse to them, and were almost *too* kind of dreamy, *too* ethereal."[44] At the time of the album's release, Phillips did a spot of promotional work as guest VJ on the VH1 programme *New Visions* in the USA, and he referred to the album as "a collection of subversive synthesiser pieces." However, nothing could be further from the truth. Sure, the synth pieces were an interesting novelty but the meat of the album still resided in the acoustic tracks which were sandwiched between them.

This album is still one of the hardest to find outside of the US, a situation aggravated by the fact that at the time of its release the record company were in the midst of financial problems which were to lead to their bankruptcy in late 1988. So, by the beginning of 1988 Phillips was faced with the dual problem of having to earn a living as a musician without an outlet for his recordings. Library and TV work had become the staff of life for many musicians and Phillips was lucky in having that outlet for some of his work. However, as an album artist it is sadly necessary to have a record company prepared to support you unless you are sufficiently wealthy to do it on your own and so, once again, what was the next option available? Ironically, it was to be a work which had been shelved in the mid 1970's during the New Wave backlash against so-called Progressive Rock which was to provide Phillips with a much need breather.

Phillips had worked with Harry Williamson (later of Gong fame) in the late '60's and early '70's on a variety of projects, including an instrumental work based around Harry's father's book *Tarka The Otter*. Phillips explains, "Around 1973-74 we started doing some more serious two acoustic guitar work and he told me about his father's book. We became terribly inspired by that, originally we hoped to get the score to the film that they were doing of *Tarka The Otter* in 1977-78, and we thought it was a good nepotistic line, Harry being Henry's son, but it was a bit far-fetched I think. Hit & Run put up some money to finish the orchestral score and it sounded pretty good actually."[45] Hit & Run were still Phillips management at the time, although they were not ultimately responsible for the completion of the project which was run by Simon MacCorkindale and Susan George. When they heard it they loved it and wanted to use it in one of their films, and even based a script re-write around it. Sadly the film, *The Dragon Under The Hill,* has yet to see the light of day, but the album *Tarka* finally emerged into the daylight on 31st October 1988.

In many ways this album was a watershed for Phillips music. First of all, it was the first of his albums to be issued on compact disc in this country, and it was the largest scale composition that he had attempted up to this point which was well received in most quarters at the time of its release. Unfortunately, he was to be dogged by bad luck on this project, within a few months of the album's release in October 1988, the record company had gone bankrupt (no doubt there was a certain feeling of déjà vu at this point).

As a stop gap measure, Phillips issued the first of what has since become a growing series of albums under the generic title of *Missing Links.* Initially it was released on his own label, Occasional Records, as a cassette-only edition, and this was also used to finance the creation of his own fan club, *The Pavilion* in 1991. The album contained a selection of his previously unheard library music and formed an excellent contrast to the other strand of archival music covered by the *Private Parts & Pieces* albums.

Phillips' career took a turn for the better in 1990 when Virgin Records signed him up for a five album deal, which began auspiciously with 1990's *Slow Dance* album which had already been composed and recorded before the deal was signed. This album proved that Phillips' talents were not just confined to small-scale work but could expand to the broader palette required for film scores. With its soaring instrumentation and lush use of orchestral and rock colour, it is to my mind one of his finest works – of which Phillips is justifiably proud. Sadly, as yet unused in a film, it remains a score "in waiting".

Phillips' connections with Virgin continued and, at last, the record company had the good sense to release the back catalogue on compact disc over a period of several months between November 1990 and October of 1991. Most of these albums had never appeared on compact disc before, and came with bonus tracks including the long lamented B-sides to the relatively few and very hard to find singles. There were also several other interesting additions, including several demos and out-takes, all of which greatly enhanced the desirability of the discs and ensured that the "Great Re-Issue Rip Off" tag levelled at so many artists could not be aimed at these releases.

The first proper new album recorded under Virgin's auspices was to be 1992's *Private Parts & Pieces VIII: New England* which continued the tradition so nobly maintained by the previous albums in this series by integrating both keyboard and guitar work into a broader picture. Sadly however, the Virgin deal was to be curtailed in 1993 when Richard Branson sold Virgin to commercial giant EMI, who took an axe to Virgin's roster of artists – sadly Phillips was one of those out in the cold again.

His work as a composer has always been Phillips' mainstay, and it was fortunate that his services were in demand and he could maintain his career this way whilst seeking an alternative outlet for his recording. Finding such an outlet proved quite difficult, and it was not until 1994 that a deal was arranged that has proven to be an infinitely more workable one which gives Phillips greater artistic freedom than he has had for many years. The deal was with Voiceprint Records, an independent record label established at the tail end of the 1980's by Rob Ayling. Its advertising slogan sums up their attitude to music quite nicely: "The best music you never heard". Determined to promote the music of composers either maligned or ignored by the mainstream, Voiceprint and its subsidiary Blueprint have enabled Phillips' work to reach a wider audience. The relationship began in 1994 with the second of the *Missing Links* albums subtitled, *The Sky Road* which continued the trend set by its predecessor by including further pieces from his television work as well as new compositions and a couple of gems from the very early days of his career.

The remainder of the 1990's have seen a continued stream of work from Phillips in a variety of styles including the soundtrack to the 1994 Whitbread Round The World Yacht Race and a compilation of music which he and fellow collaborator Jojji Hirota composed for several Anglia television programmes in the *Survival* series. 1996 saw the *Private Parts & Pieces* series reach its ninth volume, *Dragonfly Dreams,* something of a return to tradition for the series drawing upon several archival pieces as well as pieces written specifically for the album. Voiceprint's commitment could not be more aptly demonstrated than by their acquisition from Virgin of the rights to Phillips' back catalogue which they subsequently re-issued as picture disc editions retaining the added tracks of their Virgin counterparts. Finally, they re-issued the one album which had eluded Virgin, *Tarka,* with the added bonus of the missing track which had formed the b-side of the even rarer single from that album, *The Rising Spring.*

Phillips has, with his most recent album, revisited his archive to unearth a rare treat, a compilation of various out-takes and unreleased material which spans his career from its beginnings and truly lives up to its title of *The Archive Collection.* This set incorporates several pieces from his collaborations with Mike Rutherford, including the wonderful "F#" which most Genesis fans will instantly recognise as "The Musical Box", finally re-affirming Tony Banks' comments about Phillips' contribution to this Genesis classic.

With another album in the *Private Parts & Pieces* series already completed, and several television commissions currently "in progress" Phillips' career is progressing at a pace and his fans can rest assured that his music will continue to develop through the coming years. All this from a man who continuously maintains (in best Ringo Starr accent, of course); "it was just a name; we could have been called "The Shooz"!"

Anthony Phillips UK/US Discography

With Genisis

7" Vinyl Singles

The Silent sun/That's me — DECCA F12735
A winter's tale One-eyed hound — DECCA F12768
Where the sour turns to sweet In Hiding — DECCA F12949
The Knife (pt1) The Knife (pt2) — CHARISMA CB152 (PS)

VINYL AND COMPACT DISC ALBUM RELEASES WITH GENESIS

From Genesis To Revelation (Stereo) — DECCA SKL4990
From Genesis To Revelation (Mono) — DECCA KL4990
From Genesis To Revelation (CD) — MUSIC CLUB MCCD133
From Genesis To Revelation (CD) — DISKY MUSIC DC 863092
This edition contains two previously unreleased tracks: Image Blown Out and She Is Beautiful from 1968 album sessions.
Trespass — CHARISMA CAS1020
Trespass (cd) — VIRGIN CASCD 1020
Trespass (picture disc cd) — VIRGIN CASCD 1020
Trespass (Re-mastered edition) — VIRGIN CASCDX 1020

ANTHONY PHILLIPS SOLO RELEASES 7" VINYL SINGLES

We're all as we lie Sitars & Nebulous/Squirrel — ARIST 192 (UK)
We're all as we lie Sitars & Nebulous/Squirrel — PS 7914 (USA)
Um & Aargh — SOUVENIR ARIST 252 (UK) (PS)
Prelude '84 Anthem 1984 — RCA 102 (UK) (PS)
The Anthem from Tarka The Rising Spring — PYS 18 (UK) (PS)

12" VINYL SINGLES

Sally/Women Were Watching/Exocet JJ — 102-12 (UK) (PS)

COMPACT DISC SINGLES

The Anthem From Tarka (Single mix)/The Rising Spring/Excerpt From Tarka (Mvt1)/Excerpt From Tarka (Mvt3)/The Anthem From Tarka (single mix extended version) PYD 18 (UK) (PS)

VINYL ALBUMS

Beyond An Empty Dream — CHARISMA CAS1101 1975 (UK)
(Compilation album featuring 'Take This Heart' hymn co-written by Anthony and Mike Rutherford)
Intergalactic Touring Band 1977 (UK)
The Geese & The Ghost Passport — PVC8905 (US)
The Geese & The Ghost Hit & Run — HIT001 (UK)
Wise After The Event Arista — SPART1063 (UK)
Wise After The Event — PASSPORT PB9828(US)
Wise After The Event (Picture disc album) — PASSPORT PB9828 (US)
Sides — ARISTA SPART1085 (US)
Sides — PASSPORT PB9834 (US)
Private Parts & Pieces — ARISTA AFLP1 (UK)
(Limited edition with 1st 5000 copies of 'Sides)
Private Parts & Pieces — PASSPORT PVC 7909 (US)
Private Parts & Pieces II: Back to the Pavilion — PASSPORT PVC 7913 (US)
1984 — RCA RCA LP 5036 (UK)
(Initial copies contained a black and white poster of Anthony in the studio)

Private Parts & Pieces III: Antiques	RCA INTS 5228 (UK)
Private Parts & Pieces III: Antiques	PASSPORT PVC 7985 (US)
Invisible Men	PASSPORT PB 6023 (US)
Private Parts & Pieces IV: A Catch At The Tables	PASSPORT PVC 8919 (US)
Invisible Men (1 track different to US)	STREET TUNES STLP0013 (UK)
Private Parts & Pieces V: Twelve	PASSPORT PVC 8926 (US)
Harvest Of The Heart (Compilation)	CHERRY RED BRED (UK)
Private Parts & Pieces VI: Ivory Moon	PASSPORT PVC 8946 (US)
Private Parts & Pieces VII: Slow Waves Soft Stars	AUDION SYN 308 (US)
Tarka	PRT PYL 18 (UK)
Slow Dance	VIRGIN V2638 (UK)

Slow Dance was to be Anthony's last commercial album to be available on the vinyl format although his various library albums continue to be issued on vinyl although these are not available to the general public.

CASSETTE ALBUMS

The Geese & The Ghost	PASSPORT PVCC8905 (US)
The Geese & The Ghost	HIT & RUN HIT C001 (UK)
Wise After The Event	ARISTA TCART1063 (UK)
Wise After The Event	PASSPORT PBCC8928 (US)
Sides	ARISTA TCART1085 (UK)
Sides	PASSPORT PBC 9834 (US)
Private Parts & Pieces	PASSPORT PBC 9837 (US)
Private Parts & Pieces II	PASSPORT PBC 7913(US)
1984	RCA 102 (UK)
1984	PASSPORT PBC 7946 (US)
Private Parts & Pieces III	RCA INTS 5228 (UK)
Private Parts & Pieces III	PASSPORT PBC 8909 (US)
Invisible Men	PASSPORT PBC 6023 (US)
Private Parts & Pieces IV	PASSPORT PBC 8919 (US)
Invisible Men	STREET TUNES STC0013 (UK)
Private Parts & Pieces V	PASSPORT PBC 8926 (US)
Private Parts & Pieces VI	PASSPORT PBC 8946 (US)
Private Parts & Pieces VII	AUDION SYC 308 (US)
Tarka	PRT PYC 18 (UK)
Slow Dance	VIRGIN VC2638 (UK)
Missing Links Volume 1:Finger Painting (Limited edition of 1000 cassette copies)	OCCASIONAL CASSETTES (UK)
Private Parts & Pieces VIII: New England	VIRGIN TCVE319 (UK)

COMPACT DISC ALBUMS

The Geese & The Ghost	PASSPORT PVCD 8905 (US)
The Geese & The Ghost	VIRGIN CDOVD 315 (UK)
Wise after the event	VIRGIN CDOVD 322 (UK)
Sides	VIRGIN CDOVD 316 (UK)
Sides (Picture disc)	BLUEPRINT BP205CD (UK)
Private Parts & Pieces	VIRGIN CDOVD 317 (UK)
Private Parts & Pieces (picture disc)	BLUEPRINT BP202CD (UK)
1984	VIRGIN CDOVD 321(UK)
Private Parts & Pieces II	VIRGIN CDOVD 318(UK)
Private Parts & Pieces II (Picture disc)	BLUEPRINT BP203CD (UK)
Private Parts & Pieces III	VIRGIN CDOVD 319 (UK)
Private Parts & PIeces III (Picture disc)	BLUEPRINT BP204CD (UK)
Private Parts & Pieces IV	VIRGIN CDOVD 320 (UK)
Private Parts & Pieces IV (Picture disc)	BLUEPRINT BP205CD (UK)
Invisible Men	VIRGIN CDOVD 323 (UK)
Invisible Men (picture disc)	BLUEPRINT BP211CD (UK)

Private Parts & Pieces V	VIRGIN CDOVD 324 (UK)
Private Parts & Pieces V (Picture disc)	BLUEPRINT BP206CD (UK)
Private Parts & Pieces VI	VIRGIN CDOVD 325 (UK)
Private Parts & Pieces VI (Picture disc)	BLUEPRINT BP207CD (UK)
Private Parts & Pieces VII	AUDION SYNCD 308 (US)
Private Parts & Pieces VII	VIRGINCDOVD326 (UK)
Private Parts & Pieces VII (Picture disc)	BLUEPRINT BP208CD (UK)
Tarka	PRT PYC 18 (UK)
Tarka (picture disc)	BLUEPRINT BP219CD (UK)
Slowdance	VIRGIN CDV2638 (UK)
Slowdance (picture disc)	BLUEPRINT BP213CD (UK)
Missing Links Vol 1: Finger Painting	BRAINWORKS BWKD208 (UK)
Missing Links Vol 1: Finger Painting (picture disc)	BLUEPRINT BP209CD (UK)
Private Parts & Pieces VIII	VIRGIN CDVE319 (UK)
Private Parts & Pieces VIII (Picture disc)	BLUEPRINT BP212CD (UK)
Sail The World	RESURGENCE RES102CD (UK)
Missing Links Vol 2: The Sky Road	BRAINWORKS BWKD212 (UK)
The Gypsy Suite	VOICEPRINT VP189CD (UK)
Echoes (free CD with lyric book)	VOICEPRINT VP184CD (UK)
Anthology (Compilation CD)	BLUEPRINT BP201CD (UK)
The Living Room Concert (reissued Echoes CD minus booklet)	BLUEPRINT BP218CD (UK)
Private Parts & Pieces IX: Dragonfly Dreams	BLUEPRINT BP229CD (UK)
The Meadows of Englewood	ASTRAL 999CD (SPAIN)
The Giants Dance (album by R Runn & D Thomas long time friends of AP who plays on several tracks)	BLUEPRINT BP223CD (UK)
Survival – The Music of nature (Compilation)	VIRGIN VTCD148 (UK)
Missing Links III: Time & Tide	BLUEPRINT BP272CD (UK)
Live Radio Sessions (Compilation)	DISCMEDI BLAU DM15 (SPAIN)
The Archive Collection Volume One (This collection was issued free to all current members of Anthony's fan club; "The Pavilion" first 1000 copies came with additional 5 track CD EP)	BLUEPRINT BP279CD (UK)
The Archive Collection Volume One (Standard edition of above without bonus CD EP)	BLUEPRINT BP279CD (UK)
Turn It On Again... The Hits	VIRGIN GENCD7/GENMC7
Private Parts and Pieces X: Soireee	BLUEPRINT BP319CD

COMPILATION ALBUMS

Double Exposure (Double album featuring the unreleased track 'Promenade')	NO MAN'S LAND RECORDS (UK)
The Best Of Both Worlds (Audio sampler including 'Through The Black Hole' and 'Pluto Garden by Anthony)	AUDION SYN 108, (US)
Terra X (German TV series soundtrack double CD including 'Drama' and 'Aurora' from Anthony's library music)	CBS 467595 2 (GERMANY)
Touch Sampler II (Includes unreleased track 'Dansa Cucaracha)	TOUCH T02 1996 (UK)
Survival – The Music of Nature (compilation of music from Anglia TV "Survival" wildlife series 13 tracks by AP an Joji Hirota)	VIRGIN VTDCD184 1997 (UK)
Legend: Una Antologia Inedita Del Ex-Genesis	MELOPEA CDMPV1112 1997 (ARGENTINA)
Legend: Una Antologia Inedita Del Ex-Genesis (1976/1999)	ASTRAL CD39 1999 (SPAIN)

"Who Said It?"

Index of Sources of Quotations.

THE TEXT OF THIS BOOK CONTAINS REFERENCES TO WORKS OTHER THAN MY OWN AND ALSO TO WORKS CONTAINED WITHIN OTHER PUBLICATIONS. THE FOLLOWING IS A LIST OF THOSE SOURCES AND THEIR RELEVANT AUTHORS.

1. *THE SECRET HISTORY OF ANON* PUBLISHED IN #11 OF *THE PAVILION MAGAZINE* INTERVIEW WITH ANTHONY PHILLIPS BY JONATHAN DANN.
2. *THE SECRET HISTORY OF ANON.*
3. *THE SECRET HISTORY OF ANON.*
4. *THE SECRET HISTORY OF ANON.*
5. *HOW I CAME TO BE INVOLVED IN UNDERWATER ARCHERY* PUBLISHED IN #7 OF THE *WAITING ROOM MAGAZINE* ANTHONY PHILLIPS INTERVIEW WITH ALAN HEWITT.
6. *HOW I CAME TO BE INVOLVED IN UNDERWATER ARCHERY.*
7. *THE SECRET HISTORY OF ANON* (AS ABOVE).
8. *HOW I CAME TO BE INVOLVED IN UNDERWATER ARCHERY* (AS ABOVE).
9. *THE SECRET HISTORY OF ANON* (AS ABOVE).
10. *THE SECRET HISTORY OF ANON* (AS ABOVE).
12. *THE SECRET HISTORY OF ANON* (AS ABOVE).
13. *HOW I CAME TO BE INVOLVED IN UNDERWATER ARCHERY* (AS ABOVE).
14. *THE SECRET HISTORY OF ANON* (AS ABOVE).
15. *HOW I CAME TO BE INVOLVED IN UNDERWATER ARCHERY* (AS ABOVE).
16. *HOW I CAME TO BE INVOLVED IN UNDERWATER ARCHERY* (AS ABOVE).
17. HOW I CAME TO BE INVOLVED IN UNDERWATER ARCHERY" (AS ABOVE).
18. *THE A TO Z OF GENESIS (PT1)* INTERVIEW WITH TONY BANKS AS PUBLISHED IN #27 OF *THE WAITING ROOM MAGAZINE.* INTERVIEW: ALAN HEWITT/PETER MORTON/JONATHAN DANN.
19. *HOW I CAME TO BE INVOLVED IN UNDERWATER ARCHERY* (AS ABOVE)
20. *HOW I BECAME INVOLVED IN UNDERWATER ARCHERY* (AS ABOVE).
21. *THE A TO Z OF GENESIS (PT1)* (AS ABOVE).
22. *HOW I CAME TO BE INVOLVED IN UNDERWATER ARCHERY* (AS ABOVE).

22A: JOHN SILVER INTERVIEW EXTRACT FROM *GENESIS ARCHIVE 1967-75: THE INTERVIEWS* PROMOTIONAL INTERVIEW DISC FOR *GENESIS ARCHIVE 1967-75* BOXED SET. 1998.

23. *HOW I CAME TO BE INVOLVED IN UNDERWATER ARCHERY* (AS ABOVE).
24. *HOW I CAME TO BE INVOLVED IN UNDERWATER ARCHERY* (AS ABOVE).
25. *THE A TO Z OF GENESIS (PT1)* (AS ABOVE).
26. *THE A TO Z OF GENESIS (PT1)* (AS ABOVE).
27. INTERVIEW WITH PAUL WHITEHEAD PUBLISHED IN #38 OF *THE WAITING ROOM MAGAZINE.* INTERVIEW BY ALAN HEWITT/THOMAS HOLTER.
28. *ANOTHER TRIP DOWN MEMORY LANE* INTERVIEW WITH MIKE RUTHERFORD PUBLISHED IN #34

of *The Waiting Room Magazine* interview with Alan Hewitt.
29. *How I came to be involved in underwater archery* (as above).
30. *Another trip down Memory Lane* (as above).
31. *Another trip down Memory lane* (as above).
32. *Another trip down Memory Lane* (as above).
32a: John Silver interview extract from *Genesis Archive 1967-75 The Interviews* promotional interview disc for *Genesis Archive 1967-75* Boxed Set. 1998.
33. *The A to Z of Genesis* (Pt1) (as above).
34. *Another trip down Memory Lane* (as above).
35. *The A to Z of Genesis* (Pt1) (as above).
36. *How I came to be involved in underwater archery* (as above)
37. *Genesis: The Evolution of a rock band* Armando Gallo (Sidgwick & Jackson) 1978.
38. *The A to Z of Genesis* (pt2) Interview with Tony Banks for #28 of *The Waiting Room* Magazine interview by Alan Hewitt/Peter Morton/Jonathan Dann.
39. *Another trip down Memory Lane* (as above).
40. *Genesis Revelations* interview with Steve Hackett published in #33 of *The Waiting Room* Magazine interview by Alan Hewitt.
41. *The A to Z of Genesis* (Pt 2) (as above).
42. *Genesis: The evolution of a rock band* Armando Gallo (Sidgwick & Jackson) 1978.
43. *Memories of a tour promoter* Interview with Andrew Kilderry published in #39 of *The Waiting Room* Magazine interview by Tony Emmerson.
44. *Genesis Revelations* (as above).
45. *Genesis Revelations* (as above).
46. *The A to Z of Genesis* (Pt2) (as above).
47. *Melody Maker* 28/1/71.
48. *Waiting for the Big One* interview with Armando Gallo published on *The Waiting Room* Magazine's web site November 1998. Interview: Alan Hewitt/Thomas Holter.
49. *The A to Z of Genesis* (Pt1) as above).
50. *Genesis Revelations* (as above).
51. *The A to Z of Genesis* (Pt1) (as above).
52. *Genesis; The evolution of a rock band* Armando Gallo (Sidgwick & Jackson) 1978.
53. *Genesis Revelations* (as above).
54. *Recollections of Reading* Andy Wilkinson feature published in #38 of *The Waiting Room* Magazine.
55. *Waiting for the Big One* (as above).
56. *The A to Z of Genesis* (pt2) (as above).
57. *First supper* Andy Wilkinson feature in #39 of The Waiting Room Magazine.
58. *The A to Z of Genesis* (Pt2) (as above).
59. *The A to Z of Genesis* (Pt2) (as above).
60. *Genesis: The evolution of a rock band* Armando Gallo (Sidgwick & Jackson) 1978.
61. *Melody maker* 1972
62. *Genesis Revelations* (as above).
63. BBC Transcription disc.
64. *The eyes have it* interview with Dale Newman published in #12 of *The Pavilion* Magazine interview by Alan Hewitt/Simon Pound/Ian Jones.
65. *Genesis: Evolution of a rock band* Armando Gallo (Sidgwick & Jackson) 1978.
66. *The A to Z of Genesis* (Pt2) (as above).
67. *Just for the record* Interview with Steve Hackett published in #36 of *The Waiting Room* Magazine interview by Alan Hewitt.
68. *Just for the record* (as above).
69. *Just for the record* (as above).
70. *The A to Z of Genesis* (Pt2) (as above).
71. *Just for the record* (as above).
72. *How I came to be involved in underwater archery* (Pt2) Interview published in #8 of *The Waiting Room* Magazine. Interview by Alan Hewitt.
73. Andy Wlkinson feature on Genesis 1974 Lyceum concert published in #39 of *The Waiting Room* Magazine.

74. BBC Radio One interview.
75. *Waiting for the Big One* (as above).
76. *The A to Z of Genesis* (Pt3) interview with Tony Banks published in #29 of *The Waiting Room* Magazine interview by Alan Hewitt/Peter Morton/Jonathan Dann.
77. *Just for the record* (as above).
78. *The A to Z of Genesis* (Pt3) (as above).
79. *The A to Z of Genesis* (Pt3) (as above).
80. *The A to Z of Genesis* (Pt3) (as above).
81. *Portrait of an artist* interview with Kim Poor published in #38 of *The Waiting Room* Magazine interview by Alan Hewitt and Martin Dean.
82. *Lamb Memories* feature by Andy Wilkinson published in #39 of *The Waiting Room* Magazine.
83. *Lamb Memories* (as above).
84. *Genesis: A History* video Virgin Vision 1991.
85. *The Genesis of a guitarist* interview with Steve Hackett published in #37 of *The Waiting Room* Magazine interview by Alan Hewitt.
86. *The Genesis of a guitarist* (as above).
87. *The Genesis of a guitarist* (as above).
88. *The Genesis of a guitarist* (as above).
89. *The A to Z of Genesis* (Pt4) interview with Tony Banks published in #30 of *The Waiting Room* Magazine interview by Alan Hewitt/Peter Morton/Jonathan Dann.
90. *John Peel Show* BBC Radio February 1976.
91. *The A to Z of Genesis* (Pt4) (as above).
92. *The Genesis of a guitarist* (as above).
93. *The A to Z of Genesis* (Pt4) (as above).
94. *The A to Z of Genesis* (Pt4) (as above).
95. *The A to Z of Genesis* (Pt4) (as above).
96. *The Genesis of a guitarist* (as above).
97. *Melody Maker* concert review by Chris Welch January 1977.
98. Capitol Radio transcript.
99. *The A to Z of Genesis* (Pt4) (as above).
100. *The Genesis of a guitarist* (as above).
101. Genesis Information Magazine.
102. Genesis Information Magazine.
103. Genesis Information Magazine.
104. Genesis Information Magazine.
105. *The A to Z of Genesis* (Pt5) interview with Tony Banks published in #31 of *The Waiting Room* Magazine interview by Alan Hewitt/Peter Morton/Jonathan Dann.
106. Genesis Information Magazine.
107. Genesis Information Magazine.
108. *The A to Z of Genesis* (Pt5) (as above).
109. *The A to Z of Genesis* (Pt5) (as above).
110. Genesis Information Magazine.
111. *The A to Z of Genesis* (Pt6) interview with Tony Banks published in #35 of *The Waiting Room* Magazine interview by Alan Hewitt/Peter Morton/Jonathan Dann.
112. Genesis Information Magazine.
113. Genesis Information Magazine.
114. *The A to Z of Genesis* (Pt5) (as above).
115. *The A to Z of Genesis* (Pt5) (as above).
116. Phil's introduction quoted from a live recording of Hamburg concert 10/9/82.
117. Genesis Information Magazine.
118. *The A to Z of Genesis* (Pt5) (as above).
119. *The A to Z of Genesis* (Pt5) (as above).
120. Genesis Information Magazine.
121. *Genesis The Mama Tour* Video Virgin Video.
122. Genesis Information Magazine.

124. Genesis Information Magazine.
125. NME June 1986.
126. *We can't dance* press release Virgin Records.
127. *I can't dance but I can play a mean bass guitar* Interview with Mike Rutherford published in #37 of *The Waiting Room* Magazine interview by Alan Hewitt.
128. *The A to Z of Genesis* (Pt6) interview with Tony Banks published in #38 of *The Waiting Room* Magazine interview by Alan Hewitt/Peter Morton/Jonathan Dann..
129. *The A to Z of Genesis* (Pt6) (as above).
130. *The A to Z of Genesis* (Pt6) (as above).
131. Genesis Information Magazine.
132. Knebworth Park concert 2.8.92 television broadcast.
133. Virgin Records Press release *The way we walk Volume One: The Shorts.*
134. Virgin Records Press release *The way we walk Volume One: The Shorts.*
135. *An alien afternoon* interview with Tony Banks published in #35 of *The Waiting Room* Magazine interview by Alan Hewitt/Simon Pound/Ian Jones.
136. Virgin Press release announcing Phil's departure 29th March 1996.
137. *An alien afternoon* (as above).
138. *Another Chiddingfold afternoon* interview with Ray Wilson published in #36 of *The Waiting Room* Magazine interview by Alan Hewitt/Simon Pound/Ian Jones.
139. *Another Chiddingfold afternoon* (as above).
140. *Another Chiddingfold afternoon* (as above).
141 *Another Chiddingfold afternoon* (as above).
142. *Another Chiddingfold afternoon* (as above).
143. Tony Smith interview with Martin Dean and Alan Hewitt Lyon 20th February 1998 (unpublished).
144. *Another Chiddingfold afternoon* (as above).
145. Interview with Dave Hill and Chris "Privet" Hedges by Martin Dean (unpub lished).
146. Interview with Steve Hackett published in #38 of *The Waiting Room* Magazine interview by Martin Dean/Alan Hewitt.

"The Fugitive from fame" Tony Banks.

1-22. *Portrait of an artist* Interview with Tony Banks published in #27-28 of *The Waiting Room* Magazine interview by Alan Hewitt
23-27. *Strictly in conversation* Interview with Tony Banks published in #30 of *The Waiting Room* Magazine interview by Alan Hewitt/Richard Nagy/Andrew Nagy.

"No drumkit required" Phil Collins.

1. *Genesis A History* Video Virgin Video 1991.
2. BBC Radio One interview 1974.
3. Phil Collins News Magazine #1.
4. Phil Collins News Magazine #2.
5. Phil Collins News Magazine #3.
6. Genesis Information Magazine.
7. Genesis Information Magazine.

"From the cocoon to the secret world" Peter Gabriel.

1. *New Musical Express* review of Battersea Park concert 1978.
2. *Peter Gabriel: An authorized biography* Spencer Bright (Sidgwick & Jackson) 1988.
3. *The South Bank Show* ITV 31.10.82.
4. *Sounds* June 1982.
5. Genesis Information Magazine.
6. *The South Bank Show* ITV 31.10.82.
7. Various press reports on *So* album.

"The Acolyte's Voyage to a blue part of town" Steve Hackett.

1. *The Defector Speaks Out* Interview with Steve Hackett published in #26 of *The Waiting Room* Magazine interview by Alan Hewitt
2. *The Defector Speaks Out* (as above).
3. *The Defector Speaks Out* (as above).
4. *The Defector Speaks Out* (as above).
5. *The Defector Speaks Out* (as above).
6. *The Defector Speaks Out* (Pt2) interview in #27 of *The Waiting Room* Magazine.
7. *The Defector Speaks Out* (Pt2) (as above).
8. *The Defector Speaks Out* (Pt2) (as above).
9. *Sounds* Hugh Fielder interview published 16.6.80.
10. *The Defector Speaks Out*(Pt2) (as above).
11. *From the Camino Royale to the Bay of Kings* interview with Steve Hackett published in #28 of *The Waiting Room* Magazine interview by Alan Hewitt.

12-21 *The unauthorised biography of a guitar noir* interview with Steve Hackett published in #29 of *The Waiting Room* Magazine interview by Alan Hewitt.

22-25 Interview with Steve Hackett published in #30 of *The Waiting Room* Magazine interview by Alan Hewitt.

26-28 *I owe it all to the Richmond Hill tuna sandwiches!* Interview published in #31 of *The Waiting Room* Magazine interview by Alan Hewitt/Richard Nagy/Andrew Nagy.

29-31 *Widening the landscape* Interview with Steve Hackett published in #33 of *The Waiting Room* Magazine interview by Alan Hewitt/Richard Nagy/Andrew Nagy.

32-33 *Between the tape deck and the teacup* Interview with Steve Hackett published in #35 of *The Waiting Room* Magazine interview by Alan Hewitt.

34 Camino Records Press release for the *Darktown* album 1999.

"The Genesis of a Mechanic" Mike Rutherford.

1. *In the beginning there was Smallcreep* Interview with Mike Rutherford published in #31 of *The Waiting Room* Magazine by Alan Hewitt/Richard Nagy/Andrew nagy.
2. *In the beginning there was Smallcreep* (as above).
3. *Trouser Press* June 1982.
4. *In the beginning there was Smallcreep* (as above).
5. *Whistling while you work* interview with Mike & The Mechanics published in #32 of *The Waiting Room* by Alan Hewitt/Matthew Skelland/Jonathan Guntrip.
6. *Whistling while you work* (as above).
7. *From the factory floor to chief mechanic* Interview with Mike Rutherford in #30 of *The Waiting Room* Magazine by Alan Hewitt/Richard Nagy/AndrewNagy.
8. *Whistling while you work* (as above).
9. *From the factory floor to chief mechanic* (as above).
10. *From the factory floor to chief mechanic* (as above).
11. *From the factory floor to chief mechanic* (as above).
12. *Life's a beach then you write an album about one* Interview with Mike Rutherford in #29 of *The Waiting Room* interview by Alan Hewitt/Richard Nagy/Andrew Nagy.
13. *Whistling while you work* (as above).
14. Virgin Records Press release for *Hits* album.

"Putting together the parts & pieces" Anthony Phillips.

1-7 *The Geese & The Glenfiddich* interview with Anthony Phillips published in #3 of *The Pavilion* Magazine interview by Alan Hewitt/Jonathan Dann.

8 *The Humbert Ruse interview* interview with Rupert Hine published in #6 of *The Pavilion* Magazine interview by Jonathan Dann.

9 *I want to go home...I want to go home now!* interview with John G Perry published in #5 of *The Pavilion* Magazine interview by Jonathan Dann.

10 *Talking Sides* interview with Anthony Phillips published in #5 of *The Pavilion* Magazine interview by Alan Hewitt/Jonathan Dann.

11-12 *The Humbert Ruse interview* (as above).

13-15 *Talking Sides* (as above).
16-19 *Private Parts & Pieces* interview with Anthony Phillips published in #6 of *The Pavilion* Magazine interview by Alan Hewitt/Jonathan Dann.
20-28 *1984: An Antique Year* interview with Anthony Phillips published in #7 of *The Pavilion* Magazine interview by Alan Hewitt/Jonathan Dann.
29-35 *A Masquerade for Alice* Anthony Phillips interview published in #9 of *The Pavilion* Magazine interview by Alan Hewitt.
36-41 *Making the Invisible Visible* Anthony Phillips interview published in #10 of *The Pavilion* Magazine interview by Alan Hewitt.
42-45 *How I became involved in underwater archery* Anthony Phillips interview published in #8 of *The Waiting Room* Magazine interview by Alan Hewitt.

Genesis Gig Guide

1968/69 saw the band embark on the first of an increasingly gruelling series of tours to gain an audience for their music, and later to extend that audience. Live sets at this time are hard to document but it is highly likely that the band performed some or all of the following tracks… In the beginning/The serpent/Pacidy/Key to love/Visions of Angels/Going out to get you /Stagnation/Little leaf /The knife.

BBC Technical College	Evesham	UK	1968
Balmes's dance	Chobham	UK	23.9.69
Brunel University Student's Hall	Uxbridge	UK	?.10.69
Brunel University	Uxbridge	UK	1.11.69
Twickenham Technical College	London	UK	15.11.69
Kingston Hotel	London	UK	23.11.69
Warley Social Club	Birmingham	UK	14.12.69
Cheadle Hulme Social Club	Manchester	UK	16.12.69
Brunel University	Uxbridge	UK	?.12.69
Twickenham Technical College	London	UK	?.12.69
Kingston Hotel	London	UK	?.12.69
Rolleston Youth Club Rolleston	?	UK	?.12.69

1970 had many important developments for Genesis. Increasingly they were drawing an audience from the university and college circuit eager for their adventurous and imaginative music. The summer months also saw the band having to cope with the departure of two key personnel from the line-up; guitarist Anthony Phillips and drummer John Mayhew. Phillips' replacement for several months was Aylesbury guitarist Mick Barnard who was with them on their first television appearance on BBC's forerunner to *The Old Grey Whistle Test*, *Disco Two* where, in November 1970 they played The Knife. John Mayhew's replacement who joined in the Autumn of 1970 was to have a more lasting impact on Genesis. He was of course, Phil Collins. Continuing to expand their repertoire under the tutelage of Charisma Records they increased the length and scope of their music, although many of these experiments remain sadly unheard. A further selection of tracks from these halcyon days finally appeared on the first Genesis "Boxed Set" which was released on 15th June 1998 giving fans another glimpse into what might have been. The band began to pick up a live following in a big way due to their incessant touring and sets from this period would have included…Stagnation/ Going out to get you/Pacidy/Let us now make love/Shepherd/Vision of angels/Twilight alehouse/ The knife.

BBC Studios	London	UK	?.1.70
Country Club	Havesrtock Hill	UK	4.1.70
Technical College	Ewell	UK	24.1.70
Kingston Technical College	London	UK	28.1.70
Technical College	Leicester	UK	29.1.70
Locarno Ballroom	Sunderland	UK	30.1.70
Queen Mary College (*2 shows*)	London	UK	4.2.70
Brunel University	Uxbridge	UK	12.2.70
Technical College	Uxbridge	UK	13.2.70
The Dome	Brighton	UK	14.2.70
Kingston Hotel	London	UK	15.2.70

Hurlingham Tennis Club	Fulham	UK	?.2.70
BBC Studios	London	UK	22.2.70
Revolution Club	London	UK	25.2.70
Blaises Club	London	UK	26.2.70
Brunel University	Uxbridge	UK	27.2.70
Essex University	Colchester	UK	28.2.70
Farx Club	Southall	UK	1.3.70
Mistrale Club	Beckenham	UK	2.3.70
Ronnie Scott's Club	London	UK	3.3.70
Ronnie Scott's Club	London	UK	10.3.70
Roundhouse Club	London	UK	11.3.70
College of Technology	Watford	UK	14.3.70
Ronnie Scott's Club	London	UK	17.3.70
Farx Club	Southall	UK	22.3.70
Ronnie Scott's Club	London	UK	24.3.70
Ronnie Scott's Club	London	UK	31.3.70
Ronnie Scott's Club	London	UK	7.4.70
Cooksferry Inn	Edmonton	UK	9.4.70
Eel pie Island	London	UK	10.4.70
Central Hall	Chatham	UK	11.4.70
Friars Club (*2 shows*)	Aylesbury	UK	13.4.70
Ronnie Scott's Club	London	UK	14.4.70
The Temple	London	UK	17.4.70
Farx Club	Potter's Bar	UK	18.4.70
One Oak Inn	Camberley	UK	19.4.70
Imperial College	London	UK	25.4.70
Ronnie Scott's Club	London	UK	5.5.70
Eliot College	Canterbury	UK	8.5.70
Ronnie Scott's Club	London	UK	9.5.70
Great Hall Surrey University	Guildford	UK	16.5.70
Angel Inn (*Rehearsals*)	Godalming	UK	17-23.5.70
Marquee Club	London	UK	24.5.70
Angel Inn (*Rehearsals*)	Godalming	UK	25-31.5.70
Lyceum Theatre	London	UK	6.6.70
Parish Hall	Dudley	UK	8.8.70
Marquee Club	London	UK	14.6.70
Borough Assembly Room (*Friars*)	Aylesbury	UK	15.6.70
Carshalton College	Surrey	UK	20.6.70
Ronnie Scott's Club	London	UK	23.6.70
Surrey University Free Festival	Guildford	UK	27.6.70
Technical College (*evening show*)	Hackney	UK	27.6.70
Farx Club	Southall	UK	28.6.70
Ronnie Scott's Club	London	UK	30.6.70
College for Distributive Trades	London	UK	3.7.70
Polytechnic	Kingston	UK	9.7.70
St Joan's	Rickmansworth	UK	11.7.70
Star Hotel	Croydon	UK	17.7.70
King's Arms	Haywards Heath	UK	18.7.70
Gaumont Cinema	Doncaster	UK	6.8.70
Central Methodist Hall	Coventry	UK	13.8.70
Transport House	Bristol	UK	27.8.70
New Imperial Hotel	Birmingham	UK	28.8.70
Metropole Hotel	Colwyn Bay	UK	29.8.70
Marquee Club	London	UK	30.8.70
Assembly Rooms	Rotherham	UK	3.9.70
Polytechnic	Huddersfield	UK	10.9.70
?	Wakefield	UK	17.9.70

Marquee Club	London	UK	4.10.70
British Legion Hall	Princes Risborough	UK	6.10.70
Assembly Rooms	Derby	UK	7.10.70
A B C Theatre	Blackpool	UK	8.10.70
Club Liscard	Wallasey	UK	9.10.70
Sister Club	Birmingham	UK	10.10.70
Fishmonger's Arms	?	UK	13.10.70
Friars Club Addison Centre	Bedford	UK	23.10.70
Resurrection Club	Hitchin	UK	3.11.70
University	Salford	UK	6.11.70
Brunel University	Uxbridge	UK	7.11.70
Victoria Road	Chelmsford	UK	8.11.70
Marquee Club	London	UK	10.11.70
Kent University	London	UK	13.11.70
Technical College	Watford	UK	14.11.70
BBC Studios *Disco Two*	London	UK	14.11.70

Genesis's first television appearance and their only recorded appearance with Mick Barnard; Anthony Phillips's replacement in the band. This video is now sadly believed lost.

Sevens The Leas	Letchworth	UK	20.11.70
Resurrection Club	Hitchin	UK	25.11.70
Imperial College	London	UK	28.11.70
Northcote Arms	Southall	UK	29.11.70
Hebdomadal	?	UK	30.11.70
College of Education	Worcester	UK	4.12.70
City University	London	UK	16.12.70
University College	Llangollen	UK	17.12.70
Humberstone Foundation School	Cleethorpes	UK	19.12.70
Angel Hotel	Godalming	UK	20.12.70
Lyceum Theatre	London	UK	28-29.12.70

During 1971 Genesis drafted guitarist Steve Hackett into the band and with his arrival, what many fans consider to be the "classic" Genesis line-up was finally complete. The band's career was taking off with a vengeance and they appeared in two Charisma package tours titled the "Six Bob Tours" because the ticket price was pegged at 6 shillings (six "bob"). These tours took place in April and October of that year and they shared the billing with fellow Charisma artists Van der Graaf Generator and Lindisfarne, and although Genesis were the opening act on these tours they regularly outshone the other artists. The band's third album Nursery Cryme also appeared during the year and garnered several plaudits from the music press. 1971 also saw the band's first appearances outside of the UK and their first television appearances outside the UK. The live shows gradually increased in length as they headlined more and more of their own shows instead of supporting other artists and as a result, their live set increased in length too and comprised the following songs… Happy the man/ Fountain of Salmacis/Seven Stones/Twilight Alehouse/The Light/White Mountain/ The Musical Box/Harlequin/The knife/Going out to get you/ The return of the Giant Hogweed.

University Arts Laboratory	Manchester	UK	3.1.71
Slough College	Bedford	UK	8.1.71
Technical College	Ewell	UK	9.1.71
Farx Club	Southall	UK	10.1.71
University College (Hackett's 1st gig)	London	UK	14.1.71
Technical College	High Wycombe	UK	15.1.71
Tower Theatre	Blackpool	UK	17.1.71
Assembly Rooms	Derby	UK	19.1.71
City University	London	UK	22.1.71
Lyceum Theatre	London	UK	24.1.71
Town Hall	Birmingham	UK	25.1.71

Colston Hall (*Afternoon*)	Bristol	UK	26.1.71
Town Hall (*Evening*)	Watford	UK	26.1.71
City Hall	Sheffield	UK	27.1.71
St George's Hall	Bradford	UK	28.1.71
Free Trade Hall	Manchester	UK	30.1.71
City Hall	Newcastle	UK	31.1.71
?	Hatton	UK	5.2.71
Friars Club	Aylesbury	UK	6.2.71
Rainbow Theatre	London	UK	9..271
The Dome	Brighton	UK	11.2.71
Winter Gardens	Bournemouth	UK	13.2.71
City Hall	Hull	UK	18.2.71
University	Southampton	UK	20.2.71
Colston Hall	Bristol	UK	22.2.71
Blaises Club	London	UK	23.2.71
Mountford Hall	Liverpool	UK	25.2.71
University	Durham	UK	28.2.71
Tower Theatre	Blackpool	UK	4.3.71
University Great Hall	York	UK	5.3.71
Lyceum Theatre	Birmingham	UK	6.3.71
La Ferme	Woluwe St Lambert	Belgium	7.3.71
Belgian tv studios	Brussels	Belgium	8-9.3.71
University Great Hall	Essex ?	UK	13.3.71
East Street Hall	London	UK	?.3.71
Sophia Gardens	Cardiff	UK	?.3.71
Dacorum College	Hemel Hempstead	UK	2.4.71
Technical College	Farnborough	UK	3.4.71
?	Godalming	UK	?.4.71
Lyceum Theatre	London	UK	9.4.71
Fairfield Hall	Croydon	UK	11.4.71
Guildhall	Portsmouth	UK	13.4.71
Civic Hall	Guildford	UK	15.4.71
Floral Hall	Southport	UK	22.4.71
Green's Playhouse	Glasgow	UK	23.4.71
Caird Hall	Dundee	UK	24.4.71
Playhouse Theatre	Edinburgh	UK	25.4.71
Free Trade Hall	Manchester	UK	26.4.71
Arts College	Kingston	UK	30.4.71
Resurrection Club	Hitchin	UK	1.5.71
Guildhall	Portsmouth	UK	4.5.71
Marquee Club	London	UK	6.5.71
University of East Anglia	Norwich	UK	7.5.71
?	Halifax	UK	8.5.71
BBC Studios	London	UK	10.5.71
TV Studios	Brussels	Belgium	4-6.6.71
Lyceum Theatre	London	UK	8.6.71
Queen Margaret College	Edinburgh	UK	12.6.71
?	Cheltenham	UK	18.6.71
Friars Club	Aylesbury	UK	19.6.71
Kingston Hall	Watford	UK	22.5.71
Reading Festival	Reading	UK	26.6.71
Friars Club Addison Centre	Bedford	UK	2.7.71
Farx Club	Southall	UK	3.7.71
Marquee Club	London	UK	9.7.71
Lyceum Theatre	London	UK	14.7.71
?	Brussels	Belgium	7-8.8.71
Weeley Festival	Clacton	UK	28.8.71

Pavilion	Hemel Hempstead	UK	5.9.71
Civic Centre	Gravesend	UK	16.9.71
The Temple	London	UK	18.9.71
Surrey Rooms	Kennington	UK	22.9.71
Town Hall	Kensington	UK	23.9.71
Sevens The Leas	Letchworth	UK	25.9.71
Kingham Hall	Watford	UK	9.10.71
William Street Club	Windsor	UK	12.10.71
Lyceum Theatre	London	UK	14.10.71
Guildhall	Preston	UK	16.10.71
The Halls	Dorking	UK	19.10.71
Town Hall	Oxford	UK	21.10.71
University Great Hall	Exeter	UK	22.10.71
University	Essex?	UK	23.10.71
Guildhall	Southampton	UK	26.10.71
Town Hall	Birmingham	UK	27.10.71
City Hall	Newcastle	UK	28.10.71
Lake Hall	Birmingham	UK	29.10.71
Guildhall	Plymouth	UK	31.10.71
The Dome	Brighton	UK	1.11.71
Starlight Club	Crawley	UK	2.11.71
Kings Hall	Derby	UK	3.11.71
Tower Theatre	Blackpool	UK	4.11.71
College of Technology	Slough	UK	6.11.71
City Hall	Salisbury	UK	7.11.71
Community Centre	Slough	UK	19.11.71
Sevens The Leas	Letchworth	UK	20.11.71
Surrey Rooms	Kennington	UK	22.11.71
Lyceum Theatre	London	UK	24.11.71
Corn Exchange	Cambridge	UK	25.11.71
Eton College	Windsor	UK	26.11.71
City Hall	Newcastle	UK	28.11.71 ?
City Hall	Sheffield	UK	30.11.71
Lyceum Theatre	London	UK	2.12.71
Red Lion	Leytonstone	UK	3.12.71
Lawkins Centre	Cottingham	UK	4.12.71
Hobbit's Garden	Wimbledon	UK	7.12.71
Technical College	Kings Lynn	UK	8.12.71
Teeside Polytechnic	Middlesborough	UK	9.12.71
Culham College	Abingdon	UK	10.12.71
Cranbrook School	High Wycombe	UK	11.12.71
Windrush Twilight Club	High Wycombe	UK	12.12.71
Big Brother Club	Greenford	UK	15.12.71
Grammar School	Weymouth	UK	16.12.71
South Parade Pier	Portsmouth	UK	21.12.71
Kingham Hall	Watford	UK	23.12.71

1972 saw the band continuing to expand, playing their first tour of Europe and the USA and also an increasing number of television and radio appearances both at home and abroad. With the appearance in October of their fourth studio album Foxtrot, the band finally had arrived on the UK music circuit and continued to build their reputation as one of the UK's most innovative acts. The early part of 1972 saw a continuation of the set from 1971 with additions from the forthcoming new album which increased the length of the set to include Watcher of the skies/Fountain of Salmacis/Musical Box/Get 'em out by Friday/Can-Utility & The Coastliners/Supper's ready/Twilight Alehouse/The knife/Going out to get you/ The return of the Giant Hogweed.

The Roundhouse	Dagenham	UK	1.1.72

Technical College	Bradford	UK	7.1.72
Baths Hall	Epsom	UK	8.1.72
BBC Studios: Sounds of the '70's	London	UK	9.1.72
?	Brussels	Belgium	14.1.72
Salle Petite	Arlon	Belgium	15.1.72
Festival	Charleroi	Belgium	16.1.72
College of Education	Coventry	UK	19.1.72
St Johns College	Manchester	UK	20.1.72
TV studios	Brussels	Belgium	22-24.1.72
(Possibly performance for either *Pop Shop* or *Rock of the Seventies* exact details unknown at present and films not seen on tv since 1972/3)			
Toby Jug	Tolworth	UK	27.1.72
Town Hall	High Wycombe	UK	28.1.72
University of Surrey	Guildford	UK	29.1.72
Black Prince	Bexley Heath	UK	30.1.72
Queen Elizabeth Halls	London	UK	4.2.72
College of Technology	Luton	UK	5.2.72
Lancing College	Sussex?	UK	6.2.72
Rainbow Theatre	London	UK	9.2.72 ?
The Dome	Brighton	UK	10.2.72 ?
Winter Gardens	Penzance	UK	11.2.72
Van Dyke Club	Plymouth	UK	12.2.72
University College of Wales	Aberystwyth	UK	14.2.72
Green's Playhouse	Glasgow	UK	16.2.72 ?
City Hall	Sheffield	UK	17.2.72
Medway technology College	Maidstone	UK	18.2.72
Alex Disco	Salisbury	UK	19.2.72
The Greyhound	Croydon	UK	20.2.72
Winter Gardens	Cleethorpes	UK	21.2.72
City Hall	Newcastle	UK	22.2.72
Polytechnic	Leicester	UK	23.2.72
Town Hall	High Wycombe	UK	24.2.72
Locarno Ballrooms	Sunderland	UK	25.2.72
Sports Centre	Bracknell	UK	26.2.72
Civic Centre	Chelmsford	UK	28.2.72
BBC Paris Studios *In Concert*	London	UK	2.3.72
Technical College	Watford	UK	4.3.72
South Parade Pier	Portsmouth	UK	10.3.72
Friars Club	Aylesbury	UK	11.3.72
Aston University	Birmingham	UK	17.3.72
Fete Saint Gratien	Troyes	France	18.3.72
TV Studios *Pop Shop*	Brussels	Belgium	20-21.3.72
Palasport	Beluno	Italy	6.4.72
Apollo 2000 Godega di S Urbano	Treviso	Italy	7.4.72
Lem (*2 shows*)	Verona	Italy	9.4.72
Palasport	Pesaro	Italy	11.4.72
Palasport	Reggio Emillia	Italy	12.4.72
Le Rotonde	Cuorgne Turin	Italy	13.4.72
Palasport (*2 shows*)	Pavia	Italy	14.4.72
Hit Parade (*2 shows*) Lugo di Romagna	Ravenna	Italy	15.4.72
Supertivoli Travagliato	Brescia	Italy	16.4.72
Palasport	Siena	Italy	17.4.72
Piper Club (*2 shows*)	Rome	Italy	18.4.72
Teatro Mediterraneo	Naples	Italy	19.4.72
Zoom Club	Frankfurt	Germany	23.4.72
The Greyhound	Croydon	UK	25.4.72
Van Dyke Club	Plymouth	UK	26.2.72

Polytechnic	Kingston	UK	28.4.72
Polytechnic	Isleworth	UK	29.4.72
Civic Hall	Guildford	UK	30.4.72
Red Lion	Leytonstone	UK	5.5.72
Town Hall	Oxford	UK	9.5.72
Mecca Ballrooms	Newcastle	UK	19.5.72
Winter Gardens	Penzance	UK	25.5.72
Van Dyke Club	Plymouth	UK	26.5.72
Great Western Festival	Lincoln	UK	28.5.72
The Pier	Hastings	UK	2.6.72
Technical College	Luton	UK	3.6.72
Lyceum Theatre	London	UK	4.6.72
The Rock Club	Wellingborough	UK	6.6.72
Polytechnic	Leeds	UK	9.6.72
Corn Exchange	Cambridge	UK	12.6.72
Friars Club	Aylesbury	UK	16.6.72
Top Rank	Swansea	UK	19.6.72
Castle	Durham	UK	23.6.72
Pier Pavilion	Felixstowe	UK	24.6.72
Town Hall	Watford	UK	25.6.72
Olympia Theatre	Paris	France	26.6.72
Town Hall	Watford	UK	28.6.72
Town Hall	Shoreditch	UK	29.6.72
Community Centre	Slough	UK	30.6.72
The Greyhound	Croydon	UK	2.7.72
Marquee Club	London	UK	7.7.72
Uppingham School	Uppingham	UK	13.7.72
Lyceum Theatre	London	UK	14.7.72
Coatham Hotel	Redcar	UK	16.7.72
Red Lion	Leytonstone	UK	21.7.72
Alex Disco	Salisbury	UK	22.7.72
The Wake Arms	Epping	UK	23.7.72
Civic Hall	Solihull	UK	25.7.72
Winter Gardens	Cleethorpes	UK	27.7.72
Archer Hall	Billericay	UK	28.7.72
Carre Hotel	Amsterdam	Holland	7.8.72
Reading Festival	Reading	UK	11.8.72
Palasport	Reggio Emilia	Italy	15.8.72 ?
Corte Malatestana	Fano	Italy	16.8.72
Dancing Lago delle Rose	Monselice	Italy	18.8.72
Jolly Club (*2 shows*)	Ravenna	Italy	19.8.72
Piper 2000 Club (*2 shows*)	Viareggio	Italy	20.8.72
Palasport	Albegna	Italy	21.8.72
Teatro Alcione	Genoa	Italy	22.8.72
La Locanda del Lupo (*2 shows*)	Rimini	Italy	23.8.72
Civic Hall	Merton	UK	1.9.72
Friars Club	Aylesbury	UK	2.9.72
Chelsea Village	Bournemouth	UK	3.9.72
Seloncourt Festival Hall Polyvalente	Montbeliard	France	9.9.72
Big Brother Club	Greenford	UK	13-15.9.72
Sports Centre	Bracknell	UK	16.9.72
The Greyhound	Croydon	UK	17.9.72
Marquee Club	London	UK	19.9.72
Friars Club	Aylesbury	UK	22.9.72
Tatlers Hall	?	UK	23.9.72
BBC Studios *Sounds of the '70's*	London	UK	25.9.72
National Stadium	Dublin	Eire	28.9.72

Friars Club	Aylesbury	UK	29.9.72
Kennington Oval	London	UK	30.9.72
City Hall	Newcastle	UK	1.10.72
City Hall	Sheffield	UK	3.10.72
Music Hall	Aberdeen	UK	4.10.72
Green's Playhouse	Glasgow	UK	6.10.72
Empire Theatre	Edinburgh	UK	7.10.72
Free Trade Hall	Manchester	UK	10.10.72
St George's Hall	Bradford	UK	11.10.72
De Montfort Hall	Leicester	UK	12.10.72
Winter Gardens	Bournemouth	UK	13.10.72
Polytechnic	Kingston	UK	14.10.72
Coliseum	London	UK	15.10.72
Top Rank	Liverpool	UK	16.10.72
Top Rank	Watford	UK	18.10.72
Trentham Gardens	Stoke on Trent	UK	19.10.72
Top Rank	Bristol	UK	20.10.72
New Theatre	Oxford	UK	21.10.72
Guildhall	Preston	UK	22.10.72
Guildhall	Portsmouth	UK	24.10.72
Odeon Theatre	Birmingham	UK	25.10.72
Top Rank	Cardiff	UK	26.10.72
Top Rank	Brighton	UK	27.10.72
Odeon Theatre	Lewisham	UK	29.10.72
Cooksferry Inn	Edmonton	UK	30.10.72
Hard Rock Concert Theatre	Stretford	UK	2.11.72
Civic College	Ipswich	UK	3.11.72
University	Leeds	UK	4.11.72
The Wake Arms	Epping	UK	5.11.72
Brunel University	Uxbridge	UK	10.11.72
Marquee Club	London	UK	11.11.72
Fairfield Hall	Croydon	UK	12.11.72
Polytechnic	Kingston	UK	15-16.11.72
Essex University	Chelmsford	UK	17.11.72
Imperial college	London	UK	18.11.72
Town Hall	Cheltenham	UK	19.11.72
Lords Club Civic Hall	Gravesend	UK	26.11.72
Sundown Club	Mile End	UK	6.12.72
University	Southampton	UK	7.12.72
Guildhall	Plymouth	UK	11.12.72
Brandeis University	Boston	USA	16.11.72
Philharmonic Hall	New York	USA	17.12.72
Petite Halle Penfield	Mulhouse	France	19.12.72 ?
Halle Rhenus	Strasbourg	France	20.12.72 ?

In 1973 the band's stature continues to grow with their first headlining tour of the UK's larger auditoriums and an extensive tour of the east coast of the USA. The shows at Manchester's Free trade Hall and Leicester's De Montfort Hall are recorded by US radio show *The King Biscuit Flower Hour* and parts of these are subsequently issued in August as the band's first live album, Genesis Live. October sees the band record a live film at the Shepperton Film Studios, part of which was used for the putative promotional video for "I know what I like" the single from the band's new studio album Selling England by the Pound which pierces the lower reaches of the UK charts in October 1973 but sadly the remainder of the film has never seen the light of day officially. The band round off the year with six sell-out shows at Los Angeles' prestigious Roxy Theatre. By the time the band emerged with the follow up to 1972's Foxtrot album, their status as headliners meant that their show was now approaching two hours in length and comprised the following tracks with occasional "additions"…Watcher of the skies/Dancing with the moonlit knight/Cinema Show/I know what I like/Firth of fifth/Musical Box/More fool me/The battle of Epping Forest/Horizons/Supper's ready/ Harold the barrel.

The Greyhound	Croydon	UK	7.1.73
Place D'Hiver	Marseilles	France	9.1.73
Bataclan Club	Paris	France	10.1.73
Congresshalle	Hamburg	Germany	13.1.73
Festhalle	Frankfurt	Germany	14.1.73
Stadthalle	Heidelburg	Germany	15.1.73
Stadthalle	Offenbach	Germany	16.1.73
Palasport	Reggio Emilia	Italy	20.1.73
Palasport	Rome	Italy	21-22.1.73
Arts Festival	Lanchester	UK	2.2.73
Hippodrome	Bristol	UK	4.2.73
Rainbow Theatre	London	UK	9.2.73
The Dome	Brighton	UK	10.2.73
Guildhall	Plymouth	UK	12.2.73
University Great Hall	Exeter	UK	14.2.73
Green's Playhouse	Glasgow	UK	16.2.73
City Hall	Sheffield	UK	17.2.73
Town Hall	Birmingham	UK	18.2.73
New Theatre	Oxford	UK	19.2.73
University Great Hall	York	UK	21.2.73
City Hall	Newcastle	UK	22.2.73
University Great Hall	Lancaster	UK	23.2.73
Free Trade Hall	Manchester	UK	24.2.73
De Montfort Hall	Leicester	UK	25.2.73
Civic Hall	Dunstable	UK	26.2.73
US Radio "Bob Harris Show"	?	USA	1.3.73
Carnegie Hall	New York	USA	2.3.73
Grand Theatre	Quebec City	Canada	3.3.73
Montreal Forum	Montreal	Canada	4.3.73
Gusman Hall	Miami	USA	5.3.73
Carnegie Hall	New York	USA	8.3.73
Tower Theatre	Upper Darby	USA	10.3.73
Alpine Arena	Pittsburgh	USA	13.3.73
Philharmonic Hall	New York	USA	2-3.4.73
Grand Theatre	Quebec	Canada	6.4.73
Maple Leaf Gardens	Toronto	Canada	7.4.73
Community Centre	Sherbrooke	USA	8.4.73
Case Western University	Cleveland	USA	15.4.73
Henry Levitt Arena	Wichita	USA	17.4.73
Uptown Theatre	Chicago	USA	20.4.73
University	Princeton	USA	22.4.73
Brandeis University	Boston	USA	23.4.73
Olympia Theatre	Paris	France	7.5.73
Ancienne Belgique	Brussels	Belgium	8.5.73
ORTF TV Sessions	Paris	France	6.7.73
Olympia Theatre	Paris	France	7.7.73
Reading Festival	Reading	UK	26.8.73
Olympia Theatre	Paris	France	19.9.73
Munsterhalle	Munster	Germany	25.9.73
Congresshalle	Hamburg	Germany	26.9.73
?	Darmsdorff	Germany	27.9.73
Halle des fetes Beaujoire	Lausanne	Switzerland	29.9.73
Festhalle	Frankfurt	Germany	30.9.73

Opera House	Manchester	UK	6.10.73
New Theatre	Oxford	UK	7.10.73
Apollo Theatre	Glasgow	UK	9.10.73
Gaumont Theatre	Southampton	UK	11.10.73
Winter Gardens	Bournemouth	UK	12.10.73
The Dome	Brighton	UK	15.10.73
Colston Hall	Bristol	UK	16.10.73
De Montfort Hall	Leicester	UK	18.10.73
Rainbow Theatre	London	UK	19-20.10.73
Empire Theatre	Liverpool	UK	23.10.73
City Hall	Sheffield	UK	25.10.73
City Hall	Newcastle	UK	26.10.73
Hippodrome	Birmingham	UK	28.10.73
Film studios	Shepperton Vid	UK	30-31.10.73
Capitole Theatre	Quebec	Canada	7.11.73
Massey Hall	Toronto	Canada	8.11.73
Queens University Bartlett Gym	Kingston	Canada	9.11.73
University Sports Arena	Montreal	Canada	10.11.73
State University Auditorium	Buffalo	USA	11.11.73
Kosh Auditorium	Lawrence	USA	13.11.73
Tower Theatre	Upper Darby	USA	15.11.73
Tufts University Cohen Auditorium	Medford	USA	17.11.73
Bergen Community College	Paramus NJ	USA	18.11.73
Felt Forum	New York NY	USA	22.11.73
McCarter Theatre Princeton Univ.	Princeton	USA	24.11.73
Gusman Hall	Miami	USA	26.11.73
Institute of Technology	Rochester NY	USA	27.11.73
The Agora	Columbus	USA	29.11.73
Allen Theatre	Cleveland	USA	30.11.73
State University New Gym	Buffalo	USA	1.12.73
Nth Western Univ. Cahn Auditorum	Chicago	USA	3.12.73
Perdue Regional Ballroom	Fort Wayne	USA	7.12.73
Peace Auditorium	Ypsilpanti	USA	8.12.73
Hara Theatre	Toledo	USA	9.12.73
?	Detroit	USA	?.12.73
Roxy Theatre (2 shows)	Los Angeles	USA	17.12.73
Roxy Theatre (2 shows)	Los Angeles	USA	18.12.73
Roxy Theatre (2 shows)	Los Angeles	USA	19.12.73
US TV studios? *Midnight Special*	?	USA	20.12.73

With the band on an upward curve playing bigger and better shows and two successful albums under their belt, Selling England by the Pound and their most controversial album The Lamb lies down on Broadway which they play in its entirety on their biggest tour to date through late 1974 and early 1975. Originally it was to have been even bigger but the enforced cancellation of several shows due to poor ticket sales and in the case of an sixteen date tour of Italy, cancelled due to political unrest in the country at the time made it a slightly shorter affair but still their largest tour to-date. However, fans are taken by surprise by Peter Gabriel's announcement in August 1975 that he is quitting the band. A live recording of the show at the Shrine Auditorium in Los Angeles is made, part of which features as a b-side to one of the band's singles. The rest of this recording finally surfaces on the first Genesis "Boxed Set" released on 15th June 1998. The band's show continued as outlined above for 1973 until the beginning of The Lamb lies Down on Broadway tour. From that moment an entirely new set was played which comprised the entire Lamb... album with encores of one or two or two of the following tracks...Watcher Of The Skies/Musical Box/The Knife.

Hippodrome Theatre	Bristol	UK	13.1.74
Drury Lane Theatre	London	UK	15-16.1.74

Drury Lane Theatre	London	UK	18-20.1.74
Vorst Nationale	Brussels	Belgium	26.1.74
Congresshalle	Hamburg	Germany	27.1.74
Eulach Halle	Winterthur	Switzerland	28.1.74
Victoria Koncertshalle	Geneva	Switzerland	29.1.74
Philipshalle	Dusseldorf	Germany	30.1.74
Stadthalle	Offenbach	Germany	31.1.74
Palasport	Turin	Italy	3.2.74
Palasport	Reggio Emilia	Italy	4.2.74
Palasport	Rome	Italy	5.2.74
Palasport	Naples	Italy	6.2.74
Salle Vaubier	Winterthur	Switzerland	8.2.74
Palais des Sports	Marseilles	France	9.2.74
Palais d'Hiver	Lyon	France	10.2.74
TV Studios *Melody Programme*	Paris	France	12.2.74
Capitol Theatre	Passaic NJ	USA	1.3.74
Tower Theatre	Upper Darby	USA	2-3.3.74
East Wind Ballroom	Baltimore	USA	4.3.74
T P Warner Theatre	Washington D C	USA	5.3.74
Sports Arena	Fort Wayne	USA	7.3.74
Fox Theatre	Atlanta	USA	8.3.74
Gusman Philharmonic Hall	Miami	USA	9.3.74
Muthers	Nashville	USA	12.3.74
North Hall	Memphis	USA	13.3.74
Armadillo World Headquarters	Austin	USA	17.3.74
Civic Plaza Assembly Hall	Phoenix	USA	20.3.74
Civic Reunion Centre	Santa Monica	USA	21-22.3.74
Winterland Arena	San Francisco	USA	24.3.74
Arena	Seattle	USA	26.3.74
Garden Auditorium	Vancouver	Canada	27.3.74
Orpheum Theatre	Davenport	USA	3.4.74
Embassy Theatre	Fort Wayne	USA	5.4.74
Student Union Auditorium	Toledo	USA	6.4.74
The Agora	Columbus	USA	7.4.74
Community Centre	Grand Rapids	USA	8.4.74
Guthrie Theatre	Minneapolis	USA	9.4.74
Auditorium	Chicago	USA	11.4.74
Convention Centre	Indianapolis	USA	12.4.74
Kiel Theatre	St Louis	USA	13.4.74
Memorial Hall	Kansas City	USA	14.4.74
Ford Auditorium	Detroit	USA	16.4.74
McGaw Hall	?	USA	17.4.74
Centre de Congres	Quebec	Canada	18.4.74
Civic Centre	Ottawa	Canada	19.4.74
University Sports Arena	Montreal	Canada	20-21.4.74
Auditorium Theatre	Rochester NY	USA	22.4.74
Music Hall	Boston	USA	24.4.74
A G Hall	Allentown	USA	25.4.74
Century Theatre	Buffalo NY	USA	27.4.74
Allen Theatre	Cleveland	USA	28-29.4.74
Massey Hall (*2 shows*)	Toronto	Canada	2.5.74
Syria Mosque	Pittsburgh	USA	3.5.74
Academy of Music	New York	USA	4 &6.5.74
City Hall (*fan club show?*)	Newcastle	UK	29.10.74 (*)
City Hall	Newcastle	UK	30.10.74 (*)
Palace Theatre	Manchester	UK	1-2.11.74 (*)
Empire Pool	Wembley London	UK	4.11.74 (*)

Usher Hall	Edinburgh	UK	6-7.11.74 (*)
Hippodrome	Bristol	UK	8-9.11.74 (*)
Hippodrome	Birmingham	UK	11-12.11.74 (*)
(*) Original dates for UK shows cancelled as a result of Steve Hackett's hand injury			
Auditorium Theatre	Chicago	USA	20-21.11.74
Indiana Convention Centre	Indianapolis	USA	22.11.74
Ambassador Theatre	St Louis	USA	23.11.74
Allen Theatre	Cleveland	USA	25-26.11.74
Veterans Memorial Coliseum	Columbus	USA	27.11.74
Masonic Temple	Detroit	USA	28.11.74
Syria Mosque	Pittsburgh	USA	30.11.74
Lyric Theatre	Baltimore	USA	1.12.74
Warner Theatre	Washington DC	USA	2 (or) 3.12.74
Mosque	Richmond	USA	4.12.74
Tower Theatre	Upper Darby	USA	5.12.74
Academy of Music	New York	USA	6-7.12.74
Palace Theatre	Providence RI	USA	8.12.74
Orpheum Theatre	Boston	USA	9.12.74
Forum	Montreal	Canada	10.12.74
Palace Theatre	Albany	USA	11.12.74
Palace Theatre	Waterbury	USA	12.12.74
Market Square Arena	Kansas City	USA	14.12.74
Forum	Montreal	USA	15.12.74
Maple Leaf Gardens	Toronto	Canada	16.12.74
The Dome	Rochester NY	USA	17.12.74
Century Theatre	Buffalo NY	USA	18.12.74
West Palm Beach Convention Hall	Miami	USA	10.1.75
Theatre	Lakeland	USA	11.1.75
Municipal Auditorium	Atlanta	USA	12.1.75
Music Hall	New Orleans	USA	15.1.75
Music Hall	Houston	USA	17.1.75
McFarland Auditorium (*cancelled*)	Dallas	USA	18.1.75
Music Hall	Tulsa	USA	19.1.75
Civic Centre	Phoenix	USA	20.1.75
McKey Auditorium	Denver	USA	21.1.75
Community Centre	Berkeley	USA	22.1.75
Old Waldorf Astoria	San Francisco	USA	23.1.75
Shrine Auditorium	Los Angeles	USA	24.1.75
Fox Theatre	San Diego	USA	25.1.75
Civic Centre	Phoenix	USA	28.1.75
Golden Hall Community Centre	San Diego	USA	29.1.75
Queen Elizabeth Theatre (*cancelled*)	Vancouver	Canada	1.2.75
Grand Valley State College	Grand Rapids	USA	2.2.75
Allen County Memorial Coliseum	Fort Wayne	USA	3.2.75
Arie Crown Theatre McCormick Pl.	Chicago	USA	4.2.75
Ekerberghallen	Oslo	Norway	19.2.75
Falkoner Theatrit	Copenhagen	Denmark	21.2.75
Stadthalle	Hanover	Germany	23.2.75
Carre Hotel	Amsterdam	Holland	24-25.2.75
Palais des Grottes	Cambrai	France	26.2.75
Salle des Expositions	Colmar	France	28.2.75
Palais des Sports	Dijon	France	1.3.75
Palais des Sports	St Etienne	France	2..3.75
Porte de Versailles	Paris	France	3.3.75
Pavilhao dos Desportos	Lisbon	Portugal	6-7.3.75
Pabellon Nuevo	Barcelona	Spain	9-10.3.75
Pabellon Real Madrid	Madrid	Spain	11.3.75

Porte de Versailles	Paris	France	17.3.75
Salle D'Expositions	Annecy	France	22.3.75
Palasport Parco Rufino	Turin	Italy	24.3.75
Festhalle	Berne	Switzerland	29.3.75
Saarlandhalle	Saarbrucken	Germany	30.3.75
Fredrich Ebert Halle	Ludwigshafen	Germany	1.4.75
Killesberghalle 14	Stuttgart	Germany	2.4.75
Jahrhunderthalle	Frankfurt	Germany	3.4.75
Basketball Halle	Munich	Germany	4.4.75
Stadthalle	Heidelberg	Germany	5.4.75
Philipshalle	Dusseldorf	Germany	6.4.75
Westfalenhalle 3	Dortmund	Germany	7.4.75
Congresshalle	Hamburg	Germany	8.5.75
Ahoy Sportpaleis	Rotterdam	Holland	11.4.75
Vorst Nationale	Brussels	Belgium	12.4.75
Empire Pool	London	UK	14-15.4.75
Gaumont Theatre	Southampton	UK	16.4.75
Empire Theatre	Liverpool	UK	17-19.4.75
Usher Hall	Edinburgh	UK	22-23.4.75
City Hall	Newcastle	UK	24-25.4.75
Palace Theatre	Manchester	UK	27-28.4.75
Colston Hall	Bristol	UK	29-30.4.75
Hippodrome	Birmingham	UK	1-2.5.75
Ostseehalle	Kiel	Germany	10.5.75
Rhein am Main Halle	Wiesbaden	Germany	12.5.75
Stadthalle	Bremen	Germany	13.5.75
Palais des Sports	Rheims	France	15.5.75
Velodromo Anoeta	San Sebastian	Spain	18.5.75
Porte de Versailles	Paris	France	20.5.75
Palais des Grottes	Cambrai	France	21.5.75
Salle D'Expositions	Colmar	France	23.5.75
Palais des Sports	Dijon	France	25.5.75
Palais des Sports	St Etienne	France	27.5.75 ?

Genesis Gig Guide Part Two: The Phil Collins Years

1976 saw Genesis enter a new phase in their development. Peter's departure and Phil's entry into the vocalist's role gave the band a more accessible feel as evidenced by their new album A Trick of the Tail. Steve's solo success the previous year with his first solo album, Voyage of the Acolyte had proven that there was still interest in the band and their new tour was stunning. Taking over the drum seat for live performances was Yes and King Crimson stalwart Bill Bruford. The band took another stab at a live concert movie by recording their shows in Glasgow and Stafford for a film which was premiered the following summer under the title of Genesis in Concert, the premiere of which was attended by Princess Anne. From this point onwards, Genesis' live sets increasingly tended toward being the same every night with a typical 1976 set running as follows… Dance on a volcano/The lamb lies down on Broadway-Broadway melody of '74-Fly on a windshield-Carpet crawl (medley sometimes introduced as "lamb Stew" or "Lamb Casserole")/Cinema Show/Robbery Assault & Battery/WhiteMountain/Firth of fifth/Entangled/Supper's ready/Squonk/I know what I like/Los Endos/It-Watcher of the skies (instrumental).

Reunion Arena (*Rehearsals*)	Dallas	USA	?.3.76
?	London Ontario	Canada	?.3.76
Century Theatre	Buffalo NY	USA	28.3.76
Maple Leaf Gardens	Toronto	Canada	1.4.76
Forum	Montreal	Canada	2.4.76

Civic Centre	Ottawa	Canada	3.4.76
Colisee de Quebec	Quebec	Canada	4.4.76
Tower Theatre	Upper Darby	USA	7.4.76
Beacon Theatre	New York	USA	8-9.4.76
Orpheum Theatre	Boston	USA	10.4.76
Lyric Theatre	Baltimore	USA	12.4.76
Syria Mosque	Pittsburgh	USA	13.4.76
Music Hall	Cleveland	USA	14.4.76
Ohio Theatre	Columbus	USA	15.4.76
Auditorium Theatre	Chicago	USA	16-17.4.76
Ford Auditorium	Detroit	USA	20.4.76
Riverside Theatre	Milwaukee	USA	21.4.76
Civic Centre	Grand Rapids	USA	22.4.76
Ambassador Theatre	St Louis	USA	23.4.76
Cow Town Ballroom	Kansas City	USA	25.4.76
Community Centre	Berkeley	USA	29.4.76
Warner Theatre	Fresno	USA	30.4.76
Starlight Bowl	Burbank	USA	1.5.76
Will Rogers Auditorium	Fort Worth	USA	7.5.76
Hammersmith Odeon	London	UK	10-14.6.76
New Bingley Hall	Stafford	UK	15.6.76
Ahoy Sportpaleis	Rotterdam	Holland	16.6.76
Philipshalle	Dusseldorf	Germany	18.6.76
Deutshlandhalle	Berlin	Germany	19.6.76
Vorst Nationale	Brussels	Belgium	22.6.76
Pavilion de Paris	Paris	France	23.6.76
Palais des Sports	Lyon	France	24.6.76
Festhalle	Berne	Switzerland	26.6.76
Olympiahalle	Munich	Germany	27.6.76
Congresshalle	Hamburg	Germany	29..6.76
Scandinavium	Gothenburg	Sweden	30.6.76
Philipshalle	Dortmund	Germany	2.7.76
Lorelei Freiluftbuhne	St Goarshausen	Germany	3.7.76
Rhein Neckar Halle	Heidelberg	Germany	4.7.76
Apollo Theatre	Glasgow	UK	8-9.7.76
New Bingley Hall	Stafford	UK	10.7.76
Sports Centre	Luton	UK	11.7.76

1977 and Genesis are riding high on a wave of public adulation that sees them go from five nights at the 3000 seater Hammersmith Odeon to three nights at London's cavernous Earl's Court Arena and with their first ever number one album Wind & Wuthering under their belt,the band defy the critics who pan their brand of music so vehemently and continue to attract ever more fans. The year also sees the band's first shows in South America and numerous awards for their work. For live performances, the band recruit American drummer Chester Thompson who soon becomes an integral part of the Genesis live sound. Outside of the band, Phil helps to form free-jazz outfit Brand X and Mike is reunited with former guitarist Anthony Phillips on his first solo album The Geese & the Ghost. The band record their five nights at the Palais des Sports in Paris for a long overdue second live album. It is during the mixing of this album that Steve announces his decision to quit the band to pursue solo projects. The band, with typical British sense of humour title the live album Second's Out. The massive tour to promote Wind & Wuthering resulted in a couple of alternative tracks in the set which usually ran as follows… Eleventh Earl of Mar/Carpet crawl/All in a mouse's night/ Firth of fifth/Your own special way/Robbery Assault & Battery/Unquiet Slumbers for the sleepers/In that quiet earth/Afterglow/Lilywhite Lilith/Wot Gorilla?/One for the vine/Supper's ready/Squonk/Dance on a volcano/Los Endos/The lamb lies down on Broadway/Musical Box (end section). For the band's inaugural visit to Brazil Inside & Out replaced Your Own Special Way which also appeared in the set for their shows at Earls Court in June which was also where The Knife made a welcome appearance as additional encore.

Rainbow Theatre	London	UK	1-3.1.77
Odeon Theatre	Birmingham	UK	7-8.1.77
Empire Theatre (*2 shows*)	Liverpool	UK	9.1.77
Free Trade Hall	Manchester	UK	10-11.1.77
Caird Hall	Dundee	UK	14-15.1.77
City Hall	Newcastle	UK	16-17.1.77
Gaumont Theatre	Southampton	UK	19-20.1.77
De Montfort Hall	Leicester	UK	21-22.1.77
Hippodrome (*2 shows*)	Bristol	UK	23.1.77
Mackey Auditorium	Boulder	USA	2.2.77
Municipal Theatre	Tulsa	USA	4.2.77
Municipal Auditorium	Kansas City	USA	5.2.77
Kiel Auditorium	St Louis	USA	6.2.77
Orpheum Theatre	Minneapolis	USA	8.2.77
Dane County Coliseum	Madison	USA	9.2.77
Auditorium	Milwaukee	USA	10.2.77
Ballrooms	Nashville	USA	11.2.77
Masonic Auditorium	Detroit	USA	12.2.77
Wings Stadium	Kalamazoo	USA	13.2.77
Auditorium Theatre	Chicago	USA	15-17.2.77
Winnipeg Auditorium	Winnipeg	Canada	19.2.77
Memorial Auditorium	Kitchener	Canada	21.2.77
Madison Square Gardens	New York	USA	23.2.77
Bushnell Auditorium	Hartford	USA	25.2.77
Onondaga County war Memorial	Syracuse NY	USA	26.2.77
Richfield Coliseum	Cleveland	USA	27.2.77
Memorial Auditorium	Buffalo NY	USA	28.2.77
Forum	Montreal	Canada	2.3.77
Colisee de Quebec	Quebec	Canada	3.3.77
Maple Leaf Gardens	Toronto	Canada	4.3.77
Civic Centre	Ottawa	Canada	5.3.77
Maple Leaf Gardens	Toronto	Canada	6.3.77
Spectrum	Philadelphia	USA	8.3.77
Civic Centre	Baltimore	USA	9.3.77
Civic Arena	Pittsburgh	USA	10.3.77
Vanderbilt University	Nashville	USA	12.3.77
Fox Theatre	Atlanta	USA	13-14.3.77
Municipal Auditorium	New Orleans	USA	16.3.77
Sam Houston Coliseum	Houston	USA	17.3.77
Texas Hall (*cancelled*)	Arlington	USA	18.3.77
Moody Coliseum	Dallas	USA	19.3.77
Municipal Auditorium	Austin	USA	21.3.77
Forum	Los Angeles	USA	24.3.77
Winterland	San Francisco	USA	25-26.3.77
Sports Centre	San Diego	USA	27.3.77
Civic Centre	Phoenix	USA	29.3.77
Paramount Theatre	Portland	USA	1.4.77
Paramount Theatre	Seattle	Canada	2.4.77
Coliseum	Vancouver	Canada	3.4.77
Starlight Bowl	Burbank	USA	1.5.77
Gigantinho Stadium	Porto Allegre	Brazil	10-11.5.77
Maracananzinho Stadium	Rio de Janeiro	Brazil	14-15.5.77
Anhembi Stadium	Sao Paolo	Brazil	18-19.5.77
Ibirapuera Stadium	Sao Paolo	Brazil	21-22.5.77
Isstadion	Stockholm	Sweden	4.6.77

EisSporthalle	Berlin	Germany	6.6.77
Palais des Sports	Paris	France	11-14.6.77
Muengersdorfer Sportstadion	Cologne	Germany	17.6.77
Stadion Bieberer Berg	Offenbach	Germany	19.6.77
Earls Court Arena	London	UK	23-25.6.77
Vorst Nationale (*2 shows*)	Brussels	Belgium	29.6.77
Ahoy Sportpaleis	Rotterdam	Holland	30.6.77
Olympiahalle *(Hackett's last show)*	Munich	Germany	3.7.77

1978 and Genesis finally achieve another hit single. "Follow you follow me" the first release from their new album And Then There Were Three which achieves a top ten spot in the UK and elsewhere. A massive tour is undertaken in support of the album which includes three separate tours of the USA and Canada and the band's first shows in Japan. For live duties the band recruit another American, Daryl Stuermer. The tour lasts eight months and features one of the largest lighting rigs seen including six computerised mirrors and numerous laser effects and Boeing 747 landing lights – all in all the stage production costs a staggering £150,000 per day to run! The 1978 tours saw the band vary their live set depending on which territory they were in beginning with the April US tour which was as follows… Eleventh Earl of Mar/In the cage/Burning rope/Ripples/Deep in the Motherlode/Fountain of Salmacis/Down & out/One for thevine/Say it's alright, Joe/Squonk/The lady lies/Cinema Show/Follow you follow me/Dance on a volcano/Los Endos/I know what I like. The tour in Europe had a couple of alterations including rare performances of Ballad of Big. The band's Autumn US tour also saw a set change with the inclusion of Dancing with the moonlit knight. At several shows December saw the band's inaugural visit to japan for which a revised set was played…. Eleventh Earl of Mar/In the cage/Burning Rope/Ripples/Deep in the Motherlode/One for the vine/Squonk/Say it's alright, Joe/The lady lies/Cinema Show/In that quiet earth/Afterglow/Follow you follow me/Dance on a volcano/Los Endos/I know what I like.

Reunion Centre (*Showco rehearsals*)	Dallas	USA	?.3.78
Memorial Auditorium	Buffalo NY	USA	?.3.78
Community War Memorial	Rochester NY	USA	30.3.78
The Spectrum	Philadelphia	USA	31.3.78
Fieldhouse Community College	Rockland	USA	1.4.78
Penn State University	Pennsylvania	USA	2.4.78
Met Centre	Bloomington	USA	3.4.78
Wings Auditorium	Kalamazooo	USA	4,4,78
Horton Fieldhouse	Normal	USA	5.4.78
Stadium	Chicago	USA	6.4.78
Richfield Coliseum	Cleveland	USA	7.4.78
Hara Arena	Dayton Ohio	USA	8.4.78
Assembly hall Indian University	Bloomington	USA	9.4.78
Kiel Open House	St Louis	USA	10.4.78
Coliseum	Oakland	USA	14.4.78
Forum	San Diego	USA	15.4.78
Forum	Los Angeles	USA	17.4.78
Forum	Montreal	Canada	22.4.78
Sportshalle	Cologne	Germany	14.5.78
Festhalle	Frankfurt	Germany	15.5.78
Olympiahalle	Munich	Germany	16.5.78
Eistadion	Mannheim	Germany	17.5.78
Sporthalle	Cologne	Germany	18.5.78
Groenoordhal	Leiden	Holland	20.5.78
Vorst Nationale	Brussels	Belgium	21-22.5.78
J Edenhal	Amsterdam	Holland	24.5.78
Palais des Sports	Paris	France	26-29.5.78
Palais des Sports	Poitiers	France	30.5.78

Palais des Sports	Lyon	France	1.6.78
Palais de Congres	St Etienne	France	2.6.78
Palais des Sports	Dijon	France	3.6.78
Hallenstadion	Zurich	Switzerland	4.6.78
Ishallen	Malmo	Sweden	6.6.78
Scandinavium	Gothenburg	Sweden	7.6.78
Ekeberghallen	Oslo	Norway	8.6.78
Ishallen	Helsinki	Finland	9.6.78
Deutschlandhalle	Berlin	Germany	11.6.78
Stadthalle	Bremen	Germany	12.6.78
Ernst Merckt Halle	Hamburg	Germany	13.6.78
Westfalenhalle	Dortmund	Germany	14.6.78
Knebworth Park	Stevenage	UK	24.6.78
Maple Leaf Gardens	Toronto	Canada	12-13.7.78
Pine Knob Performing Arts Centre	Clarkston	USA	14.7.78
Cobo Hall	Detroit	USA	15-16.7.78
Summerfield Gardens	Milwaukee	USA	17-19.7.78
Richfield Coliseum	Cleveland	USA	21.7.78
Civic Arena	Pittsburgh	USA	22.7.78
War Memorial	Syracuse NY	USA	23.7.78
British Columbia Place	Columbia	USA	25-26.7.78
The Scope	Norfolk	USA	27.7.78
Coliseum	Hampton Roads	USA	28.7.78
Madison Square Gardens	New York	USA	29.7.78
Waterbury Theatre	Providence RI	USA	30.7.78
Performing Arts Centre	Saratoga Springs	USA	31.7.78
Stadthalle	Vienna	Austria	20..8.78
Festwiesse	Ulm	Germany	26.8.78
Stadthalle	Vienna	Austria	28.8.78 ?
Messehalle 7	Hannover	Germany	30.8.78
Fete de L'Humanite	Paris	France	1.9.78
Ludwigsparkstadion	Saarbrucken	Germany	3.9.78
Eurohal	Maastricht	Holland	4.9.78
Rijnhal	Arnhem	Holland	5.9.78
Ahoy Sportpaleis	Rotterdam	Holland	6.9.78
Palais des Sports	Paris	France	9.9.78
Sportatorium	Hollywood	USA	29.9.78
Civic Centre	Lakeland	USA	30.9.78
The Omni Centre	Atlanta	USA	4.10.78
Civic Centre	Birmingham	USA	5.10.78
Civic Arena	Baton Rouge	USA	6.10.78
Ballrooms	Tennessee	USA	8.10.78
St Johns Centre	Columbus	USA	10.10.78
University Arena	Lansing	USA	11.10.78
University of Illinois	Champaign	USA	12.10.78
Uptown Theatre	Chicago	USA	13.10.78
Civic Arena	Evansville	USA	14.10.78
Coliseum	Springfield	USA	16.10.78
Kemper Arena	Kansas City	USA	17.10.78
Edwin Nutter Centre	Norman	USA	18.10.78
Municipal Auditorium	Austin	USA	20.10.78
Reunion Centre	Dallas	USA	21.10.78
Hofheinz Pavilion Univ. of Houston	Houston	USA	22.10.78
?	Indianapolis	USA	22.11.78
Sun Plaza Hall	Tokyo	Japan	27.11.78
Kosei Nenkin Hall	Tokyo	Japan	28.11.78
Sun Plaza Hall	Tokyo	Japan	29.11.78

Castle Hall	Osaka	Japan	30.11.78
Kosei Nenkin Hall	Tokyo	Japan	2.12.78
Sun Plaza Hall	Tokyo	Japan	3.12.78

1980 and for fans who complained that the UK was being ignored at the expense of Europe and the USA there was a treat in store as the band embarked on their largest tour of the UK since the mid '70's and in theatres to boot! The new album Duke spawned several hit singles both here and in the USA where the band went from strength to strength. For once even the UK television got in on the act with this "happening" band with both ITV and BBC covering shows in the UK. During the lull in activities between the end of the 1978 tour and the start of the Duke sessions Tony and Mike take advantage of Phil's time away dealing with his family problems to finally record and release their first solo projects; Tony's A Curious Feeling appears first in 1979 followed by Mike's Smallcreep's Day early in 1980. The return to theatres also brought a revised set list which comprised the following tracks: Back in NYC/Deep in the Motherlode/Dancing with the moonlit knight/CarpetCrawl/ Squonk/One for the vine/Behind the lines/Duchess/Turn it on again/Duke's Travels/Dukes' end/Say it's alright, Joe/The lady lies/In the cage/Raven-Cinema show medley/Afterglow/ Follow you follow me/Dance on a volcano/Los Endos/I know what I like/The knife

Festival Hall	Paignton	UK	17-18.3.80
University	Exeter	UK	19-20.3.80
Civic Hall	Guildford	UK	23.3.80
Hammersmith Odeon	London	UK	27-29.3.80
New Theatre	Oxford	UK	31.3.80
Gaumont Theatre	Ipswich	UK	1.4.80
ABC Theatre	Great Yarmouth	UK	2.4.80
Odeon Theatre	Birmingham	UK	4-5.4.80
ABC Theatre	Peterborough	UK	6.4.80
Trentham Gardens	Stoke on Trent	UK	8.4.80
Sophia Gardens	Cardiff	UK	9.4.80
Gaumont Theatre	Southampton	UK	11.4.80
Conference Centre	Brighton	UK	12.4.80
ABC Theatre	Coventry	UK	13.4.80
De Montfort Hall	Leicester	UK	15.4.80
Assembly Rooms	Derby	UK	16.4.80
City Hall	Sheffield	UK	17.4.80
Apollo Theatre	Manchester	UK	18-19.4.80
St George's Hall	Bradford	UK	21.4.80
Odeon Theatre	Edinburgh	UK	23.4.80
Capitol Theatre	Aberdeen	UK	24.4.80
Caird Hall	Dundee	UK	25.4.80
Apollo Theatre	Glasgow	UK	27-28.4.80
City Hall	Newcastle	UK	29-30.4.80
Market Hall	Carlisle	UK	1.5.80
Empire Theatre	Liverpool	UK	2-3.5.80
Theatre Royal Drury Lane	London	UK	4.5.80
Lyceum Ballrooms	London	UK	6-7.5.80
Guildhall	Portsmouth	UK	9.5.80
Commonwealth Stadium	Edmonton	Canada	17.5.80
Olympic Saddledome	Calgary	Canada	18.5.80
British Columbia Place	Vancouver	Canada	20.5.80
Coliseum	Oakland	USA	23.5.80
Arena	Long Beach	USA	24.5.80
Roxy Theatre	Los Angeles	USA	25.4.80
Sports Arena	San Diego	USA	26.5.80
Greek Theatre	Los Angeles	USA	27.5.80
Hopines Pavilion	Houston	USA	30,5,80

Sanger Theatre	New Orleans	USA	31.5.80
Fox Theatre	Atlanta	USA	1.6.80
Park West	Chicago	USA	3.6.80
Kemper Arena	Kansas City	USA	4.6.80
Kiel Open House	St Louis	USA	5.6.80
Rosemont Horizon	Chicago	USA	6.6.80
Civic Arena	Milwaukee	USA	9.6.80
Cobo Hall	Detroit	USA	10.6.80
Richfield Coliseum	Cleveland	USA	11.6.80
Riverfront Stadium	Cincinatti	USA	12.6.80
Stanley Theatre	Pittsburgh	USA	13.6.80
Capitol Centre	Washington DC	USA	14.6.80
Spectrum	Philadelphia	USA	16-17.6.80
War Memorial Auditorium	Boston	USA	18.6.80
Forum	Montreal	Canada	19-20.6.80
Civic Centre	Ottawa	Canada	22.6.80
Maple Leaf Gardens	Toronto	Canada	23-24.6.80
War Memorial Auditorium	Rochester NY	USA	25.6.80
War Memorial Auditorium	Buffalo NY	USA	26.6.80
Capitol Theatre	Passaic NJ	USA	28.6.80
Madison Square Gardens	New York	USA	29.6.80
Performing Arts Centre	Saratoga Springs	USA	30.6.80

1981 the inexhaustible Genesis return with Abacab, an album that takes fans by surprise once again with its stripped down sound and the inclusion of the Earth Wind & Fire horn section on one track. The tour also saw the introduction of what is now a standard lighting effect; the vari-lite which Genesis helped create and which gave their stage show even more clout. 1981 also saw the emergence of Phil Collins as a solo artist with the release of his first solo album Face Value. In keeping with the radical new album the band's set underwent a similar reorganisation with the following tracks as part of their live show… Behind thelines/ Duchess/The lamb lies down on Broadway/Dodo/Lurker/Abacab/CarpetCrawl/Me & Sarah Jane/Misunderstanding/No reply at all/Firthof fifth/Man on the corner/Who-dunnit/In the cage/Cinema show-Raven medley/Afterglow/Turn it on again/Dance on a volcano/Los endos/I know what I like. In addition to these, at the band's shows in Spain a new song; Me & Virgil was included, and at their shows in Philadelphia and Largo Like it or not was performed where the band also trotted out The knife again as an encore at their final show in Birmingham.

Plaza de Toros Monumental	Barcelona	Spain	25.9.81
Velodromo Anoeta	San Sebastian	Spain	26.9.81
Arenes	Frejus	France	29.9.81
Parc des Expositions	Avignon	France	30.9.81
Palais des Sports	Lyon	France	1.10.81
Groenoordhal	Leiden	Holland	3-4.10.81
Stadthalle	Bremen	Germany	5.10.81
Grugahalle	Essen	Germany	6.10.81
Olympiahalle	Munich	Germany	8.10.81
Messehalle	Nuernburg	Germany	9.10.81
Karl Diehm Halle	Wuerzburg	Germany	10.10.81
EisSporthalle	Kassel	Germany	13.10.81
Ostseehalle	Kiel	Germany	14.10.81
Congresshalle	Hamburg	Germany	15.10.81
Sportshalle	Cologne	Germany	17-18.10.81
L'Hippodrome Pantin	Paris	France	19-21.10.81
Vorst Nationale	Brussels	Belgium	22.10.81
Parc des Expositions	Metz	France	23.10.81
Hallenstadion	Zurich	Switzerland	24-25.10.81

Westfalenhalle	Dortmund	Germany	27.10.81
Freidrich Eberthalle	Ludwigshafen	Germany	28.10.81
Sporthalle	Stuttgart	Germany	29.10.81
Festhalle	Frankfurt	Germany	30-31.10.81
Deutchlandhalle	Berlin	Germany	2.11.81
Dane County Coliseum	Madison	USA	12.11.81
Rosemont Horizon	Chicago	USA	13-15.11.81
Civic Arena	Milwaukee	USA	16.11.81
Notre Dame University	South Bend	USA	17.11.81
Cobo Hall	Detroit	USA	18.11.81
Civic Arena	Pittsburgh	USA	19.11.81
Riverfront Coliseum	Cincinatti	USA	21.11.81
Richfield Coliseum	Cleveland	USA	22-23.11.81
Spectrum	Philadelphia	USA	25-27.11.81
Savoy Theatre	New York	USA	28.11.81
Nassau Coliseum	Long Island NY	USA	29.11.81
Capital Centre	Landover	USA	30.11.81
Hartford Civic Centre	Hartford	USA	2.12.81
Forum	Montreal	Canada	3-4.12.81
Civic Centre	Ottawa	Canada	5.12.81
Maple Leaf Gardens	Toronto	Canada	6-7.12.81
War Memorial	Buffalo NY	Canada	8.12.81
Brendan Bryne Arena	East Rutherford	USA	10.12.81
Madison Square Gardens	New York	USA	11.12.81
Brendan Eyre Arena	EastRutherford NJ	USA	12.12.81
Wembley Arena	London	UK	17-19.12.81
National Exhibition Centre	Birmingham	UK	21-23.12.81
Civic Centre	Peoria	USA	1.8.82
Poplar Creek	Chicago	USA	2-3.8.82
Greek Theatre Berkeley	Los Angeles	USA	6-8.8.82
Forum	Los Angeles	USA	9-10.8.82
Memorial Auditorium	Phoenix	USA	11.8.82
Reunion Arena	Dallas	USA	13.8.82
The Summit	Houston	USA	14.8.82
Myriad Convention Centre	Oklahoma	USA	15.8.82
Checkerdome	St Louis	USA	16.8.82
Pine Knob Music Centre	Detroit	USA	18.8.82
Postgate Pavilion	Merryweather	USA	19.8.82
J F K Stadium	Philadelphia	USA	21.8.82
Forest Hills	New York	USA	22-23.8.82
Coliseum	New Haven	USA	25.8.82
Performing Arts Centre	Saratoga Springs	USA	26.8.82
War Memorial	Rochester	USA	27.8.82
CNE Grandstand	Toronto	Canada	28.8.82
Jarry Park	Montreal	Canada	29.8.82
Stade de Charmilles	Geneva	Switzerland	3.9.82
Amphitheatre	Frejus	France	4.9.82
Tirennia Film Studios	Pisa	Italy	6.9.82
Palasport	Rome	Italy	7-8.9.82
Wilhelm Koch Stadion	Hamburg	Germany	10.9.82
Johanneshovs Isstadion	Stockholm	Sweden	12.9.82
Broendbyhallen	Copenhagen	Denmark	13.9.82
Scandinavium	Gothenburg	Sweden	14.9.82
Vorst Nationale	Brussels	Belgium	16.9.82
Coliseum	St Austell	UK	18.9.82
Showering Pavilion	Shepton Mallet	UK	19.9.82
National Exhibition Centre	Birmingham	UK	20-21.9.82

Leisure Centre	Deeside	UK	22.9.82
Queens Hall	Leeds	UK	24.9.82
Inglistone Hall	Edinburgh	UK	25-26.9.82
Marquee Club	London	UK	27.9.82
Hammersmith Odeon	London	UK	28-30.9.82
Concert Bowl	Milton Keynes	UK	2.10.82

(*Line-up included a re-formed Genesis with Peter Gabriel and Steve Hackett/Talk Talk/The Blues Band/John Martyn*)

1983/84 and Genesis embark on their biggest tour of the USA and Canada; a massive seventy dates between November 1983 and February 1984 with their most adventurous light show to date. The five shows in the UK at the end of the tour are recorded for a video; The Mama Tour. The group's eponymous album, Genesis spawns three hit singles including the classic "Mama". Phil finds time during the tour to pen yet another hit single "Against all odds" and Tony manages to put out two solo albums, The Wicked Lady and The Fugitive. The band continued to expand their set which was now almost two and a half hours long and which for this tour usually comprised the following songs at their first show… Dodo/Carpet Crawl/That's all/Mama/Illegal Alien/Eleventh earl of Mar-Ripples-Squonk-Firth of fifth medley/Man on the corner/Who-dunnit?/Home by the sea/Second home by the sea/Keep it dark/It's gonna get better/Follow you follow me/In the cage-Cinema show-Unquiet slumbers for the sleepers-Afterglow/Abacab/Misunderstanding/Turn it on again. After this show the set generally ran as follows…Dodo/Abacab/That's all/Mama/Eleventh Earl of Mar-The lamb lies down on Broadway-Musical Box-Firth of fifth medley/illegal Alien/home by the sea/Second home by the sea/Keep it dark/It's gonna get better/Folow you follow me/In the cage/Cinema show-raven-In that quiet earth medley/Afterglow/Los Endos/Misunderstanding/Turn it on again (with Sixties medley)

Horton Fieldhouse *(cancelled)*	Normal	USA	6.11.83
Horton Fieldhouse	Normal	USA	7.11.83
Iowa state University	Ames	USA	8.11.83
Civic Centre	St Paul	USA	9.11.83
Civic Centre	Milwaukee	USA	10.11.83
Rosemont Horizon	Chicago	USA	11-13.11.83
Joe Louis Arena	Detroit	USA	14.11.83
Capital Centre	Landover	USA	16.11.83
Madison Square Gardens	New York	USA	17-18.11.83
Forum	Montreal	Canada	20-21.11.83
Maple Leaf Gardens	Toronto	Canada	22-23.11.83
Spectrum	Philadelphia	USA	25-27.11.83
Centrum	Worcester	USA	28-30.11.83
Civic Centre	Hartford	USA	1.12.83
Carrier Dome	Syracuse NY	USA	2.12.83
Municipal Auditorium	Buffalo NY	USA	3.12.83
Richfield Coliseum	Cleveland	USA	4-5.12.83
Civic Centre	Pittsburgh	USA	7.12.83
Riverfront Coliseum	Cincinnatti	USA	8.12.83
The Scope	Norfolk	USA	10.12.83
Coliseum	Greensborough	USA	11.12.83
Municipal Coliseum	Nashville	USA	12.12.83
The Omni Centre	Atlanta	USA	13.12.83
Veterans Memorial Coliseum	Jacksonville	USA	15.12.83
Expo Hall	Tampa	USA	16.12.83
Hollywood Sportatorium	Miami	USA	17.12.83
Cow Palace	San Francisco	USA	6.1.84
PNE Coliseum	Vancouver	Canada	9.1.84
Tacoma Dome	Seattle	Canada	10.1.84
Forum	Los Angeles	USA	12-14.1.84

ASU Activity Centre	Tempe	USA	15.1.84
McNichols Arena	Denver	USA	17.1.84
Lloyd Nobel Centre	Norman	USA	19.1.84
Assembly Centre	Tulsa	USA	20.1.84
Reunion Arena	Dallas	USA	21.1.84
The Summit	Houston	USA	23.1.84
Frank Erwin Centre	Austin	USA	24.1.84
Lakefront Arena	New Orleans	USA	25.1.84
Mid South Coliseum	Memphis	USA	26.1.84
MIS Arena	St Louis	USA	28.1.84
Kemper Arena	Kansas City	USA	29.1.84
Rupp Arena	Lexington	USA	31.1.84
Market Square Arena	Indianapolis	USA	1.2.84
Civic Auditorium Arena	Omaha	USA	3.2.84
Civic Centre	Peoria	USA	4.2.84
Dane County Coliseum	Madison	USA	5.2.84
Civic Centre	St Paul	USA	7.2.84
The Arena	Winnipeg	Canada	9.2.84
Olympic Saddledome	Calgary	Canada	11.2.84
Northlands Coliseum	Edmonton	Canada	12.2.84
The Pavilion Boise State University	Boise	USA	14.2.84
Lawlor Events Centre	Reno	USA	16.2.84
Thomas & Mack Centre	Las Vegas	USA	17.2.84
Coliseum	Oakland	USA	19-20.2.84
National Exhibition Centre	Birmingham	UK	25-29.2.84

1986/87 Well, where do you begin? Genesis break all records with their 1986 album, Invisible Touch. First of all the album spawned an incredible five hit singles and the tour they undertook saw them playing stadium gigs all over the world including their first in New Zealand and Australia where the regulations about employing local musicians meant that fans were treated to a string section sharing the stage with the band for versions of In too deep and Your own special way. The triumphant tour atmosphere was dampened somewhat in early 1987 with the sad news of the death of Charisma Records founder and long time supporter of the band, Tony Stratton-Smith. 1985/86 also saw Phil Collins consolidate his solo status with another sell-out tour in support of his latest solo album No Jacket Required, and Mike finally got the success he deserved with the first single from his new Mike & The Mechanics project, "Silent Running" and a successful US tour with this new band. The Genesis tour was to see several different live sets performed over its ten month course, beginning with the USA..Mama/Abacab/Land of confusion/That's all/Domino/in too deep/The Brazilian/Follow you follow me/Home by the sea/Second homeby the sea/Throwing it all away/in the cage- Unquiet slumbers for the sleepers-in that quiet earth-Apocalypse in 9/8 medley/Invisible Touch/Los Endos/Turn it on again (with Sixties medley).
This was followed by the band's inaugural shows in Australia and new Zealand for which another set was performed…Mama/Abacab/Domino/Your own special way/In too deep (or) Follow you follow me/TheBrazilian/That's all/Home by the sea/Second home by the sea/Throwing it all away/In the cage-Unquiet slumbers for the sleepers-in that quiet earth-Apocalypse in 9/8 medley/Invisible touch/Los endos/Turn it on again (with Sixties medley).
The band's US, Japanese and European shows of 1987 were fundamentally the same in each territory comprising the following tracks… Mama/Abacab/Domino/That's all/The Brazilian/In the cage/Unquiet slumbers for the sleepers-In that quiet earth-In the cage medley/Afterglow/land of confusion/Tonight tonight tonight/Throwingit all away/Home by the sea/Second home by the sea/Invisible touch/Los Endos/Turn it on again (with Sixties medley)

Joe Louis Arena	Detroit	USA	17-19.9.86
CNE Grandstand	Toronto	Canada	22.9.86

Spectrum	Philadelphia	USA	24-27.9.86
Madison Square ardens	New York	USA	29.9-3.10.86
Rosemont Horizon	Chicago	USA	5-8.10.86
Rosemont Horizon	Chicago	USA	10.10.86
Forum	Los Angeles	USA	13-17.10.86
Oakland Coliseum	Oakland	USA	19-24.10.86
Weston Springs	Auckland	New Zealand	23.11.86
Entertainment Centre	Sydney	Australia	25-27.11.86
Boondall Centre	Brisbane	Australia	29-30.11.86
Westlakes Oval	Adelaide	Australia	2.12.86
Entertainment Centre	Perth	Australia	5.12.86
Subiaco Oval	Perth	Australia	6.12.86
National Tennis Centre	Melbourne	Australia	9-11.86
Olympic Park	Melbourne	Australia	13.12.86
Entertainment Centre	Sydney	Australia	15-20.12.86
The Summit	Houston	USA	15-16.1.87
Reunion Arena	Dallas	USA	18-19.1.87
Kemper Arena	Kansas City	USA	21-22.1.87
Dean Smith Centre	Chapel Hill	USA	23.1.87
Hoosier Dome	Indianapolis	USA	24.1.87
Richfield Coliseum	Cleveland	USA	25-27.1.87
Capital Centre	Landover	USA	29.1.87
Dean Smith Arena	Chapel Hills	USA	31.1.87
Rupp Arena	Lexington	USA	1.2.87
Civic Centre	Hartford	USA	15.2.87
Centrum	Worcester	USA	16-18.2.87
Coliseum	Hampton Roads	USA	20-21.2.87
Greensboro Coliseum	Greensboro	USA	23.2.87
The Omni Centre	Atlanta	USA	25-26.2.87
Citrus Bowl	Miami	USA	28.2.87
Orange Bowl	Orlando	USA	1.3.87
Nippon Budokan Hall	Tokyo	Japan	13-16.3.87
Castle Hall	Osaka	Japan	18-19.3.87
Football Stadium	Malaga	Spain	10.5.87
Vicente Calderon Stadium	Madrid	Spain	13.5.87
San Siro Stadium	Milan	Italy	15.5.87
Casino	Montreux	Switzerland	16.5.87
Flaminio Stadium	Rome	Italy	17.5.87
Stade Sept Deniers	Toulouse	France	19.5.87
Dodgers Stadium	Los Angeles	USA	22.5.87
Three Rivers Stadium	Pittsburgh	USA	24.5.87
RFK Stadium	Washington DC	USA	26.5.87
Veterans Stadium	Philadelphia	USA	28-29.5.87
Giants Stadium	East Rutherford NJ	USA	30-31.5.87
Palais Omnisports de Bercy	Paris	France	2.6.87
L'Hippodrome de Vincennes	Paris	France	3.6.87
Gentofte Stadium	Copenhagen	Denmark	5.6.87
Niedersachsenstadion	Hanover	Germany	7.6..87
Reichstagsgelande	Berlin	Germany	8.6.87
Westfalenhalle	Dortmund	Germany	10.6.87
Feyernoord Stadium	Rotterdam	Holland	11.6.87
St Jakob Football Stadium	Basle	Switzerland	13.6.87
Marcel Picot Stadium	Nancy	France	14.6.87
Wiener Prater Stadium	Vienna	Austria	16.6.87
Nepstadion	Budapest	Hungary	18.6.87
Maimarktgelande	Mannheim	Germany	20.6.87
Olympic Stadium	Munich	Germany	21.6.87

Stade de la Beaujoire	Lyon	France	23.6.87
L'Hippodrome de Vincennes	Paris	France	24.6.87
Hampden Park Stadium	Glasgow	UK	26.6.87
Roundhay Park	Leeds	UK	28.6.87
Wembley Stadium	London	UK	1-4.7.87

The gaps between Genesis projects grew to epic proportions with only two appearances by the band between 1987 and 1992. The Atlantic Records fortieth birthday concert in 1988 at which both Phil and Genesis played, and the Silver Clef concert in 1990 in aid of the Nordoff Robbins music charity at which once again, both Genesis and Phil played separate sets. Solo success continued for both Mike and Phil with further solo outings for both musicians during the intervening years between Invisible Touch and the next Genesis project and Tony kept his hand in with two further solo albums of his own.

Madison Square Garden	New York	USA	15.5.88
Knebworth Park	Stevenage	UK	30.6.90

1992/93 saw Genesis return to the fold after their longest lay off yet. In the meantime all of the band had put out a further range of solo projects to varying degrees of success. The 1992 tour also featured another innovation the first three Sony "Jumbotron" video screens which enabled the band to play to even bigger audiences and in the open air . The We Can't Dance album continued the successful trend set by its predecessor with a whole series of hit singles and several appearances by the band on Top of the Pops. In the autumn the band undertook a short tour of theatres in the UK as a gesture to their UK fans and another video was filmed at their shows in London's Earl's Court Arena. The 1993 Cowdray Ruins charity gig also turned out to be Phil's last appearance with the band. The shows for their 1992 tour were their biggest to date with a set which comprised the following songs… Land of Confusion/No Son of Mine/Driving The Last Spike/Dance On A Volcano-The Lamb Lies Down On Broadway-Musical Box-Firth Of Fifth-I Know What I Like-That's All-Illegal Alien-Stagnation-Follow You Follow Me Medley/Throwing It All Away/Fading Lights/Jesus He Knows Me/Home By The Sea/Second Home By The Sea/Hold On My Heart/Domino/Drum Duet/I Can't Dance/Tonight Tonight Tonight/Invisible Touch/Turn It On Again.
For the band's UK indoor shows later in the year the set also included Dreaming While You Sleep and at the first of the provincial theatre shows the band also threw in the golden oldie Carpet Crawlers.

Texas Stadium	Irving	USA	8.5.92
Astrodome	Houston	USA	9.5.92
Joe Robbie Stadium	Miami	USA	16.5.92
Tampa Stadium (*cancelled*)	Tampa	USA	17.5.92
RFK Stadium	Washington DC	USA	19.5.92
Hoosier Dome	Indianapolis	USA	21.5.92
St Johns Centre	Columbus	USA	22.5.92
Silverdome	Pontiac	USA	24.5.92
Stadium	Cleveland	USA	25.5.92
Three Rivers Stadium	Pittsburgh	USA	26.5.92
Foxborough Stadium	Boston	USA	28.5.92
Stade Olympique	Montreal	USA	29.5.92
Veterans Stadium	Philadelphia	USA	31.5-1.6.92
Giants Stadium	East Rutherford NJ	USA	2-3.6.92
Carrier Dome	Syracuse NY	USA	5.6.92
Skydome	Toronto	Canada	6.6.92
Carrier Dome	Syracuse NY	USA	7.6.92
Camp Randall Stadium	Madison	USA	9.6.92
Hubert H Humphrey Metrodome	Minneapolis	USA	10.6.92
Commonwealth Stadium	Edmonton	Canada	12.6.92
British Columbia Place	Vancouver	Canada	13.6.92

Tacoma Dome	Tacoma	USA	14 & 16.6.92
Dodgers Stadium	Los Angeles	USA	18.6.92
Hornet Field	Sacramento	USA	19.6.92
Oakland Coliseum Stadium	Oakland	USA	20.6.92
Cyclone Stadium	Ames	USA	23.6.92
World Music Theatre	Chicago	USA	24-25.6.92
Festival Showground	Werchter	Belgium	28.6.92
L'Espace Tony Garnier	Lyon	France	30.6.92
Stade Gerland (*cancelled*)	Lyon	France	1.7.92
L'hippodrome de Vincennes	Paris	France	2.7.92
Parkstadion	Gelsenkirchen	Germany	3.7.92
Ring	Hockenheim	Germany	4.7.92
Olympic Stadium	Munich	Germany	5.7.92
Ullevi Stadium	Gothenburg	Sweden	7.7.92
Gentofte Stadium	Copenhagen	Denmark	8.7.92
Niedersachsenstadion	Hanover	Germany	10-11.7.92
Maifeld Stadium	Berlin	Germany	12.7.92
Niedersachsenstadiom	Hanover	Germany	13.7.92
Maimarktegelande	Mannheim	Germany	15.7.92
Wiener Pater Stadion	Vienna	Austria	16.7.92
San Siro Stadium	Milan	Italy	17.7.92
Stadio del Alpi (*cancelled*)	Turin	Italy	18.7.92
Stade de L'Ouest	Nice	France	19.7.92
L'Espace Grammont	Montpellier	France	20.7.92
Estadio Alvalade	Lisbon	Portugal	22.7.92
Estadio Vicente Calderon (*cancelled*)	Madrid	Spain	24.7.92
St Jakob Football Stadium	Basle	Switzerland	26.7.92
Muengersdorfer Sportstadion	Cologne	Germany	27.7.92
Feyernord Stadium	Rotterdam	Holland	28.7.92
Nordmark Sportfeld	Kiel	Germany	29.7.92
Roundhay Park	Leeds	UK	31.7.92
Knebworth Park (*cancelled*)	Stevenage	UK	1.8.92
Knebworth Park	Stevenage	UK	2.8.92
Mayflower Theatre	Southampton	UK	23.10.92
City Hall	Newcastle	UK	28.10.92
Playhouse	Edinburgh	UK	29.10.92
Apollo Theatre	Manchester	UK	30.10.92
Earls Court Arena	London	UK	2-4.11.92
Earls Court Arena	London	UK	6-8.11.92
Centre	Torquay	UK	10.11.92
Civic Centre	Newport	UK	11.11.92
Theatre Royal	Nottingham	UK	13.11.92
Royal Albert Hall	London	UK	16.11.92
Civic Hall	Wolverhampton	UK	17.11.92
Cowdray Ruins	Oxford	UK	18.9.93

1996/98 saw the biggest upheaval in Genesis's fortunes since the departure of Peter Gabriel. Both Mike and Phil continued to enjoy massive solo success in the intervening years and Tony also turned in his most convincing solo album in ages with 1995's underrated Strictly Inc project. The announcement on 6th June 1997 that Phil Collins had quit the band stunned fans. Holding high the spirit of Genesis, Tony and Mike decided to continue with the band and enlisted the talents of former frontman for grunge rock group Stiltslkin, Ray Wilson as their new singer and drafting in talented session musicians Nir Tsidkyahu on drums and Anthony Drennan on guitars. The result, Calling All Stations, the band's fifteenth studio album was released on 2nd September 1997 and was a welcome return to the darker and more melodramatic sound of vintage Genesis. The album entered the UK charts at the number two slot and gained respectable positions elsewhere with the notable exception of the USA where its poor showing in the charts led to a hasty re-arrangement and eventual cancellation of the proposed US tour. The band undeterred by events in the USA toured mainland Europe and the UK during January/April 1998 and turned in convincing shows proving that for Genesis there is life after Phil Collins. For their new shows billed as "Genesis through the ages" the band drew more extensively on their back catalogue for a show that included the following songs... No son of mine/Land of confusion/The lamb lies down on Broadway/Calling all stations/Carpet crawlers/There must be some other way/Alien afternoon/Domino/Firth of fifth (instrumental end section only)/Congo/Home by the sea/Second home by the sea/Dancing with the moonlit knight/Follow you follow me/Lover's leap/Not about us/Mama/The dividing line/Invisible touch/Turn it on again/Throwing it all away/I can't dance. At the band's dress rehearsal gig on 23rd January 1998 both Hold on my heart and That's all were included in the set after Calling all stations but subsequently dropped from the set.

Working men's club (*rehearsals*)	Chiddingfold	UK	?.8.97- 5.10.97
BT Tower (*album launch gig*)	Berlin	Germany	26.8.97
Kennedy Space Centre	Cape Canaveral	USA	28.8.97
RTL Studios	Paris	France	17.11.97
Danish Radio Studios	Copenhagen	Denmark	15.12.97
Pepsi Arena	Albany NY	USA	5.11.97*
Civic Arena	Pittsburgh	USA	7.11.97*
Marine Midland Arena	Buffalo NY	USA	8.11.97*
Bryce Jordan Centre	Pennsylvania	USA	9.11.97*
Edwin Nutter Centre	Dayton	USA	11.11.97*
Van Andel Arena	Grand Rapids	USA	12.11.97*
Palace of Auburn Hills	Detroit	USA	14.11.97*
Gund Arena	Cleveland	USA	15.11.97*
Dance County Coliseum	Madison	USA	18.11.97*
Bradley Centre	Milwaukee	USA	19.11.97*
Kiel Centre	St Louis	USA	21.11.97*
Rosemont Horizon	Chicago	USA	22.11.97*
Corel Arena	Ottawa	Canada	25.11.97*
Maple Leaf Gardens	Toronto	Canada	27.11.97*
Molson Centre	Montreal	Canada	28.11.97*
Colisee Arena	Quebec	Canada	30.11.97*
Madison Square Gardens	New York	USA	4.12.97*
Corestate Centre	Philadelphia	USA	5-6.12.97*
Fleet Centre	Boston	USA	9.12.97*
Civic Centre	Hartford	USA	11.12.97*
Nassau Coliseum	Uniondale LI	USA	12.12.97*
USAir Arena	Landover	USA	13.12.97*
Arena	Miami	USA	18.12.97*
Arena	Orlando	USA	19.12.97*
Ice Palace	Tampa	USA	21.12.97*

(*) *"Calling All Stations" US Arena tour cancelled dates.*

Riverside Theatre	Milwaukee	USA	5.11.97+
Braden Auditorium	Normal	USA	8.11.97+
Rosemont Theatre	Chicago	USA	9.11.97+
Fox Theatre	St Louis	USA	12.11.97+
Palace of Auburn Hills	Auburn Hills	USA	14.11.97+
Veterans Memorial Auditorium	Columbus	USA	15.11.97+
Hummingbird	Toronto	Canada	17-18.11.97+
Civic Centre theatre	Ottawa	Canada	21.11.97+
Beacon Theatre	New York	USA	23-24.11.97+
Molson Centre Theatre	Montreal	Canada	28.11.97+
Quebec Colisee	Quebec City	Canada	29.11.97+

Orpheum Theatre	Boston	USA	4.12.97+
Meadows Music Theatre	Hartford	USA	6.12.97+
Tower Theatre	Upper Darby	USA	10-11.12.97+
MCI Centre	Washington DC	USA	14.12.97+
A J Palumbo Centre	Pittsburgh	USA	15.12.97+
Van Andel Arena	Grand Rapids	USA	18.12.97+
Music Hall	Cleveland	USA	19-20.12.97+

(+) *Calling All Stations" US Theatre tour cancelled dates.*

Telecom Tower *TV Show*	Berlin	Germany	22.8.97
Kennedy Space Centre *TV Show*	Cape Canaveral	USA	26.8.97
Hotel Richmond *Radio show*	Copenhagen	Denmark	15.11.97
RTL Studios *Radio Show*	Paris	France	13.12.97
Bray Film Studios (*rehearsals*)	Windsor	UK	5.10.97-25.2.98
Bray Film Studios (*tour warm-up gig*)	Windsor	UK	23.1.98
Sportshall *warm-up gig*	Budapest	Hungary	28.1.98
Sportshall	Budapest	Hungary	29.1.98
Spodek	Katowice	Poland	31.1.98
Sportovinhala	Prague	Czech	2.2.98
Maimarktgelande	Mannheim	Germany	4.2.98
Messehalle 7	Leipzig	Germany	5.2.98
Velodrom	Berlin	Germany	6.2.98
original venue for above show was the Max Schmelling Halle			
La Galaxie	Metz	France	8.2.98
Westfalenhalle	Dortmund	Germany	10.2.98
Schleyerhalle	Stuttgart	Germany	12.2.98
Hallenstadion	Zurich	Switzerland	13.2.98
Stadthalle	Vienna	Austria	15.2.98
Palasport Casalecchio	Bologna	Italy	17.2.98
Palasport	Rome	Italy	18.2.98
Filaforum	Milan	Italy	19.2.98
Halle Tony Garnier	Lyon	France	20.2.98
Palais Omnisports de Bercy	Paris	France	23.2.98
National Exhibition Centre	Birmingham	UK	25-26.2.98
Earls Court Arena	London	UK	27.2.98
Scottish Exhibition Centre	Glasgow	UK	1.3.98
Tyneside Arena	Newcastle	UK	2.3.98
International Arena	Cardiff	UK	4-5.3.98
NYNEX Arena	Manchester	UK	6.3.98
The Point Theatre	Dublin	Eire	8.3.98
Vorst Nationale	Brussels	Belgium	10.3.98
Ahoy Sportpaleis	Rotterdam	Holland	11.3.98
Zenith	Lille	France	13.3.98
Amphitheatre 4000	Angers	France	15.3.98
Patinoire de Malley	Bordeaux	France	16.3.98
Zenith	Pau	France	18.3.98
Pabellon dos Desportos	Madrid	Spain	19.3.98
Palau St Jordi	Barcelona	Spain	20.3.98
Le Dome	Marseilles	France	22.3.98
Maison des Sports	Clermont Ferrand	France	23.3.98
Zenith	Caen	France	24.3.98
Halle Rhenus	Strasbourg	France	26.3.98
Olympiahalle	Munich	Germany	27.3.98
Messehale	Erfurt	Germany	28.3.98
Sporthalle	Hamburg	Germany	30.3.98
Seidenstickerhalle (*cancelled*)	Bielefeld	Germany	31.3.98
Forum (*cancelled*)	Copenhagen	Denmark	1.4.98

Erikhallen	Oslo	Norway	2.4.98
Globe	Stockholm	Sweden	3.4.98
Hartwell Arena	Helsinki	Finland	5.4.98
Rock in Ring Festival	Nuremburg	Germany	30.5.98
Rock in Park Festival	?	Germany	31.5.98

This gig guide has been compiled over the last ten or so years from a variety of sources. The original idea for a listing of Genesis gigs came from Peter Morton at "The Waiting Room" and has been expanded upon by the following people: Alan Hewitt (The Waiting Room), Mario Giammetti (Dusk Magazine), Helmut Janisch (It Magazine), Mal Lord, Mel Huang, Jack M Beermann, George German, Martin Dean, Mike Jackson , Jack Beermann, Thomas Holter, Vernon Parker and numerous others whose work and contributions are gratefully acknowledged.

Phil Collins Solo Gig Guide

Gigs with Brand X

London School of Economics	London	UK	?.12.75
Friars New Addison Centre	Bedford	UK	20.12.75
Marquee Club	London	UK	30.7.76
Reading Festival	Reading	UK	26.8.76
Ronnie Scott's Club	London	UK	?.9.76
Hammersmith Odeon	London	UK	12.11.76
Free Trade Hall	Manchester	UK	15.11.76
New Vic Theatre (*with Marscape*)	London	UK	20.11.76
Marquee Club	London	UK	?.4.77
Fete de L'Humanite La Courneuve	Paris	France	10.9.77
Old Waldorf Theatre	San Francisco	USA	28.11.77
Mountford Hall Students Union	Liverpool	UK	?.9.79
The Venue Club	London	UK	16.9.79
Old Waldorf Theatre (*2 shows*)	San Francisco	USA	20.9.79
Roxy Theatre (*2 shows*)	Los Angeles	USA	21-23.9.79
Park West (*2 shows*)	Chicago	USA	25.9.79
Bottom Line Club NYC	New York	USA	26.9.79
Tower Theatre	Philadelphia	USA	30.9.79
Long Island Coliseum	Long Island NY	USA	28.10.79

BRAND X TOUR 1997

Jazz Café	London	UK	14.5.97
Alley Cat	Reading	UK	18.5.97
Irish Centre	Leeds	UK	20.5.97
Music Box	Manchester	UK	21.5.97
Leadmill	Sheffield	UK	25.5.97
Zodiac	Oxford	UK	26.5.97
Fleece & Firkin	Bristol	UK	27.5.97
Arts Centre	Colchester	UK	28.5.97
Centro Culturale Polivalente	Marano sul Panaro	Italy	3.6.97
Stereorainotte Broadcast	Rome	Italy	4.6.97
Frontiera	Rome	Italy	5.6.97
Teatro Pasubio	Schio (VI)	Italy	6.6.97
Teatro Albatros	Genoa	Italy	7.6.97
Atlantis	Basle	Switzerland	8.6.97
Altes Schutzenhaus	Stuttgart	Germany	9.6.97
Schlachthof	Munich	Germany	10.6.97
E-Werk	Erlangen	Germany	11.6.97
Tunnels	Cologne	Germany	12.6.97
Sumpfblume	Hamelin	Germany	14.6.97
Sinkhasten	Frankfurt	Germany	15.6.97

1982/83 and Phil Collins solo artist bursts upon the concert scene. Consolidating his highly successful first solo album Face Value released the previous year, Phil soon takes the world by storm with his second solo album Hello; I Must Be Going released in 1982 and which

included his first number one hit; the hilarious take off of The Supremes's classic, You can't hurry love, in which he played The Supremes. Phil's first live gig was at the Concertgebouow in Holland and a tour of Europe and the USA followed including a show at Perkins Palace in Pasadena which was filmed for his first solo live video release, Live from Perkins Palace. Phil's first solo tour proved beyond doubt that he was capable of performing outside of Genesis by playing a set which drew upon material from his first two albums as well as a few classics… I don't care anymore/Thunder & Lightning/I cannot believe it's true/This must belove/Thrue these walls/I missed again/Behind the lines/You know what I mean/The roof is leaking/Don't let him steal your heart away/The west Side/If leaving me is easy/In the air tonight/ Like China/You can't hurry love/It don't matter to me/Hand in hand/And so to F../Why can't it wait til morning/ People get ready.
As if all of that wasn't enough, Phil also found the time to take part in Robert Plant's tour in the summer of 1983 as his drummer having guested on the album itself.

Hello, I Must Be Going World Tour 1982 – 1983

Concertgebouow	Den Haag	Holland	21.11.82
Olympia Theatre	Paris	France	22.11.82
Jahrhunderthalle	Frankfurt	Germany	23.11.82
Congresshalle	Hamburg	Germany	25.11.82
Vorst Nationale	Brussesls	Belgium	26.11.82
Hammersmith Odeon (*2 shows*)	London	UK	28.11.82
Hammersmith Odeon	London	UK	29.11.82
Hammersmith Odeon	London	UK	30.11.82
Hammersmith Odeon	London	UK	1.12.82
Maple leaf Gardens	Toronto	Canada	6.12.82
Ritz Theatre	New York	USA	7.12.82
Palladium Theatre	New York	USA	8.12.82
Tower Theatre	Philadelphia	USA	9-10.12.82
Holiday Star Theatre	Merriville	USA	12.12.82
Auditorium Theatre	Chicago	USA	13.12.82
Berkeley Community Theatre	San Francisco	USA	16.12.82
Universal Amphitheatre	Los Angeles	USA	17-18.12.82
Roxy Theatre	Los Angeles	USA	19.12.82
Music Hall	Houston	USA	21-22.1.83
Perkins Palace	Pasadena	USA	23.1.83
Tarrant County centre	Fort Worth	USA	24.1.83
Brady Theatre	Tulsa	USA	25.1.83
Memorial Auditorium	Kansas City	USA	26.1.83
University of Illinois	Normal	USA	28.1.83
University of Indiana	Bloomington	USA	29.1.83
Cincinnatti Gardens	Cincinnatti	USA	30.1.83
University of Minnesota	Minneapolis	USA	2.2.83
Milwaukee Auditorium	Milwaukee	USA	3.2.83
Wings Stadium	Kalamazoo	USA	4.2.83
University of Michigan	Ann Arbor	USA	5.2.83
Richfield Coliseum	Cleveland	USA	7.2.83
Civic Arena	Pittsburgh	USA	8.2.83
War Memorial Auditorium	Rochester NY	USA	10.2.83
War Memorial	Syracuse NY	USA	12.2.83
University Park	Penn State	USA	13.2.83
Stabler Arena	Allentown	USA	14.2.83
Forum	Montreal	Canada	15-16.2.83
University of Massachussetts	Amherst	USA	17.2.83
Orpheum Theatre	Boston	USA	18.2.83
Warner Theatre	Washington DC	USA	24.2.83

"The Principle of Moments Tour" with Robert Plant

Civic Centre	Peoria	USA	26.8.83
Wings Auditorium	Kalamazoo	USA	27.8.83
Rosemont Horizon	Chicago	USA	29.8.83
Kiel Auditorium	St Louis	USA	30.8.83
Civic Arena	Milwaukee	USA	31.8.83
Joe Louis Arena	Detroit	USA	3.9.83
Richfield Coliseum	Cleveland	USA	4.9.83
Reunion Centre	Dallas	USA	5.9.83 (?)
Centrum	Worcester	USA	6.9.83
Forum	Montreal	Canada	8.9.83
Memorial Auditorium	Buffalo NY	USA	9.9.83
Maple Leaf Gardens	Toronto	Canada	10.9.83
Madison Square Gardens	New York NY	USA	12.9.83
Civic Arena	Hartford	USA	13.9.83
Spectrum	Philadelphia	USA	14.9.83
Mid-South Coliseum	Memphis	USA	16.9.83
Louisiana State University	Baton Rouge	USA	18.9.83
The Summit	Houston	USA	20.9.83
Frank Erwin Centre	Austin	USA	21.9.83
Reunion Centre	Dallas	USA	22.9.83
McNichols Arena	Denver	USA	24.9.83
Sports Arena	San Diego	USA	26.9.83
Forum	Los Angeles	USA	27.9.83
Coliseum	Oakland	USA	28.9.83
Coliseum	Seattle	USA	30.9.83
PNE Coliseum	Vancouver	Canada	1.10.83

1985 Phil's rise to super stardom is assured by the release of his third solo album, No Jacket Required in February of that year coming after two years' hard graft with Genesis, and the success of the film Against All Odds which included the song of the same name. Phil's tour in support of the album took him further afield than ever including his first visit to Australia and another to Japan. Having dispelled any doubts about his solo abilities with his first tour in 1982 he continued to build on that success with a tour which included the following in the live set…I don't care anymore/Only you & I know/I cannot believe its true/This must be love/Against all odds/inside out/Who said I would?/If leaving me is easy/Sussudio/Behind thelines/Don't lose my number/The West Side/One more night/In the air tonight/Like China/ You can't hurry love/it don't matter to me/Hand in hand/Take me home/ People get ready/And so to F…

Phil's constant desire to be occupied led him in 1986/87 to work with his long time friend Eric Clapton on his Behind The Sun album and inevitably, Phil could not resist the desire to be part of the band for several shows (other commitments permitting) during the latter's several tours in support of the album as well as turning in several charity shows on behalf of the "Prince's Trust".

The No Jacket Required World Tour 1985

Royal Theatre	Nottingham	UK	11.2.85
Apollo Theatre	Manchester	UK	12.2.85
Apollo Theatre	Glasgow	UK	13.2.85
City Hall	Newcastle	UK	14.2.85
City Hall	Sheffield	UK	16.2.85
Royal Albert Hall	London	UK	17-22.2.85
National Exhibition Centre	Birmingham	UK	23.2.85
Philipshalle	Dusseldorf	Germany	25.2.85
Vorst Nationale	Brussels	Germany	26.2.85
Ahoy Sportpaleis	Rotterdam	Holland	27.2.85
Scandinavium	Gothenburg	Sweden	1.3.85

Isstadion	Stockholm	Sweden	2.3.85
Valbyhallen	Copenhagen	Denmark	3..385
Stadthalle	Bremen	Germany	4.3.85
Palais Omnisports de Bercy	Paris	France	6.3.85
Festhalle	Frankfurt	Germany	7.3.85
Olympiahalle	Munich	Germany	8.3.85
Hallenstadion	Zurich	Switzerland	10.3.85
Boeblingen	Stuttgart	Germany	11.3.85
Patinoire de Malley	Nantes	France	13.3.85
Salle D'Expositions	Bordeaux	France	14.3.85
Masion des Sports	Toulouse	France	15.3.85
L'Espace Tony Garnier	Lyon	France	16.3.85
Halle des Fetes Beaujoire	Lausanne	Switzerland	17.3.85
National Exhibition Halls	Sydney	Australia	3-4.4.85
National Exhibition Halls	Sydney	Australia	6-7.4.85
National Exhibition Halls	Sydney	Australia	10-11.4.85
Westlakes Oval	Adelaide	Australia	17.4.85
Entertainment Centre	Perth	Australia	20.4.85
The Big Egg	Tokyo	Japan	23.4.85
The Dome	Fukuoka	Japan	25.4.85
Castle Hall	Osaka	Japan	26.4.85
Rainbow Hall	Nagoya	Japan	27.4.85
Centrum	Worcester	USA	12.5.85
Forum	Montreal	Canada	13.5.85
Madison Square Gardens	New York	USA	15-17.5.85
Spectrum	Philadelphia	USA	20.5.85
Virginia Coliseum	Hampton	USA	21.5.85
Coliseum	Greensboro	USA	22.5.85
The Omni Centre	Atlanta	USA	23.5.85
Mid South Coliseum	Memphis	USA	25.5.85
Lakefront Arena	New Orleans	USA	26.5.85
Sam Houston Centre	Houston	USA	28.5.85
Reunion Centre	Dallas	USA	29.5.85
Frank Erwin Centre	Austin	USA	30.5.85
?	Phoenix	USA	1.6.85
?	Laguna Hills	USA	2.6.85
Forum	Los Angeles	USA	4-6.6.85
Forum	San Francisco	USA	7-8.6.85
?	Sacramento	USA	11.6.85
McNichols Centre	Denver	USA	13.6.85
Kemper Arena	Kansas City	USA	15.6.85
Rosemont Horizon	Chicago	USA	17.6.85
Riverfront Coliseum	Cincinnatti	USA	19.6.85
British Columbia Place	British Columbia	Canada	21.6.85
Civic Centre	Hartford	USA	22.6.85
Performing Arts Centre	Saratoga Springs	USA	23.6.85
Maple Leaf Gardens	Toronto	Canada	25.6.85
Joe Louis Arena	Detroit	USA	27.6.85
?	Cuyahoga Falls	USA	28.6.85
Madison Square Gardens	New York	USA	1.7.85

Behind the Sun Tour 1986/87 with Eric Clapton

Kalvoyre Festival (*Isle of Calves*)	Oslo	Norway	3.7.86
Roskilde Festival	Roskilde	Denmark	4.7.86
Grand Casino (*Jazz Festival*)	Montreux	Switzerland	10.7.86
Juan Les Pins Festival	Antibes	France	12.7.86
National Exhibition Centre	Birmingham	UK	14-15.7.86

Royal Albert Hall	London	UK	11-12.1.87
Coliseum	Oakland	USA	11.4.87
Pacific Amphitheatre	Costa Mesa	USA	13.4.87
Forum	Los Angeles	USA	14.4.87
Ebony Showcase Theatre (+*BB King*)	Los Angeles	USA	15.4.87
McNichols Arena (+*BB King*)	Denver	USA	16.4.87
Civic Centre	St Paul	USA	18.4.87
Rosemont Horizon	Chicago	USA	19.4.87
Limelight Club (+*BB King*)	Chicago	USA	19.4.87
Market Square Arena	Indianapolis	USA	21.4.87
Joe Louis Arena	Detroit	USA	22.4.87
Richfield Coliseum	Cleveland	USA	23.4.87
Capitol Centre	Largo	USA	25.4.87
Civic Centre	Providence RI	USA	26.4.87
Madison Square Gardens	New York NY	USA	27.4.87
Wembley Arena	London	UK	6.6.87
Civic Hall (*with Eric Clapton*)	Guildford	UK	7.2.88
Wintershall (*with Eric Clapton*)	Guildford?	UK	2.7.88
City Hall (*with Eric Clapton*)	Sheffield	UK	16.1.89
City Hall(*with Eric Clapton*)	Newcastle	UK	17.1.89
Playhouse Theatre (*with Eric Clapton*)	Edinburgh	UK	18.1.89
Royal Albert Hall (*with Eric Clapton*)	London	UK	20-26.1.89

1989/90 and Phil's star is firmly in the ascendant. His fourth solo album But Seriously hits the top of the charts worldwide and the debut single; Another day in paradise becomes a multi million selling hit. Phil's tour takes him even further around the globe than ever before and his success is assured with his most convincing shows. The 1990 tour was Phil's largest to date and the live set increased in length accordingly with a set now almost three hours long comprising the following tracks… Hand in hand/Hang in long enough/Behind thelines/Against all odds/Doesn't anybody stay together anymore?/All of my life/Don't lose my number/Do you remember?/Something happened on the way to heaven/Another day in paradise/Separate lives/I wish it would rain down/Saturday night, Sunday morning/The West Side/That's just the wayit is/Heat on the street/One more night/Colours/In the air tonight/You can't hurry love/Two hearts/Find a way to my heart/Sussudio/A groovy kind of love/Easy lover/Always/Take me home. On occasions there were changes including performances of Inside out and The roof is leaking, in place of Behind the lines or Something happened on the way to heaven.

But Seriously World Tour 1990

Seto-Shi Bunka Centre (*Rehearsal*)	Nagoya	Japan	23.2.90
Seto-Shi Bunka Centre (*Rehearsal*)	Nagoya	Japan	26.2.90
Castle Hall	Osaka	Japan	27-28.2.90
Sun Plaza hall	Hiroshima	Japan	3.3.90
Yokohama Arena	Yokohama	Japan	5.3.90
Yoyogi Olympic Pool	Tokyo	Japan	6-9.3.90
Entertainment centre	Sydney	Australia	13-15.3.90
Entertainment Centre	Brisbane	Australia	17-18.3.90
National Tennis Centre	Melbourne	Australia	21.3.90
National Tennis Centre	Melbourne	Australia	23-25.3.90
Entertainment Centre	Sydney	Australia	27-29.3.90
Memorial Drive	Adelaide	Australia	31.3.90
Entertainment Centre	Perth	Australia	4-5.4.90
Vorst Nationale	Brussels	Belgium	16.4.90
Palais Omnisports de Bercy	Paris	France	17-20.4.90*
(*) *gig on 18th cancelled.*			
Royal Albert Hall	London	UK	22.4.90

Deutschlandhalle	Berlin	Germany	24.4.90
Wembley Arena	London	UK	28.4.-2.5.90
Ahoy Sportpaleis	Rotterdam	Holland	4.5.90
Congresshalle	Hamburg	Germany	5.5.90
Scandinavium	Gothenburg	Sweden	6.5.90
Globe	Stockholm	Sweden	8.5.90
Festhalle	Frankfurt	Germany	10.5.90
Olympiahalle	Munich	Germany	12.5.90
Hallenstadion	Zurich	Switz	15.5.90
Palatrussardi	Milan	Italy	17.5.90
L'Espace Tony Garnier	Lyon	France	19.5.90
Amphitheatre	Nimes	France	20.5.90
Nuevo Pabellon	Barcelona	Spain	21.5.90
Palais Omnisports de Bercy	Paris	France	23.5.90+
(+) *replaced gig cancelled on 18th April*			
Nassau Coliseum	Long Island	USA	29.5.90
Rosemont Horizon	Chicago	USA	14-17.6.90
Great Western Forum	Los Angeles	USA	20-21.6.90
Great Western Forum	Los Angeles	USA	23-25.6.90
Knebworth Park Silver Clef Festival	Stevenage	UK	30.6.90
Inglistone Centre	Edinburgh	UK	1.7.90
The Point Theatre	Dublin	Eire	5-6.7.90
National Exhibition Centre	Birmingham	UK	7-10.7.90
Philipshalle	Dortmund	Germany	12-13.7.90
Waldebuehne	Berlin	Germany	14-15.7.90
Meadowlands Arena	New York	USA	10-11.8.90
Forum	Montreal	Canada	13-14.8.90
Palace of Auburn Hills	Auburn Hills	USA	16-17.8.90
Richfield Coliseum	Cleveland	USA	19-20.8.90
Spectrum	Philadelphia	USA	22-25.8.90
Capitol Centre	Washington DC	USA	27-28.8.90
Starlake Amphitheatre	Pittsburgh	USA	29-30.8.90
Dean E Smith Centre	Chapel Hill	USA	1.9.90
Lakewood Amphitheatre	Atlanta	USA	2.9.90
Civic Centre Coliseum	Birmingham	USA	3.9.90
Starwood Amphitheatre	Nashville	USA	4.9.90
"MTV Awards"	Los Angeles	USA	6.9.90
Summit Arena	Houston	USA	7.9.90
Starplex Amphitheatre	Dallas	USA	8-9.9.90
McNichols Arena	Denver	USA	11.9.90
PNE Coliseum	Vancouver	Canada	13.9.90
The Dome	Tacoma	USA	14-15.9.90
Shoreline Amphitheatre	San Francisco	USA	17-19.9.90
ARCO Arena	Sacramento	USA	20.9.90
Irvine Meadows Amphitheatre	Los Angeles	USA	22-23.9.90
Wiltern Theatre	Los Angeles	USA	24.9.90
Beacon Theatre	New York	USA	27.9.90
Madison Square Gardens	New York	USA	28-29.9.90
Madison Square Gardens	New York	USA	1-3.10.90

Royal Albert Hall (*with Eric Clapton*)	London	UK	5-7.2.91

Both Sides of the Story World Tour 1994

Prins van Oranje Hal	Utrecht	Holland	1-2.4.94
The Globe	Stockholm	Sweden	4.4.94
Spectrum	Oslo	Norway	6-7.4.94
Prinz van Oranje Hal	Utrecht	Holland	9-10.4.94

Flanders Expo	Ghent	Belgium	12-13.4.94
Westfalenhalle	Dortmund	Germany	15-18.4.94
La Galaxie	Metz	France	21.4.94
Hallenstadion	Zurich	Switzerland	22-23.4.94
Forum Assago	Milan	Italy	25.4.94
Patinoire de Malley	Lausanne	Switz	26.4.94
L'Espace Tony Garnier	Lyon	France	28.4.94
Palais Omnisports de Bercy	Paris	France	29.4.94
Palais Omnisports de Bercy	Paris	France	1.5.94
Palais des Sports	Toulouse	France	2.5.94
Palau St Jordi	Barcelona	Spain	4.5.94
Plaza de Toros de las Ventas	Madrid	Spain	5.5.94
Estadio Alvalade	Lisbon	Portugal	7.5.94
Sports Palace	Mexico City	Mexico	17-18.5.94
Sports Palace	Mexico City	Mexico	20-21.5.94
Amphitheatre	Monterrey	Mexico	23.5.94
Cynthia Woods-Mitchell Pavilion	The Woodlands	USA	25.5.94
The Summit	Houston	USA	26.5.94
Reunion Centre	Dallas	USA	27.5.94
Florida Thunderdome	St Petersburg	USA	29.5.94
Arena	Miami	USA	30-31.5.94
Arena	Orlando	USA	2.6.94
Lakewood Amphitheatre	Atlanta	USA	4.6.94
Blockbuster Pavilion	Charlotte	USA	5.6.94
Walnut Creek Amphitheatre	Raleigh	USA	7.6.94
Great Woods	Mansfield	USA	9-10.6.94
Performing Arts Centre	Saratoga Springs	USA	11.6.94
Forum	Montreal	Canada	13-14.6.94
Skydome	Toronto	Canada	16-17.6.94
Spectrum	Philadelphia	USA	19-20.6.94
Spectrum	Philadelphia	USA	22.6.94
US Air Arena	Landover	USA	23.6.94
Meadowlands Stadium	East Rutherford NJ	USA	25-26.6.94
Palace of Auburn Hills	Auburn Hills	USA	28-29.6.94
Star lake Amphitheatre	Burgettstown	USA	30.6.94
Jones Beach Amphitheatre	Wantagh NY	USA	3.7.94
Civic Centre	Hartford	USA	5.7.94
Madison Square Gardens	New York	USA	6-7.7.94
Richfield Coliseum	Cleveland	USA	11-12.7.94
Deer Park Amphitheatre	Noblesville	USA	14.7.94
Polaris Amphitheatre	Columbus	USA	15.7.94
Marcus Amphitheatre	Milwaukee	USA	16.7.94
Riverfront Music Centre	Cincinatti	USA	18.7.94
Rosemont Horizon	Chicago	USA	20-21.7.9
The Park	Moline	USA	22.7.94
Riverport Amphitheatre	Maryland Heights	USA	24.7.94
Sandstone Amphitheatre	Kansas City	USA	25.7.94
Fiddler's Green Amphitheatre	Englewood	USA	27.7.94
Delta Centre	Salt Lake City	USA	28.7.94
MGM Grand Garden	Las Vegas	USA	30.7.94
Desert Sky Pavilion	Phoenix	USA	31.7.94
ARCO Arena	Sacramento	USA	4.8.94
Shoreline Amphitheatre	Mountain View	USA	5.8.94
Great Western Forum	Englewood	USA	8-9.8.94
Waldebuehne (*Show cancelled*)	Berlin	Germany	31.8.94
Maifeld	Berlin	Germany	1.9.94
Niedersachsenstadion	Hanover	Germany	3-4.9.94

Niedersachsenstadion	Hanover	Germany	6-7.9.94
Palais Omnisports de Bercy	Paris	France	10.9.94
Palais Omnisports de Bercy	Paris	France	12-13.9.94
Schleyerhalle	Stuttgart	Germany	15-16.9.94
Schleyerhalle	Stuttgart	Germany	18-19.9.94
Olympiahalle	Munich	Germany	21-22.9.94
Olympiahalle	Munich	Germany	26-28.9.94
National Exhibition Centre	Birmingham	UK	3-4.10.94
King's Hall	Belfast	UK	7-8.10.94
The Point Theatre	Dublin	Eire	9-10.10.94
Arena	Sheffield	UK	23-24.11.94
Royal Albert Hall	London	UK	26.11.94
G_Mex Centre	Manchester	UK	28-29.11.94
Scottish Exhibition Centre	Glasgow	UK	1-2.12.94
National Exhibition Centre	Birmingham	UK	4-5.12.94
Wembley Arena	London	UK	7-8.12.94
Wembley Arena	London	UK	10-11.12.94
Wembley Arena	London	UK	13-14.12.94

The Far Side World Tour 1995

Ellis Park Rugby Stadium	Johannesburg	S. Africa	17.3.95
Kingsmead Cricket Ground	Durban	S. Africa	19.3.95
Indoor stadium	Singapore	Singapore	22-23.3.95
Thai Army Stadium	Bangkok	Thailand	27.3.95
Thai Army Stadium (*Show cancelled*)	Bangkok	Thailand	28.3.95
Entertainment Centre	Perth	Australia	30.3.95
Memorial Drive	Adelaide	Australia	1.4.95
National Tennis Centre	Melbourne	Australia	2-3.4.95
National Tennis Centre	Melbourne	Australia	5-6.4.95
Entertainment Centre	Brisbane	Australia	8-9.4.95
Entertainment Centre	Sydney	Australia	11-12.4.95
Entertainment Centre	Sydney	Australia	14-15.4.95

1996 and Phil takes everyone by surprise with a tour as part of a Big Band style jazz combo playing a handful of shows at prestigious jazz festivals in Europe. The show at the Royal Albert Hall is given in the presence of both HRH the Queen but also the newly elected president of South Africa, Nelson Mandela. The tour is filmed for a BBC documentary which is screened on 29thDecember 1996 and a recording is also made for future release as a live album and video. Before year's end, Phil has also released his sixth solo album Dance Into The Light The set for the jazz tour included a selection of Phil's solo material and Genesis tracks along with several jazz standards and a typical set included the following...Two hearts/That's all/The west Side/Agains all odds/Hand in hand/Tony Bennett solo set/Drum-percussion duet/Los Endos/Don't do nothin' til you hear from me/Sussudio.

Grand Casino	Geneva	Switzerland	26.1.96
Royal Albert Hall	London	UK	11.7.96
Grand Casino	Monaco	Monaco	12-13.7.96
Giardini del Frontone	Perugia	Italy	15.7.96
La Pinede	Antibes	France	16.7.96
Stavinski Auditorium	Montreux	Switzerland	17.7.96
Polediportivo de Mendizorroza	Vittoria	Spain	20.7.96
Jardine de los viveros	Valencia	Spain	21.7.96
Radio City Music Hall	New York	USA	28.10.96

1997 and Phil is on the road again this time in support of his Dance Into The Light album with an even more extravagant stage show and ever increasing band! This time the tour takes in the more traditional European and US phases although further dates were planned before

Phil's other commitments intervened and this was shelved.
The set for the Dance Into The Light Tour of 1997 was changed between the US and European legs with the two sets running as follows… (USA) Hand in hand/Hang in long enough/Don't lose my number/River so wide/Take me down/Find a way to my heart/Another day in Paradise/Against all odds/Just another story/Lorenzo/Separate lives/The times they are a-changin'/You know what I mean/One more night/In the air tonight/Timbantiocha/Loco in Acapulco/Dabce into thelight/Easy lover/Wear myhat/You cen't hurry love/Two hearts/ Something happened on the way to heaven/Sussudio/The same moon/Take me home.
(Europe/UK) Hand in hand/Hang in long enough/Don't lose my number/River so wide/Take me down/Find a way to my heart/Another day in paradise/Just another story/Againstall odds/Lorenzo/Separate lives/Both sides of the story/Do you remember?/Long long way to go/One more night/In the air tonight/Timbantiocha/Easy lover/Dance into the light/Wear my hat/You can't hurry love/Two hearts/Something happened on the way to heaven./ Sussudio/Take me home.

The Dance into the light World Tour 1997

The Arena (*Rehearsals*)	Lakeland	USA	1-25.2.97
Ice Palace (*load-in only*)	Tampa	USA	27.2.97
Ice Palace	Tampa	USA	28.2.97
Orlando Arena	Orlando	USA	1.3.97
Miami Arena	Miami	USA	3.3.97
US Air Arena	Washington DC	USA	5.3.97
Civic Arena	Pittsburgh	USA	7.3.97
Marine Midland Arena	Buffalo	USA	8.3.97
Palace of Auburn Hills	Detroit	USA	10.3.97
Edwin Nutter Centre	Dayton	USA	11.3.97
Madison Square Gardens	New York	USA	13-14.3.97
Colisee Arena	Quebec City	Canada	16.3.97
Molson Centre	Montreal	Canada	17-18.3.97
Skydome	Toronto	Canada	20.3.97
Corel Centre	Ottawa	Canada	21-22.3.97
Fleet Centre	Boston	USA	24.3.97
Pepsi (Knickerbocker) Arena	Albany NY	USA	25.3.97
Civic Centre Coliseum	Hartford	USA	27.3.97
Corestate Centre	Philadelphia	USA	29.3.97
Bryce Jordan Arena	Penn State	USA	30.3.97
Van Andel Arena	Grand Rapids	USA	3.4.97
Gund Arena	Cleveland	USA	4.4.97
Rosemont Horizon	Chicago	USA	6.4.97
Market Square Arena	Champaign	USA	8.4.97
Bradley Centre	Milwaukee	USA	10.4.97
Kiel Centre	St Louis	USA	11.4.97
Kemper Arena	Kansas City	USA	12.4.97
San Jose Arena	San Jose	USA	15.4.97
ARCO Arena	Sacramento	USA	16.4.97
America West Arena	Phoenix	USA	18.4.97
MGM Grand Garden	Las Vegas	USA	19.4.97
Arrowhead Pond	Los Angeles	USA	21.4.97
Palau St Jordi	Barcelona	Spain	7.10.97
Filaforum	Milan	Italy	9.10.97
Halle Tony Garnier	Lyon	France	11.10.97
Arena	Geneva	Switzerland	12-13.10.97
Hallenstadion	Zurich	Switzerland	15-16.10.97
Deutschlandhalle	Berlin	Germany	18-19.10.97
Festhalle	Frankfurt	Germany	21-23.10.97
Globe Arena	Stockholm	Sweden	25.10.97

Spektrum	Oslo	Norway	26.10.97
Ahoy Sportpaleis	Rotterdam	Holland	28-29.10.97
Messehalle 2	Hanover	Germany	31.10.97
Messehalle 2	Hanover	Germany	1.11.97
Flanders Expo	Ghent	Belgium	3-4.11.97
National Exhibition Centre	Birmingham	UK	6-7.11.97
Arena	Newcastle	UK	9-10.11.97
NYNEX Arena	Manchester	UK	18-19.11.97
Westfalenhalle	Dortmund	Germany	21-23.11.97
Schleyerhalle	Stuttgart	Germany	25-26.11.97
Olympiahalle	Munich	Germany	28-29.11.97
Stadthalle	Vienna	Austria	1.12.97
Sportovinhala	Prague	Czech	2.12.97
Messehalle 7	Leipzig	Germany	4-6.12.97
Palais Omnisports de Bercy	Paris	France	8-9.12.97
Westfalenhalle	Dortmund	Germany	11.12.97
Earls Court Arena	London	UK	13-14.12.97
Earls Court Arena	London	UK	16-17.12.97

1998 and Phil takes out his Big Band combo for a proper tour of the USA and Europe with a set drawing from the best of his own material and that of Genesis as well as several jazz standards. The almost three hour musical extrvaganza comprised the following tracks… Two hearts/That's all/I don't care anymore/Against all odds/The west Side/hand in hand/Rad Dudeski/Hold on my heart/In the air tonight/Chips & Salsa/Georgia on my mind/Don't lose my number/Milestones/Los Endos/Do nothin' til you hear from me/The way you look tonight/Always/Sussudio. As if that wasn't enough he also continued working on the Tarzan soundtrack and also the preparation of material for a "Greatest Hits" album released later in the year as well as several other projects. The future certainly looks busy for Mr Philip Collins Esquire!

Big Band Jazz Tour 1998.

Historic Mountain Winery	Saratoga	USA	12-13.6.98
County Bowl	Santa Barbara	USA	14.6.98
Greek Theatre	Los Angeles	USA	15.6.98
Woodlands Pavilion	Houston	USA	18.6.98
City Stages	Birmingham	USA	19.6.98
Chastain Park Amphitheatre	Atlanta	USA	20.6.98
I C Light Amphitheatre	Pittsburgh	USA	21.6.98
Nautica Stage	Cleveland	USA	22.6.98
Meadow Brook	Detroit	USA	23.6.98
Taste of Chicago	Chicago	USA	25.6.98
Summerfest	Milwaukee	USA	26.6.98
Boston Globe Jazz Festival	Harborlights	USA	28.6.98
Carnegie Hall	New York	USA	29.6.98
Tivoli Gardens Jazz Festival	Copenhagen	Denmark	7.7.98
Waldebuehne	Berlin	Germany	8.7.98
North Sea Jazz Festival	The Hague	Holland	10.7.98
Nice Jazz Festival	Nice	France	13.7.98
Montreux Jazz Festival	Montreux	Switzerland	14.7.98
Pori Fest	Helsinki	Finland	17.7.98
Villa Erba Cernobbio	Milan	Italy	19.7.98
Fourviere	Lyon	France	20.7.98
Grand Rex	Paris	France	21.7.98
Royal Festival Hall	London	UK	23.7.98
Symphony Hall	Birmingham	UK	24.7.98

Peter Gabriel Solo Gig Guide

1977 and Peter starts life as a solo artist two years after his departure from Genesis. His first solo album Peter Gabriel achieves a high chart entry and with a top ten single from it in the shape of Solsbury Hill his first tour is a great success and bodes well for his future outings.

Capitol Theatre	Passaic NJ	USA	5.3.77
Civic Auditorium	Rochester NY	USA	6.3.77
Orpheum Theatre	Davenport	USA	9.3.77
Uptown Theatre	Chicago	USA	11.3.77
Masonic Auditorium	Detroit	USA	13.3.77
Music Hall	Cleveland	USA	15.3.77
Century Hall	Buffalo NY	USA	16.3.77
Tower Theatre	Philadelphia	USA	17-18.3.77
Palladium Theatre	New York	USA	19.3.77
Massey Hall	Toronto	Canada	22.3.77
City Hall	Quebec	Canada	23.3.77
Stanley Theatre	Pittsburgh	USA	26-28.3.77
Music Hall	Cleveland	USA	29.3.77
Kiel Open House	St Louis	USA	30.3.77
Uptown Theatre	Kansas City	USA	1,4,77
Convention Centre	Dallas	USA	2.4.77
Music Hall	Houston	USA	3.4.77
Winterland Arena	San Francisco	USA	7.4.77
Roxy Club	Los Angeles	USA	9-10.4.77
Hammersmith Odeon	London	UK	24-26.4.77
Empire Theatre	Liverpool	UK	28.4.77
Apollo Theatre	Manchester	UK	29.4.77
New Vic Theatre (*2 shows*)	London	UK	30.4.77
?	Courtrai	France	2.9.77
?	Antwerp	Belgium	3.9.77
Rijnhal	Arnhem	Holland	4.9.77
Ahoy Sportpaleis	Rotterdam	Holland	7.9.77
Fete de l'Humanite	Paris	France	9.9.77
City Hall	Newcastle	UK	13-14.9.77
Apollo Theatre	Glasgow	UK	15.9.77
City Hall	Sheffield	UK	17.9.77
Trentham Gardens	Stoke on Trent	UK	18.9.77
The Dome	Brighton	UK	19.9.77
De Montfort Hall	Leicester	UK	21.9.77
St George's Hall	Bradford	UK	22.9.77
Empire Theatre	Liverpool	UK	23.9.77
Odeon Theatre	Birmingham	UK	25.9.77
Apollo Theatre	Manchester	UK	27-28.9.77
Gaumont Theatre	Southampton	UK	30.9.77
Capitol Theatre	Cardiff	UK	1.10.77
Hippodrome (*2 shows*)	Bristol	UK	2.10.77
Olympia Theatre	Paris	France	4.10.77
Halle des Fetes	Lyon	France	5.10.77

Salle D'Expositions	Colmar	France	6.10.77
Congresshalle	Hamburg	Germany	8.10.77
Tivolis Conzertsal	Copenhagen	Denmark	9.10.77
Konserthuset	Stockholm	Sweden	10-11.10.77
Munsterlandhalle	Munster	Germany	13.10.77
Rhein-Main-Halle	Wiesbanden	Germany	14.10.77
Festhalle	Berne	Switz	15.10.77
Chapiteau	Strasbourg	France	16.10.77
Sporthalle	Cologne	Germany	18.10.77
Stadthalle	Offenbach	Germany	19.10.77
Philipshalle	Dusseldorf	Germany	20.10.77
Deutschlandhalle	Berlin	Germany	21.10.77
Zirkus Krone	Munich	Germany	22.10.77
Palais des Sports	Dijon	France	24.10.77
Porte des Expositions	Nantes	France	25.10.77
Palais de Congres	Lille	France	26.10.77
Arena	Poitiers	France	27.10.77
Patinoire de Malley	Bordeaux	France	28.10.77
Palais des Sports	Toulouse	France	29.10.77
Nouvel Hippodrome	Paris	France	30.10.77
Sports & Leisure Centre	Bath	UK	1.11.77

1978 and Peter's second album, a much darker one than its predecessor is released. Also titled Peter Gabriel it includes work by King Crimson stalwart Robert Fripp who also produced the album and guested with Peter's band under the moniker of "Dusty Road". During the tour which coincided with that of Peter's former band; Genesis, Peter was briefly reunited with them during their performance of The Lamb Lies Down On Broadway at New York. The show at the Grugahalle Essen was also filmed for tv and captures the excitement of one of these shows including Peter's resurrection of his alter-ego "Rael" for a marvellous version of "The lamb.." as an encore. Peter rounds off the year with four sell-out gigs at London's prestigious Hammersmith Odeon in the company of Tom Robinson.

New Theatre	Oxford	UK	23.8.78
University Great Hall	Lancaster	UK	25.8.78
Chateau Neuf	Oslo	Norway	31.8.78
Globe	Stockholm	Sweden	1.9.78
Concerthal	Gothenburg	Sweden	2.9.78
Stadthalle	Bremen	Germany	4.9.78
Knebworth Park Festival	Stevenage	UK	9.9.78
Grugahalle	Essen	Germany	15.9.78
Roxy Club	Los Angeles	USA	30.9.-1.10.78
Bottom Line Club	New York	USA	4.10.78
Colisee de Quebec	Quebec City	Canada	13.10.78
University	Montreal	Canada	15.10.78
University	Stoneybrook	USA	21.10.78
Capitol Theatre	Passaic NJ	USA	29.10.78
Orpheum Theatre	Boston	USA	31.10.78
Palladium Theatre	New York	USA	4.11.78
Crawford Hall	Irvine	USA	18.11.78
Union Hall UCLA	Ackerman	USA	21.11.78
Terrace Theatre	Long Beach	USA	22.11.78
J Eden Hal	Amsterdam	Holland	30.11.78
Palais des Sports	Lyon	France	5.12.78
Pavilion Baltard	Nogent Marne	France	9-10.12.78
RTL French tv studios	Paris	France	10.12.78
Philipshalle	Dusseldorf	Germany	12.12.78
Congreshalle	Basle	Switzerland	16.12.78

Istadion	Geneva	Switzerland	17.12.78
Hammersmith Odeon	London	UK	20-24.12.78

1979 and only two shows at which he took the opportunity of premiering several tracks from his forthcoming third solo album which is still almost a year away.

Glastonbury Fayre	Glastonbury	UK	23.6.79
Reading Festival	Reading	UK	26.8.79

1980 and Peter's success continues this time with the brilliant "Games without frontiers" single and third solo album. For reasons which still remain uncertain, Peter titled his tour "The Tour of China 1984" maybe a veiled reference to all the artists scrambling to play behind the Iron Curtain as a status symbol. The tour is another great success.

University	Exeter	UK	20.2.80
Odeon Theatre	Taunton	UK	21.2.80
Odeon Theatre	Birmingham	UK	25.2.80
Caird Hall	Dundee	UK	27.2.80
Capitol Theatre	Aberdeen	UK	28.2.80
Apollo Theatre	Glasgow	UK	29.2.80
Odeon Theatre	Edinburgh	UK	1.3.80
City Hall	Newcastle	UK	3.3.80
Empire Theatre	Liverpool	UK	4.3.80
Apollo Theatre	Manchester	UK	5.3.80
Sophia Gardens	Cardiff	UK	7.3.80
Gaumont Theatre	Southampton	UK	8.3.80
Hammersmith Odeon	London	UK	11-13.3.80
Conference Centre	Brighton	UK	15.3.80
University	Bath	UK	16.3.80
County Bowl	Santa Monica	USA	21-23.6.80
Uptown Theatre	Chicago	USA	26.6.80
Allen Theatre	Cleveland	USA	27.6.80
Auditorium	Rochester NY	USA	28.6.80
Clensman Music Hall	Buffalo NY	USA	3-4.7.80
Parc de Jeunesse	Quebec	Canada	5.7.80
Central Park	New York	USA	7.7.80
Orpheum Theatre	Boston	USA	8.7.80
Convention Hall	Asprey	USA	9.7.80
Tower Theatre	Philadelphia	USA	10.7.80
Diplomat Hotel	New York	USA	12.7.80
Nuevo Pabellon	Barcelona	Spain	3.8.80
Erikhallen	Stockholm	Sweden	30.8.80
Scandinavium	Gothenburg	Sweden	31.8.80
Audimax	Hamburg	Germany	1.9.80
Kuppelsaal	Hanover	Germany	2.9.80
Eisporthalle	Berlin	Germany	4.9.80
Philipshalle	Dortmund	Germany	5.9.80
NeumusikCentrum	Utrecht	Holland	6.9.80
Olympia Theatre	Paris	France	10-13.9.80
Palais de Congres	Nantes	France	14.9.80
Stadthalle	Offenbach	Germany	15.9.80
Parco Cascine	Florence	Italy	28.9.80
Palasport	Genoa	Italy	29.9.80
Hallenstadion	Zurich	Switzerland	30.9.80
Parc des Expositions	Avignon	France	1.10.80

1982/83 sees Peter's fourth album released to a critically mixed reception. Its mixture of

RHYTHMS AND OVER ALL DARKER TEXTURE MAKE IT A TRYING PROPOSITION BUT THE SHOWS IN SUPPORT OF THE ALBUM BLOW AWAY ANY DOUBTS AS PETER AND HIS BAND TURN IN SUPERB PERFORMANCES WHICH ARE IMPRESSIVE ENOUGH TO PERSUADE DAVID BOWIE TO INVITE PETER ON TO THE BILL AT SEVERAL OF HIS US/CANADIAN SHOWS ON THE "SERIOUS MOONLIGHT" TOUR DURING THE SUMMER OF 1983.

Showering Pavilion	Shepton Mallet	UK	16.7.82
Showering Pavilion	Shepton Mallet	UK	18.7.82
Orpheum Theatre	Boston	USA	28.10.82
Stoneybrook University	Long Island	USA	29.10.82
?	Livingstone NJ	USA	31.10.82
Mid Hudson Civic Centre	Poughkeepsie NY	USA	1.11.82
Mohawk Valley Centre	Utica	USA	2.11.82
Horton Fieldhouse	Normal	USA	3.11.82
Colisee de Quebec	Quebec City	Canada	4.11.82
Forum	Montreal	Canada	5.11.82
Civic Centre	Ottawa	Canada	6.11.82
Maple Leaf Gardens	Toronto	Canada	8.11.82
Shea's Theatre	Buffalo NY	USA	9.11.82
War Memorial Auditorium	Rochester NY	USA	11.11.82
Orpheum Theatre	Boston	USA	12.11.82
Capitol Theatre	Passaic NJ	USA	13.11.82
Warner Theatre	Washington DC	USA	14.11.82
Spectrum	Philadelphia	USA	16.11.82
Hara Arena	Dayton	USA	18.11.82
Michigan Theatre	Ann Arbor	USA	20.11.82
University of Indiana	Bloomington	USA	21.11.82
Wings Auditorium	Kalamazoo	USA	22.11.82
Richfield Coliseum	Cleveland	USA	24.11.82
Ritz Theatre	New York	USA	25-26.11.82
Dane County Coliseum	Madison	USA	28.11.82
Performing Arts Centre	Milwaukee	USA	1.12.82
Pavilion	Chicago	USA	2.12.82
Horton Fieldhouse	Normal	USA	3.12.82
Memorial Auditorium	Kansas City	USA	4.12.82
De Kalb	Illinois	USA	6.12.82
ISU	Carbondale	USA	7.12.82
Agora	Dallas	USA	9.12.82
Music Hall	Houston	USA	10.12.82
Coliseum	Austin	USA	11.12.82
Sports Arena	San Diego	USA	14.12.82
Universal Amphitheatre	Los Angeles	USA	15-16.12.82
Civic Centre	San Francisco	USA	19.12.82
Parc des Expositions	Rouen	France	30.6.83
Palais des Sports	Paris	France	1.7.83
Tourhout Festival	Tourhout	Belgium	2.7.83
Werchter Festival	Werchter	Belgium	3.7.83
Stadio Communale	Ferrara	Italy	5.7.83
Stadio Communale	Prato	Italy	7.7.83
Selhurst Park Football Ground	London	UK	9.7.83
Landsdowne Park	Ottawa	Canada	17.7.83
CNE Bandshell	Toronto	Canada	18.7.83
Arts Centre	Holmdel	USA	22.7.83
Mann Music Centre	Philadelphia	USA	23.7.83
E M Lowe Theatre	Worcester	USA	27.7.83
Tennis centre	Forest Hills	USA	29.7.83
Poplar Creek Centre	Pine Knob	USA	31.7.83
Poplar Creek Centre	Chicago	USA	2.8.83

Hampton Roads	Vancouver	Canada	3.8.83
British Columbia Place	Vancouver	Canada	8.8.83
Paramount Theatre	Seattle	Canada	10.8.83
Civic Theatre	Berkeley	USA	12-13.8.83
Golden Hall	San Diego	USA	15.8.83
Greek Theatre	Los Angeles	USA	16-17.8.83
Coliseum	St Austell	UK	4.9.83
Gaumont Theatre	Southampton	UK	5.9.83
Hammersmith Odeon	London	UK	7-9.9.83
National Exhibition Centre	Birmingham	UK	10.9.83
Apollo Theatre	Glasgow	UK	12.9.83
Playhouse	Edinburgh	UK	14.9.83
City Hall	Newcastle	UK	15.9.83
Apollo Theatre	Manchester	UK	17.9.83
Empire Theatre	Liverpool	UK	18.9.83
Vorst Nationale	Brussels	Belgium	26.9.83
Concertgebouow (*2 shows*)	Den Haag	Holland	27.9.83
Ekeberghallen	Oslo	Norway	29.9.83
Johanneshovs Istadion	Stockholm	Sweden	30.9.83
Falkoner Theatrit	Copenhagen	Denmark	1.10.83
Congresshalle	Hamburg	Germany	2.10.83
Philipshalle	Dusseldorf	Germany	4.10.83
Alte Oper	Frankfurt	Germany	5.10.83
Zirkus Krone	Munich	Germany	6.10.83
Stadthalle	Vienna	Austria	8.10.83
Niedersachsenhalle	Hanover	Germany	10.10.83
Eisporthalle	Berlin	Germany	11.10.83
Boeblingen Sporthalle	Stuttgart	Germany	12.10.83
Halle 7	Lausanne	Switz	14.10.83
Maison des Sports	Clermont Ferrand	France	15.10.83
Palais des Sports	Toulouse	France	16.10.83
Patinoire	Bordeaux	France	17.10.83
Parc Exposition Chateau Blanc	Avignon	France	18.10.83
Alexpo	Grenoble	France	20.10.83
Chapiteau	Dijon	France	21.10.83
Chapiteau	Strasbourg	France	22.10.83
Foire de Lille Halle B	Lille	France	25.10.83
Palais de Beaujoire	Nantes	France	27.10.83
La Petite Salle Penfield	Brest	France	28.10.83

1986 sees Peter embark on his most ambitious schedule yet including two separate tours. First of all is his active participation in the "Conspiracy of Hope" tour of the US in the company of Bryan Adams, The Police, U2 and various major acts in support of the Amnesty International charity including an impromptu gig outside the UN building in New York on 15th September 1986 the 38th anniversary of the signing of the "Declaration of Human Rights".

Cow Palace	San Francisco	USA	4.6.86
Sports Arena	Los Angeles	USA	6.6.86
The Omni Centre	Atlanta	USA	11.6.86
Rosemont Horizon	Chicago	USA	13.6.86
Giants Stadium	East Rutherford NJ	USA	15.6.86
United Nations Building	New York	USA	15.9.86

Peter then embarks on his lengthiest tour to-date in support of his new album, So which sees his success reach new heights including three hit singles both in the UK and elsewhere. Peter is joined at the last night of his stint at London's Earl's Court Arena by Kate Bush for an emotional rendition of Don't Give Up.

War Memorial Auditorium	Rochester NY	USA	7.11.86
Civic Arena	Pittsburgh	USA	8.11.86
Civic Arena	Syracuse NY	USA	9.11.86
Civic Arena	New Haven	USA	11.1.186
Capitol Theatre	Largo NJ	USA	12.11.86
The Gardens	Cincinnatti	USA	14.11.86
Assembly Halls	Champaign	USA	15.11.86
Joe Louis Arena	Detroit	USA	17.11.86
Richfield Coliseum	Cleveland	USA	18.11.86
Centrum	Worcester	USA	21-22.11.86
Maple Leaf Gardens	Toronto	Canada	23.11.86
Forum	Ottawa	Canada	24.11.86
Forum	Montreal	Canada	25.11.86
Spectrum	Philadelphia	USA	29-30.11.86
Madison Square Gardens	New York	USA	1-2.12.86
Rosemont Horizon	Chicago	USA	5.12.86
Reunion Centre	Dallas	USA	8.12.86
Oakland Coliseum	San Francisco	USA	13.12.86
Forum	Los Angeles	USA	15-16.12.86
Jingu Stadium	Tokyo	Japan	20-21.12.86
Palladium Theatre	London	UK	28-29.3.87
Maison des Sports	Clermont Ferrand	France	1.6.87
Patinoire Meriadec	Bordeaux	France	2.6.87
Salle de Beaujoire	Nantes	France	3.6.87
Palais Omnisports de Bercy	Paris	France	5-7.6.87
Palatrussardi	Milan	Italy	10.6.87
Palasport	Bologna	Italy	12.6.87
Palasport	Rome	Italy	13.6.87
Olympiahalle	Munich	Germany	15.6.87
Schleyerhalle	Stuttgart	Germany	16.6.87
Frankenhalle	Nurnburg	Germany	17.6.87
Sporthalle	Cologne	Germany	19.6.87
Alster Dorfer Sporthalle	Hamburg	Germany	20.6.87
Stadthalle	Bremen	Germany	21.6.87
Scottish Exhibition Centre	Glasgow	UK	23.6.87
Earls Court Arena	London	UK	25-28.6.87
National Exhibition Centre	Birmingham	UK	29.6.-1.7.87
Tourhout Festival	Tourhout	Belgium	2.7.87
Werchter Festival	Werchter	Belgium	3.7.87
Landsdowne Park	Ottawa	Canada	10.7.87
CNE Fairgrounds	Toronto	Canada	11.7.87
Forum	Montreal	Canada	12-13.7.87
Great Woods Centre	Boston	USA	15-16.7.87
Meadowlands Stadium	East Rutherford NJ	USA	17-18.7.87
Spectrum	Philadelphia	USA	20-21.7.87
Pine Knob Music Centre	Detroit	USA	22.7.87
Performing Arts Centre	Poplar Creek	USA	24.7.87
Marcus Amphitheatre	Milwaukee	USA	25.7.87
Blossom Music Centre	Cleveland	USA	27.7.87
Postgate Pavilion	Columbia	USA	28.8.87
Hvidovre Stadium	Copenhagen	Denmark	28.8.87
Kalvoyre Festival	Isle of Calves	Norway	30.8.87
Ishallen	Helsinki	Finland	1.9.87
Johanneshovs Isstadion	Stockholm	Sweden	3.9.87
Scandinavium	Gothenburg	Sweden	6.9.87
Ahoy Sportpaleis	Rotterdam	Holland	8-9.9.87
Waldebuehne	Berlin	Germany	11.9.87

Ruhrstadion	Bochum	Germany	12.9.87
Offenbachstadion	Offenbach	Germany	13.9.87
MTK Stadium	Budapest	Hungary	15.9.87
Stadthalle	Vienna	Austria	16.9.87
Piazza Bra' Amphitheatre	Verona	Italy	18.9.87
Piazza Grande	Locarno	Switzerland	19.9.87
St Jakob Football Stadium	Basle	Switzerland	21.9.87
Patinoire de Malley	Lausanne	Switzerland	22.9.87
Chapiteau	Strasbourg	France	23.9.87
Palais des Sports	Lyon	France	24.9.87
Palais des Sports	Toulouse	France	26.9.87
Velodromo Anoeta	San Sebastian	Spain	27.9.87
Palacio de los Desportos	Barcelona	Spain	29-30.9.87
Lykabettus Hill Theatre	Athens	Greece	5-9.10.87

1988 and Peter, already well known for his activities on behalf of human rights, undertakes his most ambitious tour as part of the "Human Rights Now!" package along with Sting, Bruce Springsteen, Youssou N'Dour and Tracy Chapman. This involves a jaunt around the world spreading Amnesty International's message on human rights culminating with a gig in Buenos Aires on the 40th anniversary of the signing of the "Declaration of Human Rights".

Royal Albert Hall	London	UK	5-6.6.88
Wembley Stadium	London	UK	11.6.88
Coliseum	St Austell	UK	28.8.88
Wembley Stadium	London	UK	2.9.88
Palais Omnisports de Bercy	Paris	France	4-5.9.88
Nepstadion	Budapest	Hungary	6.9.88
Stadio Communale	Turin	Italy	8.9.88
Nou camp Stadium	Barcelona	Spain	10.9.88
Estadio Nacional	San Jose	Costa Rica	13.9.88
Maple Leaf gardens	Toronto	Canada	15.9.88
Stade Olympique	Montreal	Canada	17.9.88
J F K Stadium	Philadelphia	USA	19.9.88
Memorial coliseum	Los Angeles	USA	21.9.88
Oakland Coliseum	Oakland	USA	23.9.88
The Big Egg	Tokyo	Japan	27.9.88
Jawaharlal Nehru Stadium	Delhi	India	30.9.88
Olympiako Stadium	Athens	Greece	3.10.88
New Stadium	Harare	Zimbabwe	7.10.88
Stade Houpouet Boigny	Abidjan	Ivory C'st	9.10.88
Estadio Palmeiras	Sao Paolo	Brazil	12.10.88
Estadio Mundialista	Mendoza	Argentina	14.10.88
Estadio Rio Plata	Buenos Aires	Argentina	15.10.88

1989-1994 begin quietly enough for Peter with a handful of gigs before serious gigging begins for his new album Us released in April 1992 and for which he embarks upon his most ambitious stage set up yet and a massive world tour which sees Peter literally circumnavigate the globe playing on every continent and in many places usually missed by rock acts. The tour culminates with an appearance at the 25th anniversary celebrations of the "Woodstock Festival" in August 1994.

Since then, Peter has kept a low profile although that will probably change soon with the release of his long awaited new album and no doubt a tour in which one thing is for certain we must "Expect the unexpected" which has been Peter's trademark since day one of his solo career.

Glastonbury Fayre	Glastonbury	UK	18.6.89
Wembley Stadium	London	UK	16.4.90

Real World Studios Marquee	Bath	UK	18.8.91
Glastonbury Fayre	Glastonbury	UK	24.6.92
Rivermead Leisure Centre	Bath	UK	18.7.92
Royal Victoria Park	Bath	UK	16.8.92
Royal Victoria Park	Bath	UK	17.8.92
Botanic Park (Womadelaide)	Adelaide	Australia	19-20.2.93
Grand Slam Club (Rehearsals)	Los Angeles	USA	6-7.3.93
Academy of Music (Warm-up gig)	New York	USA	13.3.93
The Globe	Stockholm	Sweden	13.4.93
Spektrum	Oslo	Norway	14.4.93
Sporthalle	Hamburg	Germany	15.4.93
Deutschlandhalle	Berlin	Germany	17.4.93
Hallenstadion	Zurich	Switzerland	19.4.93
Festhalle	Frankfurt	Germany	20.4.93
Schleyerhalle	Stuttgart	Germany	21.4.93
Galaxie	Amneville	France	23.4.93
Le Zenith	Paris	France	24-25.4.93
Ahoy Sportpaleis	Rotterdam	Holland	27-28.4.93
Flanders Expo	Ghent	Belgium	30.4.93
Stade Couvert Reg	Lieven	Belgium	1.5.93
Halle Expo	Caen	France	2.5.93
Patinoire Meriadec	Bordeaux	France	4.5.93
WOMAD Festival	Madrid	Spain	6.5.93
WOMAD Festival	Caceres	Spain	7.5.93
Velodromo	Valencia	Spain	9.5.93
Palau St Jordi	Barcelona	Spain	10.5.93
Palais des Sports	Toulouse	France	11.5.93
Les Arenes	Nimes	France	13.5.93
Halle Tony Garnier	Lyon	France	14.5.93
Patinoire de Malley	Lausanne	Switzerland	15.5.93
Forum	Mailand	Italy	17.5.93
Palaghiaccio Marino	Rome	Italy	18.5.93
Olympiahalle	Munjch	Germany	20.5.93
Frankenhalle	Nurnburg	Germany	21.5.93
Westfalenhalle	Dortmund	Germany	22.5.93
Arena	Sheffield	UK	24.5.93
National Exhibition Centre	Birmingham	UK	25.5.93
Scottish Exhibtion Centre	Glasgow	UK	26.5.93
The Point Theatre	Dublin	Eire	27.5.93
Showground Peace Together Festival	Belfast	UK	29.5.93 *
(*) Festival cancelled.			
Earls Court Arena	London	UK	31.5.-1.6.93
War Memorial Auditorium	Rochester NY	USA	18.6.93
Centrum	Worcester	USA	19-20.6.93
Cap Centre	Landover	USA	22.6.93
Giants Stadium	East Rutherford NJ	USA	23.6.93
Madison Square Gardens	New York	USA	24.6.93
Skydome	Toronto	Canada	26.6.93
Colisee de Quebec	Quebec City	Canada	28.6.93
Forum	Montreal	Canada	29-30.6.93
Palace of Auburn Hills	Detroit	USA	2.7.93
Richfield Coliseum	Cleveland	USA	3.7.93
Spectrum	Philadephia	USA	6-8.7.93
Rosemont Horizon	Chicago	USA	10-11.7.93
Saddledome	Calgary	Canada	14.7.93
PNE Coliseum	Vancouver	Canada	16.7.93
Tacoma Dome	Seattle	USA	17.7.93

Coliseum	Oakland	USA	19-20.7.93
Great Western Forum	Los Angeles	USA	22.7.93
Sports Arena	San Diego	USA	23.7.93
America West Arena	Phoenix	USA	24.7.93
McNichols Arena	Denver	USA	27.7.93
Reunion Centre	Dallas	USA	29.7.93
Summit Arena	Houston	USA	30.7.93
The Omni Centre	Atlanta	USA	1.8.93
Orlando Arena	Orlando	USA	3.8.93
Miami Arena	Miami	USA	4.8.93
Royal Victoria Park (womad)	Bath	UK	8.8.93
Cesmes (womad)	Cesmes	Turkey	28.8.93
Estadio Alvalade (womad)	Lisbon	Portugal	29.8.93
Coliseum (womad)	St Austell	UK	30.8.93
Maple Leaf Gardens	Toronto	Canada	4.9.93
Forum (womad)	Montreal	Canada	5.9.93
Performing Arts Centre (womad)	Saratoga Springs	USA	6.9.93
Starlake Amphitheatre (womad)	Pittsburgh	USA	8.9.93
Buckeye Lake (womad)	Columbus	USA	10.9.93
World Music Theatre (womad)	Chicago	USA	11.9.93
Marcus Amphitheatre (womad)	Milwaukee	USA	12.9.93
Deer Creek	Indianapolis	USA	13.9.93
Fiddler's Green (womad)	Denver	USA	16.9.93
Velodrome (womad)	Los Angeles	USA	18.9.93
Golden Gate Park (womad)	San Francisco	USA	19.9.93
ARCO Arena	Sacramento	USA	21.9.93
Oakland Coliseum	Oakland	USA	22.9.93
Sports Palace	Mexico City	Mexico	24-26.9.93
Pista Atletica	Santiago	Chile	29.9.93
Velez Sarfeld	Cordoba	Argentina	1.10.93
Chateau Carreras Stadium	Buenos Aires	Argentina	2.10.93
Rosario stadium	Rosarui	Argentina	4.10.93
Ibirapuera	Sao Paolo	Brazil	6.10.93
Imperator	Rio de Janeiro	Argentina	7.10.96
Poliedro Parking Lot	Caracas	Venezuela	9.10.93
Maimarktgelande	Mannheim	Germany	4.11.93
Deutschlandhalle	Berlin	Germany	6.11.93
Congresshalle	Hamburg	Germany	7-8.11.93
Philipshalle	Dortmund	Germany	10.11.93
Hallenstadion	Zurich	Switzerland	12.11.93
Le Summum	Grenoble	France	13.11.93
Zenithe Omega	Toulon	France	14.11.93
Palasport	Modena	Italy	16-17.11.93
Palaghiaccio Marino	Rome	Italy	19.11.93
Palasport	Florence	Italy	20.11.93
Forum Assago	Milan	Italy	22.11.93
Palais Omnisports de Bercy	Paris	France	24.11.93
Le Zenith	Paris	France	25.11.93
Indira Gandhi Stadium	Delhi	India	11.2.94
Palace Grounds	Bangalore	India	14.2.94
Brabourne Stadium	Bombay	India	17.2.94
Entertainment Centre	Perth	Australia	21.2.94
Entertainment Centre	Adelaide	Australia	23.2.94
National Tennis Centre	Melbourne	Australia	24-25.2.94
Entertainment Centre	Brisbane	Australia	27.2.94
Entertainment Centre	Sydney	Australia	1-2.3.94

Supertop	Auckland	New Zealand	4.3.94
Budokan Hall	Tokio	Japan	7-8.3.94
Castle Hall	Osaka	Japan	10.3.94
Stadium	Hong Kong	Hong Kong	14.3.94
Messehalle	Nurnburg	Germany	19.5.94
"Rock in Reim" Festival	Munich	Germany	21.5.94
"Rock am Ring" Festival	Nuremburg	Germany	22.5.94
Nelson's Beach (womad)	Taba	Egypt	18.6.94
Hayarkon Park (womad)	Tel Aviv	Israel	19.6.94
Le Zenith	Paris	France	21.6.94
"Rock Productions"	Bratislava	Czech Republic	23.6.94
"Schulschuss" Festival	Wels	Austria	24.6.94
"Glastonbury Fayre"	Glastonbury	UK	26.6.94
"Kalvoyre Festival"	Isle of Calves	Norway	29.6.94
"Roskilde Festival"	Roskilde	Denmark	1.7.94
Tourhout Festival	Tourhout	Belgium	2.7.94
Werchter Festival	Werchter	Belgium	3.7.94
North Sea Jazz Festival	Den Haag	Holland	6.7.94
"Out in the Green" Festival	Winterthur	Switzerland	8.7.94
Forum	Mailand	Switzerland	9.7.94
Parco Acquatico	Milan	Italy	10.7.94
Lakewood Amphitheatre	Atlanta	USA	12.7.94
Polaris Amphitheatre	Columbus	USA	14.7.94
Postgate Pavilion (womad)	Merriweather	USA	15.7.94
Jones Beach (womad)	New York	USA	16.7.94
Performing Arts Centre	Saratoga Springs	USA	17.7.94
Great Woods Amphitheatre	Boston	USA	19.7.94
Stabler Arena	Allentown	USA	10.8.94
Beacon Theatre	New York	USA	11.8.94
Tower Theatre	Philadelphia	USA	12.8.94
"Woodstock 25th Anniversary"	New York State	USA	14.8.94
Palais Omnisports de Bercy	Paris	France	10.12.98

This gig guide has been compiled by Alan Hewitt with the help of Tina at "The Box" Magazine and Vernon Parker whose help has been of inestimable value.

Steve Hackett Solo Gig Guide

1978 and Steve's first solo outing which follows on the back of his second highly successful solo album "Please Don't Touch". This tour finally gives Steve the opportunity to prove himself as a solo artist.

Chateau Neuf	Oslo	Norway	4.10.78
Gota Lejon	Stockholm	Sweden	5.10.78
Konserthuset	Gothenburg	Sweden	14.10.78
Olympia Theatre	Paris	France	16.1.078
Beat Club	Bremen	Germany	17.10.78
Congresshal	Den Haag	Holland	19.10.78
University	Cardiff	UK	23.10.78
Apollo Theatre	Manchester	UK	24.10.78

Apollo Theatre	Glasgow	UK	26.10.78
Friars	Aylesbury	UK	28.10.78
Odeon Theatre	Birmingham	UK	29.10.78
Hammersmith Odeon	London	UK	30.10.78

1979 and Steve releases the album by which all his future releases will be measured. Spectral Mornings was accompanied by a highly successful tour, two tours in fact, of the UK and Europe with Steve continuing to consolidate his growing success including a stunning performance at the Reading Rock Festival.

Concerthaus	Gothenburg	Sweden	25.5.79
Chateau Neuf	Oslo	Sweden	29.5.79
Liederhalle	Stuttgart	Germany	2.6.79
Hosschulekuenste	Berlin	Germany	3.6.79
Alte Oper	Frankfurt	Germany	4.6.79
Zirkus Krone	Munich	Germany	5.6.79
Hugenottenhalle	Neu Isenburg	Germany	6.6.79
Sartory Saal	Cologne	Germany	8.6.79
Audimax	Hamburg	Germany	9.6.79
Ancienne Belgique	Brussels	Belgium	10.6.79
Pavilion de Paris	Paris	France	11.6.79
Theatre Sebastapol	Lille	France	12.6.79
La Bourse du Travail	Lyon	France	14.6.79
Theatre de Verdune	Nice	France	15.6.79
Musik Centrum	Utrecht	Holland	17.6.79
Odeon Theatre	Edinburgh	UK	21.6.79
City Hall	Sheffield	UK	22.6.79
University	Leicester	UK	23.6.79
Empire Theatre	Liverpool	UK	24.6.79
The Dome	Brighton	UK	25.6.79
Pavilion	Hemel Hempstead	UK	27.6.79
Civic Hall	Wolverhampton	UK	28.6.79
Gaumont Theatre	Southampton	UK	29.6.79
Hammersmith Odeon	London	UK	30.6.79
New Theatre	Oxford	UK	1.7.79
Reading Festival	Reading	UK	26.8.79
Capitol Theatre	Aberdeen	UK	22.10.79
Apollo Theatre	Glasgow	UK	23.10.79
Apollo Theatre	Manchester	UK	24.10.79
Royal Court Theatre	Liverpool	UK	25.10.79
Victoria Hall	Hanley	UK	26.10.79
City Hall	Newcastle	UK	27.10.79
Town Hall	Middlesborough	UK	28.10.79
St George's Hall	Bradford	UK	29.10.79
Odeon Theatre	Birmingham	UK	31.10.79
Colston Hall	Bristol	UK	1.11.79
Odeon Theatre	Chelmsford	UK	3.11.79
Gaumont Theatre	Ipswich	UK	4.11.79
Assembly Rooms	Derby	UK	5.11.79
West Runton Pavilion	Cromer	UK	6.11.79
Polytechnic	Plymouth	UK	8.11.79
Brunel University	Uxbridge	UK	9.11.79
Theatre Royal Drury Lane	London	UK	11.11.79
Arts Centre	Poole	UK	12.11.79

1980 sees Steve continuing to attract audiences to his own brand of rock with a new album, Defector. The year also sees him put in an appearance at the prestigious Montreux Jazz

FESTIVAL AND ALSO PERFORM HIS FIRST SOLO SHOWS IN THE USA.

Assembly Rooms	Derby	UK	11.6.80
Playhouse	Edinburgh	UK	13.6.80
Apollo Theatre	Glasgow	UK	14.6.80
City Hall	Newcastle	UK	15.6.80
Apollo Theatre	Manchester	UK	16.6.80
City Hall	Sheffield	UK	17.6.80
Princess Theatre	Hull	UK	19.6.80
Guildhall	Preston	UK	20.6.80
Odeon Theatre	Birmingham	UK	21.6.80
New Theatre	Oxford	UK	22.6.80
De Montfort Hall	Leicester	UK	23.6.80
Davenport Arts Centre	Coventry	UK	24.6.80
Civic Centre	Guildford	UK	26.6.80
Gaumont Theatre	Southampton	UK	27.6.80
Arts Centre	Poole	UK	28.6.80
Top Rank	Cardiff	UK	29.6.80
Royal Court Theatre	Liverpool	UK	1.7.80
Odeon Theatre	Canterbury	UK	4-5.7.80
Grand Casino	Montreux	Switzerland	13.8.80
Warner Theatre	San Francisco	USA	?.9.80
Bayou	Washington DC	USA	15.9.80
Paradise	Boston	USA	24.9.80
Hardo's Theatre	Detroit	USA	9.10.80
Tempe Theatre	Phoenix	USA	14.10.80
Roxy Theatre	Los Angeles	USA	15-16.10.80
(Other US dates were played but details are currently unavailable)			
Chateau Neuf	Oslo	Norway	11.11.80
Rijnhal	Arnhem	Holland	14.11.80
Musik Centrum	Utrecht	Holland	15.11.80
Palasport	Cantu	Italy	24.11.80
Palasport	Bologna	Italy	25.11.80
Palasport	Rome	Italy	26.11.80
Palasport	Turin	Italy	28.11.80
Palasport	Brescia	Italy	30.11.80
Palasport	Genoa	Italy	1.12.80

1981 SAW STEVE OUT AGAIN WITH ANOTHER ALBUM, CURED, WHICH SAW HIS FIRST ATTEMPTS AT SINGING VOCALS HIMSELF. GENERALLY WELL RECEIVED, THE TOUR SAW STEVE CONTINUE TO BROADEN THE SPECTRUM OF HIS AUDIENCES BY PLAYING THE FIRST GIGS BY ANY MEMBER OF GENESIS BEHIND THE IRON CURTAIN IN YUGOSLAVIA AS WELL AS FURTHER DATES IN THE USA.

Leas Cliff Pavilion	Southend	UK	22.8.81
Arts Centre	Poole	UK	23.8.81
Coliseum	St Austell	UK	24.8.81
Gaumont Theatre	Ipswich	UK	26.8.81
Rock City	Nottingham	UK	27.8.81
Reading Festival	Reading	UK	28.8.81
Carre Theatre	Amsterdam	Holland	31.8.81
Vorst Nationale	Brussels	Belgium	1.9.81
Hallenstadion	Zurich	Switzerland	3.9.81
Palasport	Milan	Italy	5.9.81
Festival	San Remo	Italy	6.9.81
Festival	Trento	Italy	7.9.81
Festival	Bolzano	Italy	8.9.81
Rolling Stone Theatre	Milan	Italy	9.9.81

Palasport	Reggio Emilia	Italy	10.9.81
Palasport	Viareggio	Italy	11.9.81
Festival	Udine	Yugoslavia	13.9.81
?	Zagreb	Yugoslavia	15.9.81
Parco Viscegliano	Naples	Italy	16.9.81
Zirkus Krone	Munich	Germany	17.9.81
Festhalle	Mannheim	Germany	18.9.81
SalleD'Expositions	Colmar	France	19.9.81
Congreshalle	Hamburg	Germany	20.9.81
Ostseehalle	Kiel	Germany	21.9.81
Waldebuehne	Berlin	Germany	22.9.81
Grugahalle	Essen	Germany	23.9.81
Festhalle	Frankfurt	Germany	24.9.81
Concerthal	Den Haag	Holland	25.9.81
Casino (2 shows)	Hertogenbosch	Holland	26.9.81
L' Hippodrome Pantin	Paris	France	27.9.81
Guildhall	Portsmouth	UK	29.9.81
Colston Hall	Bristol	UK	30.9.81
Leisure Centre	Gloucester	UK	1.10.81
Victoria Hall	Hanley	UK	2.10.81
Empire Theatre	Liverpool	UK	3.10.81
City Hall	Newcastle	UK	4.10.81
Playhouse	Edinburgh	UK	5.10.81
City Hall	Sheffield	UK	6.10.81
Odeon Theatre	Birmingham	UK	7.10.81
Apollo Theatre	Manchester	UK	8.10.81
University Great Hall	York	UK	9.10.81
Hammersmith Odeon	London	UK	11-12.10.81
Hugenottenhalle	Neuisenburg	Germany	24.10.81
Fox Theatre	Atlanta	USA	?.10.81
War Memorial	Rochester NY	USA	30.10.81
Triangle Theatre	New York	USA	31.10.81
?	Oswego	USA	3.11.81
Agora	Cleveland	USA	7.11.81
Paradise	Boston	USA	11.11.81
Roxy Club	Los Angeles	USA	27-28.11.81
Commodore Ballroom	Vancouver	Canada	7.12.81

(*Other US dates were played but details are currently unavailable*)

1982 and 1983 saw Steve hard at work with no less than two albums appearing in 1983, the electric Highly Strung was first out in March with another highly successful UK tour and a hit single in the shape of "Cell 151". The autumn saw Steve's second release, the acoustic Bay Of Kings album for which Steve embarked upon a tour of the university and college circuit in the UK and played in places which hadn't seen an artist of his calibre since the early days of Genesis. The gig at Guildford in January 1983 also saw Steve reunited again with Peter Gabriel and Mike Rutherford for a charity show in aid of Tadworth Children's Hospital.

Elixii festival	?	France	15.7.82
Venue Club	London	UK	18.12.82
Civic Centre	Guildford	UK	29.1.83
Pavilion	Worthing	UK	19.4.83
Odeon Theatre	Birmingham	UK	20.4.83
City Hall	Newcastle	UK	21.4.83
Apollo Theatre	Manchester	UK	22.4.83
Playhouse	Edinburgh	UK	24.4.83
University	Bradford	UK	25.4.83
Empire Theatre	Liverpool	UK	26.4.83

Colston Hall	Bristol	UK	27.4.83
Queensway Hall	Dunstable	UK	28.4.83
Gaumont Theatre	Southampton	UK	29.4.83
Hammersmith Odeon	London	UK	30.4.-1.5.83
Cliffs Pavilion	Southend	UK	2.5.83
Derngate Centre	Northampton	UK	4.5.83
City Hall	Sheffield	UK	5.5.83
Royal Centre	Nottingham	UK	6.5.83
Winter Gardens	Margate	UK	7.5.83
Arts Centre	Poole	UK	8.5.83
University of East Anglia	Norwich	UK	9.5.83
University	Warwick	UK	26.10.83
Mountford Hall	Liverpool	UK	27.10.83
University	Nottingham	UK	28.10.83
? (Cancelled)	Ashton-under-Lyne	UK	29.10.83
University	Leeds	UK	30.10.83
University	Loughborough	UK	31.10.83
Polytechnic	Plymouth	UK	1.11.83
University	Keele	UK	2.11.83
University	Newcastle	UK	3.11.83
Heriot Watt University	Edinburgh	UK	4.11.83
University	Dundee	UK	5.11.83
Civic Centre	Corby	UK	6.11.83
Barbican Centre	London	UK	7.11.83
Leisure Centre	Mansfield	UK	13.11.83
Taliesin Centre	Swansea	UK	14.11.83
St Davids Hall	Cardiff	UK	15.11.83
University	Oxford	UK	16.11.83
Civic Centre	Guildford	UK	17.11.83
Town Hall	Birmingham	UK	18.11.83
Leas Cliff Pavilion	Folkestone	UK	19.11.83
University	York	UK	21.11.83

There was to be a two year gap between these tours and Steve's next outing and when he next appeared it was as part of the AOR supergroup GTR with Steve Howe! Hackett had released another album in 1984; the sadly underrated (and un-toured) Til We Have Faces. Steve's involvement with GTR led to a highly successful album and another hit single "When the heart rules the mind" and a high profile tour of the USA and Europe.

Lyric Theatre	Baltimore	USA	20.6.86
Stanley Theatre	Utica NY	USA	21.6.86
Ulster Performing Arts Centre	New York	USA	22.6.86
Orpheum Theatre	Boston	USA	23.6.86
Beacon Theatre	New York	USA	25.6.86
Palace Theatre	Newhaven	USA	27.6.86
Tower Theatre	Philadelphia	USA	28.6.86
Constitution Hall	Washington DC	USA	29.6.86
Convention Centre	Quebec	Canada	2.7.86
Congress Centre	Ottawa	Canada	3.7.86
Verdune	Montreal	Canada	4.7.86
Massey Hall	Toronto	Canada	5.7.86
Music Hall	Cleveland	USA	6.7.86
Syria Mosque	Pittsburgh	USA	8.7.86
State Theatre	Detroit	USA	9.7.86
Riviera Theatre	Chicago	USA	10.7.86
Performing Arts Centre	Milwaukee	USA	11.7.86
The Orpheum	Minneapolis	USA	12.7.86

Music Hall	Omaha	USA	13.7.86
Mc Nichols Centre	Denver	USA	15.7.86
Warfield Theatre	San Francisco	USA	18.7.86
Wilton Theatre	Los Angeles	USA	19.7.86
California Theatre	San Diego	USA	21.7.86
?	Mesa	USA	22.7.86
Coliseum	Austin	USA	24.7.86
Bronco Bowl	Dallas	USA	25.7.86
Music Hall	Houston	USA	26.7.86
Sam Gore Theatre	New Orleans	USA	27.7.86
?	St Petersburg	USA	30.7.86
Arena	Miami	USA	31.7.86
Apollo Theatre	Manchester	UK	8.9.86
Odeon Theatre	Birmingham	UK	10.9.86
Hammersmith Odeon	London	UK	12.9.86
Alabamahalle	Munich	Germany	22.9.86
Hammersmith Odeon	London	UK	29.9.86

(*Other European dates were played but details are currently unavailable*)

Rehearsals	London	UK	23.4.88
Town Hall	Cheltenham	UK	25.4.88
Leas Cliff Pavilion	Folkestone	UK	26.4.88
University	Warwick	UK	27.4.88
University of East Anglia	Norwich	UK	28.4.88
The Dome	Brighton	UK	29.4.88
Essex University	Colchester	UK	30.4.88
Opera House	Manchester	UK	1.5.88
Derngate Arena	Northampton	UK	2.5.88
Colston Hall	Bristol	UK	3.5.88
Polytechnic	Leicester	UK	4.5.88
Wessex Hall	Poole	UK	5.5.88
The Forum	Hatfield	UK	6.5.88
Saddlers Wells Opera House	London	UK	7.5.88
Cliffs Pavilion	Southend	UK	8.5.88
Corn Exchange	Cambridge	UK	10.5.88
Civic Hall	Guildford	UK	11.5.88
St Davids Hall	Cardiff	UK	12.5.88
Concert Hall	Lewisham	UK	13.5.88
Royal Centre	Nottingham	UK	14.5.88
Alexandra Theatre	Birmingham	UK	15.5.88
The Orchard Theatre	Dartford	UK	16.5.88
Hexagon Theatre	Reading	UK	17.5.88
Teatro Colosseo	Turin	Italy	19.5.88
Teatro Orseo	Milan	Italy	20.5.88
Teatro Verdi	Genoa	Italy	21.5.88
Teatro Tenda a Strisce	Rome	Italy	22.5.88
Osterpoort	Groningen	Holland	24.5.88
Music Centrum	Utrecht	Holland	25.5.88
Paradiso Theatre	Amsterdam	Holland	26.5.88
De Doelen	Rotterdam	Holland	27.5.88
Het Noorderlight	Tilburg	Holland	28.5.88
Ancienne Belgique	Brussels	Belgium	29.5.88
Craigtoun Park	St Andrews	UK	24.7.88
Central Tejo	Lisbon	Portugal	3.9.88
Teatro Rivoli	Opporto	Portugal	4.9.88
Sardines	Oslo	Norway	8.9.88
Gota Lejon	Stockholm	Sweden	9.9.88

Saga Theatre	Copenhagen	Denmark	11.9.88
Quartier Latin	Berlin	Germany	12.9.88
Markthalle	Hamburg	Germany	15.9.88
Zeche	Bochum	Germany	16.9.88
Scala	Ludwigsburg	Germany	17.9.88
New Morning	Paris	France	19.9.88

Fans were amazed by Steve's acoustic tour in support of the Momentum album which achieved top ten status in the classical charts and drew favourable comments from music virtuoso Yehudi Menuhin. Steve also fulfilled an ambition to play Vivaldi's Guitar Concerto as guest of the London Chamber Orchestra proving once again that there was more to Steve Hackett than meets the eye! There was a four year wait before Steve returned to the live circuit again. In the meantime, he continued to work on building his own studio and the only releases to appear were a long overdue live album ironically titled Timelapse and a compilation album by Virgin Records titled The Unauthorised Biography.

Steve's touring schedule increased dramatically during 1992/93 with a lengthy tour of the USA and UK as well as several shows in Brazil (Steve's first in that country since the 1977 Genesis tour). Another new album, Guitar Noir was well received by fans and critics alike and Steve's profile remained high throughout the period.

Le Spectrum	Montreal	Canada	14.8.92
El Mocambo	Toronto	Canada	15.8.92
D'Auteuil	Quebec	Canada	16.8.92
Bottom Line Club	New York	USA	18.8.92
Birchmere Auditorium	Alexandria	USA	19.8.92
The Penguin	Ottawa	Canada	22.8.92
Impaxx Concert Theatre	Buffalo NY	USA	23.8.92
Shank Hall	Milwaukee	USA	25.8.92
The Agora	Cleveland	USA	27.8.92
The Marquee	Detroit	USA	28.8.92
City Limits	Dallas	USA	2.9.92
Concert Theatre	Ventura	USA	5.9.92
The Cave	Las Vegas	USA	7.9.92
The Strand	Redondo Beach	USA	8.9.92
Coach House	San Juan Capistrano	USA	9.9.92
Mason Jar	Tempe	USA	10.9.92
Cabaret	San Jose	USA	12.9.92
Club Soda	Montreal	Canada	19.9.92
Bottom Line Club	New York	USA	20.9.92
Max's on Broadway	Baltimore	USA	23.9.92
23 East Cabaret	Philadelphia	USA	24.9.92
Club Bene	South Amboy NJ	USA	27.9.92

Grand Rex Theatre	Buenos Aires	Brazil	16-17.4.93
Canecao	Rio de Janeiro	Brazil	20.4.93
Palace Theatre	Sao Paolo	Brazil	22.4.93
Town Hall (*Rehearsals*)	Whitchurch	UK	20.5.93
Neptune Theatre	Liverpool	UK	21.5.93
Renfrew Ferry	Glasgow	UK	22.5.93
Coatham Bowl	Redcar	UK	23.5.93
Spring Street Theatre	Hull	UK	24.5.93
Hop & Grape	Manchester	UK	25..5.93
The Old Bourbon (*Cancelled*)	Harrogate	UK	26.5.93
Wulfrun Hall	Wolverhampton	UK	27.5.93
De Montfort Hall	Leicester	UK	28.5.93
University of East Anglia	Norwich	UK	29.5.93
Lead Mill	Sheffield	UK	31.5.93

Assembly Halls	Worthing	UK	1.6.93
Princess Hall	Aldershot	UK	2.6.93
Leas Cliff Pavilion	Folkestone	UK	3.6.93
Polygon	Southampton	UK	4.6.93
Wedgewood Rooms	Portsmouth	UK	5.6.93
The Swan Theatre	High Wycombe	UK	6.6.93
Bierkeller	Bristol	UK	7.6.93
The Grand Theatre Clapham	London	UK	8,6,93
Arts Centre	Kendal	UK	11.6.93
Woughton Centre	Milton Keynes	UK	12.6.93
St George's Hall (*Cancelled*)	Bradford	UK	13.6.93
Villa Torlonia	Frascati	Italy	5.7.93
Centro Sportivo	Selvazzano nr Padua	Italy	6.7.93
Castello	Brescia	Italy	7.7.93
Stadio del Pini	Sassari	Italy	9.7.93
Stadietto San Gaviro	Ozieri	Italy	10.7.93
Teatro Tenda	Cagliari	Italy	11.7.93
Irving Plaza	New York	USA	26.10.93
Charity's	Clifton Park NY	USA	28.10.93
The Icon	Buffalo NY	USA	29.10.93
El Mocambo	Toronto	Canada	30.10.93
Café du Palais	Sherbrooke	Canada	1.11.93
D'Auteuil (2 shows per night)	Quebec	Canada	2-3.11.93
Club Soda	Montreal	Canada	4-5.11.93
The Penguin	Ottawa	Canada	6.11.93
The Town Pump	Vancouver	Canada	8.11.93
Chillers	San Diego	USA	10.11.93
The Coach House	San Juan Capistrano	USA	11.11.93
Cabaret	San Jose	USA	12.11.93
The Strand	Redondo Beach	USA	13.11.93
Ventura Theatre	Ventura	USA	14.11.93

1994 saw Steve continue to perform including shows as part of the David Palmer presentation of music by Pink Floyd, Genesis, and Jethro Tull. Steve also indulged his love of The Blues with an album of blues standards and new tracks written in the blues style titled Blues With A Feeling although no tour was undertaken to promote this album. Later in the year Steve's acoustic tour in Italy was recorded and released as a live acoustic album under the title There Are Many Sides To The Night.

Vorst Nationale	Brussels	Belgium	3.5.94*
?	Caracas	Venezuela	7-8.5.94*
Planet Pul Festival	Uden	Holland	4.6.94
Stadthalle	Vienna	Austria	8.6.94*
Tanzbrunnen	Cologne	Germany	12.6.94*
Rock Summer Festival	Tallinn	Estonia	17.6.94
Golden Stag TV Festival	Brasov	Romania	7.9.94
Standard	Barcelona	Spain	12.11.94
Sonny Boy	Treviso	Italy	24.11.94
Teatro C T M	Brescia	Italy	25.11.94
Teatro Aurora	Como	Italy	26.11.94
Teatro Michetti	Pescara	Italy	28.11.94
Teatro Palladium	Rome	Italy	29.11.94
Piper's Club	Rome	Italy	30.11.94
Teatro Metropolitan	Palermo	Italy	1.12.94
Teatro Nuovo	Catania	Italy	2.12.94

(*) *shows as part of David Palmer's Orchestral presentation of the music of Pink Floyd, Genesis* *and Jethro Tull*

1995/98 saw Steve increasingly prolific; a re-issue of the King Biscuit Flower Hour's recording of the 1986 GTR set revived interest in that band and Steve followed that with an orchestral interpretation of Shakespeare's "A Midsummer Night's Dream" for the Classics division of EMI Records. Steve also found time to indulge in a little nostalgia by putting together an album of re-worked Genesis classics and several new pieces and a couple of previously unheard tracks under the title of Genesis Revisited initially released in Japan in 1996 and subsequently elsewhere in 1997. Steve put together a band to perform a handful of shows in Japan in December 1996 and the resulting recording titled The Tokyo Tapes is his third live album and with his other new studio album Darktown released at the end of April and several other projects under way at the moment Steve's career is very much an ongoing adventure.

Sun Plaza Hall	Tokyo	Japan	16-17.12.96
Castle Hall	Osaka	Japan	19.12.96
Rainbow Hall	Nagoya	Japan	20.12.96

This part of the gig guide has been compiled by Alan Hewitt with the help and assistance of Billy Budis, Vernon Parker, Phil Morris and Pam Bay of "The Steve Howe Appreciation Society"

Mike & The Mechanics Gig Guide

Mike is the late developer in terms of solo performances. His first outing in 1986 was on the back of his third solo album, the highly successful Mike & The Mechanics debut album which appeared in 1985. The tour was a USA/Canada only affair between stints with Genesis, and fans in Europe and the UK had to wait a further three years to see Mike's "part-time" band in action.

Sunrise Theatre	Miami	USA	5.6.86
?	Tampa Bay	USA	6.6.86
Southern Star Amphitheatre	Atlanta	USA	8.6.86
?	Memphis	USA	10.6.86
Kiel Open House	St Louis	USA	11.6.86
Midland Theatre	Kansas	USA	12.6.86
Holiday Star	Merrivale	USA	14.6.86
Timber Wharf	Cincinatti	USA	15.6.86
Allen Theatre	Cleveland	USA	16.6.86
Kingswood	Toronto	Canada	17.6.86
Tower Theatre	Philadelphia	USA	19.6.86
Finger lakes Performing Arts Centre	Rochester NY	USA	21.6.86
Syria Mosque	Pittsburgh	USA	22.6.86
The Pier	New York	USA	23-24.6.86
Six Flags over Texas	Dallas	USA	27.6.86
Seven Stars Amphitheatre	Houston	USA	30.6.86
Universal Amphitheatre	Los Angeles	USA	1.7.86
Pavilion	Concord	USA	5.7.86
Paramount Theatre	Seattle	Canada	8.6.86
Expo Theatre	Vancouver	Canada	9.7.86

1988 saw Mike & The Mechanics hit the big time with a worldwide number one hit single with the title track to the second album, Living Years. Number one everywhere except mysteriously in the UK where it weighed in at number two. With two solid albums under their belts and a settled line-up, the band undertook an extensive tour of Europe where they were supported by progressive rockers IQ. Two US tours followed and a handful of shows were planned for Australia but these were cancelled at the last minute. Nonetheless, 1989 saw Mike & The Mechanics arrive on the concert stage and play for keeps. A third album Word Of Mouth followed in 1991 although Mike was unable to capitalise on the band's profile for this one, due to other commitments with Genesis and it was to be a further four years before the Mechanics hit the road again.

Volkshaus	Zurich	Switzerland	22.2.89
Palatrussardi	Milan	Italy	23.2.89
Forum	Ludwigsburg	Germany	24.2.89
Niedersachsenhalle	Hanover	Germany	26.2.89
Philipshalle	Dusseldorf	Germany	27.2.89
Broendbyhallen	Copenhagen	Denmark	1.3.89
Gota Lejon	Stockholm	Sweden	2.3.89
Apollo Theatre	Manchester	UK	5.3.89
Hammersmith Odeon	London	UK	6.3.89
Leas Cliff Pavilion	Folkestone	UK	7.3.89
Deutsches Museum	Munich	Germany	9..3.89
Rheingoldhalle	Mainz	Germany	10.3.89
Salle des Fetes Thonex	Geneva	Switzerland	11.3.89
Olympia Theatre	Paris	France	13.3.89
Ancienne Belgique	Brussels	Belgium	14.3.89
Vredenburg	Utrecht	Holland	15.3.89
Playhouse	Edinburgh	UK	17.3.89
City Hall	Newcastle	UK	18.3.89
Hammersmith Odeon	London	UK	19.3.89
?	Dayton	USA	23.3.89
?	Miami	USA	24.3.89
?	St Petersburg	USA	25.3.89
The Omni Centre	Atlanta	USA	26.3.89
?	Raleigh	USA	27.3.89
?	Washington DC	USA	28.3.89
Lyric Theatre	Baltimore	USA	29.3.89
Tower Theatre	Philadelphia	USA	30.3.89
The Scope	Norfolk	USA	2.4.89
Orpheum Theatre	Boston	USA	7.4.89
Bally's Grand Grandstand	Atlantic City	USA	10.4.89
Coliseum	Springfield	USA	12.4.89
?	Courtland State NY	USA	14.4.89
?	Albany NY	USA	15.4.89
War Memorial	Rochester NY	USA	17.4.89
Hamilton Place	Ontario	Canada	21.4.89
Tower Theatre	Philadelphia	USA	22.4.89
Allen Theatre	Cleveland	USA	24.4.89
?	Ann Arbor	USA	25.4.89
Holiday Star	Merriville	USA	26.4.89
?	Milwaukee	USA	27.4.89
?	Minneapolis	USA	28.4.89
?	Warrensburg	USA	29.4.89
Roxy Theatre	Los Angeles	USA	30.4.89
Lake Compounce	Bristol	USA	28.7.89
L'Agora	Quebec	Canada	29.7.89
La Ronde	Montreal	Canada	30.7.89

Ontario Place Forum	Toronto	Canada	31.7.-1.8.89
Garden State Arts Centre	Holmdel	USA	3.8.89
Jones beach Amphitheatre	Wantaugh	USA	4.8.89
Bally's Grand Grandstand	Atlantic City	USA	5.8.89
Amphitheatre	Doswell	USA	6.8.89
Merryweather Post Pavilion	Columbia	USA	7.8.89
Ohio State Fair Grandstand	Columbus	USA	8.8.89
Pine Knob Music Theatre	Clarkston	USA	10.8.89
Timberwolf Amphitheatre	King's Island	USA	11.8.89
Old Glory Theatre	St Louis	USA	12.8.89
Poplar Creek Music Theatre	Hoffman Estates	USA	13.8.89
Grandstand Stagefair	Springfield	USA	15.8.89
Lakewood Amphitheatre	Atlanta	USA	17.8.89
The Summit	Houston	USA	19.8.89
Music Mill Amphitheatre	Arlington	USA	20.8.89
Ventura County Theatre	Ventura	USA	23.8.89
Concord Concord	Concord	USA	24.8.89
Greek Theatre	Los Angeles	USA	25.8.89
Pacific Amphitheatre	Costa Mesa	USA	27.8.89
Entertainment Centre	Sydney	Australia	1.9.89*
Entertainment Centre	Brisbane	Australia	4.9.89*
National Tennis Centre	Melbourne	Australia	6.9.89*
Apollo Entertainment Centre	Adelaide	Australia	8.9.89*
Superdome	Perth	Australia	10.9.89*

(*) *Australian tour dates cancelled.*

1994/95 saw Mike's "other" band take off in a big way with the hugely successful Beggar On A Beach Of Gold album which produced no less than three top ten singles. The tour took them to South Africa in time for the Rugby World Cup before returning to Europe and the UK. To capitalise on this success, Mike's record company released the Hits album in 1996 and organised the band's biggest tour of the UK, a 31 date tour round the theatres and city halls to packed audiences. Mike then returned to his "Full time" band Genesis to begin work on what would become their seventeenth studio album in 1997.

The manor Studios (Virgin Records 21st birthday)	Oxford	UK	24.8.94
Victory Club (album launch gig)	London	UK	18.1.95
World Earth Day Festival	Boston	USA	22.4.95
Standard Bank Arena	Johannesburg	South Africa	1-2.6.95
Village Green	Durban	South Africa	3.6.95
Sandton Towers	Johannesburg	South Africa	5.6.95
Saambo Arena	Pretoria	South Africa	6.6.95
Freiluftbuhne	Lorlei	Germany	10.6.95
Capitol Theatre	Hanover	Germany	11.6.95
Offenbach Theatre	Frankfurt	Germany	12.6.95
Guildhall	Portsmouth	UK	14.6.95
Royal Concert Hall	Nottingham	UK	15.6.95
Wembley Stadium (Supporting R Stewart)	London	UK	17.6.95
International Centre	Bournemouth	UK	18.6.95
Trinity College	Cambridge	UK	19.6.95
Apollo Theatre	Oxford	UK	20.6.95
Civic Hall	Wolverhampton	UK	21.6.95
St David's Hall	Cardiff	UK	22.6.95
St Gallen Festival	Zurich	Switzerland	24.6.95
Park Pop Festival	?	Holland	25.6.95
Congreshalle	Hamburg	Germany	27.6.95
Tivolis Conzertsal	Copenhagen	Denmark	28.6.95
Metron	Gothenburg	Sweden	29.6.95

Midtfyns Festival	?	Sweden	1.7.95
Lalauna	Brussels	Belgium	4.7.95
Demain Du Monde	Paris	France	5.7.95
Culture Tent	Luxembourg	Luxembourg	6.7.95
Festival	Imst	Austria	8.7.95
Prague Festival (Cancelled)	Prague	Czechoslovakia	9.7.95
Colston Hall	Bristol	UK	11.7.95
Pavilion	Plymouth	UK	12.7.95
The Dome	Brighton	UK	13.7.95
Summer Rock Festival	Tallinn	Estonia	15.7.95
The Island	Ilford	UK	17.7.95
Shepherds Bush Empire	London	UK	18.7.95
Coliseum	Watford	UK	19.7.95
Roundhay Park "Heineken festival"	Leeds	UK	21.7.95
City Hall	Newcastle	UK	23.7.95
Sands Centre	Carlisle	UK	24.7.95
Assembly Rooms	Derby	UK	25.7.95
Festival	Langelands	Denmark	27.7.95
Mean Fiddler	Dublin	Eire	29-30.7.95
Festival	Jubeck	Germany	12.8.95
?	?	Belgium	13.8.95

The "Hits" tour proved to be Mike + The Mechanics' biggest success to date with sell-out shows across the UK and with a hit album under their belts the Mechanics were to go their separate ways to concentrate on their various solo projects.

Working Men's Club (*Rehearsals*)	Chiddingfold	UK	21-27.2.96
The Island	Ilford	UK	28.2.96
Mayfield Leisure Centre	Belfast	UK	1.3.96
Stadium	Dublin	Eire	2.3.96
Guildhall	Portsmouth	UK	4.3.96
Colston Hall	Bristol	UK	5.3.96
Royal Concert Hall	Nottingham	UK	7-8.3.96
Apollo Theatre	Manchester	UK	9.3.96
City Hall	Sheffield	UK	11.3.96
City Hall	Newcastle	UK	12.3.96
Sands Centre	Carlisle	UK	13.3.96
Usher Hall	Edinburgh	UK	14.3.96
Capitol Theatre	Aberdeen	UK	16.3.96
Royal Concert Hall	Glasgow	UK	18.3.96
St George's Hall	Bradford	UK	19.3.96
Civic Hall	Wolverhampton	UK	21.3.96
Corn Exchange	Cambridge	UK	23-24.3.96
Assembly Rooms	Derby	UK	5.4.96
Apollo Theatre	Oxford	UK	6.4.96
Hexagon	Reading	UK	7.4.96
Centre	Brighton	UK	9.4.96
International Centre	Bournemouth	UK	10.4.96
De Montfort Hall	Leicester	UK	11.4.96
Apollo Theatre	Manchester	UK	12.4.96
Empire Theatre	Liverpool	UK	14.4.96
St David's Hall	Cardiff	UK	15.4.96
Fairfield Halls	Croydon	UK	16.4.96
Royal Albert Hall	London	UK	18-19.4.96
"Rock am Ring Festival"	Hockenheim	Germany	24.5.96
"Rock in Park Festival"	?	Germany	25.5.96

The years between the last album by the Mechanics and the release in May 1999 of their fifth studio album have been eventful ones for Mike and for Genesis in general. However, the Mechanics' success continues with the new album.

Hanover Club (Warm-up show)	London	UK	10.5.99
Barbican Centre	York	UK	13.5.99
Apollo Theatre	Manchester	UK	14.5.99
Apollo Theatre	Manchester	UK	15.5.99
City Hall	Sheffield	UK	17.5.99
City Hall	Sheffield	UK	18.5.99
International Conference Centre	Bournemouth	UK	20.5.99
The Conference Centre	Brighton	UK	21.5.99
Corn Exchange	Cambridge	UK	22.5.99
Royal Albert Hall	London	UK	24-25.5.99
The Pavilion	Plymouth	UK	26.5.99
Colston Hall	Bristol	UK	28.5.99
St Davids Hall	Cardiff	UK	29.5.99
St David's Hall	Cardiff	UK	30.5.99
The Royal Theatre	Hanley	UK	31.5.99
Symphony Hall	Birmingham	UK	1.6.99
Symphony Hall	Birmingham	UK	2.6.99
Fairfield Hall	Croydon	UK	3.6.99
Armadillo Centre	Glasgow	UK	5.6.99
Royal Centre	Nottingham	UK	6.6.99
St George's Hall	Bradford	UK	8.6.99
City Hall	Newcastle	UK	9.6.99
City Hall	Newcastle	UK	10.6.99
Stadtpark Festival	Hamburg	Germany	13.6.99
Museumsmeile	Bonn	Germany	18.6.99
Guildhall	Portsmouth	UK	20.6.99
Fairfield Halls	Croydon	UK	21.6.99

This gig guide has been compiled by Alan Hewitt with help from Carol Willis Impey at Hit & Run Music

Ray Wilson / Cut Gig Guide

Since joining Genesis in 1997, Ray Wilson has not only fronted one of the largest rock bands in the world, but also found time to form his own solo band: Cut whose first album Millionairhead was released by Virgin Germany in March 1999. This band were in fact already established before Ray joined Genesis and this will be an ongoing project. Prior to joining Genesis, Ray had also enjoyed some success with grunge rockers Stiltskin whose single "Inside" was a Top ten hit in 1994. Ray also appears in another earlier band: Guaranteed Pure whose album Swing Your Bag is now a highly sought after item.

Room at the Top Nightclub	Bathgate	UK	27.4.99
Eisstadion	Deggendorf	Germany	30.4.99
Congress Centrum	Suhl	Germany	1.5.99
Festhalle	Frankfurt	Germany	3.5.99
Schleyerhalle	Stuttgart	Germany	4.5.99
Frankenhalle	Nurnberg	Germany	6.5.99

Olympiahalle	Munich	Germany	8.5.99
Messehalle	Leipzig	Germany	10.5.99
Boerdelandhalle	Magdeburg	Germany	11.5.99
Sporthalle	Hamburg	Germany	12.5.99
Gerry-Weber-Stadion	Halle	Germany	14.5.99
Koln Arena	Cologne	Germany	15.5.99
Arena	Berlin	Germany	17.5.99
Arena	Oberhausen	Germany	18.5.99
Eissporthalle	Memmingen	Germany	20.5.99
Freilictbuhne	Wiesmoor	Germany	22.5.99

Titles available from SAF, Firefly and Helter Skelter Publishing

No More Mr Nice Guy: The Inside Story of The Alice Cooper Group
By Michael Bruce and Billy James (reprint due soon)
The dead babies, the drinking, executions and, of course, the rock 'n' roll.

Procol Harum: Beyond The Pale
by Claes Johansen UK Price £12.99 (available early 2000)
Distinctive, ground breaking and enigmatic British band from the 60s.

An American Band: The Story of Grand Funk Railroad
By Billy James UK Price £12.99
One of the biggest grossing US rock 'n' roll acts of the 70s - selling millions of records and playing sold out arenas the world over. Hype, Politics & rock 'n' roll - unbeatable!

Wish The World Away: Mark Eitzel and American Music Club
by Sean Body UK Price £12.99
Sean Body has written a fascinating biography of Eitzel which portrays an artist tortured by demons, yet redeemed by the aching beauty of his songs.

Ginger Geezer: Vivian Stanshall and the Bonzo Dog Band
by Chris Welch and Lucian Randall UK Price £12.99 (available spring 2000)
Stanshall was one of pop music's true eccentrics. An account of his incredible life from playing pranks with The Who's Keith Moon to depression, alcoholism, & sad demise.

Go Ahead John! The Music of John McLaughlin
by Paul Stump UK Price £12.99
One of the greatest jazz musicians of all time. Includes his work with Miles Davis, Mahavishnu Orchestra, Shakti. Full of insights into all stages of his career.

Lunar Notes: Zoot Horn Rollo's Captain Beefheart Experience
by Bill Harkleroad and Billy James UK Price £11.95
For the first time we get the insider's story of what it was like to record, play and live with an eccentric genius such as Beefheart, written by Bill Harkleroad - Zoot himself!

Meet The Residents: America's Most Eccentric Band
by Ian Shirley UK Price £11.95
An outsider's view of The Residents' operations, exposing a world where nothing is as it seems. It is a fascinating tale of musical anarchy and cartoon wackiness. Reprinted to coincide with the recent world tour.

Digital Gothic: A Critical Discography of Tangerine Dream
by Paul Stump UK Price £9.95
For the very first time German electronic pioneers, Tangerine Dream mammoth output is placed within an ordered perspective.

The One and Only - Homme Fatale: Peter Perrett & The Only Ones
by Nina Antonia UK Price £11.95
An extraordinary journey through crime, punishment and the decadent times of British punk band leader, Peter Perrett of The Only Ones

Plunderphonics, 'Pataphysics and Pop Mechanics
The Leading Exponents of Musique Actuelle
By Andrew Jones UK Price £12.95
Chris Cutler, Fred Frith, Henry Threadgill, John Oswald, John Zorn, etc.

Kraftwerk: Man, Machine and Music
By Pascal Bussy UK Price £11.95
The full story behind one of the most influential bands in the history of rock.

Wrong Movements: A Robert Wyatt History
by Mike King UK Price £14.95
A journey through Wyatt's 30 year career with Soft Machine, Matching Mole & solo artist.

Wire: Everybody Loves A History
by Kevin Eden UK Price £9.95
British punk's most endearing and enduring bands combining Art and Attitude

Tape Delay: A Documentary of Industrial Music
by Charles Neal (out of print)
Marc Almond, Cabaret Voltaire, Nick Cave, Chris & Cosey, Coil, Foetus, Neubauten, Non, The Fall, New Order, Psychic TV, Rollins, Sonic Youth, Swans, Test Dept and many more...

Dark Entries: Bauhaus and Beyond
by Ian Shirley UK Price £11.95
The gothic rise of Bauhaus, Love & Rockets, Tones on Tail, Murphy, J, and Ash solo.

Poison Heart: Surviving The Ramones
by Dee Dee Ramone and Veronica KofmanUK Price £11.95
Dee Dee's crushingly honest account of life as junkie and Ramone. A great rock story!

Minstrels In The Gallery: A History Of Jethro Tull
by David Rees UK Price £12.99
At Last! To coincide with their 30th anniversary, a full history of one of the most popular and inventive bands of the past three decades

DANCEMUSICSEXROMANCE: Prince - The First Decade
by Per Nilsen UK Price £12.99
A portrait of Prince's reign as the most exciting black performer to emerge since James Brown and Jimi Hendrix.

SOUL SACRIFICE: THE SANTANA STORY
by Simon Leng UK Price £12.99
In depth study of seventies Latin guitar legend whose career began at Woodstock through to a 1999 number one US album.

WAITING FOR THE MAN: THE STORY OF DRUGS AND POPULAR MUSIC
by Harry Shapiro UK Price £12.99
Fully revised edition of the classic story of two intertwining billion dollar industries. "Wise and witty." The Guardian

THE SHARPER WORD: A MOD READER
Edited by Paolo Hewitt (available November 1999) UK price:£12.99
Hugely readable collection of articles documenting one of the most misunderstood cultural movements

DYLAN'S DAEMON LOVER: THE TANGLED TALE OF A 450-YEAR OLD POP BALLAD
by Clinton Heylin UK price £12.00
Written as a detective story, Heylin unearths the mystery of why Dylan knew enough to return "The House Carpenter" to its 16th century source.

GET BACK: THE BEATLES' LET IT BE DISASTER
by Doug Sulpy & Ray Schweighardt UK price £12.99
No-holds barred account of the power struggles, the bickering, and the bitterness that led to the break-up of the greatest band in the history of rock 'n' roll. "One of the most poignant Beatles books ever." Mojo

XTC: SONG STORIES - THE EXCLUSIVE & AUTHORISED STORY
by XTC and Neville Farmer UK Price £12.99
"A cheerful celebration of the minutiae surrounding XTC's music with the band's musical passion intact … high in setting-the-record-straight anecdotes. Superbright, funny, commanding." Mojo

LIKE THE NIGHT: BOB DYLAN AND THE ROAD TO THE MANCHESTER FREE TRADE HALL
by CP Lee UK Price £12.00
In 1966 at the height of Dylan's protest-singing popularity he plugged in an electric guitar to the outrage of folk fans who booed and jeered. Finally, in Manchester, fans branded him Judas. "Essential Reading" Uncut

BORN IN THE USA: BRUCE SPRINGSTEEN AND THE AMERICAN TRADITION
by Jim Cullen UK Price £9.99
"Cullen has written an excellent treatise expressing exactly how and why Springsteen translated his uneducated hicktown American-ness into music and stories that touched hearts and souls around the world." Q****

BACK TO THE BEACH: A BRIAN WILSON AND THE BEACH BOYS READER
Ed Kingsley Abbott UK Price £12.99
"A detailed study and comprehensive overview of the BBs' lives and music, even including a foreword from Wilson himself by way of validation. Most impressively,

Abbott manages to appeal to both die-hard fans and rather less obsessive newcomers." Time Out "Rivetting!" **** Q "An essential purchase." Mojo

A Journey Through America with the Rolling Stones
by Robert Greenfield UK Price £12.00
This is the definitive account of their legendary '72 tour.
"Filled with finely-rendered detail ... a fascinating tale of times we shall never see again" Mojo

Bob Dylan
by Anthony Scaduto UK Price £12.99
The first and best biography of Dylan. "The best book ever written on Dylan" Record Collector "Now in a welcome reprint it's a real treat to read the still-classic Bobography". Q*****

Mail Order